UNCERTAINTY

UNCERTAINTY

Behavioral and Social Dimensions

Edited by
Seymour Fiddle

PRAEGER

PRAEGER SPECIAL STUDIES • PRAEGER SCIENTIFIC

Published in 1980 by Praeger Publishers
CBS Educational and Professional Publishing
A Division of CBS, Inc.
521 Fifth Avenue, New York, New York 10017 U.S.A.

© 1980 by Praeger Publishers

All rights reserved

Library of Congress Catalog Card Number: 80-82073

0123456789 038 987654321

Printed in the United States of America

For Adele

CONTENTS

PART I: GENERAL THEORETICAL ANALYSIS

Chapter		Page
1	GENERAL INTRODUCTION Seymour Fiddle	3
2	UNCERTAINTY AS A SCIENTIFIC CONCEPT AND ITS APPLICATION TO THE STUDY OF OCCUPATIONS AND ORGANIZATIONS Paul Montagna	9
3	ORIENTATION TO AMBIGUITY Allen Lerner	43
4	SOME COMMENTS ON THE ROLE OF SOCIAL PSYCHOLOGY IN FORECASTING Marie Jahoda	59
5	UNCERTAINTY, ACTION, AND COMPETENCE: SOME ALTERNATIVES TO OMNISCIENCE IN COMPLEX PROBLEM-SOLVING Terry Connolly	69
6	A SOCIAL BEHAVIORIST MODEL OF UNCERTAINTY IN THE PROCESS OF SYMBOLIC INTERACTIONS Richard E. Sykes	92
7	ORGANIZATIONAL AND INDIVIDUAL RESPONSES TO ENVIRONMENTAL UNCERTAINTY James G. Hougland and Jon M. Shepard	102
8	COST-BENEFIT ANALYSIS: AN UNCERTAIN GUIDE TO PUBLIC POLICY Baruch Fischhoff	120
9	UNCERTAINTY Emmanuel Demby	139

PART II: THEORETICAL ANALYSIS IN SPECIFIC SUBJECT AREAS

Chapter		Page
10	HEALTH, UNCERTAINTY, AND THE ACTION SITUATION Talcott Parsons	145
11	MACRO AND MICRO UNCERTAINTY George Katona	163
12	UNCERTAINTY AND MODELS OF URBAN TRAVEL BEHAVIOR Vincent B. Robinson	176
13	UNCERTAINTY IN PUBLIC OPINION ASSESSMENT Robert Mason and G. David Faulkenberry	192
14	RISK AND UNCERTAINTY IN POLITICAL CHOICE Eugene J. Alpert	205
15	UNCERTAINTY IN FAMILY LIFE Andrew Cherlin	231
16	CLINICAL CHOICE UNDER UNCERTAINTY: ITS SIGNIFICANCE FOR REGULATING HOSPITALIZATION RATES C. E. Brian Frost	247

PART III: SPECIFICALLY EMPIRICAL STUDIES IN PERSONAL OR ORGANIZATIONAL UNCERTAINTY

17	UNCERTAIN TIMETABLES: A CASE OF SPARE-PART SURGERY Daniel J. Klenow and Fabio B. Dasilva	269
18	APPLIED BEHAVIOR UNDER UNCERTAINTY Peter Lorenzi	284
19	REDUCING UNCERTAINTY AND BUILDING TRUST: THE SPECIAL CASE OF AUCTIONS Robert E. Clark and Larry Halford	305

Chapter		Page
20	BEHAVIORAL DETERMINANTS OF MARKET FAILURE: THE CASE OF DISASTER INSURANCE Ralph Ginsberg and Howard Kunreuther	323
21	HESITATION PHENOMENA AND CONVERSATIONAL STYLE: INDICATIONS OF UNCERTAINTY IN FAMILY SITUATIONS Fern L. Johnson and Leslie K. Davis	347
22	UNCERTAINTY IN VOLUNTARY ORGANIZATIONS: THE CASE OF CONSUMER FOOD COOPERATIVES Michael Nagy	369

ABOUT THE EDITOR AND CONTRIBUTORS   399

1
GENERAL THEORETICAL ANALYSIS

1
GENERAL INTRODUCTION
Seymour Fiddle

INTRODUCTION TO BOOK

The twentieth century has been colored by the principle of uncertainty, taken both in its original Heisenberg meaning of 1927, to refer to a fundamental incommensurability, and in its broadest sense, as a general characteristic of the life of modern man since Einstein's miracle year of 1905 and the killing of the archduke in 1914. Along with relativity, uncertainty is a sort of charismatic concept, exciting those who filter conventional concepts and data through its perspectives.

This book is a venture at showing how the various social sciences have reacted to that encounter. Since there is not, nor likely to be in the near future, an all-embracing theory of uncertainty (although some cues are on the horizon), the book starts with chapters of relatively general import. Paul Montagna's chapter helpfully sets the stage by giving one version of the trinity—uncertainty, risk, and probability—working out a particular body of concepts in two areas, occupations and organizations. Allen Lerner perceptively reminds us of a fourth partner, ambiguity. He develops a general set of orientation patterns, unexpectedly linking uncertainty theory to the celebrated researches on Machiavellianism. Marie Jahoda sketches out some of the social psychological (that is, realistic) problems of forecasting, one preoccupation of modern man. Working out of research on police-civilian encounters and its methodology, Richard Sykes has daringly constructed a "transition probabilities" model of social interaction, which also generalizes some of George H. Mead's social behaviorism.

An informal synthesis of Emmanuel Demby's reflections summarize his learnings and experiences in a long career of applied

4 / UNCERTAINTY

and market research, in which interdisciplinary efforts at reducing costly uncertainty have to be worked out. Terry Connolly's "offbeat" chapter considers the question, which he phrases in a technical though literate way, How is it that despite the odds and current opinion, a surprising number of the world's complex decision-making problems are settled in what participants call a successful way? He sets up a number of original models, which give the reader an insight into the most advanced work about decisional uncertainty. James Houghland and Jon Shepard's chapter exemplifies Connolly's focus in part, showing how organizations develop strategies for coping with perceived environmental uncertainty, concluding that "secure organizations" have relatively high probability of responding adaptively. Completing the general theoretical analysis, Baruch Fischhoff searches out the limits of some current conventional seemingly rational methods of uncertainty management. His comments may perhaps deflate some of the optimistic protagonists of the "cost-benefit" school.

The more specialized theoretical discussions are fittingly led off by what turned out to be Talcott Parsons' last written statement of his general theoretical position, as he thought it applied to medical uncertainty. Making use of the notion of stable and unstable internal environments, he perceived health as a "generalized medium of exchange," a novel concept suggestive of a variety of uncertainty-theoretical issues. George Katona sketches out the sphere of consumer volatility and hesitation in the presence of different prospective futures. He offers one set of indicators for subsequent empirical research.

Vincent Robinson demonstrates that urban geographers can create models of urban travel behavior. Distinguishing between conditions of maximum and minimum uncertainty, he argues that previous geographical thinking has taken an observer's standpoint, one that may be purblind to actual decision making under uncertainty. He develops mathematical models that express the traveler's own point of view. Robert Mason and G. David Faulkenberry examine and clarify poll respondents' "don't know" and "no opinion" answers, which bedevil survey research with "metauncertainty." Their analysis has strong implications for all the social sciences insofar as they have to differentiate shades of incomplete information. Eugene Alpert's chapter is a systematic analysis of research on political choice uncertainty to date. In addition, his Bayesian examination of competing models ought to be helpful, indeed exciting, to those who are attracted to Bayes's persistent renewal. Andrew Cherlin outlines some not so obvious applications of uncertainty in family life, linking his conceptual analysis to a wide range of hitherto unconnected empirical materials. Brian Frost applies an uncertainty perspective to the problem of regulating hospitalization rates under different payment practices.

Part III, on specifically empirical uncertainty studies, opens with the Klenow-Dasilva study of how patients waiting—they do not know for how long—for a renal transplant handle their uncertainty and disappointment. Those who would investigate the connections between uncertainty and temporal perspectives, a general social science problem, will find much to reflect on in this poignant issue. From a rather different vantage point, Peter Lorenzi shows how experimentation contributes to uncertainty research, as he fits together uncertainty and "applied behavior" and visualizes strategies for dealing with these problems. Robert Clark and Larry Halford examine uncertainty and trust in an archetypal situation, auction bidding, one in which at least some buyers cannot employ their customary consumer cues. Their close analysis studies the building of trust. Ralph Ginzberg and Howard Kunreuther's chapter represents the most advanced concepts and research methodology on the thorny question of how people adapt to the possibilities of a flood or an earthquake. Would not a rational family purchase cheap security? Ginzberg and Kunreuther explore the sources for consumer unenthusiastic response and reemphasize the pivotal place of consumer's information-gathering processes and "computational heuristics," echoing Fischhoff's analysis.

Fern Johnson and Leslie Davis examine the linguistic expression of hesitation phenomena as a modality of uncertainty, testing its presence and forms in differentiated conversational styles and situations. Their effort will be of especial interest to those who believe that naturalistic studies of conversation yield valuable insight into uncertainty on a micro social level.

Finally, Michael Nagy had the opportunity to study voluntary organizations in their "takeoff" stage, in which we would expect to find a welter of contingencies and fumbling explanatory efforts to reduce confusion. His analysis and data will be illuminating for those who wish to take the risks of building within alternative frames of social organization.

Representing the spectrum of social science, blending the technical and the humanistic, the book allows one to glimpse some of the fertile perspectives of the general uncertainty principle and invites its readers to follow their own ways and versions of uncertainty in their lives and efforts to understand them in a fresh way.

GENERAL INTRODUCTION

This book developed as a by-product of a manuscript (still incomplete) on the sociological analysis of uncertainty. I had completed a study of the "Son of Sam" murders, one of whose themes was the complex nature of mystery in an assertedly secular world. For a number of reasons, I was led to generalize this theme into the focus on uncertainty and quite by accident stumbled upon what now seems obvious to me: (1) that all the social sciences, in different measure and manner, have been struggling with the place of uncertainty as an aspect of their research and theory; (2) that there was no one universally accepted general and testable theory of uncertainty; and (3) most interesting of all, that many of the scholars and scientists doing uncertainty work appeared to be minimally aware of their unseen colleagues' activities.

This last striking phenomenon, in which a few key names were continually being cited and hundreds went about doing relatively unheralded work, had its converse. A Duke anthropologist might cite the uncertainty research of an Oregon psychologist, but the latter would not know about this use of his research unless, as in this case, I was in touch with both. There was much evidence that uncertainty students were not members of a single invisible college, if by this term we refer to a group of scientists who share and develop a field by informal media of communication from which others are generally excluded. Uncertainty workers were doubly invisible: much of what they did was read only by fellow professionals, who need not necessarily have conceptualized the work as an instance of a developing body of uncertainty theory, and moreover, they displayed the "pluralistic ignorance" cited above.

Accordingly, it seemed useful to try to bring some of these widely differing perspectives together on one elephant, so to speak. My first notion was to have a special number of the Journal of Social Issues, but it is a kind of evidence for the size of this doubly invisible community that the book outgrew any ordinary journal format. Though many contacted scholars declined, and some who agreed did not contribute, the book's two dozen or so chapters reveal the fertility of this way of looking at the world.

One may almost make a game of the ways in which these chapters' contents can mesh with each other as exemplars of thinking about uncertainty. Could Katona, who presents us with his current thinking about the way in which men and women do or do not defer purchasing goods, have made use of the model urged upon us by Johnson and Davis, in their study of hesitation patterns in family speech? May we not visualize micro social studies of family buying-planning decision-making using their categories? Could these categories in turn be expanded to include economic indicators?

Or consider Clark's study of auction bidding—a participant observer's examination of how different types of bidders attempt to minimize their uncertainty about what is happening before them and how, correlatively, different auctioneers seek to build trust in their audiences. Could these materials be reprocessed through Sykes's transition probabilities model, a development of selected ideas of George H. Mead applied to uncertainty theory?

Or finally (not to deprive the reader of the enjoyment of playing this "mind-game"), note that Nagy's study of farm cooperatives leads him to emphasize the place of formalization as an uncertainty reducing device, a point, among others, at which his empirical analysis converges with some of Montagna's theoretical reasoning.

Unquestionably, this book should be understood to be a fairly primitive effort. It requires little imagination to say that looking back from 2000 A.D., these chapters will appear to be relatively timorous efforts. We may foresee specialized studies of collective, official, interpersonal, and personal uncertainty and not merely studies connecting uncertainty reduction to social organization. The Lorenzi, Ginzberg-Kunreuther, and Fischhoff chapters represent different avenues toward that goal, but in this respect, my own personal preference, and therefore hope, is for participant observational studies of different uncertainty forms and situations, as exemplified in the Clark-Halford chapter.

If I may hazard an intellectual prediction, it seems to me quite likely that the very useful notion of perceived environmental uncertainty (PEU), which shows up in this book in the Hougland-Shepard chapter, will be expanded beyond its current jurisdictional limits, set by administrative science and organizational sociology. If I may borrow from James Gibson, I would guess that an "ecological" study of uncertainty will develop. For one thing, structural anthropology can obviously contribute the idea that classes of people in (say) a changing urban environment have to learn to "decode" the urban scene for its variable, sometimes blurred social messages. Hence, PEU studies from that perspective would encourage research on such ecological problems, as well as their solutions, among different classes, such as the recurrent situations in which two ethnic or other cultural strata reveal that they are not sure what is the "real" status of a border neighborhood because the terms <u>going up</u>, <u>going down</u>, and <u>I don't know</u> are applied to it. For another thing, PEU can be redirected, a portable telescope back down into the decoders themselves. Supplementing Parsons' provocative speculations on the stabilities and instabilities of the human organism in its exchanges with its milieus, studies will probably seek out the changing and varied criteria by which different social types judge their inner spaces: bodies, health, illness, and the foods they take in (junk, health foods, conventional foods, and scientific pill food). Do mobile ethnic groups differ in the amount and focus of their uncertainty about these cultural boundaries and definitions for these "biological" phenomena?

Perhaps I might express this notion in more general terms: by the year 2000, uncertainty theory will have broken out of its contemporary cognitive psychological assumptions, according to which uncertainty is a by-product of "constructivist" activity, and will have been replaced by an "ecological" psychology and sociology of knowledge, for which uncertainties correspond to problematical aspects of human adaptation to complexly and variably structured environment; PEU would refer to an environment affording unreliable supports, if not something worse. In a time of inflation and military alarums, questions of an impending "crash" or "collisions" (between great powers) will be recognized as grist for the ecological mill.

Thinking in ecological terms also helps us make sense of the considerable research connecting power and uncertainty, exemplified in Montagna's lead chapter. If organizational or personal environments grow turbulent, strategy and special skills and information are at a premium to facilitate adaptation. Conversely, so far as possible, professionals and subgroups within organizations will find it expedient to "discover," perhaps even "model" or idealize, both the ecological uncertainty and their claimed skills at reducing or even transcending it. For organizations, that environment may be competing organizations, substitute organizations, suppliers, labor unions, consumer groups, various layers of government, and even foreign states. In the modern world, as the recurrent oil situation shows, power can be demonstrated by the ability to transmit or even produce uncertainty for others. At any rate, the vogue of such research is itself a sign of an underlying search for a more rational ecological perspective with respect to organizations and people.

One more point: I would not want to join the legions engaged in the wars of, Whose-paradigm-is-best? but I also would not want to close these lines without asserting my belief that uncertainty-certainty can become the axis of an alternative general social science perspective. Much of the division in social science, for example, conflict versus consensus in sociology and neoclassical economics versus Marxism, seem to echo the nineteenth century. Uncertainty is of our time and the times ahead; its cultivation as a scientific perspective puts us closer to our actual and possible lives.

2
UNCERTAINTY AS A SCIENTIFIC CONCEPT AND ITS APPLICATION TO THE STUDY OF OCCUPATIONS AND ORGANIZATIONS
Paul Montagna

The concept of uncertainty has a long and complex history in both the liberal arts and the sciences. However, only recently has it received attention from social scientists, often in close correspondence with other equally broad constructs, such as risk, decision-making, choice, and probability. For example, uncertainty has been used to describe human behavior under probability conditions, that is, either mathematical, statistical, or subjective probability. Since one or more of these probability types is a dominant feature in the development or explication of a great many social theories, a general review is conducted of how these types were and are defined and applied. The analysis is then expanded by relating the types to the underlying methodological approaches in social science (positivist, subjectivist, and critical). Examples are taken from the literature dealing with the study of organizations, including occupations as one kind of organization. In sum, this chapter attempts to delineate how uncertainty is used to describe human behavior in organized groups, with specific emphasis on the development of theory and analysis in the study of occupations and organizations.

I am indebted to Eliot Freidson, Laura Kitch, and Sharon Zukin for their invaluable criticisms.

UNCERTAINTY, RISK, AND PROBABILITY IN THE SOCIAL SCIENCES

Uncertainty has an exciting though rather ambiguous record as a concept in twentieth-century philosophy and science. In the sciences, it was a basic concept in the development of the theory of quantum mechanics, where the contradictions of simultaneity of wave and particle action were seen to result in an ultimate indeterminacy of physical processes. The action of particles can only be partially defined; events could no longer be specified in determinate sequences—there are only complementary forms in a world of possibilities. This was the crux of Heisenberg's principle of uncertainty (Heisenberg 1958) and of the philosophical notion of irreducible uncertainty (see, for example, Watkins 1957). From this conceptual crucible, a host of theories and discoveries has mushroomed in atomic and subatomic physics. Their applications have done more to affect the direction of human history than any other structure of thought during the twentieth century.

This major physical-philosophical reassessment has had a tremendous effect on the social sciences as well. In his book <u>The Human Use of Human Beings</u> (1954), the mathematician Norbert Wiener gave further legitimacy to Weber's assertion (Weber 1949) that social science is probabilistic in nature. Wiener stated that innovation in systems approaches the highest probability in randomly generated types, which create chaos. Complete randomness is the state of entropy, or total uncertainty, which follows the second law of thermodynamics: confusion increases and order decreases in the universe. Yet, there are islands of decreasing entropy—most notably, living organisms and organizations of interacting people. These are examples of the "least probable" state, the state of information in which forms and distinctions exist and seek purpose, where uncertainty is in the process of decreasing (Wiener 1954; Prigogine 1975; Prigogine and Rice 1975).

Working from this base, social scientists have been slow to apply the concept of uncertainty to their own theories. Where it has been used, it has been defined in several different ways. The British economist Anthony Downs (1957) has defined uncertainty as "any lack of sure knowledge about the course of past, present, future, or hypothetical events." Thus, we might visualize a continuum of uncertainty, ranging from "perfect certainty"* to complete uncertainty.

---

*The phrase is tautological. However, some analysts use it to separate out nonrefutable, a priori, ideal-type certainty from the looser empirical meaning of certainty. For example, see Ayer (1956, p. 25) and Dewey (1929, p. 128).

Another British economist, G. L. S. Shackle (1961), has specified two levels of uncertainty: <u>distributional uncertainty</u>, where statistical probability estimates can be drawn, and <u>nondistributional uncertainty</u>, where the amount of knowledge is insufficient to make a decision on the basis of probability estimates. Instead, a "possibility" situation occurs, in which one's "good judgment" must be applied.* In his classic work <u>Risk, Uncertainty and Profit</u> (1933), the U.S. economist Frank Knight earlier suggested that in the latter type of uncertainty, more risk is involved on the part of the decision maker, and there is no guarantee of correctness of the decision (Knight 1921, p. 231). According to Knight (1921, pp. 238-40), this view of uncertainty could be perceived as a continuum.† An attempt to visualize this is made in the following diagram:

decreasing probability		increasing probability
UNCERTAINTY		CERTAINTY
subjective probability (possibility)	statistical probability	mathematical probability

Mathematical probability is probability in which no judgment enters into the calculation. It is the least probable state, based on "a logic-tight system of elements and relationships, all of which are univocally defined" (Guilford 1956, p. 204) and which follow nature so closely that mathematical logic can be applied to events. In the normal distribution curve, the exact degree of probability is known in advance; the probability of winning in a lottery is known exactly. No uncertainty is involved; there is only one alternative, one best way. Mathematical probability exemplifies the ideal-type situation— human behavior as an emergent form cannot be considered. In

---

*The psychologist John Cohen (1964) uses a similar structure for many unusual examples: the mentally ill, diviners, suicides, sporting events, and gambling.

†Reviews of the literature (Edwards 1954; Foldes 1958) suggest the arrangement of probability on a continuum of decision-making. The association of the term <u>uncertainty</u> with probability derives from the historical roots of the former in the development of science. Some of its unfortunate consequences are spelled out in this chapter.

mathematical probability, all alternatives of action in a specified universe are known. The utility of all values is maximized. "The [mathematical] decision-maker maximizes expected utility by choosing the alternative that has a utility larger than all the others" (Luce and Raiffa 1957, p. 31).* Risk, on the other hand, is by definition subjective and perceptual. It is always tied to social structure and process. "A decision is risky if the individual involved believes it to be" (Milburn and Billings 1976, p. 116). For the logical positivist, uncertainty is an objective consequence describing degrees of lack of knowledge of the social and physical environment. Yet, risk can still occur if the individual or group involved is not aware of the logical system of explanation of the phenomenon in question.

In statistical probability situations, uncertainty is present. For example, insurance rates are based on statistical tables in which classes of events (death rates, accident rates, and so forth) are estimated. Goals are clear, and expected consequences can be quantified (Mack 1971, p. 9). Judgments must be made on the number of variables to be considered and the weights given each in reaching a decision on the classification of groups. The variables and their weights are chosen on the basis of limited knowledge of available alternatives.

The risk involved in these cases of controlled uncertainty may or may not be considerable. Even though the outcomes are limited and are _known_ to be limited by the individual or group involved in choosing, the resulting consequences (the outcomes) are _perceived_ to be more extreme or less extreme; thus, the risk is seen as greater or lesser. In addition, the _preference_ for one consequence over another results in the feeling that the more negative the consequence, the greater the risk. Also, different people have different preferences regarding their need for certainty, as well as different perceptions of uncertainty (Milburn and Billings 1976). Thus, perceived risk and uncertainty preferences will vary with the situation in which social interaction takes place.

In a landmark book on organizational theory, James Thompson uses a two-dimensional model to indicate four outcomes, ranging

---

*The work on applications of mathematical probability was introduced by John von Neumann and Oskar Morgenstern (1953). Following von Neumann and Morgenstern, Luce and Raiffa (1957, app. 1) emphasize that human behavior is "less probabilistic," that is, contains uncertainty. In the field of decision-making, Simon (1957, 1958) has shown how mathematical probability is a totally inaccurate technique for analysis of social behavior—that is, the human being does not operate perfectly logically.

from complete certainty to high uncertainty. The model portrays decision-making as revolving around beliefs about cause-effect relations and preferences regarding possible outcomes (Thompson 1967, pp. 134-35). If a decision is made with complete certainty regarding both beliefs and outcomes, a situation of <u>computational strategy</u> occurs, a computer-precise response synonymous with mathematical probability. When uncertainty exists only in outcome preferences, a <u>judgmental strategy</u> exists, and when it exists only in cause/effect beliefs, a <u>compromise strategy</u> occurs. Finally, <u>inspirational strategies</u> occur when uncertainty surrounds both dimensions, a situation of subjective probability proportions. It is important to note here that the various types of uncertainty include both rational and nonrational elements of the decision-making process. Perceptions and preferences, up to this point limited to the definition of risk, are now an integral part of the concept of uncertainty. As I shall explain below, this is an important step in its development.

High uncertainty is characteristic of <u>subjective probability</u> situations. Decisions are unitary and nonrepeatable. Often, ends must be created, and only the extremes of the alternatives available are kept in mind by the decision maker (Shackle 1961, pp. 272-73). "It becomes . . . impossible . . . to assert on any objective ground that there is even approximately a certain fractional 'chance' of any particular result" (Knight 1934, vol. 13, p. 394). The rules of statistical probability do not operate. For example, in the social organization of political economy, capitalists argue that in addition to profits, the subjective probability (that is, the maintenance of uncertainty) that exists in free market competition provides the necessary incentive to keep the society viable—an equality of opportunity. On the other hand, the plea of socialists is that the reduction of uncertainty (perhaps to statistical probability?) will permit better planning for production, distribution, and earnings, leading to an equality of results.

These apparently contradictory statements of subjective probability are belief systems. What is fact for one is not fact for another. The question of "rightness" is in human behavior separate from the question of logical consistency.* These two worlds, the

---

*Barton and Parsons (1977, p. 179) have discussed this problem with the following example:

> A critic of democratic socialist beliefs may say that democratic socialism is a "contradiction in terms," but what he really means is that it is empirically

positivist one of instrumental knowledge and the normative one of human reflexivity, have been given unusual attention recently in philosophy in the work of Saul Kripke (1975, 1977). Kripke distinguishes between <u>possible truths</u> (subjective probability) and <u>necessary truths</u> (mathematical probability). Possible truths are comprised of statements that are true for one world (or society or social system) but may not be for another. Necessary truths take the form of statements that are true in all possible worlds. The latter is in the bailiwick of analytic philosophers, who deal with those statements that are true by definition, that is, mathematical axioms, the world of logic. Led by the seminal work of Bertrand Russell and Ludwig Wittgenstein, analytic philosophy attempts to logically examine reality through the meaning and structure of language.

In contrast, the world of experience (possible truths) deals with the knowledge of human experience. Phenomenology and existentialism are two major currents in this branch of learning. Beliefs and emotions are important factors to consider in the examination of reality. Contrary to the views of analytic philosophy, human experience can hold contradictions. This Hegelian primitive that reality is not free of contradiction is totally rejected by physical science, which adheres to the "laws of [the nonacceptance of] contradiction."* It is likewise rejected by analytic philosophy, which often appears to be attempting to pattern itself as a scientific discipline. Kripke, in attempting to synthesize the two worlds, states that beliefs and their resulting actions (or nonactions) may have sensations attached. What these sensations may be and how they can be measured is the central problem to solve.†

---

impossible because if everyone works for the government, people are not free to oppose the government. The socialist will say that democratic capitalism is a contradiction, because the concentration of wealth and power make democracy impossible.

*For a summary of this position, see Popper (1962, pp. 312-35). Popper emphasizes that the opposite of this law, the dialectical method, can be used to describe the history and development of scientific theories, but not to science itself. It merely describes polarities of a situation that in fact may be better examined by means of the trial-and-error method of science. Reality does not necessarily always develop dialectically.

†For a summary of Kripke's recent work in this area, see Branch (1977). Kripke's reliance on a hypothetical common denominator of measurement eliminates the notion of qualitative dif-

However, the desire to synthesize faces the ultimate epistemological problem, stated by Mannheim (1936), that those who attempt to describe reality objectively are themselves influenced by the values and beliefs of their own social position. Therefore, all knowledge is biased.* At best, one can only agree with the statement that

> perhaps the development of knowledge is, in fact, the successive growth and replacement of old errors by newer ones, but that these errors constitute the framework of social existence at any given time or place. Perhaps all we can do is become conscious of the efforts of the past as we move on (Bensman and Lillienfeld 1973, p. 4).

Subjective probability in human behavior is a separate, independent, and significant way of knowing. Knowledge that is ideology is separate from knowledge that is "physically" uncertain. The guiding (domain) assumption of social science is qualitatively different from that of physical science. The knowledge of the former varies with the historicity of its subject matter and by context and meaning in the constitution of data (London 1977).† In his discussion of subjec-

---

ferences and assumes comparability of the two philosophies. The sociologist Jurgen Habermas has been criticized for not successfully carrying out what he intended to do—a synthesis of the two (Giddens 1977, p. 211).

*Although Popper (1962, p. 226) states that "the very idea of error, or of doubt . . . implies the idea of an objective truth which we may fail to reach," Carveth's (1977, pp. 93-96) way of coming to grips with this dilemma is to advocate the position of realism and a "critical empiricism," which can indicate a "limited degree of orderliness in experience . . . sufficient to sustain life." Although we will always live with the uncertainty inherent in the larger questions of ultimate concern, with the development of knowledge, the scope of permissible belief can be narrowed, and we may attain closer approximations to "the truth of this world and modify it in a humanly gratifying manner."

†Movahedi and Ogles (1977) emphasize the qualitative distinctions between the three types of probability. "Subjective probability is a measure of the individual's strength of belief or confidence in a proposition which describes the world of experience." It is a function of the degree of confidence of the individual about a proposition;

tivity, Blumer (1969) emphasizes that human nature is truly emergent. People define activities as they act. Their interpretations are not an automatic application of established meanings, but a formative process in which meanings are used and revised in light of actions of self and others and their perceptions.

It remains that subjective probability in social scientific explanation is not "operationalized," that is, it is not compatible with the objective measures of physical science.* As Schutz (1967, p. 152) emphasized, subjective probability refers to "the subjective expectation on the part of one party that the other will manifest a reciprocal orientation." It is not the outside observer's "objective" judgment that establishes this probability. Indeed, there is no external point of observation—"The investigator is implicated in and has an effect upon any observation" (Gay 1978, p. 32).

UNCERTAINTY AS APPLIED TO
OCCUPATIONS AND ORGANIZATIONS

As described in the three types of probability above, uncertainty is utilized as a powerful conceptual tool by social scientists. These types serve as explanatory mechanisms in the major methodological approaches in social theory: positivist, subjectivist, and critical.† Although all three kinds of probability explanation may be

---

there are as many probabilities as there are individuals who express their beliefs about them. Mathematical (logical) and statistical (relative) probability are examples of logical statements independent of experience.

*Confusion over the terminology persists. Lem (1978) states that <u>subjective probability</u> by definition implies that certainty can be achieved—that the only reason we cannot predict human behavior is the technical impossibility of collecting the amount of data needed and not that the data do not exist. Homans (1962, 1963) holds this to be true for social science. On the other hand, says Lem (1978, p. 38), <u>objective probability</u> is a case where uncertainty lies within the province of the events themselves. "There is between the asker and all other people no physical difference that will explain the existential one. . . . No one knows and no one can know."

†Boguslaw and Vickers (1977) use these terms to distinguish them from the slightly different <u>functional</u>, <u>interactionist</u>, and <u>conflict</u> terms. Positivism emphasizes prediction and control of the basically unchanging natural laws of social behavior (exemplified by

found in any specific theory stemming from any one of these broad approaches, it is usually the case that mathematical probability is emphasized in positivism, statistical probability in subjectivism, and subjective probability in the critical approach. These tendencies are described in the following review and discussion of the relevant literature in occupations and organizations.

Positivist Theories

Positivist theories of organization have a long history of development, stemming from Auguste Comte's natural laws of social order, Herbert Spencer's organismic sociology, and Emile Durkheim's functionalism. The emphasis of these writers was to attempt to predict social behavior by examining the overall structure of societies. Modern structural-functionalism continued in this tradition, emphasizing equilibrium between interdependent parts. The social system, from small groups through international societies, became the focus for analysis. Even though Parsons himself is equivocal regarding voluntarism in human behavior (Scott 1963), his theories are utilized by systems theorists, the most highly positivistic group to emerge recently. Systems theory views the world or some part of it as a logical, closed system in which all behavior can be measured accurately enough for all actions to be predicted—a form of mathematical probability. The input (actions, values, beliefs, and so forth) can be analyzed, frequently through computerized programs, and the output will provide the correct information for social policy. When carried to its logical conclusion, systems theory states that near-certainty can ultimately be attained through improvement of statistical probability estimates.

---

structural-functionalism, behaviorism, and exchange theory). Subjectivism emphasizes the role of persons in shaping social behavior—that different people have different conceptions of what is real (phenomenology, symbolic interactionism, and conflict sociology). The critical approach emphasizes social change in terms of dialectical processes and what is historical and reflexive (Marxist and critical theories). There are different ways of breaking up the theoretical pie. For example, Ritzer (1975) depicts three groupings, or paradigms, as: social facts (structural-functionalism and conflict theory); social definition (symbolic interactionism, social action, and ethnomethodology); and social behavior (social behaviorism and exchange theory). Mitroff and Kilmann (1978), Cohen (1968), and Zollschan and Hirsch (1964) propose still other typologies.

18 / UNCERTAINTY

Systems theory is the logical result of positivist thinking in organization theory. However, most work in organizations and occupations has not been carried this far. Researchers in the positivist and voluntarist tradition have found the number of variables and their combinations too large (and in many cases impossible to measure) to accept the theory. Instead, their focus is on interdependence and stability, viewing organizations and occupations more or less as stable communities, with occasional encroachment from other groups (Goode 1957; Moore 1970; Parsons 1978). They are more concerned with the state of existing knowledge. For example, Fox (1957, p. 208) suggests three kinds of uncertainty faced by medical students: first, limitations in the body of knowledge; second, incomplete or imperfect mastery of available knowledge; and third, the difficulty in distinguishing between the first two. Merton and Barber (1963) discuss client ambivalence about professional behavior, based on the institutionally patterned relations between the two rather than deviant practices of professionals. Conflicting normative expectations of the client experienced in everyday relations with professionals generate distrust and hostility. Emphasis is on conflicts and uncertainties created in individual role performances rather than on the organizational conflicts and uncertainties within the profession and between the profession and outside groups, although Merton (1975) acknowledges the importance of the latter in the analysis of the former in his review of structural analysis in sociology.

The social science that presently comes closest to the mathematical probability model is economics.* The neoclassical model in economics depicts individuals as rational, self-interested beings selecting freely from among known alternatives of action in order to maximize their marginal productivity. Freedom to choose is freedom from control by the government and other institutions. Placing the burden of choice completely on the individual supports the argument that those who are in disadvantageous positions in society are there because of the choices they have made. The choices made are based on the amount of knowledge individuals have accumulated.

Theory and practice in the public accounting profession is a good example of the application of neoclassical economics to everyday problems. Through "objective" accounting principles and pro-

---

*Organizational theory, which has been dominated by the positivist model of the goal-oriented, bounded, rational organization, is a subdiscipline found in several social sciences and related disciplines.

cedures, uncertainty is reduced by quantifying information in a social system. The reduction of ignorance (through increased knowledge of the system) results in an equilibrated organization in which individuals perform as utility maximizers who expend the energy necessary to maintain the system as it is (Montagna 1971, pp. 145-47). The recently developed social audit extends this functionalist model into the macro economic realm of social and environmental ecology.

As Thurow (1977) has noted, the econometric model has failed to take into account certain parts of the reward system, such as power, prestige, friendship, and feelings of accomplishment. These and other stochastic (random) shocks to the system contribute a great deal of variance, enough so that economists should realize that "although it is possible to predict the center of mass of a distribution of stocks (atoms), it is not possible to predict the movement of any particular stock (atom)." Thurow appeals to economists to drop their largely unsuccessful attempt to explain economic reality through mathematical probabilities and to return to social scientific principles, at least of the statistical probability type.

Subjectivist Theories

Subjectivists are more concerned with the creation of new knowledge than with the reduction of ignorance. Dahrendorf describes a principle of uncertainty, in which no knowledge is indubitably true (Dahrendorf 1968, p. 240) and in which new knowledge is generated in and through the system either by emergent properties and/or by conflict. Occupations are viewed as temporary coalitions (Bucher and Strauss 1961) rather than as stable communities. Viewed historically, these work organizations often fragment and even dissolve (Strauss 1971, p. 77). This view is directly antithetical to the "positive mysticism" of Western religions, which are society oriented rather than individual oriented and which emphasize the perfectability of the system by rewarding people according to the risks they take to improve human nature and the environment (Horowitz 1966). Coming from a different perspective but arriving at the same position are the utopian socialist theories. The future is "perfect," the "one best way" of plan-rational orientation, where all needs are anticipated and the means of satisfying them are prescribed. Dahrendorf (1968, p. 240) summarizes his critique of this perspective by stating that the most important moral consequence of the principle of uncertainty is

> the necessity of maintaining a plurality of decision patterns, and an opportunity for them to interact and

compete. . . . Uncertainty demands variety and competition. <u>From the assumption of a fundamental uncertainty about what is right, there follows the necessity of conflict.</u>

The French sociologist, Michel Crozier, theorizes along the lines of the second law of thermodynamics, presenting bureaucratic organization as the opposite of uncertainty. The extreme rationalization created by bureaucracy produces a high degree of predictability in the organization.* Yet, no matter how bureaucratic the organization (or occupation), there remain areas of uncertainty, areas as yet unnoticed or too difficult for bureaucratization (Crozier 1964). These are areas where influence of a group within the organization can be expanded because control over the source of uncertainty means control over a position affected by this uncertainty. Johnson (1972, pp. 41-43) has discussed this phenomenon for occupations by emphasizing the social distance maintained by professionalizing occupations. The emphasis on the esoteric knowledge results in the dependence upon the professional's skills and has the effect of "reducing the common area of shared experience and knowledge." The autonomy and power of the occupation will be determined by the level of uncertainty, or "indeterminacy," maintained by its members (Jamous and Peloille 1970).

The power of a group is reduced when its source of uncertainty has been rationalized, especially with regard to the amount, specificity, and extent of rules and procedures. In time, this previously private knowledge becomes part of the public domain. In order to gain new power to replace that lost, a group will seek a new source of uncertainty. Groups are reciprocally dependent on power relations, power being ever-present in the organization because of "the impossibility of eliminating uncertainty in the context of bounded rationality which is ours" (Crozier 1964, p. 158).

All social situations require some degree of risk-taking, of dealing with the perceived unknown. People have power over other people because they control and apportion areas of uncertainty in which risk-taking is involved. This apportionment can filter down through the various levels of an organization because, as Blau indicates (1964, p. 219), responsibility for uncertainty is not neces-

---

*Rationalization is defined as organization according to the canons of logic and efficiency. It involves standardization, formalization, codification, systemization, accessibility, and availability of knowledge (see Heydebrand and Noell 1973).

sarily confined only to the top of organizations but can exist throughout their hierarchies.*

The element of trust is important in the organizational/occupational relationship. Kanter (1977) has pointed out that uncertainty in management positions in corporations creates pressures for conformity and the development of exclusive management circles. Uncertainty requires trust because "the greater the uncertainty the greater the pressures for those who have to trust each other to form a homogeneous group." The higher the position in this group, the greater the amount of uncertainty (nonroutine events and/or lack of information). "Issues such as 'direction' and 'purpose' cannot be reduced to rational formulae" (Kanter 1979, pp. 49, 52). The reduction of uncertainty reduces the need for homogeneity. Trust is no longer necessary because the impersonal bureaucratic mechanisms of routinization and the rationalization of areas of uncertainty ensure reliability in organizational control. Loyalty and conformity to the organization take the place of trust between colleagues, and the ranks can be opened to former undesirables. However, management often does discriminate because the more closed the circle is initially, the more difficult it is for outsiders to break in. Kanter points out that this protectionism may backfire. The very difficulty of gaining access to the higher ranks may be interpreted as a sign of incompetence of those trying to obtain entry. This justifies the action of keeping the ranks closed, with no new blood to share the power. This means continued emphasis on conformity and reduction of uncertainty, that is, less personal discretion and, thus, increased rationality. If there is no break in the circle, the organization ultimately disintegrates.

An important process in organizing and controlling uncertainty is professionalization. A profession is an organization of workers who control the terms, conditions, and content of their work in the settings where that work is performed. A profession has gained a monopoly over the right to control its own labor (Freidson 1977, p. 16). Professional control is attained in several ways: by licensing developed knowledge, by encroaching on the knowledge of other occupations, and by developing and controlling new knowledge. All of these are ways of expanding and controlling uncertainty (Montagna

---

*Although Blau concentrates on the social psychological correlates of power in this analysis, he later modifies his focus to what he considers to be the main thrust of sociology, the macro sociological perspective (Blau 1973, preface; Blau 1977). Blau's analyses are located within the positivist framework.

1977, p. 235). As established bodies of knowledge become rationalized, the profession looks for new areas where judgment must be exercised, where people will pay for the risk that the professional must take.* As professional knowledge becomes rationalized, less risk is required on the part of the professional in the decision-making process. Licensing, which entitles exclusive use of the knowledge, initially protects the profession from encroachment by client and other outside organizations. However, in the long run, many professional activities are rationalized and deskilled and are legislated into the public domain. Professional methods and techniques become accessible to nonprofessionals. As discussed in the examination of the critical approach, this tends to set up a process of professional change.

Those of the subjectivist persuasion would agree with the statement that the more professionalized the occupation, the more uncertainty and, thus, the more autonomy. However, autonomy is limited by the organizations in which professionals work. In professional organizations, workers set their own goals and carry them out. In industrial bureaucracies, skills tend to be segmented and controlled by management (Freidson 1973; Form and Huber 1976, pp. 785-86). Professionals in industrial bureaucracies or in highly rationalized professional firms tend to find themselves constricted by a bureaucratized system, though considerably less than their nonprofessional fellow employees (Engel and Hall 1973; Hall 1968; Montagna 1968; Smigel 1964; Blau 1963). Germane to this analysis is the finding of Lawrence and Lorsch (1967) that power tends to collect in subsystems that have a less bureaucratic structure, that is, those with uncertain environments.

It is only those occupations which can maintain a considerable amount of indeterminacy that will be able to withstand the tremendous rationalizing pressures of modern industrial society. Yet, there is a balance that must be maintained. Professionals can manipulate their knowledge base. Generating too much uncertainty (new knowledge) produces situations too unpredictable for risk-taking;

---

*One point of view (Riesman 1951) states that the client pays to remain ignorant so that s/he will be protected through licensing from the moral burden of such judgments. However, this has its drawbacks. As Nilson (1979) emphasizes, the public pays for the costs of professional incompetency—for example, in medicine, higher fees are charged to finance unnecessary surgery and malpractice insurance and litigation. The risk is in fact low and the gains are high when professionals are in full control of their knowledge base.

professionals are unwilling to engage in high-risk ventures—or it produces a situation of too much power, that is, public authorities fear monopolization of too large an area of professional control. On the other hand, too little uncertainty would result in situations of detailed rules and consequent rigidity (Wilensky 1964, pp. 148-49; Crozier 1964, p. 186; Montagna 1968, pp. 144-45).

Many authors fail to distinguish between uncertainty generated by technical-material factors and uncertainty created by people's perceptions. As techniques are rationalized, the amount of uncertainty (lack of knowledge of operations) will decrease. But at the same time, what is perceived to be uncertain may be a matter of the social control of knowledge. Perceived uncertainty is a social construct; it represents a choice of the professional or client regarding what s/he perceives as problematic. Therefore, the social conditions of knowledge development and control must be considered when examining indeterminate relations among persons in organizations and occupations. Critical theory attempts to accomplish this task.

Critical Theory

Critical theory states that society operates in a dialectical fashion, that is, our knowledge of social life affects (resonates with) the development of that life. Rather than a conflict between true opposites, there is a _tendency_ toward, and not the _necessity_ or _inevitability_ of, the development of contradictions between social activity (social relations and structures) and its outcome, that is, the forces of production (Heydebrand 1977, pp. 86-89). There is historical possibility of contradiction and not objective probability without contradiction (Wilson 1977, pp. 5, 238).* As Sewart (1978, p. 21) describes it, "We must examine the relationship between the practice

---

*Contrary to the point of view of modern analytic philosophy, one does not have to "define the value of his speech in terms of its capacity to be anonymous, for it would mean that the justification for speaking resided not in him but in externalities whose clarification and description is to be considered its only legitimate occasion." For the analytic philosopher, speech becomes more objective (truthful) as we overcome our values and biases through discipline (Wilson 1977, p. 236). For the critical theorist speech is truthful when viewed as human action which must be considered as changeable and in change. Speech cannot be grasped independently of its being lived (Wilson 1977, pp. 241-52).

of social scientific research and how our knowledge about social life affects the evolution of that life." Social scientific knowledge cannot be separated from the object it studies. Facts, as they are presently constituted, are not to be accepted uncritically to explain social reality. For if facts are separated from values, they tend to reify existing social reality—the continuing reproduction of existing relationships—and reflexivity and praxis are prohibited. Instead, critical theory emphasizes history as a human process capable of being influenced by human activity rather than as a natural process governed by natural laws. Critical theory merges reason and action, reflection and commitment (Sewart 1978, p. 19).

From the critical perspective, science, as a social system, operates in a dynamic process of transformation, that is, dialectically (Feyerabend 1975, p. 23). The development of scientific knowledge has been described as a rapid, often revolutionary struggle between contradictory, or at the least alternative, paradigms (Kuhn 1970; Foucault 1972). Nonscientific forms of organization can also be seen to develop along paradigmatic lines. Paradigms provide the possibility of contradictions in the epistemological sense, that is, organizational change, like scientific change, is a matter of change in the knowledge used in that setting (Imershein 1977, p. 34). Knowledge as consciousness affects the material conditions of existence. It has been suggested (Brown 1978, p. 373) that organizations are in fact paradigms in operation; that they provide roles to be enacted in certain ways and in certain settings and in relation to other roles. They are the "concrete structural manifestations of social institutions . . . the more or less established outcome of historically specific human practical activity" (Heydebrand 1977, p. 101).

Occupations as one type of organization, if viewed historically, tend to develop contradictions both internally and externally. Within an occupation, at any given time, there may be one or more competing paradigms or methods of practice at various stages of rationalization.* For example, in the public accounting profession, auditing,

---

*Kuhn's definition of paradigm is limited to the level of the exemplar, that is, the puzzle-solving, concrete applications of a highly structured body of belief specific to a substantive area as held by a subgroup (a specialized community) within a scientific discipline. That so many disciplines, both scientific and nonscientific, have used the term indicates the need for a concept to symbolize the processes discussed here.

This concept of the paradigm should not be confused with the methodological approaches used above, that is, positivist, subjectiv-

management advisory services, and offshoots of management-advisory services, such as actuarial practice, are found at various stages of computerization, rule-making, rule enforcement, and the like (Montagna 1968, 1974). The same dialectical procedure is described both within and between organizations by Benson (1977, p. 15). By mapping the historical sequence of changes in professional knowledge and power, the time order of events and their utility in social change are given reflection. At another level, that between occupations, there may exist competition for control of a paradigm. Occupations compete in the marketplace with opposing "domain proposals" (Benson 1973, p. 389). They innovate in structures of uncertainty while at the same time their established bodies of knowledge are being rationalized. The process of rationalization itself tends to instigate its opposite, namely, uncertainty (Montagna 1974, p. 172; Imershein 1977)—that is, professionals find it in their interests to pursue areas of new knowledge or what is perceived to be new knowledge by the client in order to maintain work autonomy. It is a rare case in which this pursuit goes uncontested by some other occupation. The result is the emergence of a new theory, a new paradigm for the occupation, or even a new occupation for the paradigm. The emphasis is on the historical development of power relations, on occupational change. Bensman and Lilienfeld (1973, pp. 90-103) point to the conflict of history, mathematics, politics, and sociology with philosophy. As each of these new disciplines developed, they began to form new or greatly revised paradigms that were often antagonistic to, or defiant of, philosophy. In part, philosophy has attempted to recoup its losses by maintaining a "professional jurisdiction," if not its intellectual preeminence. Thus were developed the areas of political philosophy, philosophy of history, social philosophy, philosophy of science, and so forth. Becker (1978) analyzes the conflict between ceramists and fine artists in the discovery of new paradigms, and Montagna (1971) investigates the competition between public accountants, management consultants, and administrative scientists for control of the existing paradigm of systems theory.

    At a third level is the analysis of the contradictions between occupations and organizations. Professionals in bureaucratic organizations are the classic example. As rationalization occurs in occupations, there is a transfer of power and control from the occu-

---

ist, and critical. These approaches are lower level belief systems and have been referred to variously as domain assumptions (Gouldner 1970, p. 35), themata (Holton 1975, p. 334), and metaparadigmatic disciplinary matrices (Eckberg and Hill 1979, p. 934).

pation to the organization* and from lower participants in the organization to higher participants. A recent analysis (Heydebrand 1977) specifies the contradictions between work groups, listing three major types of control structures in work organizations in historical sequence: (1) "occupational status groups," comprising the professions and the crafts, which sell judgment; (2) "legal-bureaucratic groups," comprising private corporate and public bureaucracies, in which routinization of tasks and procedures is accomplished through legitimated rational methods;† and (3) the "self-organization of labor," that is, grass roots labor organizations, consumer groups, and client groups, which are self-governed and cut across categories in the division of labor. They include several occupations and act in the public interest and not in the interests of the client. Each of these structures tends to come into contradiction with the previous control structure and the new productive forces in which labor develops (Heydebrand 1977, p. 93).‡

At a fourth level is the emphasis on how existing occupational and organizational structures are in contradiction to the dominant political economy. Braverman (1974, pp. 112-20) traces the history of the routinization of occupational tasks, which he says is not endemic to all societies, but specifically to capitalist societies. It is capitalist organizations that emphasize management control over work processes in order to maximize profits by exploiting labor power. If it could, management would completely deskill professional work; it has already gone a long way in its goal to do so

---

*Freidson (1973) has called these the occupational principle (control primarily through professional associations and unions) and the administrative principle (control through bureaucratic management).

†These two types are basically synonymous with the occupational and administrative principles of control.

‡Haug (1977, p. 225) suggests that there are a series of historical events and social changes which will render professional control obsolete, that is, the worldwide increase in educational levels; the deskilling of professional tasks, resulting in the use of lesser-trained personnel; growing emphasis on an ideology of accountability to the public and occupational equality; client consciousness, created by centralization of professional services in bureaucratic organizations; the rationalization of professional knowledge through computerization; and as a result of these, the demystification and consequent accessibility and control of much professional knowledge by the public.

(Kraft 1977).* Jacoby (1976) elaborates on this process, stating that just as profit decreases as capitalism matures, so too does intelligence (intelligence being the critical substance of thought, the spontaneous, creative aspect—in other words, that element of personality from which uncertainty in the form of new knowledge develops). In academia, for example, the goal is more "accumulate or perish" than "publish or perish." New schools, innovations, advances, and breakthroughs are announced like new brands, Marxism not excepted, in order to corner a piece of the market. Obsolescence is so rapid that one must produce anew to keep one's name in the literature. Emphasis is on quantity rather than quality: there is a falling rate of intelligence. Likewise, in the media, early periods were characterized by creativity and competition. But with concentration and centralization and "constant capital," the rate of intelligence fell. Jacoby suggests this is true of capitalist society as a whole—that this form of "secondary exploitation" results in a powerful tendency toward class unconsciousness.

One group of critical theorists believe the antithesis of capitalism is not socialism but bureaucracy (Baptista 1974; Leforte 1975). The bureaucratic structure of advanced industrial societies is the only dichotomous structure able to manage present-day large-scale, complex societies. Whereas professionals can move from one enterprise to another by virtue of the autonomy received through their control over their body of knowledge, bureaucrats are not mobile. They are dependent on their specific place in the organization of the enterprise. Success is measured by the range of authority over people and machines. Administration of the means of production is the major differentiating factor between bourgeoisie and proletariat (Leforte 1974, p. 49). Bureaucracy is not just a parasitical organ but a new form of social class lodged in the mass institutions of society: the political parties, labor unions, and production organizations. It becomes a class for itself by subordinating itself to the state, which, in turn, protects the bureaucratic group through a police state and ideology. Bureaucratization is not merely a result of economic rationalization: it is part and parcel of a system of domination that develops economic rationalization, that is, decreasing

---

*Lasch (1977, p. 24) suggests that games, as a form of play, have taken on added meaning in modern society because they provide what work used to provide—risk, daring, and uncertainty. Modern industry and culture have rationalized work, religion, and even warfare to the point where the elements of risk and uncertainty are practically eliminated.

uncertainty, and, in the process, exploits labor (Leforte 1974, pp. 52-54). In other words, capitalist rationalization is superseded by bureaucratic rationalization, which will, in turn, lead to a bureaucratic state of "gentle totalitarianism." Implied in this analysis is the contradiction between occupational autonomy and organizational control.

Whereas Marx emphasized the transitory nature of bureaucracy, as being but a contradictory form of organization on the road to communism, Weber depicted it as the most powerful and ultimate expression of rationalization. Critical theorists elaborate that the vicious circle of bureaucracy can only be broken by the "emancipatory cognitive interest" of individuals engaging in open communication and self-reflection (Habermas 1971, pp. 308-15). There is emancipation through choice. People can seek to maximize their personal utilities, their preferences. What is utility for one may not be for another (O'Brien and Stern 1978, pp. 83-84; Held 1977). Technological-material interests can be accompanied by a cultural revolution of expansion of ends. Hearn (1978) describes how Marxist China attempted this melding by politicizing consciousness. The Great Leap Forward and the Cultural Revolution were attempts to control the growing bureaucracy by introducing decentralized decision-making through teams of workers, administrators, and technicians—to politicize bureaucracy. All organizational decisions were seen to have political significance. Study and discussion groups were necessary. Managers and technicians were periodically reassigned to workers' jobs, and a strong dialogue was established between the three groups. However, in practice, public communication was not free, but foisted on workers and controlled by leaders.*

In his analysis of professions, Johnson (1977) warns us of the dangers of this one-dimensional thinking in using the concept of uncertainty. We must recognize that in addition to the more "objective" uncertainty generated by technological factors of production, there is a perceived uncertainty, an ideology that is class based. The indeterminacy developed by the professions depends on their relation to capital. Those who work to aid the control of capital at its highest advisory levels are able, because of their proximity to capital, to control the indeterminacy of their work situation, that is, both technical and perceived uncertainty. Those not directly related to capital are relegated to the objective uncertainty of limiting

---

*For a discussion of the totalitarian aspects of this system, see Bettelheim (1978), Leys (1977), Tz'ong (1978), and Lee (1977).

technical functions. Consequently, one finds differences within a profession between the elite and the workers. For example, in public accounting, large-firm partners are engaged in advising on major policy decisions for their corporate clients. Yet, the same function of servicing capital stresses the technical aspects of their subordinate colleagues' work, creating the conditions for rationalization and ultimate work devaluation (Johnson 1977, p. 108). Considering only the technical base of a profession, that is, its body of knowledge, is insufficient. One needs to examine "the social meaning of knowledge and the social conditions which allow practitioners to control their knowledge" (Klegon 1978, p. 272).

Technology and task are not objective forces totally independent of human action (Montagna 1977, p. 187). Uncertainty represents a <u>choice</u>, for example, as a power group, professionals can to a considerable extent determine to what degree their work will be routinized and deskilled. However, the limits of their choice are culturally determined. Burrage (1972) describes how one society (Great Britain) may decide to protect the mystique of what its physicians practice by means of ideological generalizations and in another (United States) the decision is to expand through innovation because rationalization of technique is not as easily controlled. In the latter society, there are weaker group sanctions on individual behavior, and within the profession, there is less emphasis on early occupational socialization—a guildlike relation between physician and patient does not exist.

Societal priorities, then, also play an important role in limiting the amount of uncertainty to be generated and controlled. For example, in advanced capitalist societies, there is strong <u>public support</u> for standardized summaries of information on corporate financial transactions. In the United States, this has been enacted into federal law. The Securities Exchange Act of 1934 requires that all publicly traded corporations be audited annually by a certified public accountant (CPA). As CPAs come to perceive the danger of the deskilling of the audit, they are moving in two directions: first, to protect their control over the setting of accounting regulations and determination of auditing procedures; second, to develop a field of "management advisory services." The first attempts to protect the profession from government incursion in an area of traditionally secret knowledge; the second attempts to gain control of new and already developed knowledge. Thus, <u>public control</u> of information on corporate financial transactions is averted. It is highly likely that capitalist ideology will permit this control to remain in a profession that generally supports that ideology. The automated audit may not forever be averted, but what will constitute that audit CPAs fervently intend to have left to their discretion. Certain management services may be able to extend the audit to nonrationalized, non-computerized areas of competence.

On the other hand, state interference, as is the case with social work, does permit public control and limits the amount of uncertainty preferred by professionals and perceived by clients. With increased client involvement created by state interference, there may be less client willingness to conform to its traditional role of "patient," thus seriously limiting the <u>dialogue</u> necessary for free communication. Communication thus remains at the level of institutionalized discourse (Bauman 1976, pp. 104-6); there is no critique of reality—unless, that is, professionals are perceived as part of the ruling class and clients as part of the working class, which is a much oversimplified model of reality.

In their enduring optimism, critical theorists hold that no communications problems are forever unsolvable. Therefore, emancipation may ultimately occur through a slow "diffuse dissemination of insights" (Habermas 1974, p. 32). If a meaningful dialogue finally does take place between parties, then ultimately professions as we know them would disappear, for authenticity (the critical stage) demands equality (Bauman 1976, p. 108). But will this emancipation result in a necessarily less repressive society? How much government control will citizens accept in professional areas where matters of life and death or varying degrees of inequality are at stake? How will open discussion be maintained if expertise must in the last analysis be honored?

Although it is a comprehensive method for explaining social reality, critical theory remains idealistic in its assumptions as to outcomes. It is this ambiguity that in the end leaves it as just another alternative critique of society. As a critique of the theory of knowledge, however, it is extremely helpful in examining social structure and process. It is much more indeterministic than the dominant scientific method of positivism. Its "intrinsic inconclusiveness" is evident in its postulates of uncorrectible error and the changeability of human culture. Uncertainty, in the form of the requirement of personal judgment in dialogue, is necessary to attain the conditions of liberty. The basic affirmation of critical theory is that human behavior is constantly changing and that "the limits of such changeability can be tested only in practical trial" (Bauman 1976, p. 110).

UNCERTAINTY AT THE MICRO LEVEL

Uncertainty frequently has been used as a concept to examine those theories that concentrate on the relationships between individuals—the theories of many social psychologists, symbolic interactionists, ethnomethodologists, human capital theorists, and so forth. As Goffman (1973) points out, most of these theories argue that people are prompted to reduce uncertainty because they have an intolerance of ambiguity. Social norms serve as standards to reduce uncertainty and prevent paralysis of action. Roth's (1963) development of timetables, Malinowski's (1926) treatment of ritual, and Lane's (1962) use of ideologies to explain political attitudes all describe methods utilized by the actor to reduce uncertainty. Traditionally, uncertainty has been used to analyze situations of unequal power, where capricious acts are more common. For example, Homans (1961, p. 298) emphasizes that people attempt to reduce the anxiety of uncertainty by acquiring "risk capital." They come to depend on knowledge of what to expect in situations in order to obtain rewards and avoid punishments. Homans' exchange theory works at the level of statistical probability. The propositions of sociology can ultimately be reduced to those of elementary economics and psychology (Homans 1962).

However, the approach of ethnomethodology takes an entirely different point of view. It depicts the nonrationality of rational thought. Behavior is often problematic and loaded with uncertainty (Garfinkel 1967). Rationality itself is a social construction. People employ rationality retrospectively, following actions that were initially chaotic or stumbling (Brown 1978). As Brown explains (1978, pp. 369-70), organizations act similarly. The plan of action is an ideological device that imposes management's definition of reality on the communication and conduct of those in the organization. The plan of action produces problems that generate responses, which are then reconceptualized—after the responses are given—to fit organizational goals. A recently developed "garbage can model" of behavior in organizations follows this approach (Cohen, March, and Olsen 1972; March and Olsen 1976). There are certain cognitive limits on rationality. To borrow a term from the economist Leibenstein (1976), the selective rationality of rational maximizing behavior and nonrational impulsive behavior operates. In organizational settings, this creates a great deal of ambiguity. The garbage can model describes how problems, solutions, and people are mixed together in mostly unexpected and unpredictable sequences—for example, past mistakes are reconstructed and reinterpreted through after-the-fact planning, and solutions look for problems so that they (the solutions) may be utilized.

In sum, discussions using uncertainty at the micro level have provided many insights into human behavior. But as with nearly all studies in this perspective, there are severe structural limitations. Important organizational and interorganizational (including comparative and cross-national) relations are omitted. Such phenomena as professionalization and bureaucratization are not considered, or, if they are, they are limited to individual case studies or, at most, to small group analysis. One area that does hold promise is the application of ethnomethodological principles to large-scale organizations. However, few empirical studies have yet been conducted using this approach.

CONCLUSIONS

Uncertainty is a concept that is basic to the development of theory in the physical and social sciences. In the study of human behavior, the concept as taken from physical science has been very helpful in analogies—for example, in the attempt of economists to move away from the highly deterministic models of econometrics (emphasizing mathematical probability) to stochastic models. However, these analogies are quite limited because of basic differences between the two scientific realms—most importantly, by the distinction of the emergent quality of human behavior in social science. Positivism, the dominant school in most social sciences, does not recognize this distinction. Its utilization of mathematical and statistical probability applied to social phenomena, such as organizations or occupations, produces a sterile reductionism. Only when emergence is considered and reflexivity practiced will there be effective measurement of social phenomena.

As an example, the clash between occupational autonomy and organizational control is explicated by theorists of all persuasions. Positivists generally view this struggle as one that takes place within the system and which will in its resolution strengthen that system through a process of feedback resulting from those functions that will best maintain system balance. Mathematical and statistical probability estimates are often made to explain deviations in occupational and organizational behavior. Subjectivists concentrate on the relations of power between groups in areas of irreducible uncertainty, the sources of that power, and the changes created by control over those sources. A balance between forces may or may not be the outcome. Critical theorists emphasize the tendency toward contradictions established in social life. Actions counterposed by theory will generate historical process and transcendence of original social situations through this process. Ideology has a limited ability to examine its assumptions and the assumptions underlying those assumptions, ad infinitum (Gouldner 1976, pp. 48-49). But the dialectic sets up the questioning and criticism of others' and one's own assumptions. In the process, it demystifies the taken-for-granted belief and value systems "lost" in the social structure. The dialectical analysis of class interests, of intelligence, of language, of bureaucracy, and the like are cases in point. In conceptual terms, there is established a dialectic of rationalization and uncertainty, the specific nature of the contradiction determined by the particular dominant paradigm (rationalizing mechanism) and the challenging paradigm (uncertainty-producing mechanism). However, to leave the process at this level of analysis invites a facile interpretation of technological determinism. Occupational and organizational control systems rationalize in practice, whereas the development of knowledge (theory) attempts to overcome this rationalization, only to be in turn rationalized. Technology is the dominating feature. But praxis contains perceived uncertainty and preferences in choice, which themselves are sources of new possibilities. Rationality contains the seeds of its own destruction.

The concept of uncertainty has been used to explain the nature of organizational reality by all manner of theorists. It would seem that the broadest and most sensitive use of the concept is in theories of the critical perspective, where history and holism are emphasized.

REFERENCES

Ayer, A. J. 1956. The Problem of Knowledge. Middlesex, England: Penguin.

Baptista, José. 1974. "Bureaucracy, Political System, and Social Dynamic." Telos 22 (Winter): 66-84.

Barton, Allen H., and Parsons, R. Wayne. 1977. "Measuring Belief System Structure." Public Opinion Quarterly 41 (Summer): 159-80.

Bauman, Zygmunt. 1976. Towards a Critical Sociology. London: Routledge & Kegan Paul.

Becker, Howard S. 1978. "Arts and Crafts." American Journal of Sociology 83 (January): 862-89.

Bensman, Joseph, and Lillienfeld, Robert. 1973. Craft and Consciousness: Occupational Technique and the Development of World Images. New York: Wiley.

Benson, J. Kenneth. 1973. "The Analysis of Bureaucratic-Professional Conflict: Functional Versus Dialectical Approaches." The Sociological Quarterly 14 (Summer): 376-94.

_____. 1977. "Organizations: A Dialectical View." Administrative Science Quarterly 22 (March): 1-22.

Bettelheim, Charles. 1978. "The Great Leap Backward." Monthly Review 30 (July-August): 37-130.

Blau, Peter M. 1963. The Dynamics of Bureaucracy. Chicago: University of Chicago Press.

_____. 1964. Exchange and Power in Social Life. New York: Wiley.

_____. 1973. The Organization of Academic Work. New York: Wiley.

_____. 1977. "A Macrosociological Theory of Social Structure." American Journal of Sociology 83 (July): 26-54.

Blumer, Herbert. 1969. Symbolic Interactionism: Perspective and Method. Englewood Cliffs, N.J.: Prentice-Hall.

Boguslaw, Robert, and Vickers, George R. 1977. Prologue to Sociology. Santa Monica, Calif.: Goodyear.

Branch, Taylor. 1977. "New Frontiers in American Philosophy." The New York Times Magazine, August 14, 1977, pp. 12-14, 47-53.

Braverman, Harry. 1974. Labor and Monopoly Capital: The Degradation of Work in the Twentieth Century. New York: Monthly Review Press.

Brown, Richard Harvey. 1978. "Bureaucracy as Praxis: Toward a Political Phenomenology of Formal Organizations." Administrative Science Quarterly 23 (September): 365-82.

Bucher, Rue, and Strauss, Anselm. 1961. "Professions in Process." American Journal of Sociology 66 (January): 325-34.

Burrage, Michael. 1972. "Democracy and the Mystery of the Crafts: Observations on Work Relations in America and Britain." Daedalus 101 (Fall): 141-62.

Carveth, Donald L. 1977. "The Disembodied Dialectic: A Critique of Sociological Relativism." Theory and Society 4 (Spring): 71-102.

Cohen, John. 1964. *Behaviour in Uncertainty*. London: Allen & Unwin.

Cohen, Michael D.; March, James G.; and Olsen, Johan P. 1972. "A Garbage Can Model of Organizational Choice." *Administrative Science Quarterly* 17 (March): 1-25.

Cohen, Percy S. 1968. *Modern Social Theory*. New York: Basic Books.

Crozier, Michel. 1964. *The Bureaucratic Phenomenon*. Chicago: University of Chicago Press.

Dahrendorf, Ralf. 1968. *Essays in the Theory of Society*. Stanford, Calif.: Stanford University Press.

Dewey, John. 1929. *The Quest for Certainty*. New York: Capricorn Books.

Downs, Anthony. 1957. *An Economic Theory of Democracy*. New York: Harper's.

Eckberg, Douglas Lee, and Hill, Lester, Jr. 1979. "The Paradigm Concept in Sociology: A Critical Review." *American Sociological Review* 44 (December): 925-36.

Edwards, Ward. 1954. "The Theory of Decision-Making." *Psychological Bulletin* 51: 380-417.

Engel, Gloria V., and Hall, Richard H. 1973. "The Growing Industrialization of the Professions." In *The Professions and Their Prospects*, edited by Eliot Freidson, pp. 75-88. Beverly Hills, Calif.: Sage.

Feyerabend, Paul. 1975. *Against Method: Outline of an Anarchist Theory of Knowledge*. London: New Left Books.

Foldes, Lucien. 1958. "Uncertainty, Probability and Potential Surprise." *Economica* 25 (August): 253-72.

Form, William H., and Huber, Joan Althous. 1976. "Occupational Power." In *Handbook of Work, Organization, and Society*, edited by Robert Dubin, pp. 751-806. Chicago: Rand McNally.

Foucault, Michel. 1972. The Archeology of Knowledge. London: Tavistock.

―――. 1978. Discipline and Punish: The Birth of the Prison. New York: Pantheon Books.

Fox, Renée C. 1957. "Training for Uncertainty. In The Student Physician, edited by Robert K. Merton, George C. Reader, and Patricia L. Kendall, pp. 198-217. Cambridge, Mass.: Harvard University Press.

Freidson, Eliot. 1973. "Professions and the Occupational Principle." In The Professions and Their Prospects, edited by Eliot Freidson, pp. 19-38. Beverly Hills, Calif.: Sage.

―――. 1977. "The Futures of Professionalisation." In Health and the Division of Labor, edited by M. Stacey et al., pp. 14-38. London: Croom Helm.

Garfinkel, Harold. 1967. Studies in Ethnomethodology. Englewood Cliffs, N.J.: Prentice-Hall.

Gay, William C. 1978. "Probability in the Social Sciences: A Critique of Weber and Schutz." Human Studies 1 (January): 16-37.

Giddens, Anthony. 1977. "Review Essay: Habermas's Social and Political Theory." American Journal of Sociology 83 (July): 198-212.

Goffman, I. W. 1973. "Notes on Uncertainty in Social Research." Mimeographed. New York University, Department of Sociology.

Goode, William J. 1957. "Community within a Community: The Professions." American Sociological Review 22 (April): 194-200.

Gouldner, Alvin W. 1970. The Coming Crisis of Western Sociology. New York: Basic Books.

―――. 1976. The Dialectic of Ideology and Technology. New York: Seabury Press.

Guilford, J. P. 1956. Fundamental Statistics in Psychology and Education. New York: McGraw-Hill.

Habermas, Jurgen. 1971. *Knowledge and Human Interests*. Boston: Beacon Press.

_____. 1974. *Theory and Practice*. London: Heinemann.

Hall, Richard H. 1968. "Professionalization and Bureaucratization." *American Sociological Review* 33 (February): 92-104.

Haug, Marie. 1977. "Computer Technology and the Obsolescence of the Concept of Profession." In *Work and Technology*, edited by Marie Haug and Jacques Dofney, pp. 195-214. Beverly Hills, Calif.: Sage.

Hearn, Francis. 1978. "Rationality and Bureaucracy: Maoist Contributions to a Marxist Theory of Bureaucracy." *The Sociological Quarterly* 19 (Winter): 37-54.

Heisenberg, Werner. 1958. *Physics and Philosophy*. New York: Harper & Row.

Held, Virginia. 1977. "Rationality and Reasonable Cooperation." *Social Research* 44 (Winter): 708-44.

Heydebrand, Wolf V. 1977. "Organizational Contradictions in Public Bureaucracies: Toward a Marxian Theory of Organizations." *The Sociological Quarterly* 18 (Winter): 83-107.

Heydebrand, Wolf V., and Noell, James J. 1973. "Task Structure and Innovation in Professional Organizations." In *Comparative Organizations: The Results of Empirical Research*, edited by Wolf V. Heydebrand, pp. 294-321. Englewood Cliffs, N.J.: Prentice-Hall.

Holton, Gerald. 1975. "On the Role of Themata in Scientific Thought." *Science* 188: 328-34.

Homans, George. 1961. *Social Behavior: Its Elementary Forms*. New York: Harcourt, Brace & World.

_____. 1962. *Sentiments and Activities: Essays in Social Science*. London: Routledge and Kegan Paul.

_____. 1963. "Schlesinger on Humanism and Empirical Research." Commentary in *American Sociological Review* 28 (February): 99-100.

Horowitz, Irving Louis. 1966. Three Worlds of Development: The Theory and Practice of International Stratification. New York: Oxford University Press.

Imershein, Allen W. 1977. "Organizational Change as a Paradigm Shift." The Sociological Quarterly 18 (Winter): 33-43.

Jacoby, Russell. 1976. "A Falling Rate of Intelligence?" Telos 27 (Spring): 141-46.

Jamous, H., and Peloille, B. 1970. "Professions or Self-Perpetuating Systems? Changes in the French University-Hospital System." In Professions and Professionalization, edited by J. A. Jackson, pp. 109-52. New York: Cambridge University Press.

Johnson, Terence J. 1972. Professions and Power. London: Macmillan.

_____. 1977. "Professions in the Class Structure." In Industrial Society: Class, Cleavage, and Control, edited by Richard Scase, pp. 93-110. New York: St. Martin's Press.

Kanter, Rosabeth Moss. 1977. Men and Women of the Corporation. New York: Basic Books.

Klegon, Douglas. 1978. "The Sociology of Professions: An Emerging Perspective." Sociology of Work and Occupations 5 (August): 259-83.

Knight, Frank H. 1921. Risk, Uncertainty and Profit. Boston: Houghton Mifflin.

_____. 1934. "Risk." In The Encyclopedia of the Social Sciences, vol. 13, pp. 393-95. New York: Macmillan.

Kraft, Philip. 1977. Programmers and Managers: The Routinization of Computer Programmers in the United States. New York: Springer-Verlag.

Kripke, Saul. 1975. "Outline of a Theory of Truth." The Journal of Philosophy 72 (November 6): 690-716.

_____. 1977. "Speaker's Reference and Semantic Reference." Midwest Studies in Philosophy, 2: 255-67.

Kuhn, Thomas S. 1970. *The Structure of Scientific Revolutions.* Rev. ed. Chicago: University of Chicago Press.

Lane, Robert E. 1962. *Political Ideology: Why the American Common Man Believes What He Does.* New York: Free Press.

Lasch, Christopher. 1977. "The Corruption of Sports." *The New York Review of Books* 24 (April 28): 22-25.

Lawrence, Paul R., and Lorsch, Jay W. 1967. "Differentiation and Integration in Complex Organizations." *Administrative Science Quarterly* 12 (June): 2-31.

Lee, Sarel. 1977. "Subterranean Individualism: Contradictions of Politicization." *Telos* 33 (Fall) 5-26.

Leforte, Claude. 1974. "What Is Bureaucracy?" *Telos* 22 (Winter): 31-65.

Leibenstein, Harvey. 1976. *Beyond Economic Man: A New Framework for Microeconomics.* Cambridge, Mass.: Harvard University Press.

Lem, Stanislaw. 1978. "Odds." *The New Yorker*, December 11, 1978.

Leys, Simon. 1977. "Chinese Shadows: Bureaucracy, Happiness, History." *The New York Review of Books* 24 (June 9): 17-28.

London, Ivan D. 1977. "Convergent and Divergent Amplification and Its Meaning for Social Science." *Psychological Reports* 41: 111-23.

Luce, R. Duncan, and Raiffa, Howard. 1957. *Games and Decisions.* New York: Wiley.

Mack, Ruth P. 1971. *Planning on Uncertainty: Decision Making in Business and Government Administration.* New York: Wiley Interscience.

Malinowski, Bronislaw. 1926. *Crime and Custom in Savage Society.* London: Routledge & Kegan Paul.

Mannheim, Karl. 1936. *Ideology and Utopia.* New York: International Library.

March, James G., and Olsen, Johan P. 1976. *Ambiguity and Choice in Organizations*. Oslo, Norway: Universitet Sforlaget.

Merton, Robert K. 1975. "Structural Analysis in Sociology." In *Approaches to the Study of Social Structure*, edited by Peter M. Blau, pp. 21-52. New York: Free Press.

Merton, Robert K., and Barber, Elinor. 1963. "Sociological Ambivalence." In *Sociological Theory, Values, and Sociological Change: Essays in Honor of Pitirim A. Sorokin*, edited by Edward A. Tiryadian, pp. 91-120. New York: Free Press.

Milburn, Thomas W., and Billings, Robert S. 1976. "Decision Making Perspectives from Psychology: Dealing with Risk and Uncertainty." *American Behavioral Scientist* 20 (October): 111-26.

Mitroff, Ian I., and Kilmann, Ralph H. 1978. *Methodological Approaches to Social Science*. San Francisco: Jossey-Bass.

Montagna, Paul D. 1968. "Professionalization and Bureaucratization in Large Professional Organizations." *American Journal of Sociology* 74 (September): 138-45.

——. 1971. "Certified Public Accounting: Organization, Ideology, and Social Power." *American Behavioral Scientist* 14 (March/April): 475-91.

——. 1974. *Certified Public Accounting: A Sociological View of a Profession in Change*. Houston: Scholars Books.

——. 1977. *Occupations and Society: Toward a Sociology of the Labor Market*. New York: Wiley.

Moore, Wilbert E., in collaboration with Gerald W. Rosenblum. 1970. *The Professions: Rules and Roles*. New York: Russell Sage Foundation.

Movahedi, Siamak, and Ogles, Richard H. 1977. "Probability of a Hypothesis or of a Theory: Some Uses and Misuses of the Concept of Probability." *Sociology and Social Research* 62 (October): 43-62.

Nilson, Linda Burzotta. 1979. "An Application of the Occupational 'Uncertainty Principle' to the Professions." *Social Problems* 26 (June): 570-81.

O'Brien, David J., and Stern, Richard S. 1978. "Sociology and Choice." Humanity and Society 2 (May): 75-89.

Parsons, Talcott. 1978. "A Paradigm of the Human Condition." In Action Theory and the Human Condition, edited by Talcott Parsons, pp. 352-433. New York: Free Press.

Popper, Karl. 1962. Conjectures and Refutations: The Growth of Scientific Knowledge. New York: Basic Books.

Prigogine, Ilya. 1975. "Dissipative Structures, Dynamics, and Entropy." International Journal of Quantum Chemistry 9: 443-56.

Prigogine, Ilya, and Rice, Stuart A., eds. 1975. Advances in Chemical Physics, Vol. 30: Molecular Scattering: Physical and Chemical Applications. Chichester, England: Wiley Interscience.

Riesman, David. 1951. "Toward an Anthropological Science of Law and the Legal Profession." American Journal of Sociology 57 (September): 121-35.

Ritzer, George. 1975. Sociology: A Multiple Paradigm Science. Boston: Allyn & Bacon.

Roth, Julius. 1963. Timetables: Structuring the Passage of Time in Hospital Treatment and Other Careers. Chicago: Bobbs-Merrill.

Schutz, Alfred. 1967. The Phenomenology of the Social World. Evanston, Ill.: Northwestern University Press.

Scott, John Finley. 1963. "The Changing Foundations of the Parsonian Action Scheme." American Sociological Review 28 (October): 716-34.

Sewart, John J. 1978. "Critical Theory and the Critique of Conservative Method." The American Sociologist 13 (February): 15-22.

Shackle, G. L. S. 1961. Decision Order and Time in Human Affairs. Cambridge: Cambridge University Press.

Simon, Herbert A. 1957. Models of Man. New York: Wiley.

―――. 1958. "The Role of Expectations in an Adaptive or Behavioristic Model." In Expectations, Uncertainty, and Business Behavior, edited by Mary Jane Bowman, pp. 49-58. New York: Social Science Research Council.

Smigel, Erwin O. 1964. The Wall Street Lawyer: Professional Organization Man? New York: Free Press.

Strauss, Anselm. 1971. Professions, Work and Careers. San Francisco: Sociology Press.

Thompson, James D. 1967. Organizations in Action. New York: McGraw-Hill.

Thurow, Lester C. 1977. "Economics 1977." Daedalus 106 (Fall): 79-94.

Tz'ong, Mi. 1978. "The Trial of a Counterrevolutionary." Dissent 25 (Summer): 261-69.

Von Neumann, John, and Morgenstern, Oskar. 1953. Theory of Games and Economic Behavior. 3rd ed. Princeton, N.J.: Princeton University Press.

Watkins, J. W. N. 1957. "Decisions and Uncertainty." In Uncertainty and Business Decisions, edited by C. F. Carter, G. P. Meredith, and G. L. S. Shackle, pp. 116-37. Liverpool: Liverpool University Press.

Weber, Max. 1949. The Methodology of the Social Sciences. Translated and edited by Edward A. Shils and Henry A. Finch. New York: Free Press.

Wiener, Norbert. 1954. The Human Use of Human Beings. 2d rev. ed. Garden City, N.Y.: Doubleday Anchor Books.

Wilensky, Harold. 1964. "The Professionalization of Everyone?" American Journal of Sociology 70 (September): 137-58.

Wilson, H. T. 1977. The American Ideology: Science, Technology and Organization as Modes of Rationality in Advanced Industrial Societies. London: Routledge & Kegan Paul.

Zollschan, George K., and Hirsch, Walter, eds. 1964. Explorations in Social Change. Boston: Houghton Mifflin.

3
ORIENTATION TO AMBIGUITY
Allen Lerner

No society—certainly no modern society—can provide its members with a sense of total certainty. An analyst working with the notion of an ambiguous social context must accept that the definitional question of just <u>how much</u> ambiguity makes for an ambiguous social context can be a persistent and troublesome question. It is not a question that can be answered directly, but we may avoid prohibitive difficulties by emphasizing two ideas at the outset.

First, the notion of an ambiguous social context is inherently relative. It is used here to denote a society with patterns of norms that are perceived by members to be fluid and unclear. Members perceive (or better, sense) it to be a vague social context, heavily riddled with inconsistency and with indefinite signals.

Second, to keep the definitional problem in bounds, we must stress the assumption that while a climate of such perceptions may characterize the broad social environment as a whole, individuals and collectivities within such an environment may vary in their adjustments to this climate (Lerner 1978). The nature of variations in adjustments may be such as to allow some individuals and collectivities to cope more effectively than others. The aim of this chapter is to suggest that we may distinguish two broad types of orientations to ambiguity by individuals and collectivities and that these types of orientations imply a distinct actor profile in each case.

AMBIGUITY AND COPING

Coping takes on a specific meaning in ambiguous contexts. While popular usage has made coping a cliché synonym for survival, that is an especially unproductive sense for work in the ambiguous context. Except in the most draconian circumstances, survival is not perceived as a prominent issue. Draconian circumstances would presumably be too clear a set of signals to expect for an ambiguous social context, by definition. For our purposes, then, a more useful sense of an ability to cope is to see it as an ability to identify and pursue goals. The greater the ability to cope in the ambiguous social context, the greater the ability to both retain a sense of purpose and act effectively with it.

A number of orientations in political science and sociology, and perhaps all of economics, build their images of actors on this notion of goal formation and implementation attempts. These are the approaches that rest on an epistemological decision to treat the actor as a rational decision maker. The actor-as-decision-maker orientation entails the view that actors take what may be called a predominantly cognitive orientation to their environments. They are problem solvers. Such actors are treated at least "as if" they could understand their environments as a web of causes and effects. They are treated as if they could conceptualize desired future states, could identify access points for intervention in the cause-effect web, and could fashion strategies of intervention, all richly enough to deal with some degree of contingency. In assuming that actors not only can act but do act, there is also implied a sense of efficacy. Indeed, this is a modest additional assumption once we have endowed an actor with a capacity to discern the causal web and to discriminate points of access guided by a strategy for intervention related to a goal.

Actors as decision makers must be capable of cognitively "mapping" their environments; they must have a basis for plotting positions and interventions. The presumption of an ambiguous social context requires that we relax the assumption of actors as rational decision makers in several respects. The more ambiguity, the more trouble mapping. The environment presents a reality that is unclear.

If the lack of clarity presented by an ambiguous context is thought of as an interference with the mapping process, it might be argued that rational decision-making always occurs in the presence of some uncertainty, which simply suggests some attention to work with probabilities. An important element in the notion of an ambiguous context, however, is that the uncertainty it engenders is characteristically pervasive. It is not that there are blank spots on the map or delineated areas of ignorance in the context of a perceived reliable instrument. Rather, the map is vaguely suspicious throughout. The uncertainty of ambiguity is more diffused than the uncertainty of ignorance, albeit also less intense than the uncertainty of ignorance. Assuming that the ambiguous context is distinguishable from the relatively unambiguous context empirically, that is, assuming that there is a justification for the actor's perspective, the analyst's assumption is that the inconsistency in pattern and indefiniteness in signals is a pervasive, structural characteristic of the system in the case of the ambiguous context. Again, of course, this is a relative notion and a question of degree.

To assume an empirical context where actors generally do, and with justification, orient to a vague and pervasive <u>systemic</u> uncertainty raises an epistemological question early in analysis. Given an ambiguous social context, how much may we rely on the notion of a predominantly <u>cognitive</u> orientation for actors, as the term was used above, in the sense of the rational decision maker?

HIGH AND LOW COGNITIVE ORIENTATION

The suggestion in this chapter is that the adoption of such an orientation in the ambiguous social context be viewed as problematic. The simplest way to do this, and a way that is appropriate to an initial, exploratory view, is to dichotomize the notion of orientation to ambiguity in this regard. Let us posit two broad categories of orientation to ambiguity: one characterized by a felt high degree of cognitive control, <u>high cognitive orientation</u>; the other by a felt low degree of cognitive control, <u>low cognitive orientation</u>. While this is a relative distinction, dichotomizing for exploratory purposes suggests treatment as polar opposites, which may be developed as pure types. Thus, while their empirical manifestations would always be imperfect illustrations to some degree, the categories can be useful organizing ideas (Pinder and Moore 1979).

The labels, <u>high cognitive orientation</u> and <u>low cognitive orientation</u>, are preferable to labels retaining the rational decision-making phrasing, despite the importance of that notion in bringing us to this juncture. We suspected that the rational decision-maker notion should be treated problematically rather than paradigmatically in the ambiguous context. This suggested that some elements implicit in the rational decision-maker construct would still be useful components in an analysis of orientations to ambiguity. But we also contended that the rational decision-maker construct presumed an action context that limited "mapping" capability only through the persistence of uncertainty as a delineable ignorance, not as a diffused ambiguity. This suggests that the rational decision-maker image carries too many connotations linked to its generic context, the unambiguous context. By fashioning our categories of orientation to the ambiguous context with <u>some</u> components of the rational decision-maker construct, instead of the entire notion and some sense of its opposite, we can avoid having to frequently comb our

types of excess meanings. We can deal directly with the implications for contrasting orientations, which the idea of an ambiguous context throws into sharpest relief.

In stressing the relative basis of a distinction between high and low cognitive control, or <u>felt</u> control as the notions were phrased, the commitment to deal with perceptions is underscored. A felt high degree of cognitive control does not have the empirical prerequisite of a demonstrable ability to formulate successful solutions to problems, or "winning strategies" in competitive terms. Positing a felt high degree of cognitive control for an actor simply attributes to the actor the belief that s/he can approach the environment with such strategies. It is the description of a posture—not necessarily a capability, from our view. Some actors with a felt high degree of cognitive control may misunderstand their environment. They may act on strategies that are doomed to be losing strategies, empirically, though their misunderstanding leads them to anticipate the opposite. They might even be so far from an accurate view of the cause-effect web of their environment that their thinking could be called <u>magical</u>, though this is a limiting case, as we shall see. In the main, if they act purposefully in the "magical" world in terms of formulating goals, strategies, and points of intervention, as a result of which they attribute to themselves the capability of securing the intended response from the environment with a probability that makes the effort worthwhile to them, they might seem to deserve the high cognitive orientation label we are assigning, as it has been developed to this juncture.

In this sense, attributing a felt high degree of cognitive control to an actor attributes the disposition to act strategically. Our basis for definition is preferable to empirical success or empirical accuracy of actor perceptions as a basis for definition. It avoids confounding a discussion of orientations with measurements of success, which may be influenced by many extraneous factors, including luck. It also avoids confounding a discussion of orientations with difficult discussions of objectivity.

The only additional characteristics of actor perceptions that must be added in describing the high cognitive control orientation has to do with processing feedback. We want to assume for all action contexts that they are rich enough, and actors are frail enough, that any actor strategy may need revision while in progress. In the case of extremely erroneous world views, extreme enough to approach magical thinking, the actor's cause-effect images guiding his/her empirical assumptions may be so tautological and sealed from disconfirmation that negative feedback is categorically undetectable as such. For actors so far from a pragmatic capability, rationale becomes impenetrable rationalization, immune from empirical disconfirmation to the actor. It seems better to treat such limiting cases as a type of low cognitive orientation (specifically, a true believer, as noted below) (Hoffer 1951). Thus, we will posit the additional requirement for the high cognitive orientation of an ability to identify and absorb negative feedback. This is a reality-testing capability, an ability to show pragmatism. (See Figure 3.1.)

FIGURE 3.1

Orientations to the Ambiguous Context

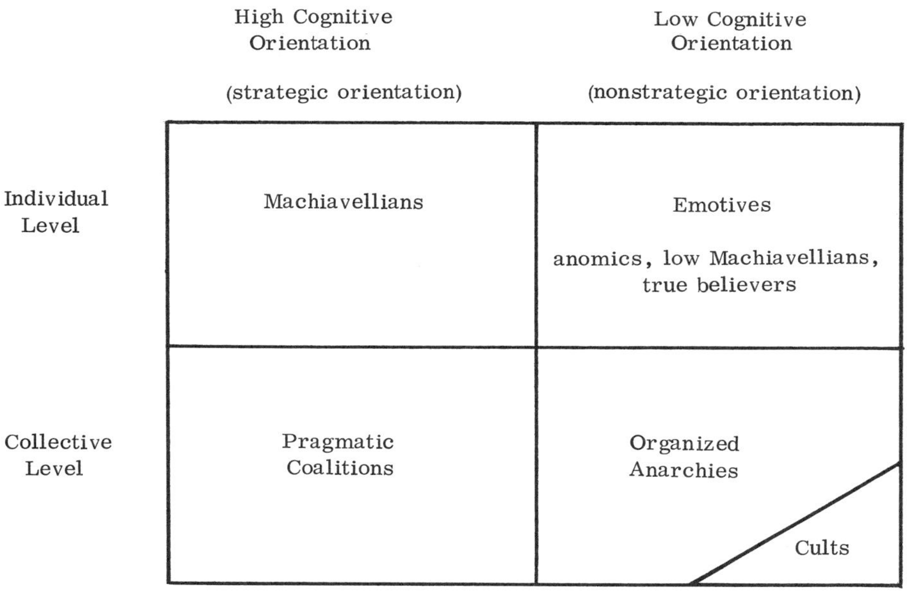

	High Cognitive Orientation (strategic orientation)	Low Cognitive Orientation (nonstrategic orientation)
Individual Level	Machiavellians	Emotives anomics, low Machiavellians, true believers
Collective Level	Pragmatic Coalitions	Organized Anarchies Cults

Source: Compiled by the author.

INDIVIDUAL-LEVEL ORIENTATIONS

Machiavellians

As Figure 3.1 indicates, one suggestion in this chapter is that for individuals, the contrast between high and low cognitive orientation to ambiguous contexts may be thought of as a contrast between a

Machiavellian and an emotive orientation. Laboratory and survey work on Machiavellianism have indicated several broad features of the Machiavellian orientation (Christie and Geis 1970):

(a) a comparative freedom from conventional morality;
(b) less of a tendency to feel dissonance, or at least less need for dissonance reduction;
(c) a tendency to strike "game theory" solutions in bargaining situations, rather than solutions based on some broader sense of social equity;
(d) greater enjoyment of the "game" per se, in situations with a competitive element;
(e) less affective distraction in task-oriented activity;
(f) greater tendency to initiate structure in situations with ambiguous elements, and to initiate structure to their advantage.

The last two points are the obvious points of departure in suggesting that a Machiavellian posture be the core concept in a profile of the high cognitive orientation by individuals in the ambiguous context. Experimental work on the ability of high Machiavellians to exploit an ambiguous setting suggests that high Machiavellian winning can be frustrated if the structure of games is made comprehensive, clear, and inflexible. In contrast, as subjects are left free to improvise rules and strike bargains in a more ambiguous setting, high Machiavellians begin to win, and win dramatically (Christie and Geis 1970).

Discerning a world view from laboratory data has its limitations, and transposing such a world view for discussion in a setting broader than what the laboratory work intended certainly has its limitations—but in a work concerned with preliminary speculation, some license may be granted. Consider then a possible line of inference regarding the notion of a Machiavellian orientation to the ambiguous context at the societal level.

In conceptualizing a high cognitive orientation to an environment of unclear signals and fluid norm patterns, the essential characteristic was the retention of a purposive, means-ends orientation. This is retention of the pure rational decision-making orientation of economic man.* Machiavellianism reflects this in the tendency to

---

*Machiavellian- "ism" constructs are sometimes used to describe a preoccupation with power (Wagner and Swanson 1979). This is not the issue here.

produce game theoretic solutions to coalition problems. Freedom from conventional morality should further facilitate retention of a problem-solving (that is, strategic) orientation to the environment if we assume that the ambiguous context is perceived by an implicit comparison with stable, conventional, and now bygone states of the given action system. Fidelity to conventional morality in the ambiguous context may be understood as retention of an outdated orientation. A conventional morality for a context that is by definition no longer reliably conventional suggests a limited capacity to adapt strategically. It constrains action to precedents drawn from a context for which clear analogies are not available, by definition. In contrast, readiness to think the unthinkable widens options, especially when the unthinkable is now one more vague and thus permeable category.

Similarly, greater freedom from the need to reconcile current behavior with beliefs and past actions facilitates a widening of the behavioral repertoire and, so, enhances strategic adaptability. It not only mandates less screening tests for contemplated behaviors but, also, opens more categories of action out of which to fashion such behaviors. Presumably, such a freedom to break remnant patterns from the unambiguous context could also be combined with a freedom from excessive concern for establishing some new pattern of constraints to be imposed on the self prior to action.

The suggestion that Machiavellians also enjoy the competitive, strategizing game per se augurs well for strategic adaptation in the ambiguous context. Obviously, it would suggest an added, intrinsic incentive to approach the environment strategically, beyond the problem-specific rewards associated with a particular goal. What might be straining for the nonstrategic orientation is exciting instead.*

Emotives

What we are calling the nonstrategic, our low cognitive, orientation to the ambiguous social context is partly suggested by the contrast between high and low Machiavellians in the discussions of experimental findings. The high Machiavellian, as noted above, is not distracted by the affective dimension in task activity. Low

---

*The more usual tack is to treat ambiguity as a source of stress (Kahn et al. 1964). The implication here is that its stressfulness is problematic.

Machiavellians are: one might say they act as if they accepted a Kantian categorical imperative. In contrast, high Machiavellians, though they operate with few imperatives, would presumably opt for an "instrumental imperative," were we to press the contrast with such language (Lerner 1976).

The low Machiavellian undertakes rational strategies but does not compete successfully against high Machiavellians. The affective responsiveness of the low Machiavellian is part of an integrated task and emotional orientation. Our concern here is with an ambiguous context per se rather than a specific contrived game with some ambiguous (better, uncertain in our vocabulary) aspects of rule structure. Thus, it seems wise to consider greater variety in predominantly emotive orientations, or low cognitive orientations, as we have called them. Specifically, we may consider emotive extremes that reflect anticognitive, antirational postures. Such postures under the rubric of emotive, low cognitive orientation would imply less task-responsive capacity than simple low Machiavellians, who still can strategize rationally albeit within the constraints of affective sensitivity. Two more extreme postures under the emotive rubric are the true believer and the anomic (Hoffer 1951; Riesman 1950).

As an emotive orientation to the ambiguous social context, the true believer develops a strong affective tie to a particular cause, often personified by a revered leader. Associated with the true believer profile is a low sense of self-esteem; we may presume, therefore, potentially little sense of efficacy if ever cut loose from the cause. Discussion is polemical and emotional; negative feedback is impossible to absorb. Individual goals with clear operational meaning, independently determined and pragmatically pursued, are beyond the true believer's repertory. The theme is exclusively emotive, with commitment and intensity.

Consider an anomic to be the true believer without a belief. There is no sense of efficacy, no pragmatic task capability. Orientation, or better disorientation, is defined on an emotive dimension, but here, the emphasis is on emotive incapacity. Task incapacity is a correlate of passivity in disorientation. Thus, the Machiavellian's strong sense of self, efficacy, and task identification are absent. While these contrasts among individual orientations to ambiguous contexts invite several interesting observations, it may be useful to develop some notion of contrasting orientations by collectivities before discussing the individual level any further.

COLLECTIVE-LEVEL ORIENTATIONS

Pragmatic Coalitions

We can pursue the question of collectivities' orientations to the ambiguous context—again in terms of high cognitive control and low cognitive control—by seeking collective-level analogies to the individual-level orientations we have discussed. From this perspective, it would seem that a collectivity orienting itself to an ambiguous societal context in a way analogous to a Machiavellian orientation by individuals might well be described as a pragmatic coalition.

Consider the properties of an ambiguous context and the features that might be expected for a collectivity adopting a high cognitive control orientation to this context. In contrast to the unambiguous context, the ambiguous context should be one in which affiliation, and certainly extended affiliation, is difficult. Values display ambivalence. Identifications should thus be loose and comparatively superficial. Behavioral objectives and goals should be short-term and modest. They would be confined perhaps to discontinuous, relatively short chains of incremental task ambitions. The ambiguous context is not a propitious environment for comprehensive task activity or sustained programmatic action by collectivities. On the collective level, this is an environment of expedient shifting coalitions. Success in such an environment should be understood in relative terms—as the accomplishment of limited objectives associated with minimal agendas. Thus, collectivities that are effectively task oriented, that is, high cognitive control in orientation, should tend to be small, pragmatically disposed groups, held together by a common task interest, albeit an interest expressed in terms of limited objectives, and consequently for limited duration (Frohlich 1975). This image seems fairly reflected in the notion of a pragmatic coalition.

Cults and Organized Anarchies

On the collective level, the image of the ambiguous context is so infused with notions suggesting near anarchy (though a tepid anarchy to be sure) that one may well ask why collectivities that would merit classification as low cognitive orientation should aggregate at all. Individuals are born and so must orient; those not displaying a high cognitive control orientation must be addressed by a typology, through some parametric description. Individuals may orient passively, poorly, or irrationally, but they do not evaporate. The latter is a possibility, however, on the collective level (Olson 1965). If a pragmatic, efficacious, task-focused high cognitive control orientation is problematic on the collective level, as well as on the individual level, in the ambiguous context, the analytic category of a low cognitive control orientation, in contrast, might be presumed to have an empty set. It could be argued that the blandness of the environment, and the atomistic tendencies it fosters, inhibit potential groups' formation, so that those groups unlikely to orient with high cognitive control are unlikely to form at all.

Our scheme ought to take this into account in some way. Thus, it may be assumed from our perspective that collectivities rarely form with a low cognitive control orientation in periods where ambiguity characterizes the societal context. The exception in this vein would be aggregations of true believers in cults. It seems not unreasonable to assume further that anomics in the ambiguous context are the potential recruitment pool for true believers, assembled by an extreme Machiavellian should it suit one's purpose, or focused on one truest believer with rhetorical gifts or some other basis for personal appeal compelling to the extreme emotives (Willner 1968). But assuming cults to be a fringe and, hence, small set of collectivities with a low cognitive orientation to the ambiguous environment, any numerically and socially significant population of collectivities with a low cognitive orientation should be fashioned out of collective structures already in place prior to an environmental transformation to the perceived ambiguous mode.

In another section (below), we will discuss the possibility of relating the typology of actors in the ambiguous context to antecedent categories of actors proper to the unambiguous context. For now, on the strength of the observation that except for cults, any collectivities with low cognitive orientation to the ambiguous context must be formed from collective structures in place, consider the notion of organized anarchies (March and Olsen 1976). March, Olsen, and their colleagues have developed the image of organized anarchies making "garbage can" decisions to describe the behavior of large organizations in ambiguous situations. The nuances are considerable, but for our purposes, the essential point is that the traditional view of organizational decision-making as "rational," however bounded, is inaccurate in the ambiguous case. Decision-making in such a context is better thought of as "an outcome or an interpretation of several relatively independent 'streams' within an organization" (p. 26). March and Olsen (1976, pp. 26-27) focus on four such streams:

1. Problems, which are "distinct from choices; and they may not be resolved when choices are made."
2. Solutions, a solution being "somebody's product. . . . It is an answer actively looking for a question . . . you often do not know the question in organizational problem solving until you know the answer."
3. "Participants, [who] come and go. . . . Substantial variation in participation stems from other demands on the participants' time (rather than from features of the decision under study)."
4. "Choice opportunities, . . . occasions when an organization is expected to produce behavior that can be called a decision. . . . Although the streams are not completely independent of each other, an organizational choice is a somewhat fortuitous confluence. It is a highly contextual event, depending substantially on the pattern of flows in the several streams."

In developing the profile of organized anarchies, né organizations, now displaying such behavior, it is observed that there is a distinctive emphasis on ceremonial participation by members of the collectivity. Drawing heavily on Edelman (1964), the symbolic value of participation and of the objects of discussion are stressed. It is observed that members are frequently indifferent to any implementation of decisions, and the affective dimension of member relation to the organization is of special importance in explaining behavior.

Though I prefer to reserve a fuller critique of the garbage can notion for another time, it is useful to note here that garbage can explanations are held to be most powerful by their proponents in those aspects of organizational behavior noted to be least bureaucratic, least Weberian. For those areas of organizational activity, hierarchy and even power struggle explain less than "biases" representing socialization cues from the larger environment, which undercut the importance of formal organizational procedure in determining individual behavior in the erstwhile organizational context (March and Olsen 1976, p. 311).

One of the problems of garbage can theorizing may be that it is impressed with the fact that organizations do not behave with bureaucratic rationality if they are not bureaucracies. In the garbage can cases (often universities and free schools), organizational "rationality" is not detectable, but individual rationality tempered by heavy doses of socialization—we may say <u>acculturation</u>—is. The rub, and therefore finding, in the garbage can mode of analysis seems to lie primarily in the fact that people retain the collectivity affiliation, but collective-level rationality is undetectable.

Instead, individual-level rationality guided by a socialization to extraorganizational (often professional) group values predominates. The individual appears to be the last level of actor showing clearly purposive behavior, albeit in pursuit of symbolic satisfactions. The collective level is really more an environment that is irrational only if viewed as an actor. It must be stressed, however, that the collectivity is an acknowledged common action context in the sense of a community nested in a larger environment. The community is a context of rewards, analyzed primarily in terms of symbolic values. Viewed in these terms, the notions are familiar.

While the garbage can/organized anarchy view as some countermodel of organizational behavior may be troubled, for our purposes, its basic image is valuable in fashioning an image of a collectivity with a low cognitive control orientation to the ambiguous context. Simply put, bureaucracies unable to adapt to a developing ambiguous context may exhibit the features of such organized anarchies if the individual identifications with the bureaucracy and acculturation to its ways can persist in the minds of participants though its powers as a rational, goal-oriented collectivity in the traditional sense are largely defunct. In a kind of ultimate goal displacement, fidelity to ritual, ceremony, and symbolism not only replace goals but also eventually replace fidelity to a specific structure of routines, as program coordination is lost. The image is that of fragments of routine distorted to enlarge their symbolic value by a calculus, if any, of individual affective needs rooted in (usually professional) role stereotypes reinforced by groups outside the collectivity. In this sense, the organized anarchy producing garbage can decisions is essentially a web of emotive ties expressed through modern organizational rituals. The rituals are fashioned from what were once integrated programs of behavior logically mapped to collective goals identified with common, pragmatically chosen purposes.

With this understanding of organized anarchies, we may consider them to be a second, and the major form, of collective-level orientation of low cognitive control to the ambiguous social context. They eschew problem action in favor of choice ceremony. The latter is pursued for symbolic rather than tangible rewards; the organized anarchy represents an emotive orientation. It may be thought of as a collective format fashioned from the remnant structure of a bureaucracy or, at least, a purposive, task-oriented organization already in place. We can explain the existence of organized anarchies without having to posit a starting mechanism or aggregating process that would have to operate in the context of a low cognitive orientation already prevalent. This yields a type of low cognitive collectivity in the ambiguous context that should be more frequent and more important than the cult. It is the latter that may actually aggregate in the emotive mode.

TRANSFORMATION OF CONTEXT: ANALOGUES FROM THE UNAMBIGUOUS CONTEXT

Given the format limitations for this chapter, I would like to conclude with two brief observations concerning the notion of transformation from the unambiguous to the ambiguous context. Let us confine our discussion now to the so-called postindustrial, or technological or organizational, society, all of which is to say, our society. Focusing on the connotations emphasized by the <u>organizational society</u> label, the expectation is that the large-scale formal organization is the prevalent form of collective actor. Regarding the transformation issue, the question is whether such organizations in the comparatively unambiguous context will transform into organized anarchies or a collection of pragmatic coalitions, as the context shifts to the ambiguous mode. From the perspective of this chapter (see Figure 3.2), the expectation would be that organizations are more likely to yield a collection of pragmatic coalitions if the task orientation of the organization, its collective purpose, was the effective predominant theme of organization. In contrast, an organized anarchy should result if the institutionalization of participation and commitment to role performance were so thorough prior to the onset of pervasive ambiguity that considerable goal displacement and ritualization had taken place.

In general terms, adaptation to the ambiguous context would presumably entail enhancement of the predominant organizational theme prior to the change in context. Thus, the predominantly task-oriented organization would be expected to yield a task-oriented high cognitive orientation analogue in the ambiguous mode, that is, pragmatic coalitions. The organization that is less effectively task oriented, and in effect more ritual dependent, or secularly ceremonial, should yield a comparatively less task-oriented low cognitive control analogue, that is, an organized anarchy. It would perhaps be a fair corollary observation that the first organizations to show signs of organized anarchy would be those populated by members who bring a predominantly emotive, affect-focused orientation to their participation—or to turn things about, organizations that stress such themes in their role relations at the expense of more task-based themes.

On the individual actor level, the transformation issue may be raised in terms of the following question: What are the unambiguous context analogues of Machiavellians and emotives? It would seem that the unambiguous context counterparts should be thought of as types likely for a relatively more stable (as actors would perceive it) affiliation-conducive environment. Such an environment should not generate extreme types compared with the ambiguous context.

FIGURE 3.2

Orientation to Ambiguity

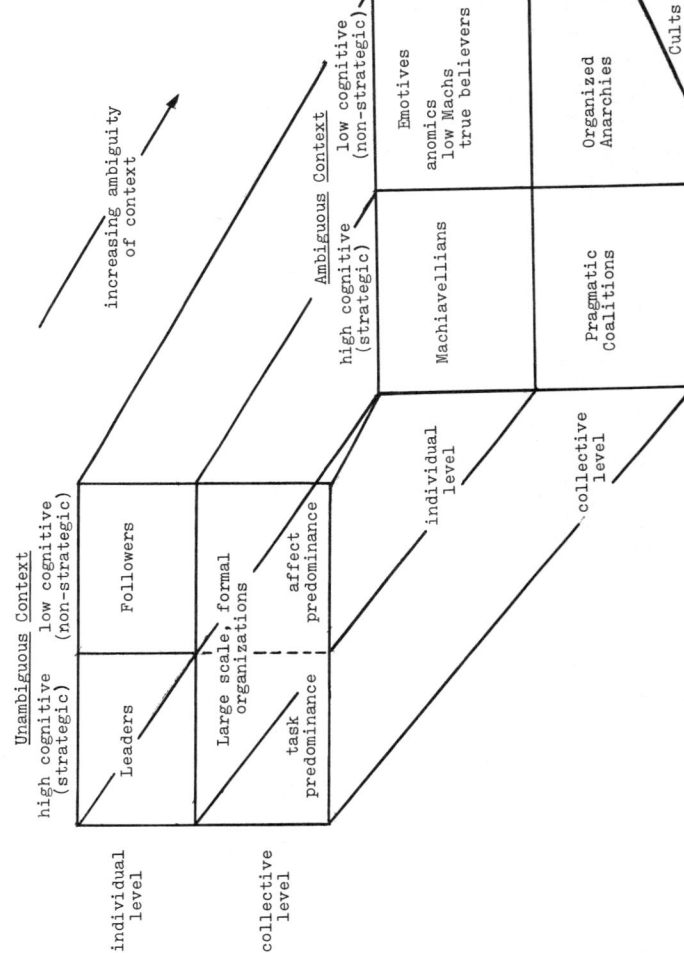

Source: Compiled by the author.

From this perspective, my own sense of the unambiguous context analogues of Machiavellians and emotives is that they may be thought of as leaders and followers. The latter contrast seems to capture the task versus emotive contrast in emphasis. It suggests a relationship that fits the notion of increased affiliation without violating the contrast between high cognitive control and low cognitive control orientations. Thus, other things being equal, leaders in the unambiguous context may become the Machiavellians of the ambiguous context. Followers in the unambiguous context may become the emotives of the ambiguous context. In the latter case, the "choice" of emotive type would presumably depend on the combined effects of individual psychology, the perceived rate and severity of the contextual transformation to ambiguity, and contact with various "cause" peddlers (Steiner and Edmunds 1979; Schultz 1975).

This discussion of some aspects of context transformation does not imply that such transformations are irreversible, always in a given direction, or even complete for an entire system. These are questions worth pursuing, but in broadest terms, the primary intention of this chapter is simply to suggest that there may be some value in viewing the ambiguous societal context as a distinct action context.

REFERENCES

Christie, R., and Geis, F. L. 1970. Studies in Machiavellianism. New York: Academic Press.

Edelman, M. 1964. The Symbolic Uses of Politics. Urbana: University of Illinois.

Frolich, N. 1975. "The Instability of Minimum Winning Coalitions." American Political Science Review 69 (September): 943-46.

Hoffer, E. 1951. The True Believer: Thoughts on the Nature of Mass Movements. New York: Harper.

Kahn, R. L. et al. 1964. Organizational Stress: Studies in Role Ambiguity. New York: Wiley.

Lerner, A. W. 1976. The Politics of Decision-Making: Strategy, Cooperation, and Conflict. Beverly Hills, Calif.: Sage.

_____. 1978. "On Ambiguity and Organizations." Administration and Society 10 (May): 3-33.

March, J. G., and Olsen, J. P. 1976. *Ambiguity and Choice in Organizations*. New York: Columbia University Press.

Olson, M. 1965. *The Logic of Collective Action: Public Goods and the Theory of Groups*. Cambridge, Mass.: Harvard University Press.

Pinder, C. C., and Moore, L. F. 1979. "The Resurrection of Taxonomy to Aid the Development of Middle Range Theories of Organizational Behavior." *Administrative Science Quarterly* 24 (March): 99-118.

Riesman, D. 1950. *The Lonely Crowd*. New Haven, Conn.: Yale University Press.

Shultz, G. P. 1975. *Leaders and Followers in an Age of Ambiguity*. New York: New York University Press.

Steiner, J. F., and Edmunds, S. W. 1979. "Ascientific Beliefs About Large Organizations and Adaptation to Change." *The Academy of Management Review* 4 (January): 107-12.

Van Wagner, Karen, and Swanson, Cheryl. 1979. "From Machiavelli to Ms.: Differences in Male-Female Power Styles," *Public Administration* 39, no. 1 (Jan./Feb.): 66-72.

Willner, A. R. 1968. *Charismatic Political Leadership: A Theory*. Princeton, N.J.: Princeton University Center of International Studies.

4
SOME COMMENTS ON THE ROLE OF SOCIAL PSYCHOLOGY IN FORECASTING
Marie Jahoda

To predict the historical future is one of mankind's oldest yet unfulfillable desires. For thousands of years, the basis of forecasting were divine revelations, oracles, astrology, crystal gazing, and dreams. Such predictions were not always unsuccessful, partly because sophisticated ambiguity, as that of the Delphic oracle, for example, could be interpreted to fit any subsequent outcome, partly because forecasts brought into operation the mechanism of self-fulfilling prophecies, and partly by fluke. While modern forecasting is based on more systematic and rationally more justifiable procedures, these three mechanisms have not stopped operating. Forecasting is for these and other reasons inevitably an intellectually hazardous enterprise, permanently beset by uncertainty. As Young (1968) said, "It is (far more happily than unhappily for mankind) part of the definition of the future that it is unknown."

Nonetheless, there are now all over the industrialized world (including the Soviet Union) natural and social scientists who, jointly or separately, engage in forecasting what the future may hold for the planet. A recent analysis of 17 major efforts in that direction (Cole 1978) yielded very diverse anticipations based on diverse assumptions, values, methods, and purposes, united only by the virtual absence of systematic psychological thought or research in these imaginative enterprises. The exception to this disregard for psychology is Heilbroner's <u>An Inquiry into the Human Prospect</u> (1974), where he justifies his pessimistic expectation of authoritarian regimes and wars about the world's resources partly by reference to Freud, from whom he deduces "biopsychological underpinnings of political submissiveness" (p. 106).

There are, of course, implicit psychological assumptions in many other forecasts. When Kahn (1967), for example, foresees for an even more affluent United States in the year 2000 a vast increase in the alienation experienced by its citizens, he makes such an assumption. Schumacher's "Small is Beautiful" implies assumptions about human aspiration levels. Maslow's need hierarchy, sometimes referred to explicitly, is one example among many of underlying assumptions in forecasting about motivation. In fact, it is virtually impossible to engage in policy sciences—and forecasting is, of course, policy oriented—without an implicit conception about social psychological processes. However, it is equally true that these conceptions are, as a rule, naive and hardly ever spelled out or critically examined. One reason for this state of affairs is that only a very few psychologists are interested in forecasting, even though it is concerned with human experience and behavior under a variety of social and physical environmental conditions, a problem, par excellence, for social psychology. Why is this the case?

There are at least three possible answers to this question: (1) forecasting on a global level for longer periods—say, to the end of the century—is so dubious an enterprise, containing so many uncertainties, that self-respecting social scientists rightly wash their hands of it; (2) social psychology itself has no contribution to make to forecasting; and (3) the integration of social psychological thought and research into a combination of macro economic events, demographic developments, and geophysical and geopolitical issues presents methodological problems of interdisciplinary cooperation with which social psychologists could perhaps come to grips, though they have as yet only rarely done so. Each of the first two answers has some validity, but it is the qualification of these kernels of truth that may perhaps induce more social psychologists to devote attention to the third possibility. I shall briefly discuss the rationale for each of these positions.

Is forecasting for inevitable uncertainty, then, an intellectually legitimate undertaking? The answer is less simple than one would like it to be. Only one matter is certain: any forecast presented as a prediction of what must necessarily happen in the future is intellectually suspect because such prediction is implicitly based on the assumption of a total and rigid determinism of historical events. It is easy to avoid entering the philosophical controversy on this point by reference to an undisputable fact: even if we can imagine, as Laplace did in his famous assumption, a universal intelligence that knows everything in the here and now—and therefore also all the past and future (for example, Wartofsky 1968)— no such universal intelligence has so far appeared or seems likely to be realized. As a result, there is no comprehensive theory from which the future could be predicted as the inevitable result of the past and the present; only in the most vulgar misinterpretations of Marx is historical materialism so presented—had Marx believed it, he could have abandoned his unceasing efforts to persuade others to engage in actions.

It would be wrong, however, to conclude that since there is no universal deterministic theory for forecasting that it needs to engage in blind empiricism. Indeed, a good case can be made for blind empiricism being virtually as impossible in forecasting as a universal theory. For whatever "blind" collection of facts is presented as relevant to the future, doing so implies a theoretical stance—most often, the assumption of a continuation of the status quo.

Having said what forecasting should not pretend to be—not prediction, not based on a global theory, not blindly empirical—it now is necessary to say what it should be. Instead of prediction, forecasting can spell out alternative possible developments and identify the contingencies that increase the probability of one alternative versus another. Forecasting is different from science fiction in that it is committed to examine the possibility of various scenarios for the future. Only what can be shown to be in the realm of social and physical possibility on this globe deserves further examination in terms of probability and desirability. Forecasting can use theories where they exist, but it must be recognized that the way we view the world—theoretically or practically—is not neutral or value free. In all the social sciences, fundamental assumptions, often left implicit, about what to study, what variables to select, and what procedures to use or what purposes to serve with one's research have as much weight as the state and logic of a given discipline. Since the choice between such world views is not in itself subject to scientific criteria, all that can be done is to make the implicit assumptions explicit and follow them through in their consequences. Miles (1978) has done this for forecasting and has developed a systematic method for the construction of scenarios. He used three dominant world views—conservative, reformist, and radical—that underlie social, economic, historical, and political theories and lead to differences in the understanding of social change and emphasize different goals and values. Since we cannot say which assumptions will in the retrospection of future historians emerge as corresponding best to actual events, all world views should be spelled out in their consequences, so that total uncertainty about the future can be reduced to a set of alternatives and tested in the normal scientific way for, say, energy requirements, food supply, trade conditions, political organization, and so forth.

Of course, there is still a lot of guesswork involved in establishing such scenarios, but as long as the assumptions on which such informed guesses are made are fully stated, the emerging possibilities for the future can be qualified by others and improved where possible.

Granted that there is more guessing in forecasting than in ordinary scientific activity, there are two major reasons that justify the participation of scientists in long-term forecasting in my view: one is that the complexities of modern life make it inevitable. Social, political, and economic decisions in the here and now commit the future and reduce the available choices. Such decisions are for political convenience sometimes made with only the immediate consequences in mind; others—for example, investment in public transport facilities—are recognized as producing desired effects only in a more distant future. Like every purposeful social action, they have unanticipated consequences beyond the desired goal (Merton 1957). Forecasting can aim at anticipating the unanticipated consequences of policy decisions.

The second reason is of equal importance: it is, after all, not only policy makers who make choices—we all do. Even though a large proportion of our collective fate is shaped by factors over which we have little control, what little there is left is very important. What is more, it can be enlarged. To the extent that forecasts of possible alternatives for the future, including aspects of a future quality of life, become subject to a wide-ranging public debate, more and more people will be able to engage in deliberate actions with the more distant future in mind.

The question now arises whether social psychology has a specific contribution to make in multidisciplinary and long-term forecasting exercises. Here, there is a paradox: on the one hand, social psychology, broadly conceived, deals with the interaction of people and their environment—and the crucial question that motivates all forecasts (even when they are narrowly concerned with estimating if and when, say, copper deposits, will be exhausted) is, How will people live with such an anticipated environment? This would assign a crucial role to social psychology. On the other hand, however, the assumptions that underlie much social psychological research and the procedures which it employs separate it sharply from concern with the long-term future. It sometimes seems that many social psychologists, who, like everybody else, have to live with uncertainty in their daily lives, seek compensation for this by retiring into the relative certainty of their theories and laboratories to the exclusion of everything else.

This should not be understood as a slur on theories and experiments, which are the mainstay of social psychology. But it is one thing to acknowledge that these procedures are the best guide for sharpening thought and controlling flights of fancy; it is quite another thing to maintain that this is all that social psychologists could do. For notwithstanding all the assets of the dominant procedures, they also have their inevitable limitations. In his recent book, Bandura (1977) states, "Theories must demonstrate predictive power." Of course they must, within the confines of the laboratory. Experimental results are valid always with the qualification "other things being equal." Concern with external validity invariably reveals that other things are not equal, often not even with a large grain of salt. Many social psychological theories can comply with Bandura's "must" only by virtue of ignoring the world outside the laboratory, which makes it difficult to use them in forecasting.

Related to the lack of concern with external validity, mainstream social psychology ignores a matter of major concern in forecasting by virtue of its commitment to the experimental method: social and psychological change over extended time spans. The experiment deals with the immediate present, manipulating in the here and now whatever independent variable can be manipulated. The experimental results, even within the confines of internal validity only, are assumed to be stable over time. This is a reasonable assumption in natural science and biological research, but it is surely unwarranted in social psychology. We all know in our guts that social and psychological realities change, though not always at the same speed, but much faster than evolution or the physical character of the universe. It is these relatively rapid changes that preoccupy forecasting and which are rarely considered in social psychological work.

There are exceptions, of course, of which Katona's work (1975) in economic forecasting based on surveys of intentions and attitudes is an outstanding example, demonstrating the use of the concepts and methods of social psychology in an externally valid future-oriented manner, at least over relatively short time spans. Such replications of surveys, or, for that matter, replications of experiments (Wally and Cook 1966), clearly show that other things do not remain equal in social psychological affairs. This is one of the reasons that induced Gergen (1973) to suggest against the mainstream of social psychology that social psychology may not be able to propose theories of more or less timeless validity, but that it should be regarded as a historical descriptive enterprise. This need not imply blind empiricism; social psychological theories have their function in collecting contemporary data, even if they are not suited for historical prediction.

Given that replication over time or culture indicates some areas of changed interaction between macro social and micro psychological phenomena, and given that we have fairly extensive conceptual tools for dealing with the psychological side of the interaction, we still have very little notion about how to identify psychologically relevant aspects of the macro environment. We know, for example, from studies of the psychological impact of unemployment during the years of the Great Depression that it undermined the unemployed men's self-respect. The unemployed today live under different circumstances: they enjoy better economic support, live longer and in better health, and have better education and higher aspirations: Will the effect be the same? There are neither theories nor sufficient empirical data that could provide an answer. Thinking about this specific question (Jahoda 1979) made me realize several things. First, the poverty of existing social psychological theory, which has simply nothing to say on the issue. Second, it led me to modify Gergen's challenging dichotomy between history and a universally valid science. Even though all our data, the social as well as the psychological, are liable to change over time, some change faster and some change slower; the need for self-respect gained from work may well outlast the historical process that reduced the absolute deprivation of the unemployed. Third, the macro social changes enumerated are ad hoc suggestions and are given in no particular order. Even if we knew what one or the other implied for the experience of daily living, their relative weight in a simultaneous occurrence remains an unknown aspect. Yet, many forecasters agree that the level of employment will probably be one of the major social, political, and economic problems for the next two decades or so. There is here a vast field for social psychological research that deserves more attention.

Yet, notwithstanding the realization of how little we know, there is ample evidence that social psychology, mainstream and otherwise, is already in a position to enrich the thinking of forecasters. It is now in order to identify these contributions explicitly.

Above all, the very existence of social psychology as an intellectual discipline concerned with the complexity and diversity of human interaction with the environment can act as a safeguard against the oversimplified forecasts that are based on physical attributes of the environment only. Meadows's <u>The Limits to Growth</u> (1972) suffered from just such oversimplification, and it was social psychology—not a specific theory or piece of research, but a social psychological way of thinking about the world—which led to the most sustained critique of this influential work (Cole et al. 1973). This way of thinking need not be applied only critically; constructively, it has, for example, contributed both to the conception of world views mentioned before and the effort to spell out the quality of life that can be expected to dominate in any of the possible scenarios (Miles 1978). Another contribution, for which Katona's work is one example, consists in the use, for the purposes of forecasting, of the concepts and methods developed by social psychologists. These are largely inadvertent contributions, as it were; that is, it needs only a few social psychologists turned forecasters to exploit the ideas and methods designed for other purposes. But I am pleading for a more widespread "advertent" concern among social psychologists with forecasting in the conviction that this would not only lead to more sophistication in thinking about the future but would also be in the interest of the development of the discipline itself, by enforcing a recognition of the uncertainties inherent, though hidden, in our theoretical formulations.

One of the most frustrating aspects in thinking about the future is the realization that social analysts in, say, 50 years may well discover in their past—our present—the germs of their present and be able to describe how the future developed out of the manifold possibilities that now exist because some had either taken deliberate action or failed to do so, because these germs remained undetected or were identified in good time. It is in the discovery and analysis of presently hardly perceptible but existing alternatives that contemporary social psychological theory and research could help, whether based on experiments or surveys, national or cross-cultural data. A wide field of social psychological knowledge could become relevant under two conditions: that those who fail to confirm a hypothesis be accorded as much attention in the interpretation of results as those who do and that the conditions and consequences of the deviant pattern becoming the dominant pattern be considered. In all conformity studies, there are some who remain independent; in every experiment designed to heighten competition, there are some cooperators; in every other-directed culture, there exist also different character structures; there are dissidents in authoritarian regimes, as there are fascists in democracies. To search for an understanding of such deviances both from a psychological and a sociological point of view would considerably enrich social psychology, even though it would also increase its indeterminancy.

However, the task of developing such a social psychology is daunting. For even if we abandon the attractive apparent certainty of knowledge that stems from limited theories experimentally tested, there are several intellectual problems which are as yet unsolved and not often seriously confronted. I shall mention only two: the question of interdisciplinarity and the related issue of how to combine micro and macro data.

Interdisciplinarity has for decades been a fashionable slogan. But if one looks around for examples of interdisciplinary work of genuine merit, one has to look very hard indeed. Even social psychology exists in two versions, a psychological and a sociological one. Sociobiology, the newest seemingly interdisciplinary enterprise, is of course pure biology in its explanations. Much the same is true for psychohistory, which is psychology to the extent it tries to explain (not history). However interdisciplinary the intention of a research group, explanations appear as a rule to be formulated from the point of view of a single discipline. Theories that "predict and control behavior"—Lieberman (1979) regards this as the proper goal of psychology—are, by definition, single-discipline oriented and, as has been pointed out, of limited external validity. The explicandum may lend itself to research approaches from several disciplines; the explanatory terms come from one. I do not know whether truly interdisciplinary theories are possible, but I am convinced that their logic has not yet been spelled out.

One reason for the difficulty of arriving at interdisciplinary explanations lies in the fact that the units of observation and analysis in various disciplines are incommensurable and require different methods. To take an example: to explain the manner in which individuals acquire values and the degree to which their actions are guided by them requires a psychological approach; the different value hierarchies incorporated in the institutions of various political systems require an approach from political science or sociology. The interdisciplinary problem of the interaction between institutionalized and personal values can be illuminated by theories of either discipline, but, as far as I can see, resists a common integrated explanation. As long as this is the case, it would be more true to what actually happens to speak of multidisciplinary explanations than of interdisciplinarity.

To tackle these problems as well as the question of the degree of transhistorical and transcultural validity of social psychological research is not easy. The price to be paid for such a social psychology is that in this area, it must abandon the "predict and control" ideal of the natural sciences; the prize to be gained is its own further development, as much as its potential contribution to a humanization of forecasting, which remains all too often enmeshed in technological determinism, as if a "good society" could be judged by anything but the quality of life it enables people to enjoy.

REFERENCES

Bandura, A. 1977. <u>Social Learning Theory</u>. Englewood Cliffs, N.J.: Prentice-Hall.

Cole, H. S. D.; Freeman, Christopher; Jahoda, Marie; Pavitt, K. L. R. (eds.) 1973. <u>Models of Doom</u>. New York: Universe Books.

Cole, Sam. 1978. "The Global Futures Debate 1965-1976." In <u>World Futures: The Great Debate</u>, edited by C. Freeman and M. Jahoda, pp. 9-49. London: Martin Robertson/ New York: Universe Books.

Gergen, K. 1973. "Social Psychology as History." <u>Journal of Personality and Social Psychology</u> 26, no. 2, pp. 309-20.

Heilbroner, R. 1974. <u>An Inquiry into the Human Prospect</u>. New York: Norton.

Jahoda, M. 1979. "The Impact of Unemployment in the 1930's and the 1970's." <u>Bulletin of the British Psychological Society</u> 32 (August): 309-14.

Kahn, H., and Wiener, A. J. 1967. <u>The Year 2000</u>. London: Macmillan.

Katona, George. 1975. <u>Psychological Economics</u>. New York: Elsevier.

Lieberman, David A. 1979. "Behaviourism and the Mind: A (Limited) Call for a Return to Introspection." <u>American Psychologist</u> 64 (April): 319-33.

Meadows, Donella H.; Meadows, Dennis L.; Randers, Jørgen; and Behrens III, William W. 1972. <u>The Limits to Growth</u>. New York: Universe Books.

Merton, R. K. 1957. <u>Social Theory and Social Structure</u>. Glencoe, Ill.: Free Press, chap. 1, pp. 21-28.

Miles, I. 1978. "Worldviews and Scenarios." In <u>World Futures: The Great Debate</u>, edited by C. Freeman and M. Jahoda, pp. 233-79. London: Martin Robertson/ New York: Universe Books.

Petrinovich, Lewis. 1979. "Probabilistic Functionalism: A Conception of Research Method." American Psychologist (May).

Wally, Patricia, and Cook, Stuart W. 1966. "Attitude as a Determinant of Learning and Memory: A Failure to Confirm," Journal of Personality and Social Psychology 4.

Wartofsky, M. W. 1968. Conceptual Foundations of Scientific Thought. New York and London.

Young, M., ed. 1968. Forecasting and the Social Sciences. London.

S. Fiddle (ed): <u>Uncertainty: Behavioral and Social Dimensions</u>
New York: Praeger, 1980

5
UNCERTAINTY, ACTION, AND COMPETENCE: SOME ALTERNATIVES TO OMNISCIENCE IN COMPLEX PROBLEM-SOLVING
Terry Connolly

INTRODUCTION

Instances of important failures in solving complex problems are commonly observed, discussed, and deplored in both popular and scholarly literatures. Less widely remarked, but in many ways more remarkable, is the frequency with which such problems are successfully solved or, at least, adequately handled. Physicians frequently make correct diagnoses; industrial corporations often handle profitably complex problems of production and distribution; political coalitions are successfully maintained in the face of rapid change and extensive uncertainty; and quite ordinary citizens behave (at least in the aggregate) in ways that approximate the stern demands of economic rationality. While such decisional successes are, of course, far from universal, they appear not uncommonly in everyday affairs.

What makes these decisional successes so striking is the gross disparity between the (apparently) rather small capacity of the human mind for analysis and the (apparently) very large analytic demands of the decision problems. On the one hand, we appear able to retain in short-term memory only relatively tiny amounts of information (Miller 1956), routinely make logical errors in the simplest of syllogisms (Henle 1962), make sizable (and predictable) errors in estimating probabilities (Tversky and Kahneman 1974), and learn simple combinatorial tasks only very slowly (Hammond 1971). On the other hand, a careful description of our daily lives, both personal and professional, suggests that we routinely face, and often cope adequately with, decision problems involving very large numbers of variables, complex interactions, extensive uncertainties, and so on. In short, we often seem to do much better than either our cognitive equipment or our knowledge of the world would justify.

One's sense of the inadequacy of the unaided intellect to even quite small decision problems is sharpened by a little reflection on what would be required to live one's life rationally. Should I purchase this lettuce at this price? How shall I get to work? Shall I have another cup of coffee? Even a rough attempt to resolve such tiny decisions rationally would require the gathering of quite large amounts of information, the invention and assessment of many alternatives, the specification of complex personal utilities, estimation of difficult probabilities, and large intellectual effort in structuring the problem and in computing the values of each alternative. Fortunately (for both our productivity and our sanity), few of us ever attempt such an effort, or even press rationality to the extent of assessing whether or not the effort would be justified. We just drive to work the way we normally drive to work, until forced (say, by sudden rises in gasoline prices) to find some other more-or-less acceptable alternative. We must select the targets for our attempts at rationality with considerable care. In most cases, the payoffs are too small or the uncertainties too large for even the most rational person to attempt rationality.

In classical decision theory, the notion of uncertainty carries a rather restrictive meaning. Decision problems are treated as "given," in the sense that one is to choose from a specified set of alternatives in terms of the future consequences of each, assessed against some fixed preferences. <u>Certainty</u> is then defined as the case in which all consequences of all alternative actions are known, <u>risk</u> as that in which the probabilities of each consequence are known, and <u>uncertainty</u> as that in which these probabilities are not known. This use of the word is rather far from the everyday usage, where one's sense of "being less than certain" frequently extends even to doubt as to whether or not one is faced with a decision problem, let alone whether or not there are any alternative actions available, what evaluative criteria should be applied and with what weights, and what streams of consequences might flow from any given action (Conrath 1967; Connolly 1977a). While uncertainty in the restricted sense produces difficulties for the decision theorist, uncertainty in the everyday sense seems likely to produce either paralysis or catastrophe for the layperson (manager, consumer, parent, or whatever)—paralysis, from contemplating the insolubility of the problems; catastrophe, from acting without this awareness.

The broad subject matter of this chapter is the perverse phenomenon of decisional success in the face of large uncertainty. A steady stream of research increasingly emphasizes the unsuspected complexities of even quite mundane decision problems and the limitations of the human mind in grappling with them. Why, then, does the world appear to operate at least tolerably well?

As noted at the outset, there are grounds for doubt as to whether or not the phenomenon exists at all. It is not obvious how one would set about assessing the world decisional batting average, and the impression of rather frequent success may be confined to the author alone—and that only on his more optimistic days. For more determined pessimists, there are good grounds for arguing that the appearance of decisional success is frequently a misperception or, when success is genuine, that it is not attributable to the competence of the decision maker. A number of mechanisms by which such misperceptions and misattributions might arise are considered in the first part of the chapter. The second part of the chapter supposes at least some residual of unjustified decisional success not compellingly explained by these mechanisms and proposes an alternative general mechanism by which it might come about.

MISPERCEPTIONS AND MISATTRIBUTIONS OF DECISIONAL SUCCESS

Bogus Wisdom and Selective Structures

Promotion to senior decision-making ranks in large organizations is frequently made on the basis of the candidates' prior track records, among other criteria. In the course of their careers, people make a number (perhaps not a very large number) of what might be termed critical decisions. Selecting for promotion those individuals whose critical decisions have proved always, or nearly always, correct appears to be an entirely sensible process. The justification, should one be demanded, is that such a procedure serves to identify individuals whose judgment in critical matters has been tested in the fire and has proved sound. It serves, in short, to place individuals of proven wisdom in the positions in which such wisdom is most required.

As Deutsch and Madow (1961) point out, the expectation that such procedures will guarantee the wisdom of the chosen candidate may or may not be well-founded. Suppose, for example, that managers were to make their critical decisions, not on the basis of judgment and wisdom, but on chance—say, by tossing a coin. Then, so long as the number of entrants to the process is reasonably large and the number of critical decisions reasonably small, it is quite likely that one will later find one or more individuals with perfect track records, people who invariably made the correct decision at each critical decision point. Merely by simple probability, a group of m managers making correct decisions with probability p would be expected to produce mp^n individuals with perfect track after n decisions. If, for example, all decisions are binary and are made by coin-tossing, then exactly one individual from an entering class of size 256 would be expected to have a perfect track record after eight critical decisions. Presumably, this individual would now be promoted to the vacant senior position; and the organization's affairs would, despite the evidence so far, remain at the mercy of subsequent coin tosses. The appearance of wisdom is bogus.

Clearly, the decision-making process postulated for the candidate managers is "improper," in that no grasp of their decision problems was required for them to toss their coins. On the other hand, the decision process of the promotion committee may have been perfectly "proper." With full understanding of the problem they face, they would know that no manager is better (or worse) than another. A president is required and choice on the basis of track record may be defensible (on grounds such as perceived fairness, the confidence-inspiring value of a perfect track record, or a desire not to appear arbitrary). (They may, still more properly, wish to save a large executive salary and to generate random decisions by other means, but this is outside the terms of their decision problem as we have defined it.) Further, if the model is extended to allow even a little expertise or judgment, as well as a large random term, then selection on track record will maximize the probability of capturing what expertise there is available.

The bogus wisdom model thus offers examples both of proper and improper decision-making. It is improper to the extent that individual managers are considered as making their decisions randomly. The selection-promotion itself, however, is perfectly proper, as long as additional criteria for promotion are introduced or the assumption of purely random decision-making by the candidates is relaxed even mildly.

The ambitious manager moving through such a process may be able to enhance his or her promotion chances by a variety of strategies. Some possibilities are outlined in the next section.

Retrospective Rationality and Selective Recall

As an explanation for our focal phenomenon, unjustified decisional success, the bogus wisdom model mainly asserts that it does not exist. Decisional success is, in fact, just as rare as would be implied by the contrast of decisional demands and human capabilities. Selective promotion merely serves to distract us from the sampling bias involved, making the (rare) instances of decisional success more salient and failures less so.

An important feature of highly complex, highly uncertain decision environments is that they offer considerable latitude for individuals to manipulate their decisional track records. In these environments, actions taken lead to complex chains of consequences that, over time, become entangled with other decision outcomes and random fluctuations. As long as the actions taken do not generate dramatic, immediate, and obviously traceable results, the responsible individual has excellent opportunities to reinterpret history so as to make prior decisions appear well-founded.

The essence of such a strategy is for the individual to develop and promulgate an interpretation of the record that emphasizes the connection between his or her prior actions and other later events presently regarded as "good," while deemphasizing connections of past actions to current "bads." To the extent that action-consequence-evaluation sequences are loosely coupled, high in ambiguity, or imperfectly recorded, there is wide scope for self-interested sense-making. Obvious possibilities include the following: (1) invention (or denial) of originating actions or of the individual's responsibility for them; (2) emphasis (or deemphasis) of some consequences rather than others or of the causal connection between originating actions and consequences; (3) emphasis (or deemphasis) of criteria by which consequences are evaluated.

A large body of empirical evidence suggests the prevalence of such processes. The vast literature on cognitive dissonance and self-justification phenomena (for example, Festinger 1962; Aronson 1976) suggests that retrospective sense-making may be a very common activity. Recent interest in myth-making and other efforts at plausible reinventions of organizational histories (for example, Clark 1972) places the process firmly in an organizational context, as well as in the individual's private mind. Studies of "escalation" in the allocation of further resources to failing enterprises (for example, Staw and Ross 1978) suggest that the process is not purely retrospective but may drive future action as well.

In short, the looseness of the action-consequence-evaluation sequence in highly complex, high uncertainty environments allows large scope for retrospective sense-making, both conscious and unconscious. Unjustified decisional success, in this perspective, is again seen as a misperception phenomenon. Where bogus wisdom emphasizes the sampling bias built into the assessment of decisional track records, retrospective rationality emphasizes the manipulability of such records in the actor's interests.

Self-Fulfilling Prophecies and Enactment

A third category of apparently successful, but improper, decision-making is in situations of self-fulfilling prophecy (for example, Archibald 1974; Merton 1948). Psychiatric (or legal) judgments of mental disturbance (or criminality) may lead to incarceration in settings likely to produce exactly the characteristic originally judged. Anticipations of positive or negative interactions may lead to behavior that does, in fact, produce such interactions. Assessments of potential for graduate work lead to admission to (or exclusion from) excellent graduate programs and, thus, to excellent (or poor or no) graduate school achievement. Expectations of gasoline shortages lead to panic buying and actual shortage. Worries about bank failures lead to bank failures.

It is apparent that the term self-fulfilling prophecy is a broad, perhaps overbroad, label loosely applied to a rather wide range of phenomena, only some of which fall within our present focus on improper but successful decision-making. For example, the statement: "I shall find something to enjoy in this exhibition" may be read as a prediction that may or may not be borne out in the experience. Replacing shall with will implies a resolve, a determination either to continue one's search or to explore additional criteria until enjoyment results. In neither case does any decisional impropriety necessarily arise. Neither prediction nor determination constitutes improper decision-making in the sense we are examining here.

The shared feature of the examples listed above is that in each case, the listener is expected to react with surprise to the prophet's retrospective and exasperating, "I told you so." When the self-fulfilling nature of the prophecy is seen, the surprise disappears. Of course, people who are told they are crazy, and treated as such, become crazy. Of course, banks fail if depositors withdraw their money in a rush. Of course, you cannot do good graduate work if you never get the chance. In each case, the prophet is claiming a decisional success, a correct and surprising choice of an action that leads to desired consequences, when no such surprise is merited. The prophet is obscuring his or her power either to force certain consequences to flow from certain actions (as in graduate school admissions and gas panics) or to construct evaluative criteria that will ensure that any of a range of consequences will be labeled a success.

The notion has been developed at considerable length by Weick (1969, 1977) in his examination of enactment processes. In Weick's analysis, sense-making is not merely retrospective but also has an important reflexive component, in that the material from which sense is made may be largely the product of the actor's prior activities. By acting as though the external world were a certain way, one ensures that data available at some later stage will be structured so as to confirm the initial hypothesis. The raw materials from which sense is to be made are not merely "given" by some external reality: they are imposed upon a plastic environment by means of prior actions. Environments are "enacted."

We do not need to probe here the subtleties of this analysis. Our current purposes are served by merely noting that self-fulfilling prophecies and enactment processes, like retrospective rationality and bogus wisdom, offer a possible explanation for the appearance of unjustified decisional success: that it is merely an appearance. While acknowledging that at least some of the instances can be explained (or, rather, explained away) by one or another of these means, we are reluctant to accept such explanations in every case. In the following sections, we shall examine a number of examples in which decisional success is genuine and in which decision processes are, in one way or another, improper.

Desert Survival

An interesting example of a decision process which, though in some ways improper, can be highly effective, is suggested by Simon (1956). It concerns the probability of survival of a rather simple creature in a sparse environment in which small piles of food are randomly distributed. A simple survival-probability model may be constructed as follows. We can consider the environment as a network of paths, with d paths leaving any node. Suppose that food is available at some small fraction, p, of all nodes. The creature is described by two parameters: v, its range of vision (measured in "steps" from the node at which it currently stands), and H, its storage capacity for food (again measured in steps or "moves").

Any one move opens up d^v new nodes for the creature to examine. In one move, then, its probability of seeing food is p^{d^v}, and its probability of not seeing food is $(1 - p)^{d^v}$. Thus, the probability of not finding food after (H - v) moves, the creature's maximum range, is:

Probability of starvation = $(1 - p)^{(H-v)d^v}$

Note that of the four parameters affecting this probability, two (H and v) describe the creature, while two (p and d) describe the environment.

The sensitivity of the model to changes in its parameter values is suggestive. For example, if one sets up a rather sparse environment (say, $p = 10^{-4}$, so food is found at only one node in 10,000), with d = 10 paths per node, then the probability of survival for different values of H and v is as shown in Table 5.1. Note that even with large storage capacity, a blind creature (v = 0) is virtually certain to starve. In contrast, with even modest ranges of vision (v = 2 or 3), and moderate or better storage, the beast is almost certain to survive. Of the two parameters, vision, v, is hugely the more significant.

TABLE 5.1

Probability of Starvation as a Function of H and v

v (number of moves animal can see)	H (number of moves on stored food)		
	10	100	1,000
0	.999	.990	.905
1	.991	.906	.368
2	.923	.375	$2/10^4$
3	.497	$6/10^5$	$5/10^{44}$
4	.002	$2/10^{42}$	Quite small

Note: Environment: d = 10; p = .0001.
Source: Compiled by the author.

To what extent is the creature's decision-making proper? As outlined, its decision rule is certainly simple: Go where you like, and eat what you see. This rule certainly seems improper, in the sense we have been using that term: it implies no reflective understanding of the consequences of alternative actions in light of the structure of the decision problem. On the other hand, it is difficult to see what rule would be more proper: the environment is, in fact, random; there is little insight or understanding to be had.

Proper or not, there is an important aspect in which the creature faces what we earlier identified as one of the crucial problems facing the proper decision maker: as v increases, so does information-processing load. For every unit by which v increases, ten times as many nodes need to be searched for food. Admittedly, this is not a complex task, in that food is assumed either to be present (and visible) at a node or not. No complex understanding or inference is required of the creature. It does, however, need to be able to examine a large number of simple alternatives in unit time if it is to have a decent probability of survival (that is, if its v parameter is larger than 0 or 1).

In short, the desert survival model provides an example of a highly successful, but at least somewhat improper, decision strategy. The decision maker need not have any complex understanding of the problem it faces or of the consequences of its actions. Very simple decision rules generate successful decisions. We shall therefore tentatively assign this example to the category of improper, but genuinely successful, decision-making.

(In no heretical spirit, I cannot resist pointing out the possible relevance of this model to the leader of a tribe wandering in the desert, with water holes sparsely distributed. If the leader can see even one step farther than the rest of the tribe, (s)he will enjoy a well-deserved reputation for omniscient leadership. Perhaps an occasional trip up some convenient mountain would serve a very secular purpose.)

Flat Maximum Problems

A defining characteristic of proper decision-making is that those making decisions in this way should, on the average, do better than those who do not—but how much better? If, for example, a formally optimal strategy for some problem generates solutions very little better than do other nonoptimal strategies, then improper strategies may turn out to be sensible, particularly when large extra effort is required for optimality.

The problem may be pushed further. Suppose that the contrast is between an optimal solution strategy based, say, on fallible data versus a nonoptimal strategy not so based. Suppose, for example, that one is comparing the track record of an optimal inventory-holding model, in which several parameters must be estimated from fallible data, with the performance of an experienced stockroom manager, whose decisions are entirely based on experience. It is clearly possible that the "optimal" strategy, handicapped by the poor parameter estimates, might perform less well than does the improper seat-of-the-pants method. It needs to be borne in mind that <u>optimal</u> in such contexts is invariably used to describe a characteristic of the model, not of the real-world setting. It is perfectly possible to "optimize" one's model without the implementation of that model performing better than, or even as well as, some other nonoptimal strategy.

There are, then, two issues here: How rapidly does the payoff function decline as one moves away from optimality? and, How close to an identified "optimal" solution is one likely to get, given real-world constraints, model simplifications, and so on. A third question, particularly relevant for our current purposes, is, How often are solutions arrived at by improper (nonoptimal) methods as good as, or better than, those arrived at properly?

There is evidence that the answer to this last question may be: a lot more often than one would expect. In the operations research literature, for example, one can find occasional reports (for example, Woolsey 1972) of complex and expensive optimization approaches being outperformed, or at least matched, by the legendary little old lady in tennis shoes. (Given the emphasis placed in that literature on optimal solution, one suspects that the infrequent reports of such matters may be the tip of a much larger iceberg.) A more extensive body of evidence is provided by the research in applied psychology on <u>improper linear models</u> and <u>unit-weighting schemes</u> (for example, Dawes 1979; Dawes and Corrigan 1974; Einhorn and Hogarth 1975). The evidence in this area is so striking that a short review might be useful here.

In a wide variety of practical settings, the need arises for an estimate or prediction of one variable from a number of measures or predictors. Examples include the estimation of a patient's health from various clinical indicators, the prediction of a student's performance in graduate school from various application materials, and the estimation of an individual's intelligence from scores on several IQ tests. In most of these areas, it is customary to use an "expert judgment" of some sort (a medical doctor, an admissions committee) to combine the information. Interest in the mechanisms of expert judgment led to many attempts to represent the expert by means of simple linear models, generally using some form of regression analysis to explore the relative weights applied by the expert to each input in forming the output variable.

A striking finding from many such studies was that the simple model representing the expert's weighting scheme invariably outperformed the expert, as evaluated against some later criterion (such as actual performance in graduate school or actual survival time for patients). This was initially interpreted as "bootstrapping," with the model capturing the judge's wisdom and applying it systematically, without the day-to-day variation to be expected from human operators. However, an alternative explanation is possible—and, in fact, now appears correct. It is that virtually any linear model, and almost always one in which simple unit weights are used, will so perform. The clear implication—that in a wide range of these problems, simple unit-weighted models should be used in preference to either an expert or a model with weights developed from regression analysis—has been trenchantly argued, most recently by Dawes (1979).

This surprising conclusion appears to turn on a combination of the two mechanisms noted earlier. First, linear models are surprisingly insensitive to variations in the weights applied to the several independent variables, particularly when these variables are positively correlated. The phenomenon has been known at least since 1938 (Wilks 1938) and has been rediscovered with varying degrees of delight since then (see, for example, Wainer 1976). This implies that predictions from differently weighted linear models will tend to be highly correlated with one another. For many settings, then, a model with simple unit weights will be highly correlated with many more complex schemes (such as might be employed by experts). (The author has recently attempted to explore the conditions under which such equal-weighted models do and do not perform well: see Connolly 1979). Further, they correlate highly with at least some clearly nonlinear generating processes (Yntema and Torgerson 1961).

On the one hand, then, these processes appear to have strikingly flat maxima. Even if experts are using differential weights in linear processes, or are using nonlinear combination schemes, unit-weight linear models will provide a good approximation. If we now add the further complications—that experts are subject to hangovers and interruptions, that regression models require large sample sizes before coefficient estimates become stable, and that measurement of both independent and dependent variables often contains large error terms—the conclusions offered by Dawes (1979) and by Einhorn and Hogarth (1975) have surprising generality. A clearly improper decision process—taking the relevant predictors and averaging their standardized values—will often outperform the apparently more proper processes of either expert combination or regression-weighted combination.

(It should be noted in passing that the body of evidence assembled by these authors is not particularly encouraging of our initial postulate: that humans frequently enjoy reasonable success in making complex decisions. For the class of decisions they consider, there is no good evidence for an expert outperforming a unit-weighted model. This class of decisions is, clearly, not all-encompassing; but the author's impression of the frequency of unjustified decisional success is certainly not bolstered by the empirical evidence generated in these investigations.)

Process Solutions

There remains a final category in which the appearance of decisional success might be misinterpreted as suggesting widespread decisional competence. These are multiperson decision processes in which success, or even elegance, of the final solution is not attributable to the propriety of any person's decision processes. The obvious example is, of course, the free market of economic theory, in which the most complex problems of resource allocation and distribution are "solved" by the aggregate of individual decisions directed to other ends. Related examples may be found in the operation of large political systems, in decisions made in large organizations, and in other multiperson processes, such as science, treated as a social inquiring process (for example, Campbell 1969a). There is, of course, no guarantee that multiperson decision processes will result in optimal, or even tolerable, solutions. Arrow (1951) has shown that voting processes have no such property outside of quite limited cases, and Schelling (1978) provides numerous examples of malign decision solutions flowing from processes in which all individuals act with good intentions.

We do not wish to explore this territory in any detail here. We note only that the emergence of excellent solutions is not sufficient evidence for inferring "propriety" in the decision-making of any of the individuals involved in making the decisions. They may, in fact, be pursuing goals irrelevant (or even hostile) to the decision the observer notes as so elegantly solved. The propriety of the solution does not require the propriety of the solver.

Thus far, we have suggested six possible mechanisms that singly or in combination may explain the appearance of rather frequent decisional success, even when such success would not be expected in light of the complexity of the problems and the inadequacy of the human mind. Such appearance may be just that—an appearance caused by selective recall of successes or the selective properties of hierarchical systems, by the tendency of individuals to devise plausible retrospective interpretations of decision-making sequences so as to produce the appearance of prospective rationality, or by their ability to enforce success in some form of self-fulfilling prophecy. Alternatively, the author may be misattributing decisional competence to individuals when, in fact, the process generating the decisions is merely a fortuitous match to the properties of the decision problem (as in the desert survival model), in which almost any reasonable strategy will do as well as, or better than, an analytic optimum or in which the quality of the solution is attributable to the interpersonal arrangements of the decision process, not to the intrapersonal processes of the participants.

It is, perhaps, presumptuous to suppose that there remains in the reader's mind any residual phenomenon to be explained. Yet, there remains a further, and possibly more general, argument to be explored, an argument that overlaps and extends much of the preceding discussion. The argument is, in essence, that a rather generally defensible reaction to a highly complex, highly uncertain decision problem is to act—that is, an implication of what we have been calling proper decision-making is that predecisional reflection should increase as problems become more and more complex or uncertain. In the final section of the chapter, we shall present the case for the reverse argument: that in case of doubt, one should think less and act more.

ACTION AS AN ALTERNATIVE TO REFLECTION

Proper decision-making requires a period of reflection before action is taken. The decision problem must be identified and analyzed, evaluative criteria for possible solutions must be clarified, and relative weights established, feasible alternative actions identified, and their consequences projected, and so on. As more complexity and uncertainty is added to the decision problem, the amount of such reflection required to maintain propriety increases rapidly. The thesis of the present argument is that this increase rapidly overtakes human capability for information-processing and that the period of reflection becomes indefinitely long. Given that action is commonly required within finite, and possibly quite short, periods of time, reflection is inevitably truncated, and the decision process becomes improper.

In many cases, action taken after no, or only a relatively small, amount of reflection may lead to better decision solutions. Some everyday examples may suggest the line of argument we shall take in making this case:

1. Hedge clipping: Faced with an overgrown hedge, the proper problem solver has some rather tricky calculations to make in selecting points at which to cut each branch. The position of the branches finally left will change as a complex function of the weight of the portion to be cut off, so that considerable knowledge is required as to the cantilever characteristics of branches, the weights of different woods, and so on. In contrast, the action-first hedge clipper starts by taking a few modest snips, sees where the branches settle, snips a little more, and so on, quickly arriving at an acceptable solution. S/he will do more cutting, but a lot less thinking, than will the proper problem solver.

2. Attic insulating: Proper solutions to the problem of insulating one's attic are reasonably straightforward, though data-hungry. Some of the data (such as manufacturers' claims of the coverage yielded by their products) are liable to be unreliable, some

to be difficult or unpleasant to acquire (such as the exact dimensions of one's attic, which requires a preliminary crawl around). In contrast, the action-firster buys a carload, rolls it in, measures what's left, and gets an exact solution with much less effort (and only one crawl around the attic!).

3. Spouse neglect: The proper problem solver, realizing that his or her spouse is feeling neglected, may spend considerable time evaluating the relative merits of flowers, candy, or a dinner out as alternative solutions. The action-firster merely selects the first option that comes to mind—with optimal results, since the problem is equally well-solved by any of the alternatives.

4. Cavities: The proper parent is likely to react to news of a child with several cavities by concern, consultation with dentists, journal reading, and other information-gathering. The improper parent presents the child with a new toothbrush and waits six months. For at least a fraction of the latter, the problem goes away. The instability of time-series data, such as cavities per dental inspection, is liable to trigger more intervention than is called for if action is triggered by any single observation outside a present range. In parenting, as in policy experiments, the threat of regression artifacts is ever-present.

In all four examples, the improper problem solver evades the information-processing load burdening the proper approach and arrives at solutions generally as good, or better, and in less time. Other benefits also accrue. For hedge-clipping, a proper solution may have to be deferred while the householder completes graduate work in mechanical engineering. The proper attic insulator is quite likely to be back at the hardware store anyway, to return (or purchase) insulation corresponding to the error in the data or calculations. The spouse neglector may by impropriety reap a bonus in the form of spontaneity. And the dental noninterventionist avoids expensive, and probably unnecessary, efforts to solve a nonproblem. Action first saves the time, effort, and possible errors of extended reflection; also, incidental bonuses of one sort or another often accrue.

The suggestion that action may offer an alternative to reflection is certainly not entirely novel.

Satisficing

Simon's (1955) notion of <u>satisficing</u>, as opposed to <u>optimizing</u> represents an important retreat from the heroic demands of rationality and in the direction of empirically accurate description of real decision-making. In its most familiar aspect, the notion involves the collapsing of continuous utility functions into binary, acceptable/ unacceptable regions—a modification that offers huge reductions in the information-processing load placed on the decision maker. Less emphasized in discussions of satisficing are the two related processes of search and resetting levels of aspiration. Having chosen some alternative as "acceptable," the decision maker monitors the implementation of the solution. If it appears successful, his/her level of aspiration may be reset upward, if unsuccessful downward, and a second solution attempted. For reasonably well-behaved objective functions, such iterative cycles can be shown to converge on optimal solutions. It should be emphasized, however, that action is needed at each point in order that feasibility can be assessed in the region around the chosen solutions. Satisficing, then, turns not just on the simplification of one's utility functions but also requires action.

Disjointed Incrementalism

For much the same reasons as those presented here, public policy incrementalists (Lindblom 1965; Braybrooke and Lindblom 1963) have argued that the pursuit of comprehensive rationality in the public policy sphere is misguided. Predicting the consequences of any large public policy intervention is fraught with uncertainty, both as to the direction and scope of anticipated changes and as to the extent of unanticipated changes. Agreement on evaluative criteria between the multiple parties involved is unlikely and, at best, extremely time-consuming. Instead, Lindblom advocates a disjointed incremental, or muddling through, approach, in which each agency takes relatively small policy steps in light of its own parochial appraisal of the alternatives available close to current practice, a bounded set of first-order consequences, and a limited set of evaluative criteria. Ability to extract agreement on the specific action steps proposed from other involved agencies is treated as the major test of promise, and is certainly more likely than is agreement in principle. Monitoring of consequences, and advocacy of remedial action, is treated as a normal part of parochial monitoring of bounded sets of impacts and criteria. By such muddling through, Lindblom argues, we are likely to achieve a greater measure of rationality, and of comprehensiveness, than is offered by the direct attempt at comprehensive rationality. The taking of action is the key, both to achieving what agreement is required on criteria and to achieving comprehensive monitoring of results.

Much the same emphasis on action in the face of pervasive uncertainty is found in the writings of Campbell on the experimenting society (Campbell 1969). In Campbell's view, the critical issue is the unpredictability of consequences that will flow from a given policy intervention. His prescription is that we move tentatively in policy innovation, carefully designing "policy experiments" by which we can assess the impacts, intended and otherwise, of different approaches to a given problem. Much of Campbell's effort has been devoted to the development of suitable experimental and quasi-experimental designs by which such assessment can be conducted (Campbell and Stanley 1963; Cook and Campbell 1979).

For all the differences in emphasis between Campbell's experimenting society and Lindblom's muddling through, it is clear that both reject the feasibility of comprehensive rationality, what we have been referring to as proper decision-making, as a means to solve large social problems. Indeed, it is not too difficult to outline the elements of a synthesis between the two views, with Campbell's powerful technology for the discovery of effects married to Lindblom's rich grasp of the political process (see Connolly 1977b for a sketch of such a synthesis). Importantly, both views lead to an understanding of the importance of action as an uncertainty-reducing device, as well as a possible solution to the problem. Action is both for learning about and for solving problems, with the former payoff emphasized in situations of high uncertainty, the latter when the situation is more firmly grasped.

Organizational Decision-Making

A similar retreat from the demands of heroic rationality is noticeable in recent writings on the processes by which decisions are made in organizations. Traditional mythology on the subject pictures raw information flowing from the lowest organizational levels, through various processes of sifting, collation, and analysis, to appropriately senior levels, at which rationality prevails and from which command directions flow back down the organization. Important heresies concerning the boundedness of human rationality and the retrospective nature of its application have been noted already. More recently, the processes have been characterized as loosely coupled systems (Weick 1976), as organized anarchies with garbage can decision methodologies (Cohen, March, and Olsen 1972), and the challenge facing the designer as akin to that of constructing a structure suitable for "camping on seesaws" (Hedberg, Nystrom, and Starbuck 1976). The empirical work of Mintzberg (1973) portrays the manager's life as leaving little time for reflection and analysis in the midst of a press of short-term, interrupted, and somewhat chaotic activity.

Mintzberg's data are, in fact, strongly supportive of the emphasis placed here on the importance of action, rather than reflection, in solving complex problems. In his samples of managers, the mere duration of the average activity—typically nine minutes or less—seems to preclude any extensive reflection, deliberation, or analysis. Mintzberg also provides other important clues: for example, managers rely heavily on spoken, rather than written, communication. This may, of course, be nothing more than a reflection of the speed with which they must work. However, it may also reflect the selection of a fast-feedback communication channel by which the consequences of actions can be quickly monitored. When action is taken on little reflection, error is to be expected, and self-correcting processes are vital. Where Campbell advocates formal experimentation, the working manager depends on fast feedback. (Staw [personal communication] has offered the interesting speculation that such enhancement of feedback may be a primary impact of "sensitivity training," making managers more adept at observing the consequences of their actions.)

In short, the present emphasis on the central role of action in dealing with highly complex highly uncertain decision problems can be identified in a wide body of recent literature, ranging from public policy analysis to observation of managerial work. Action, of itself, does not, of course, solve problems. In proper decision-making, it achieves its effects by being well-directed from the start, so that action is the termination of the decision-making process. In the action-first approach, correctness of aim is less dependent on initial direction (though, clearly, it helps if the shot is aimed in the right direction). Direction is monitored and corrected as the consequences unfold, as opportunities for further impact are revealed, as new actors find their interests involved and bring pressure to bear, and as undesirable side effects are manifested.

Our emphasis so far has been on the easing of cognitive load— the reduction in the amount of information an individual must think about—that flows from action-first strategies. As a side benefit, it is worth pointing out that memory load is similarly reduced. Having, for example, dealt with a subordinate's problem by suggesting an action (intendedly, though not necessarily, a sound one), I do not need to remember much of the episode. Perhaps the problem will go away, either because of the wisdom of my suggestion or because the problem was a one-time extreme case. If, however, it persists, I can be reasonably sure that the subordinate will later reappear, armed with additional information about the problem

86 / UNCERTAINTY

(notably, what happened or failed to happen when the attempt at solution was made). In the interim, problem-relevant information was "stored" in the organizational analogue of the acoustic-delay memory used in early electronic computers.

Prerequisites and Limitations

Having tried to paint a somewhat rosy picture of the general efficacy of action-first decision strategies, we must sketch, if only briefly, the requirements for such an approach to work and the types of problems for which it will probably fail. The following listing is not comprehensive, but may suggest the types of issues involved.

1. No feedback problems: As noted above, improper decision strategies generally depend heavily on the availability of feedback as the action consequences unfold. A number of approaches to enhancing such feedback have been suggested, from formal experimentation to improved interpersonal sensitivity. If no feedback is available, self-correction is impossible, and one is forced to do the best possible job of deciding correctly at the outset. It is not clear how broad this category of problems must be, but the limitations of the careless parachute packer's defense ("I've never had any complaints") must be borne in mind.

2. Short-fuse problems: When there is time for only one solution attempt before catastrophe, the virtues of self-correcting feedback strategies disappear. So, of course, do those of proper problem-solving: the fuse will reach the powder keg before a proper analysis can be made. If, on the other hand, the problem can be "frozen" while expertise is brought to bear, then proper problem-solving is clearly the method of choice. No example comes readily to mind.

3. Inter-solution problems: there are clearly a range of important problems, including nuclear wars and childbearing, in which it is not possible to "try a little one and see how it goes." In such cases, however, it is not clear that proper decision-making offers any very large improvement, since most of the analysis must be founded on assumptions, rather than on factual information, about the specific decision context.

4. Cumulative-poison problems: If, by some complex concatenation of linkages, the use of DDT is decimating the eagle population by weakening the shells of their eggs, it is unlikely that even the most careful monitoring of decision-consequence feedback will reveal this. However, it is again unclear that this is a drawback

unique to the action-first strategy, since the same omission would almost certainly be made in the proper decision analysis, unless omniscience is assumed for the latter.

5. Defensible-solution problems: For senior managers, as for journal editors, the adequacy of one's solutions may be less important than the correctness of one's methodology. In such settings, there is no question that proper decision-making is the method of choice. As argued here, such settings may, indeed, be the only ones in which this unquestioned dominance exists.

CONCLUSION

The central concern of this chapter is the puzzling, perhaps even paradoxical, observation that people often cope with difficult decisions quite well. If we take seriously the descriptions of what is required to understand, analyze, and evaluate decision alternatives in settings where complexity and uncertainty are present in nontrivial amounts, the demands appear disproportional to what we know of human intellectual capabilities. It seems unlikely that the degree of success we observe is the result of widespread proper decision-making.

At least some of the puzzle is the result of failures of observation: people appear to make good decisions more often than they actually do. Such mechanisms as the bogus wisdom model, as well as processes of retrospective and self-fulfilling rationality, would tend to exaggerate impressions of decisional success. In other cases, including those illustrated here in the desert survival example, the flat maximum problem and the various problems that are solved by multiperson processes, the attribution of large competence to the decision maker is mistaken. These are settings in which even the modestly endowed can perform very well, or at least appear to do so.

However, there appears (at least to this observer) a sizable residual category in which good decisions are made by "improper" processes, and often in settings in which "proper" decision processes seem unlikely of success. The central feature of these is that the actor acts much more, and reflects much less, than would be required or allowed by proper decision making. The heretical suggestion offered is that such improper decision making may, in fact, be a perfectly defensible decision strategy, perhaps even the strategy of choice for many situations. Numerous benefits accrue if action is moved from the termination of a lengthy, possibly infinite, process of reflection, analysis, and evaluation and placed much closer to the beginning of the sequence. Action-first (or almost first) is proposed as a potentially viable strategy in its own right, not merely a second-class expedient to which a hard-pressed decision maker may be forced by external pressures. Action-first has its own distinct merits, capable of development and refinement, and potentially of wide and useful application.

Bateson (1972, p. 1) offers the notion of a metalogue: "a conversation about some problematic subject . . . such that not only do the participants discuss the problem but the structure of the conversation as a whole is also relevant to the same subject." Something rather similar is intended here. The present chapter falls far short of the standards of "proper" scholarship in definitional preciseness, comprehensiveness of literature review, and so on. Indeed, an attempt at "propriety" along these dimensions would require a work of essentially limitless length. This is not to suggest that editorial impositions are the cause of the chapter's shortcomings: it is the author's inadequacy in the face of the complex and uncertain issues raised that is to blame. Given such failure of reflection, action (here in the form of publication) is the response suggested by this work. It awaits the corrective feedback of interested colleagues.

REFERENCES

Archibald, W. P. 1974. "Alternative Explanations for the Self-Fulfilling Prophecy." Psychological Bulletin 81: 74-84.

Aronson, E. 1976. The Social Animal. 2d ed. San Francisco: Freeman.

Arrow, K. 1951. Social Choice and Individual Values. New York: Wiley.

Bateson, G. 1972. Steps to an Ecology of Mind. New York: Ballantine.

Braybrooke, D., and Lindblom, C. 1963. A Strategy of Decision: Policy Evaluation as a Social Process. New York: Macmillan.

Campbell, D. T. 1969. "Ethnocentrism of Disciplines and the Fish-Scale Model of Omniscience." In Interdisciplinary Relations in the Social Sciences, edited by M. Sharif and C. W. Sharif, pp. 328-48. Chicago: Aldine.

_____. 1969. "Reforms as Experiments." American Psychologist 24: 409-29.

Campbell, D. T., and Stanley, J. C. 1963. Experimental and Quasi-Experimental Designs for Research. Chicago: Rand McNally.

Clark, B. R. 1972. "The Organizational Saga in Higher Education." Administrative Science Quarterly 17: 175-84.

Cohen, N. D.; March, J. G.; and Olsen, J. P. 1972. "A Garbage Can Model of Organizational Choice." Administrative Science Quarterly 1: 1-25.

Connolly, T. 1977a. "Information Processing and Decision Making in Organizations." In New Directions in Organizational Behavior, edited by B. M. Staw and G. R. Salancik, pp. 205-34. Chicago: St. Clair Press.

———. 1977b. "A Note on the Policy-Relevance of Evaluation." In Interdisciplinary Dimensions of Accounting for Social Goals and Social Organizations, edited by H. W. Melton and D. J. H. Watson, pp. 135-38. Columbus, Ohio: Grid.

———. 1979. "A Measurement Model Approach to the Construction of Simple Linear Composite Measures." Mimeographed. Atlanta: Georgia Institute of Technology.

Conrath, D. W. 1967. Organizational Decision Making under Varying Conditions of Uncertainty." Management Science 13: B487-500.

Cook, T. D., and Campbell, D. T. 1979. Quasi-Experimentation: Design and Analysis Issues for Field Settings. Chicago: Rand McNally.

Dawes, R. M. 1979. "The Robust Beauty of Improper Linear Models in Decision Making." American Psychologist 34: 571-82.

Dawes, R. M., and Corrigan, B. 1974. "Linear Models in Decision Making." Psychological Bulletin 81: 95-106.

Deutsch, K. W., and Madow, W. G. 1961. "A Note on the Appearance of Wisdom in Large Bureaucratic Organizations." Behavioral Science 6 (January): 72-78.

Einhorn, H. J., and Hogarth, R. M. 1975. "Unit Weighting Schemes for Decision Making." Organizational Behavior and Human Performance. 13: 171-92.

Festinger, L. 1962. "Cognitive Dissonance." Scientific American 207, no. 4: 93-106.

Hammond, K. R. 1971. "Computer Graphics as an Aid to Learning." Science 172: 903-8.

Hedberg, B. L. T.; Nystrom, P. C.; and Starbuck, W. H. 1976. "Camping on Seesaws: Prescriptions for a Self-Designing Organization." Administrative Science Quarterly 21: 41-65.

Henle, M. 1962. "On the Relation between Logic and Thinking." Psychological Review 69: 366-78.

Lindblom, C. 1965. The Intelligence of Democracy. New York: Macmillan.

Merton, R. K. 1978. "The Self-Fulfilling Prophecy." Antioch Review 8: 193-210.

Miller, G. A. 1956. "The Magical Number Seven, Plus or Minus Two: Some Limits on Our Capacity for Processing Information." Psychological Review 63: 81-97.

Mintzberg, H. 1973. The Nature of Managerial Work. New York: Harper & Row.

Schelling, T. C. 1978. Micromotives and Macrobehavior. New York: Norton.

Simon, H. A. 1955. "A Behavioral Model of Rational Choice." Quarterly Journal of Economics 69: 99-118.

_____. 1956. "Rational Choice and the Structure of the Environment." Psychological Review 63: 129-38.

Staw, B. M., and Ross, J. 1978. "Commitment to a Policy Decision: A Multi-Theoretical Perspective." Administrative Science Quarterly 23: 40-64.

Tversky, A., and Kahneman, D. 1974. "Judgment under Uncertainty: Heuristics and Biases." Science 185: 1124-31.

Wainer, H. 1976. "Estimating Coefficients in Linear Models: It Don't Make No Nevermind." Psychological Bulletin 83: 312-17.

Weick, K. E. 1969. The Social Psychology of Organizing. Reading, Mass.: Addison-Wesley.

_____. 1976. "Educational Organizations as Loosely Coupled Systems." Administrative Science Quarterly 21: 1-19.

_____. 1977. "Enactment Processes." In New Directions in Organizational Behavior, edited by B. M. Staw and G. R. Salancik, pp. 267-300. Chicago: St. Clair Press.

Wilks, S. S. 1938. "Weighting Schemes for Linear Functions of Correlated Variables When There Is No Dependent Variable." Psychometrika 8: 23-40.

Woolsey, R. E. D. 1972. "A Candle to Saint Jude, or Four Real World Applications of Integer Programming." Interfaces 2: 20-27.

Yntema, D. B., and Torgerson, W. S. 1961. "Man-Computer Cooperation in Decisions Requiring Common Sense." IRE Transactions on Human Factors in Electronics 2: 20-26.

6
A SOCIAL BEHAVIORIST MODEL OF UNCERTAINTY IN THE PROCESS OF SYMBOLIC INTERACTIONS
Richard E. Sykes

INTRODUCTION

Uncertainty is an inevitable concomitant of interaction. Persons engaged in interaction seek to protect themselves from its uncertainty. The attempt to be protected, in itself, influences the process, but does not always decrease the uncertainty. This chapter, though based on long contemplation of detailed interaction data, is focused on developing a "theory" of uncertainty.

THE NATURE OF INTERACTION

Mind

Interaction is cooccurring verbal or nonverbal behavior of two or more persons acting in an arena of potential mutual awareness. The extent to which the interaction is coordinated or mutually contingent is an empirical, not a theoretical, question. Contingency is not a necessary predicate of interaction. It is assumed that contingency is a variable and that any particular behavior may be more or less contingent upon any other.

The behavior that is a part of interaction is an actualization of the decisions and habits of the actor. Preceding actualization, mind self-takes, other-takes, and group-takes. The latter two concepts are merely shorter terms for Mead's (1934, pp. 254-55, 155-56) taking the role of the other and taking the role of the generalized other. "An actor occupying a particular position imaginatively anticipates what someone occupying another position expects of him, in the first instance, or, in the second instance, what a particular group expects of him." It has been less often noted that it is not obvious what identity the actor wishes to choose to indicate in actualizing a particular behavior. S/he must, as it were, decide what self to be on his or her own terms, not just those of the other or group. Taking one's self into account is self-taking.

It is a mistake to overintellectualize interaction. Much interaction for many persons in specific situations is so repetitive and well-rehearsed that I assume (with Dewey 1957) it occurs with little imaginative effort and little self-, other-, or group-taking, except perhaps at an initial point, where a decision to commit oneself to a situation is made. A politician standing in a reception line and greeting 1,000 persons is probably manifesting the behaviors of shaking hands, saying, "How do you do?," and smiling with little imaginative effort, though s/he simultaneously may be making an effort to remember names and previous contacts with, and interests of, those who approach him/her in the line. In fact, the relatively habitual greeting behavior may manifest itself while the imaginative effort is focused on others further back in the line.

Repertoire

The behaviors that persons actualize are part of a repertoire of behaviors which are both typical in themselves and the actualization of typifications (Schutz 1970, pp. 63-64, and Wagner 1970) made by the actor. These typifications are a fruition of individual-in-position-in situation-in culture-in society (Secord and Backman 1974, p. 520).

> These typifications are made by an individual occupying a particular position, who is brought up within a particular culture and society, and who, at the moment, finds himself in a particular situation. Thus a person who is a member of a union, a baseball team player and a bowler will typify an event as a "strike" depending upon which position-situation is salient. The meaning of the typification is distinguishable only to someone who understands our language, the customs of our society, and which position-situation is in the mind of the speaker.

They are not determined or inevitable, but are the outcome of the process of interpretation in which the individual imaginatively engages. One such typification is isolated by Sudnow (1965) describing the activities of the public defender. Another, used by police officers, is dealt with succinctly by Van Maanen in "The Asshole" (1978).

94 / UNCERTAINTY

Typifications may be made in response to self and group as much as in response to other.

I assume that there is no one-to-one relationship between typifications and typical acts, but that before typical acts occur, except for habitual acts, that typification and perhaps imaginative rehearsal take place. A schematic of the process is displayed in Figure 6.1.

FIGURE 6.1

A Schematic of the Process Leading to Behavior by One Actor

Actor's Posited

Source of Event

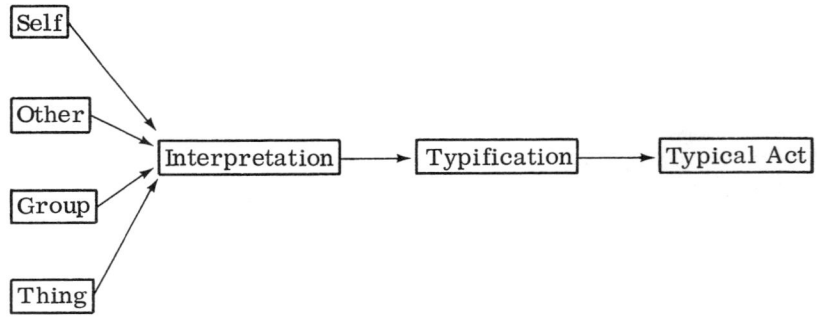

Source: Compiled by the author.

Typical acts are not necessarily described by the actor as "typical." Such acts are merely what-I-decided-to-do-given-my-goals-and-the-other-person-in-that-situation. They are merely "what anyone would do." They are taken for granted and unremarkable.

I assume this process occurs in an individual mental world in which what I term <u>perceptual sampling</u> (Brunswick 1957) takes place. In Mead's terminology (1938, pp. 3-4), a perceptual act is taking place. This implies that between some source event and typification, there occurs a process by means of which different aspects of the event are selected for attention and evaluation. While there is, ultimately, an "objective" event, it is never known to the human actor. The same event occurring in the same situation-culture-society will still elicit variation in the aspects of the event to which the actor chooses to attend. The same event will give rise to different typifications—inevitably. The famous parable of the blindfolded men and the elephant is apt. One man was led to the elephant and grabbed his tail; another, his trunk; and a third, his foot. When asked what the object was, each gave a different answer. The experiences of all three were "real"; but each had sampled a different aspect of the event, so each gave a different answer.

If a person occupying a position in the world of work is observed, then, gradually, the observer will learn both the typifications of the observed, usually expressed in the argot of his/her work group, and the typical acts, less often verbalized when reference is made to the micro level of interaction, but often verbalized in terms of overall import or outcome of the event. Inclusion of the process of perceptual sampling on which interpretation and typification are based leads to a revised schematic of the process, displayed in Figure 6.2.

A particular event may be sampled differently by the same actor at different times or by different actors at the same time. The outcome of perceptual sampling and interpretation leads to a range of typifications. Each typification leads to a range of typical acts. As a result of observation, an observer may compile a list of typical acts. With sufficient data, an estimate may be made of the probability of each act in the list, though I assume that the list is never exhaustive. Depending on the observer's interests, the list may be either of the typifications by the actor of his/her own acts or the observer's typifications of the actor's act. The total number of typical acts may be calculated, and their probability estimated, by dividing the frequency of each typical act by the total number of acts sampled. Thus, there results a probability vector of typical acts.

Coordinated Interaction

So far, I have considered only one actor. But I defined interaction as cooccurring behavior of two or more persons acting in an arena of mutual awareness. Now, I may specify the meaning of mutual awareness by requiring that the actors act within an arena

FIGURE 6.2

From Event to Action: The Revised Process

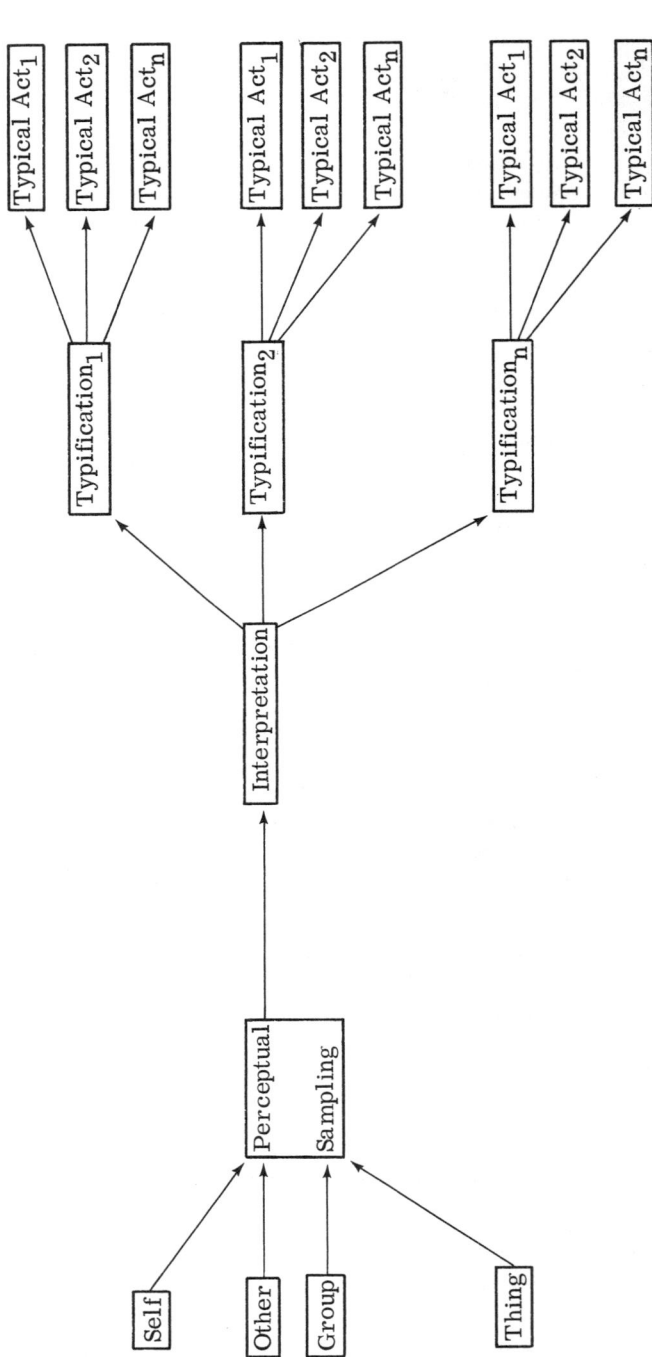

Source: Compiled by the author.

in which perceptual sampling of the other's typical acts is possible.
Typical acts are themselves sampled, interpreted, typified, and
then followed by some typical act. The repertoire of typical acts
of each actor may be the same or different. However, since each
list may be considered a probability vector, and since the typical
acts of the first actor may be observed, as well as those of the
second actor, it is possible to represent the sequence of acts of the
two actors in a matrix:

		Actor 2			
		Act_1	Act_2	Act_n	
	Act_1	n	n	n	
Actor 1	Act_2	n	n	n	(1)
	Act_n	n	n	n	

This matrix may be converted into a stochastic matrix simply by
converting <u>each</u> row into a probability vector, that is, by dividing
the total n for each row into the n for each cell in the row.

It is now possible to define <u>coordinated</u> interaction. Coordinated interaction occurs when the typical acts of each actor are
contingent upon those of the other actor, that is, when they are
dependent.

But the process cannot usually be represented by one matrix.
In (1) above, actor 2's acts follow those of actor 1. The magnitude
of the contingency between the acts of 1 and acts of 2 may be different from that between actor 2 and actor 1. For instance actor 2
may be likely to follow actor 1's act 1 with his/her act 2, while actor
1 may be more likely to follow actor 2's act 1 with his/her act 1.
Thus, interaction may be represented by the following matrix:

		Actor 1			Actor 2				
		Act 1	Act 2	Act n	Act 1	Act 2	Act n		
	Act 1				p	p	p	m_1	
Actor 1	Act 2				p	p	p	m_2	
	Act n				p	p	p	m_3	(2)
	Act 1	p	p	p				m_4	
Actor 2	Act 2	p	p	p				m_5	
	Act n	p	p	p				m_6	

98 / UNCERTAINTY

In the upper right quadrant, actor 2's typical acts <u>following</u> those of actor 1 are represented, and in the lower left quadrant, vice versa.

From (2), we may now distinguish the <u>absolute probability</u> of either actor issuing an act from <u>transition probabilities</u> between actors. The absolute values are calculated from the marginals for each actor converted to probabilities, for example, a particular row <u>total</u> divided by the total number of acts for that actor (for example, $m_1 \div m_1 + m_2 + m_3$ would give such a probability for act 1 of actor 1). Transition values are the probabilities that if actor 1 actualized a particular act, say, act_1, actor 2 will follow with another particular act, say, act 2. If actor 1 actualizes act 1, then actor 2 may follow with act_1 or act_2 or act_3 from his/her repertoire, but each with a different probability. These probabilities are called <u>transition probabilities</u>. To the extent that these probabilities depart significantly from chance, the interaction of actor 1 and actor 2 may be said to be coordinated. Not only this, but since the transition probabilities represent a <u>relation</u> between the two actors, it would appear that the greater the probability that actor 2 will respond to a typical act of actor 1 with a specific typical act, or vice versa, the more we are justified in hypothesizing that the relationship between the two acts is the manifestation of a norm or rule of conduct. The greater the probability relating the typical acts, the greater the likelihood of such a rule. In fact, it is now possible to define a rule as simply a high (threshold undefined) probability that a particular typical act will be followed by another particular act.

The fact that the initial act may be followed by several possible acts of different probabilities prevents us from assuming a deterministic or causal perspective. Even if there is one strong probability (rule), other probabilities remain. Perhaps there is a set of optional responses from which choices may be made, or perhaps there is a hierarchy; perhaps some options in the repertoire are deviant and an account would be forthcoming if challenged. In any event, whatever the other position, there always remains the uncertainty of response, even in the presence of an empirically established rule.

The most intriguing source of uncertainty inheres in the relationship between the relatively stable predispositions to respond to a particular act of the other by a particular act (transition probabilities) and by the relatively stable but differing absolute proportions of particular acts that particular positions will actualize.

Let us take, for example, the position of police officer. As an officer (not a person), s/he might respond as follows (these figures are entirely hypothetical):

Civilian	Officer		
Prior Typical Act	Probability of Typical Subsequent Act		
	Elaborate Respect	Respect	Disrespect
Elaborate respect	.20	.70	.10
Respect	.05	.80	.15
Disrespect	.05	.55	.40

From the above, we would infer that (1) the rule is to respond to elaborate respect or respect with respect, and (2) that the overall expectation would be for an officer to respond with respect. Let us, in fact, hypothesize that the above set of transition probabilities represents the rule for officers. This rule at the level of interpersonal relations constitutes a social psychological symbolic construct analogous to a psychological construct, such as trait. We may also assume some absolute distribution of the proportion of typical acts of the officer:

Absolute Proportions	
Elaborate respect	.05
Respect	.80
Disrespect	.15

These proportions are independent of the transition probabilities. But in this instance, one would still expect the officer to actualize primarily respectful typical acts.

Now let us assume that the officer intereacts with several different other positions, each of which manifests a *different* set of *absolute* proportions of their typical acts. For instance:

Complainant		Suspect	
Elaborate respect	.07	Elaborate respect	.02
Respect	.90	Respect	.70
Disrespext	.03	Disrespect	.28

Since police interact with complainants probably four times more than with suspects, the chances are high that officers will be observed actualizing typical acts of respect. When, then, one reads about or observes an act of police disrespect or brutality, it will appear to be a violation of the norm. In fact, it is not, because, although the transition predisposition remains exactly the same, the officer is interacting with a position that actualizes a higher proportion of disrespectful acts. Instead of civil interaction, confrontational interaction will ensue.

It follows that perhaps the most interesting source of uncertainty in interaction is not the "freedom" which the actor manifests to actualize a range of responses to a particular act of the other, even in the presence of a rule, but, rather, the independent tendency of different positions to actualize different absolute proportions of their repertoires of acts. Since these differences are consciously unknown to the actors, and in some cases, practically speaking, unknowable, every new dyad must be entered in uncertainty because different sets of absolute proportions interacting with the same set of transition probabilities produces phenomenologically different results. That which is basically orderly appears phenomenologically eccentric.

So far, I have spoken of both the absolute proportion of acts and the stable predisposition toward certain sets of transition probabilities from one act to another in regard to positions. My assumption is that the behavior of incumbents in any position is partially guided by rules and that a matrix of transition probabilities such as (2) reflects those rules. However, in real life, we are dealing with individuals-in positions-in situations. For example, a police officer (position) is expected to respond differently to a young male who has been injured in an auto accident than to one who is running out of a supermarket with cash in one hand a gun in the other. Situations constitute parameters that may modify the matrix, and individuality is a unique parameter which must modify each matrix to an unknown extent. Thus, the position matrix "masks" individuality, although individual predispositions must also affect the fate and increase the uncertainty of every dyad. I do not assume human beings to be oversocialized, and therefore, I assume that individuality enters into every series of interactions, but to an unknown extent, since it is impossible to know the differences for all individuals.

So far, I have identified three sources of uncertainty intrinsic to interaction: The first is perceptual sampling—even of typical acts—as a result of which some are perceived as atypical and some which are atypical are perceived as typical. The second concerns the possession of a range of alternate typical acts that the actor can choose as a response. The initial absolute distribution of acts, as well as the transition probabilities, are a result of aggregation, and to apply them to a particular act-act sequence is to make an error analogous to the ecological fallacy. At the individual level, the process always is indeterminate.

Finally, even if a position manifests a stable set of predispositions to respond, the actual responses are dependent upon the absolute proportion of typical acts in the other's repertoire. This proportion differs between positions and, for each position, probably between individuals and situations. Since this pertains to both positions in any interaction, it means that despite the predictability that might seem to exist because of the stable response dispositions of each position, in fact, each series of interactions may give the appearance of being completely different from that which was expected. The police officer, for instance, who appeared to be a "nice guy" may suddenly appear brutal, and likewise the civilian with whom s/he is dealing. Interaction has emergent properties, for which knowledge of individuals or positions alone cannot account.

While my own studies have focused primarily on police, I believe the conditions that I describe pertain to all symbolic interaction.

REFERENCES

Brunswick, Egon. 1957. "Scope and Aspects of the Cognitive Problem." In Cognition: The Colorado Symposium, edited by H. Gruber, R. Jessor, and K. Hammond. Cambridge, Mass.: Harvard University Press, pp. 137-62.

Dewey, John. 1957. Human Nature and Conduct. New York: Modern Library.

Mead, George H. 1972. The Philosophy of the Act. Chicago: University of Chicago Press.

―――. 1974. Mind, Self, and Society. Chicago: University of Chicago Press.

Schutz, Alfred. 1970. Reflections on the Problem of Relevance. New Haven, Conn.: Yale University Press.

Secord, Paul F., and Backman, Carl W. 1974. Social Psychology. 2d ed. New York: McGraw-Hill.

Sudnow, David. 1965. "Normal Crimes: Sociological Features of the Penal Code in a Public Defender Office." Social Problems 12 (Winter): 225-76.

Van Maanen, John. 1978. "The Asshole." In Policing: A View from the Street, edited by P. K. Manning and J. Van Maanen, pp. 221-38. Santa Monica, Calif.: Goodyear.

Wagner, Helmut, ed. 1970. Alfred Schutz on Phenomenology and Selected Writings. Chicago: University of Chicago Press.

7
ORGANIZATIONAL AND INDIVIDUAL RESPONSES TO ENVIRONMENTAL UNCERTAINTY
James G. Hougland, Jr.
Jon M. Shepard

INTRODUCTION

Most organizations strive for autonomy because autonomous organizations are able to maximize control over internal processes while avoiding external influence. In fact, Thompson (1967) argues that organizations attempt to be autonomous by insulating important aspects of their operations from external forces. However, Thompson is also among many theorists who have noted that organizations cannot operate as closed systems, unaffected by their surroundings. Organizations need resources in order to operate, and most of them can survive only if enough external actors are willing to receive their output. Thus, despite a desire for autonomy, organizations are "pushed" into systems of interdependence with external actors (Aiken and Hage 1968).

Because of organizations' interdependence with external actors, the environment—the set of actors and conditions outside an organization—has been identified as a contingency factor having important implications for organizational design (Mintzberg 1979). Thus, the environment is an important aspect of contingency theory, which

> seeks to understand the interrelationships within and among subsystems as well as between the organization and its environment and to define patterns of relationships or configurations of variables. It emphasizes the multivariate nature of organizations and attempts to understand how organizations operate under varying conditions and in specific circumstances (Kast and Rosenzweig 1973, p. ix).

Assessing the implications of the environment for organizations is often difficult for both researchers and practitioners because of the existence of environmental uncertainty—a situation in which events are occurring that cannot be forecast by an organization (Pfeffer 1978a, p. 133).

Uncertainty may reflect unpredictable relationships between environmental elements, inadequate perceptions of the relationships that exist, or some combination of the two (Aldrich and Mindlin 1978). In either case, environmental uncertainty may have important effects on decisions about organizational design and strategy. Even if decision makers choose to ignore environmental conditions, they may ultimately be affected by the greater success of other organizations that have acted in ways more compatible with environmental conditions (Hannan and Freeman 1977; Aldrich 1979). In this chapter, we examine some ways in which organizations respond to environmental uncertainty, the effectiveness of those responses, and organizational members' reactions to organizational changes brought about by responses to environmental uncertainty.

ORGANIZATIONAL RESPONSES TO ENVIRONMENTAL UNCERTAINTY

It was once believed that exposure to uncertainty would lead to an abandonment of traditional organization techniques (for example, Bennis 1965). This, in fact, has not happened (Shariff 1979; Bennis 1979; Meyer 1979). Organizations may respond to environmental uncertainty in a variety of ways, ranging from ignoring it altogether to transforming the organizational structure. While hardly forming an exhaustive typology of potential responses, the following responses are among the most common strategies organizations use to cope with environmental uncertainty (also see Pfeffer 1978a, pp. 133-37).

Ignoring Uncertainty

According to Starbuck (1976), organizations tend to create their own "environments" by selecting from the external world exactly what they wish to see. While this view underestimates the potential for negative feedback stemming from inaccurate perceptions and actions regarding the environment (Aldrich 1979, p. 157), the tendency does exist for environments to be perceived in terms the observer can comfortably interpret. Consequently, organizational expectations are often based on available information and established repertoires. Many organizations seek to avoid uncertainty—and, thus, to avoid challenges to existing expectations—by solving pressing problems rather than developing long-run strategies (Cyert and March 1963). Such techniques as standard operating procedures and reliance on industry tradition are frequently used to avoid dealing with uncertainties.

Since uncertainty avoidance involves ignoring potentially important conditions, it represents a major departure from rational models of organizational action. The basis for such practices, however, can be understood because of the necessity for organizations to provide incentives to a coalition of participants representing a diversity of demands. Some participants may be strongly attached to organizations, but many are attracted only because they perceive the organization as being successful in attaining some specific objectives and in providing easily recognized benefits (Rogers 1971). New ventures with uncertain payoffs are unlikely to impress such participants.

Pressures exist, then, toward ignoring uncertainty. Despite such pressures, however, uncertainty avoidance is not always an available organizational strategy. Organizations are forced to deal with uncertainty if they are highly dependent on external actors, who push them into new activities and relationships, or if powerful internal actors encourage dealing with uncertainty. As Aldrich (1972), Pfeffer (1972), and Benson (1975) have argued, organizations must act on the basis of their dependence on other organizations for needed resources. For organizations in positions of dependence, establishing favorable relations with the organizations controlling essential resources is a major problem, and such organizations must frequently expose themselves to new sources of uncertainty to secure such favorable relations. For example, the Tennessee Valley Authority allowed potentially hostile actors to occupy decision-making positions within the organization in an effort to win their support (Selznick 1949).

Even if dependence on external actors is not a major problem, some organizations take relatively risky actions, thereby introducing uncertainty, because such actions are "pushed" by powerful actors within the organization. For example, some ministers and denominational officials have encouraged churches to take more daring stands on such policies as civil rights than many members would have preferred. Efforts to push organizations into such new areas of uncertainty appear to be more likely to influence policy to the extent that the internal polity gives some legitimacy to the actors pushing for the change (Wood 1975).

The likelihood of sticking with a strategy of uncertainty avoidance, then, appears to depend on the external and internal polity of an organization (Zald 1970b). Organizations are likely to make a policy of avoiding uncertainty unless external or internal actors are able to gain the power to overcome the force of habit and tradition. Despite the importance of strategic choice by internal leaders (Child 1972) and dependence on external actors (Benson 1975), the tendency for organizations in many industries to retain traditional forms even after technological and other conditions change (Stinchcomb 1965) suggests that uncertainty avoidance is a very common strategy.

Creating a Segmented Organizational Structure

Despite tendencies to avoid uncertainty, many organizations are virtually forced to deal with it. Particularly if comparable organizations are adjusting to environmental changes, an organization that fails to do so is likely to lose the support of potential clients. However, in many cases, dealing with uncertainty apparently does not lead to a far-reaching change in organizational structure. In his influential work, Thompson (1967, p. 20) suggested that, "Under norms of rationality, organizations seek to buffer environmental influences by surrounding their technical cores with input and output components." Among the techniques cited by Thompson are stockpiling and the use of personnel in boundary roles who "monitor" the environment and "absorb" uncertainty for the organization.

In broader terms, organizations often attempt to confine the effects of environmental disturbances to specific segments of the organization. The development of a loosely coupled system, in which the connections between parts of the organization are relatively weak, allows disturbances affecting a part of an organization to be confined to that one part (Weick 1976). In a discussion that anticipated the recent attention to loosely coupled systems, Litwak (1961) noted that while some parts of an organization dealt with uniform tasks, another part of the same organization may deal with uncertain, nonuniform tasks. For example, many organizations have both manufacturing and research divisions. The research division is likely to respond to uncertainty, but its effort may have no effect whatsoever on procedures in the manufacturing division. The main problem faced by such an organization, according to Litwak, is the establishment of mechanisms of segregation which prevent the often incompatible activities and orientations of different parts of the organization from interfering with each other.

Many organizations face the dilemma of being dependent on outside or inside actors, who push for change or risky action, while simultaneously depending on the ongoing effort of members, whose activities or incentives would be disrupted by departures from established practice. The segmented organization provides a structural mechanism through which an organization's leaders can attempt to pursue change and continuity simultaneously. As the recent attention to loosely coupled systems attests, such techniques are likely to receive increasing recognition.

Creating Organic-Adaptive Structures

Bennis (1965, pp. 34-35) has suggested that because of the increased interdependence and turbulence of environments, most organizations will begin to experience major changes:

> The key word will be "temporary;" there will be adaptive, rapidly changing <u>temporary systems</u>. These will be "task forces" organized around problem-to-be-solved. The problems will be solved by groups of relative strangers who represent a set of diverse professional skills. The group will be arranged on organic rather than mechanical models; they will evolve in response to the problem rather than to programmed role expectations. The "executive" thus becomes <u>coordinator</u> or "linking pin" between various task forces. . . . People will be differentiated not vertically, according to rank and role, but flexibly and functionally according to skill and professional training.

Bennis's predictions have, in fact, received some support. Burns and Stalker (1966), Lawrence and Lorsch (1967), and Duncan (1972) have reported that organizations in uncertain environments are more effective to the extent that they depart from traditional bureaucratic structures. While these findings fall short of Bennis's "end of bureaucracy" predictions, they do indicate that if environments become increasingly uncertain, bureaucracy will become a less and less viable organizational form.

This area of research, however, must be treated with caution. Some efforts to find relationships between environmental uncertainty and organizational structure have failed to support the proposed relationship (Pennings 1975). Some of the original studies have been subjected to severe methodological criticisms. Tosi, Aldag, and Storey (1973) and Downey, Hellriegel, and Slocum (1975) reported difficulty achieving acceptable reliability levels for Lawrence and Lorsch's scales. Even after reconceptualizing the scales,

Downey, Hellriegel, and Slocum (1975) found a lack of significant relationships between the Lawrence and Lorsch uncertainty subscales. Two of Duncan's subscales—lack of information and lack of effect knowledge—were found to be related, but neither of these was significantly related to Duncan's third subscale, ability to assign probabilities. Thus, it is possible that neither study has succeeded in tapping total uncertainty. In the absence of stronger evidence, the assertion that organic-adaptive systems perform more successfully than bureaucracies in conditions of uncertainty must remain rather speculative.

Such measurement problems might ultimately be resolved. Even if they are, however, the assumption that organizations will respond to environmental uncertainty with the thought of maximizing the organization's performance is open to question. It is probably more plausible to suggest that an organization's members will differ in their objectives and their definitions of reality (Pfeffer 1978a). If so, an organization's reaction to uncertainty may depend on the agendas and perceptions of powerful actors either inside or outside the organization. Like the tendencies toward uncertainty avoidance discussed above, the likelihood that environmental uncertainty will lead to an organic-adaptive structure may ultimately be a political question.

Environmental Uncertainty, Organizational
Response, and Contingency Theory

Probably the best known assertion made by contingency theorists is that there is no "one best way" to organize. Despite this assertion, contingency theorists have stopped far short of saying that "anything goes." Their contention has been that appropriate organizing techniques depend on the situation faced by an organization. The proposition that organic-adaptive systems are appropriate responses to environmental uncertainty is a prominent example of the kinds of predictions developed by contingency theorists. However, as most contingency theorists would probably agree, such a proposition is only a first step toward understanding reality because other characteristics of the internal and external circumstances faced by the organization may combine with environmental uncertainty to influence the organization's response.

Organizations whose competitors—those organizations with which they will be compared—are ignoring environmental uncertainty may be in a position to engage in uncertainty avoidance themselves. Those that are combinations of loosely coupled parts may use organic-adaptive strategies in some areas of operation, while retaining traditional bureaucratic procedures elsewhere. Only those whose operations are permeated by uncertainty are likely to develop organic-adaptive structures throughout the organization. Even in these organizations, the structure may be modififed by pressures leading to the institutionalization of successful practices (Hughes 1937; Zucker 1977) or by the consolidation of power on the part of the organization (Perrow 1979).

In short, environmental uncertainty is only one of many factors likely to affect organizational structure and process. It cannot be viewed in isolation.

> [T]here has been a pronounced tendency to examine the various determinants of structure one at a time, with one study examining technology, another the environment, and still another size. The possibility exists, however, that these various determinants affect the structure in an interactive, rather than an additive, fashion (Pfeffer 1978b, p. 33).

Rather than being content with refining measures and conceptualizations of environmental uncertainty, future researchers should try to examine the ways in which it interacts with other contingency factors (such as the organization's size, its past practices, the nature of its technology, the extent to which it has consolidated power, and so forth) in influencing organizational structure and process.

CONSEQUENCES OF ORGANIZATIONAL RESPONSES TO THE ENVIRONMENT

If organizations are affected by their environment, how can we assess the consequences of their responses? Consequences are likely to be experienced both on the level of the organization as a whole and on the level of the individual member. This portion of the chapter will address both levels of consequences.

The Nature of Organizational Effectiveness

Any assessment of the effects of environmental uncertainty on the organization as a whole requires some consideration of organizational effectiveness. Effectiveness, in turn, is often evaluated in terms of the organization's degree of success in goal achievement (Etzioni 1964, p. 8). However, most organizations possess multiple goals, not all of which are compatible. Consequently, "effectiveness in one set of endeavors may lead to ineffectiveness in another" (Hall 1977, p. 85). Selznick (1957, p. 54) has called attention to the importance of an organization's "character"—its "built-in capabilities and limitations," which, in combination, make it a distinct entity. While character remains a somewhat vague concept, it has the virtue of calling attention to the combination of goals, policy, and tradition that set an organization apart from others. Selznick argues that an organization's "leaders must take account of the environment, adapting to its limitations as well as to its opportunities, but we must beware of institutional surrender [lack of attention to the organization's core values] made in the name of organizational survival" (1957, p. 145). Roe and Wood (1975) suggest that "adaptive innovation" occurs when an organization makes an adjustment in its practices that improves its relationship to its environment without weakening the organization's character. In these terms, then, an adaptive innovation would represent a highly effective response to environmental conditions, while institutional surrender would represent a highly ineffective response.

Conditions Promoting Effective Responses to the Environment

Nature of the Environment

A key factor affecting the likelihood that an organization will respond effectively to its environment is the nature of the environment itself. Considerable attention has been devoted to types of environmental conditions (for example, Emery and Trist 1965; Terreberry 1968; Jurkovich 1974; Aldrich 1979, pp. 63-73). Much of this work has been concerned with discussing the difficulties associated with responding to unstable, turbulent environments. Instability—stemming from the addition of competing organizations— and turbulence—a condition in which one's understanding of the environment is obscure because of increasing interconnection between relevant elements in the environment—both increase the difficulty of responding to environmental conditions because links between strategies and effective outcomes become unclear (Emery and Trist 1965). Strategies that under more stable conditions would promote effectiveness are likely to be offset by actions of competitors or unpredicted changes in the environmental field. Under these conditions, problem-<u>solving</u> is likely to be replaced by problem-<u>coping</u> (Jurkovich 1974), but the adoption of such strategies as environmental-monitoring and attention to information-processing systems are likely to benefit the organization (Terreberry 1968).

Organizational Resources and Past Success

Despite their importance, environmental characteristics provide only a starting point for predicting the nature and effectiveness of an organization's response to environmental conditions. Some organizations may not be able to make what would initially appear to be an appropriate response to environmental conditions, and others may not need to. As Aldrich (1979, p. 63) notes, an organization's discretion regarding the use of such mechanisms as environmental monitoring and information-processing systems may be affected by "the relative level of resources available to an organization within its environment" or "the extent to which an organization has to expand its area of operation to obtain the resources it requires." Aldrich argues that environments with relatively "lean" capacities reward the efficient use of resources. But it may be more crucial to note that resources must be acquired before they can be efficiently used, and the acquisition of resources is a major problem under lean conditions. Thus, as Aldrich says, lean environments promote such strategies as hoarding and stockpiling. In broader terms, lean environments are likely to promote institutional surrender by organizations. When needed resources are scarce, the organization's need to continue receiving them is likely to be more salient to its members than the somewhat abstract matter of preserving the organization's character.

Within any given environment, the likelihood that an organization will engage in adaptive innovation rather than institutional surrender may depend on its past success in securing resources. Extremely marginal organizational organizations are likely to be forced to innovate, but their innovativeness is likely to reflect a desperate attempt to survive rather than an attempt to enhance their character. Thus, the Townsend organizations responded to environmental changes by deemphasizing their efforts to promote economic reform in favor of selling consumer products and providing recreational activities (Messinger 1955). Many adult education programs have allowed their course offerings to be determined by customer wishes rather than by a coherent educational policy involving a balanced curriculum (Clark 1968).

In contrast, the Young Men's Christian Association (YMCA) has apparently succeeded in changing from an evangelistic to a general service organization in a manner consistent with the values of its members and leaders (Zald 1970a), and some college sororities have risked short-term financial losses to allow members more freedom about where to live (Roe and Wood 1975). Such actions can be viewed as adaptive because they have enhanced the prestige of organizations without disrupting their basic character.

The modification of sororities' housing policies, for example, allowed them to attract mature members, who placed a high value on freedom of life-style at a time when such freedom was valued by college students in general. However, such actions have not been taken by all sororities. Roe and Wood (1975) found that this type of adaptive innovation was most likely to be tried by sororities that were relatively secure in terms of financial solvency, prestige, and recent success in recruitment. Similarly, the YMCA adopted changes representing a "revitalization of organizational mission" (Zald 1970a, p. 158) after it had already enjoyed considerable success.

It is commonly asserted that "necessity is the mother of invention," but, as Roe and Wood (1975) note, immediate necessity is not very likely to lead to adaptive innovation. The examples reviewed above indicate past success gives organizational decision makers the opportunity to evaluate plans in terms of their long-term implications in addition to their short-term payoff.

Members' Reactions to Organizational Change

Effectiveness is a crucial aspect of the consequences of an organization's response to environmental uncertainty, but it is also crucial to recognize that an organization can maintain its effectiveness only if its members continue to provide the organization with their services. It is therefore important to recognize that members of an organization will be affected by changes in the organization's policies and procedures. The possibility that they will respond negatively to what might initially seem to be an appropriate change is an important one because participants were originally attracted to the organization by an incentive system established prior to the change.

Contingency theories focusing on individuals have suggested a need to introduce members' characteristics and orientations as intervening variables in the relationship between organizational characteristics and members' responses (Hulin 1971). Such incidents as the periodic disturbances at the Lordstown plant of General Motors Corporation and the Episcopal church's loss of members following its advocacy of several controversial social causes show that inadequate attention to members' characteristics and orientations can have detrimental consequences for organizations. Since organizations' responses to environmental uncertainty may require their members to cope with considerable ambiguity, the question of individual responses is a very important one. Burns and Stalker (1966) are best known for recommending the organic form as appropriate for conditions of uncertainty, but they have also acknowledged that it introduced problems for managers:

> The organic form by departing from the familiar clarity and fixity of the hierarchic structure, is often experienced by the individual manager as an uneasy, embarrassed, or chronically anxious quest for knowledge about what he should be doing, or what is expected of him, and similar apprehensiveness about what others are doing. . . . In these situations, all managers some of the time, and many managers all the time, yearn for more definition and structure (Burns and Stalker 1966, pp. 122-23).

Such findings suggest what at first seems to be an irreconcilable dilemma: many organizations are simultaneously faced with pressures from an uncertain environment and from members who expect some definition and structure to guide their activities. The severity of the dilemma, however, may have been exaggerated by some analysts. Evidence exists that individuals are capable of changing on the basis of organizational experience. Kohn and Schooler (1978), for example, found from a longitudinal study that the effects of a job's substantive complexity on workers' intellectual flexibility was larger than the reciprocal effect of the worker on the job. In another longitudinal study, Mortimer and Lorence (1979) found that the work experiences of male college graduates over a ten-year period were capable of altering work-related values. As Shepard and Hougland (1978, p. 418) concluded on the basis of their review of the literature:

> This study suggests that individuals are capable of changing in response to their job situation. Such results should not be surprising. Early experiments in gestalt psychology indicated that "personality traits . . . were dependent variables, significantly altered by the organization of the group into authoritarian, democratic, or laissez-faire structures" (Blumberg, 1968, p. 109). More generally, Blau (1960) showed that structural pressures cause individuals to behave in ways contrary to their initial attitudes. Festinger (1957) highlighted the potential significance of such structurally induced behavior by suggesting that behavior which is initially contrary to one's attitudes will often result in consistency-producing attitude change. Thus, by confronting individuals with demands

which must be met, jobs are likely to affect perceptions, values, and thinking processes. Since the studies reviewed indicate that jobs do affect the adult socialization process, the potential for change over time must not be overlooked.

Attention to individual characteristics should not overshadow the possibility that individuals' attitudes are affected by their organizational experience. Individuals' reactions to organizations should not be overlooked, but the stronger direction of influence is probably from the organization to the individual. Thus, such techniques as employee orientation and training programs are frequently recommended as means of achieving compatibility between members' orientations and organizational characteristics whenever such compatibility has not been achieved by the recruitment process (Mealiea and Lee 1979).

An important qualification must be added, however, because some organizations are more successful than others in achieving an integration of individual and organizational characteristics. Organizational security—which was shown above to be an important predictor of an organization's ability to respond effectively to environmental characteristics—is also likely to influence an organization's success in maintaining members' incentives. When some members of an organization object to a change, leaders and other members often deal with the objection through such techniques as "quasi-resolution of conflict," in which sequential attention to goals and concessions on secondary issues divert attention from conflict of interest (Cyert and March 1963), and "goal submergence," a gradual shift in organizational policy, which allows leaders to deemphasize a traditional goal to members who find it disturbing, while continuing to stress it to other members who value it (Hougland, Woods, and Mueller 1974). However, such strategies require a diversion of some resources from operations essential to organizational survival into efforts to pacify a segment of the organizational membership. Under conditions of scarcity, when the acquisition of resources is problematic, such uses of resources are likely to be resisted by members of the dominant coalition, and holders of competing viewpoints will perceive each other as threats. The organization's ability to reconcile its policies with the previously acquired attitudes and values of resisting members will be seriously diminished. Zald (1970a, p. 227) has provided a helpful summary of these phenomena in terms of a politics of scarcity and a politics of abundance:

> A politics of scarcity almost always involves a zero-sum game in which one person's or group's gain

requires another's equivalent loss; competitive strategies are obviously encouraged and political elites must mediate between competing claims. The politics of abundance, however, resembles a non-zero game in that alternatives exist through which both parties can achieve results above zero; cooperative strategies are thus encouraged and elites need not penalize one person or group to reward another or to change allocations.

A politics of abundance is, of course, analogous to organizational security. The organization that has already experienced some success, then, is in a better position than others to deal with internal problems related to adjusting to environmental conditions.

CONCLUSION

As was stated at the beginning of this chapter, organizations' strivings for autonomy are almost inevitably thwarted by a variety of forces. Contingency researchers have provided valuable guidelines for dealing with pressures from external actors and the probable responses of internal actors. Environmental uncertainty is among the factors emphasized by contingency theorists. Environmental uncertainty, however, must be viewed in combination with other factors. In this chapter, we have tried to show the existence of a range of possible responses to environmental uncertainty, and we have argued that the effectiveness of the organization's response to uncertainty—both for the organization as a whole, as well as for its individual members—will reflect organizational security. Ironically, the greatest success in responding to environmental uncertainty is likely to be enjoyed by those organizations that are already experiencing success.

REFERENCES

Aiken, M., and Hage, J. 1968. "Organizational Interdependence and Intraorganizational Structure." American Sociological Review 33: 912-30.

Aldrich, H. E. 1972. "An Organization-Environment Perspective on Co-operation and Conflict in the Manpower Training Program." In Conflict and Power in Complex Organizations, edited by A. Negandhi, pp. 11-37. Kent, Ohio: Center for Business and Economic Research.

_____. 1979. *Organizations and Environments*. Englewood Cliffs, N.J.: Prentice-Hall.

Aldrich, H. E., and Mindlin, S. 1978. "Uncertainty and Dependence: Two Perspectives on Environment." In *Organization and Environment: Theory, Issues and Reality*, edited by L. Karpik, pp. 149-70. Beverly Hills, Calif.: Sage.

Bennis, W. G. 1965. "Beyond Bureaucracy." *Trans-action* 2 (July/August): 31-35.

_____. 1979. "Response to Shariff: Beyond Bureaucracy Baiting." *Social Science Quarterly* 60 (June): 20-24.

Benson, J. K. 1975. "The Interorganizational Network as a Political Economy." *Administrative Science Quarterly* 20 (June): 229-49.

Blau, P. M. 1960. "Structural Effects." *American Sociological Review* 25 (April): 178-93.

Blumberg, P. 1968. *Industrial Democracy: The Sociology of Participation*. London: Constable.

Burns, T., and Stalker, G. M. 1966. *The Management of Innovation*. 2d ed. London: Tavistock.

Child, J. 1972. "Organization Structure, Environment, and Performance—The Role of Strategic Choice." *Sociology* 6 (January): 1-22.

Clark, B. 1968. *Adult Education in Transition*. Berkeley: University of California Press.

Cyert, R. M., and March, J. G. 1963. *A Behavioral Theory of the Firm*. Englewood Cliffs, N.J.: Prentice-Hall.

Downey, H. K.; Hellriegel, D.; and Slocum, J. 1975. "Environmental Uncertainty: The Construct and Its Application." *Administrative Science Quarterly* 20 (December): 613-29.

Duncan, R. B. 1972. "Characteristics of Organizational Environments and Perceived Environmental Uncertainty." *Administrative Science Quarterly* 17 (September): 313-27.

Emery, F. E., and Trist, E. L. 1965. "The Causal Texture of Organizational Environments." Human Relations 18 (February): 21-32.

Etzioni, A. 1964. Modern Organizations. Englewood Cliffs, N.J.: Prentice-Hall.

Festinger, L. 1957. A Theory of Cognitive Dissonance. New York: Harper & Row.

Hall, R. H. 1977. Organizations: Structure and Process. 2d ed. Englewood Cliffs, N.J.: Prentice-Hall.

Hannan, M., and Freeman, J. 1977. "The Population Ecology of Organizations." American Journal of Sociology 82 (March): 929-64.

Hougland, J. G., Jr.; Wood, J. R.; and Mueller, S. A. 1974. "Organizational 'Goal Submergence': The Methodist Church and the Failure of the Temperance Movement." Sociology and Social Research 58 (July): 408-16.

Hughes, E. C. 1937. "Institutional Office and the Person." American Journal of Sociology 43 (November): 404-13.

Hulin, C. L. 1971. "Individual Differences and Job Enrichment—The Case Against General Treatments." In New Perspectives in Job Enrichment, edited by J. R. Maher. New York: Van Norstrand Reinhold.

Jurkovich, R. 1974. "A Core Typology of Organizational Environments." Administrative Science Quarterly 19 (September): 380-94.

Kast, F. E., and Rosenzweig, J. E., eds. 1973. Contingency Views of Organization and Management. Chicago: Science Research Associates.

Kohn, M. L., and Schooler, C. 1978. "The Reciprocal Effects of the Substantive Complexity of Work and Intellectual Flexibility: A Longitudinal Assessment." American Journal of Sociology 84 (July): 24-52.

Lawrence, P. R., and Lorsch, J. W. 1967. Organization and Environment: Managing Differentiation and Integration. Boston:

Division of Research, Graduate School of Business Administration, Harvard University.

Litwak, E. 1961. "Models of Bureaucracy which Permit Conflict." American Journal of Sociology 67 (September): 177-84.

Mealiea, L. W., and Lee, D. 1979. "An Alternative to Macro-Micro Contingency Theories: An Integrative Model." Academy of Management Review 4 (July): 333-45.

Messinger, S. L. 1955. "Organizational Transformation: A Case Study of a Declining Social Movement." American Sociological Review 20 (February): 3-10.

Meyer, M. W. 1979. "Debureaucratization?" Social Science Quarterly 60 (June): 25-34.

Mintzberg, H. 1979. The Structuring of Organizations. Englewood Cliffs, N.J.: Prentice-Hall.

Mortimer, J. T., and Lorence, J. 1979. "Work Experience and Occupational Value Socialization: A Longitudinal Study." American Journal of Sociology 84 (May): 1361-85.

Pennings, J. M. 1975. "The Relevance of the Structural-Contingency Model for Organizational Effectiveness." Administrative Science Quarterly 20 (September): 393-410.

Perrow, C. 1979. Complex Organizations: A Critical Essay. 2d ed. Glenview, Ill.: Scott Foresman.

Pfeffer, J. 1972. "Merger as a Response to Organizational Interdependence." Administrative Science Quarterly 17 (September): 382-94.

──────. 1978a. Organizational Design. Arlington Heights, Ill.: AHM Publishing.

──────. 1978b. "The Micropolitics of Organizations. In Environments and Organizations, edited by M. W. Meyer et al., pp. 29-50. San Francisco: Jossey-Bass.

Roe, B. B., and Wood, J. R. 1975. "'Adaptive Innovation' and Organizational Security." Pacific Sociological Review 18 (July): 310-26.

Rogers, D. L. 1971. "Contrasts between Behavioral and Affective Involvement in Voluntary Associations: An Exploratory Analysis." *Rural Sociology* 36 (September): 340-58.

Selznick, P. 1949. *TVA and the Grass Roots*. Berkeley: University of California Press.

———. 1957. *Leadership in Administration*. New York: Harper & Row.

Shariff, Z. 1979. "The Persistence of Bureaucracy." *Social Science Quarterly* 60 (June): 3-19.

Shepard, J. M., and Hougland, J. G., Jr. 1978. "Contingency Theory: 'Complex Man' or 'Complex Organization'?" *Academy of Management Review* 3: 413-27.

Starbuck, W. 1976. "Organizations and Their Environments." In *Handbook of Organizational and Industrial Psychology*, edited by M. Dunnette, pp. 1069-1123. Chicago: Rand McNally.

Stinchcombe, A. L. 1965. "Social Structure and Organizations." In *Handbook of Organizations*, edited by J. C. March, pp. 142-93. Chicago: Rand McNally.

Terreberry, S. 1968. "The Evolution of Organizational Environments." *Administrative Science Quarterly* 12 (March): 590-613.

Thompson, J. D. 1967. *Organizations in Action*. New York: McGraw-Hill.

Tosi, H.; Aldag, R.; and Storey, R. 1973. "On the Measurement of the Environment: An Assessment of the Lawrence and Lorsch Environment Subscale." *Administrative Science Quarterly* 18 (March): 27-36.

Weick, K. 1966. "Educational Organizations as Loosely Coupled Systems." *Administrative Science Quarterly* 21 (March): 1-19.

Wood, J. R. 1975. "Legitimate Control and 'Organizational Transcendence.'" *Social Forces* 54 (September): 199-211.

Zald, M. N. 1970a. *Organizational Change: The Political Economy of the YMCA.* Chicago: University of Chicago Press.

_____. 1970b. "Political Economy: A Framework for Comparative Analysis." In *Power in Organizations*, edited by M. N. Zald, pp. 221-61. Nashville, Tenn.: Vanderbilt University Press.

Zucker, L. G. 1977. "The Role of Institutionalization in Cultural Persistence." *American Sociological Review* 42 (October): 726-43.

8
COST-BENEFIT ANALYSIS: AN UNCERTAIN GUIDE TO PUBLIC POLICY
Baruch Fischhoff

The costs and benefits of large-scale interventions into people's lives (for example, social reforms and new technologies) are almost inevitably clouded with uncertainty. Such projects typically seem to bring some benefit and to entail some risk, but the extent of each and the acceptability of the tradeoff is difficult to determine. A variety of approaches have been proposed for resolving these uncertainties. The most prominent of these approaches are variants of cost-benefit analysis; they ask, in effect, whether or not the expected benefits outweigh the expected costs.

The expected cost of a project is determined by enumerating all aversive consequences that might arise from its implementation (for example, increased occupational hazard), assessing the probability that each will occur, and estimating the cost or loss to society should each occur. Next, the expected loss from each possible consequence is calculated by multiplying the amount of the loss by the probability that it will be incurred. The expected loss of the entire project is computed by summing the expected losses associated with the various possible consequences. An analogous procedure produces an estimate of the expected benefits. Figure 8.1 works out one hypothetical example. Prominent variants on this procedure are cost-effective analysis (which compares the relative benefits of alternative actions), risk-benefit analysis (in which the major costs are risks to life, limb, or property), and decision analysis (which avoids the need to reduce all consequences to monetary units by directly eliciting value judgments).*

---

*Excellent expositions of these procedures may be found in a number of sources, including Keeney and Raiffa (1976), Layard (1974), Stokey and Zeckhauser (1978), and Raiffa (1968).

FIGURE 8.1

Cost-Benefit Analysis

Consider a fictitious new product, Veg-E-Wax, designed to coat fresh fruits and vegetables. Its demonstrated advantages are reducing losses in storage and preserving nutritive value. Aside from the cost of application, its disadvantages are making food look less appetizing and possibly causing cancer to workers who apply it and to consumers who fail to wash fruit. A highly simplified cost-benefit analysis of the decision to apply Veg-E-Wax to a $10 million (market value) shipment of pears bound for storage might appear as follows:

	$ million
Advantages (benefits)	
Guaranteed reduction in storage loss from 30% to 20%	1.0
Improved nutritive value (translating into a 10% increase in market value in the 80% that is not lost in storage).	.8
Total benefits	1.8
Disadvantages (costs)	
Cost of application	.1
Cancer in .1% of 100 workers (@ $1 million per case)	.1
Cancer to users (1 million consumers, of whom 10% fail to wash fruit, of whom .0001/ contract cancer as a result, @ $1 million per case).	.1
Unappetizing appearance (20% loss in market value of pears not lost in storage).	1.6
Total costs	1.9

In this calculation, the costs slightly outweigh the benefits, and the packer should decide not to use Veg-E-Wax. The viability of this conclusion depends upon its capacity to withstand small changes in the figures. If there were only an 18% loss in market value due to the waxy look of the fruit (translating into a cost of $1.44 million), the balance would tip the other way. It might be impossible to predict this loss with the precision needed to take confident action.

Even larger effects may accompany changes in fundamental assumptions. A packer with no social conscience might decide not to worry about the $200,000 in cancer costs, reducing total costs to $1.7 million. Other interested parties, such as consumers interested in maximizing value and minimizing personal risk, might structure the problem entirely differently.

Source: B. Fischhoff, P. Slovic, and S. Lichtenstein, "Weighing the Risks," Environment 21 (1979): 17-20, 32-38.

Between them, they have garnered a considerable following among bureaucrats seeking systematic approaches to management. These, in turn, have generated a vigorous contract research industry, entrusted with the implementation of these analyses. Proponents of formal analysis as a guide to public policy can point to the intuitive appeal of balancing costs and benefits and to the great flexibility of such analyses; in principle, they can be revised to incorporate new options and new information. Furthermore, the whole procedure is open to public scrutiny. Each quantitative input or qualitative assumption is available for all to see and evaluate, as are the computational rules used to combine them.

Unfortunately, these procedures have a number of characteristic limits on their usefulness as management tools. These limits arise when the mathematical formalisms confront the fallible individuals who must conduct, accept, or implement them. Be they technical experts, lay interveners, or government regulators, these individuals all have, to some extent, limited capacity to process technical information, restricted resources to devote to the project at hand, irrational apprehensions about its consequences, intransigent prejudices about the facts of the matter, ulterior motives, and incoherent and unstable values on critical issues.

When uncertainty is inherent in the human condition, the best that formal analysis, or any other scheme for managing society, can hope to do is get the most out of what we do know and make us sensitive to what we do not. To do that, even an approach that is conceptually sound, as cost-benefit analysis appears to be at first blush, will be of little use unless it is designed with people in mind. People must accept its logic and its conclusions, provide its inputs, carry out its calculations, understand its limitations, and respond wisely when its dictates impinge upon their lives. Table 8.1 provides one summary of the features one would like in a policy-setting tool designed to work with people.

When one considers the people in the cost-benefit ointment, three distinct sets of limits arise. One set of limits is imposed by the unavailability of necessary inputs to the analysis. Without those inputs, the implementability of cost-benefit analysis must be seriously questioned. A second set of limits comes from the inability of the analysts to assess the validity of their work and incorporate that assessment into their guides to action. The absence of such appraisals creates problems for the logical soundness of such analyses and their ability to protect the public from unanticipated side effects. The third set of limits comes from the failure of these methods to address critical management issues. These include the acceptability of the political philosophy underlying the procedures and the feasibility of implementing their recommendations.

TABLE 8.1

Desiderata for a Policy-Making Tool

1. Conceptually sound
   (a) Comprehensive, coherent
   (b) Derived from axioms formalizing assumptions and justifying conclusions
   (c) Considers alternative actions (including inaction)
   (d) Acknowledges uncertainty
   (e) Flexible enough to incorporate new information
   (f) Leads to resolution (an answer)
   (g) Ethically acceptable in terms of broadly accepted principles

2. Implementable
   (a) Adequate inputs available
   (b) Cadres of competent technical people available
   (c) Can be translated to operational terms
   (d) Can be completed in reasonable period of time
   (e) Will degrade well when done imperfectly

3. Politically acceptable
   (a) Relatively invulnerable to criticism
   (b) Either responsive to powerful interest or deliberately designed to withstand their pressure
   (c) Allows meaningful participation without facilitating obstructionism
   (d) Respects social contract

4. Open to evaluation
   (a) Assumptions transparent
   (b) Avoids disciplinary blinders by eliciting varied critiques
   (c) Facilitates iteration
   (d) Failures detectable (correctable)

5. Respects institutional constraints
   (a) Relevant institutions have the legal mandate to implement the approach and its conclusions
   (b) Can our legal and legislative legacy accommodate its innovations?
   (c) No easily exploitable loopholes

6. Creates no side effects
   (a) Unwanted changes in social and political institutions
   (b) Neglect of some solutions or some problems
   (c) Reduction of social resilience (for example, freezing on current solutions, reduction of innovation or society's ability to experiment)

7. Promotes long-term effective management
   (a) Cumulative record created of deliberations and precedents
   (b) Educates participants
   (c) Subsequent decisions need not start from scratch
   (d) Treats classes of problems

AVAILABILITY OF INPUTS

Performing a full-dress analysis assumes, among other things, that (1) all possible events and all significant consequences can be enumerated in advance; (2) meaningful probability, cost, and benefit values can be produced and assigned to them; and (3) the often disparate costs and benefits can somehow be compared to one another.

Unfortunately, some of these tasks cannot be completed at all, while for others, the results are hardly to be trusted. Despite the enormous scientific progress of the last decade or two, we still do not know all of the possible physical, biological, psychological, and social consequences of any large-scale project. Where we know what the consequences are, we often do not, or cannot, know their likelihoods. For example, although we know that a nuclear reactor core melt-down is unlikely, we will not know quite how unlikely until we accumulate much more on-line experience. Even then, we will be able to utilize that knowledge only if we can assume that the system and its surrounding conditions remain the same (for example, there will be no changes in the incidence of terrorism or the availability of trained personnel). For many situations, even when a danger is known to be present, its extent cannot be known. Whenever low-level radiation or exposure to toxic substances is involved, consequences can be assessed only by somewhat tenuous extrapolation from the consequences of high-level exposure to humans or low-level exposure to animals (Harriss, Hohenemser, and Kates 1978).

In all these cases, we must rely upon unaided human judgment to guide or supplant our formal methods. Research into the psychological processes involved in producing such judgments offers reasons for pessimism. A rather robust result is that people have a great deal of difficulty both in comprehending information under conditions of complexity and uncertainty and in making valid inferences from such information. The fallibility of such judgment stems in part from the counterintuitive nature of many probabilistic processes, in part from the lack of hands-on experience with low-probability and high-consequence events, and in part from the mental overload created by many problems (Slovic, Fischhoff, and Lichtenstein 1977).

The failings of our intuitions are shown in persistent tendencies to neglect various kinds of normatively important information, such as population base rates (indicating how common a particular event is), sample size (indicating how reliable evidence is), and predictive validity. Other kinds of information are attended to, but given inappropriate interpretations. People tend to be more confident making predictions on the basis of redundant information than with independent information (although the latter has greater predictive validity), they readily find interpretable patterns in random sequences, and they assume that more information guarantees better performance even when it only generates confusion. When asked to synthesize information from their experience, people tend to misjudge the risks to which they are exposed, they remember themselves to have been more foresightful—and others to have been less foresightful—in past judgments than was actually the case, and they sometimes persevere in erroneous beliefs despite mounting, even overwhelming, contrary evidence (Fischhoff 1975; Ross 1977; Tversky and Kahneman 1974).

To the best of our understanding, these judgmental biases do not reflect folly, but the occasional (or frequent) inadequacies of people's best attempts to muddle through difficult problems. Often, these attempts reflect the use of judgmental heuristics or rules of thumb that embody moderately valid appraisals of regularities in the world around us. In situations allowing a trial-and-error successive-correction approach to decision problems, these heuristics often work pretty well. However, where we (as planners or consumers) must get our decisions right the first time or suffer severe consequences, the limits of these heuristics may spell real problems.

These problematic tendencies are typically observed in situations where people's sole motivation would seem to be making the best, most "objective," judgment possible. Such situations are designed to avoid the additional problems engendered by the coloring of judgments by wishful thinking, self-serving motives, selective attention, cognitive dissonance, and the like. Although the evidence is sketchy, there is at the moment no good empirical reason to believe that these problems are appreciably reduced when the judgment in question carries high (personal or societal) stakes or when the judge is a substantive expert forced to go beyond the available data and rely on intuition (Fischhoff 1977; Slovic, Fischhoff, and Lichtenstein 1977).

Such results provide strong evidence for using formal methods for producing and combining information whenever possible—and for treating the results of such analyses with considerable caution because of their inevitable judgmental component.

Once the consequences have been enumerated and their likelihood assessed, a price tag (in dollars or utiles) must be placed on them. When it comes to tradeoffs between deaths today and in the future, between sterility and black lung disease, or between profits and lives, both the exigencies of our political processes and the indeterminate nature of cost-benefit logic force us to ask people for their opinions.

Such questions of value would seem to be the last redoubt of intuitive judgment. Unfortunately, however, subtle changes in how questions are posed can have a major impact on the opinions elicited.

Worse yet, in situations where alternative questioning procedures elicit different preferences, the normative theory often offers no guide as to which of the different judgments is to be preferred. When people's judgments show this sort of lability, the method may become the message, leading to decisions not in the decision makers' best interest, to action when caution is desirable (or the opposite), or to the obfuscation of poorly articulated views (Fischhoff, Slovic, and Lichtenstein in press).

Many of these effects have been known since the antiquity of experimental psychology in the mid-1800s. Early psychologists concerned with the relationship between sensations and judgments about them found that both the threshold for discerning a sensation and the threshold for discriminating between two sensations depended on a variety of subtle aspects of how stimuli were presented and how responses were elicited. Different judgments were attached to the same stimuli as a function of whether those stimuli were presented in ascending (increasing on a physical continuum) or descending order, whether the set of stimuli was homogeneous or diverse, whether particular regions on the continuum were densely or sparsely represented, whether sequentially presented stimuli were relatively similar or disparate, whether values near the threshold of detection were included or not, and whether the respondent made one or many judgments. Even when the same presentation was used, different judgments might be obtained with a numerical or comparative (ordinal) response mode, with implicit instructions motivating speed versus accuracy, with a bounded or unbounded response set, with small or large numbers (subsequently normalized), or with verbal or numerical labels. The instability of judgment is heightened by the fact that perception is inherently accompanied by some random error and by idiosyncratic tendencies, such as fatigue, locking in on stereotypic ways of viewing a problem, second-guessing the elicitor (What am I supposed to say?), and linking variables that should be independent (halo effects).

All of these problems emerge when people are questioned about their values or preferences. The elicitor must decide how many questions to ask and how to word them, how many alternatives to consider and in what order to present them, and what response format to use and how much time to allot for it. The preferences expressed will reflect in part the respondent's true beliefs and in part the method used to uncover them. Indeed, no decision is so clear-cut in its options, events, and attributions, no respondent is so mechanical, that these problems can be avoided entirely.

Lability may be particularly troublesome when people are asked about value issues raised by many proposed technologies (for example, the breeder). For such new and complex issues, with subtle interactions and gargantuan effects, people may have no articulated preferences. In some fundamental sense, their values are incoherent, not thought through. The desires they express at any given time are those tapped by the particular question posed. That question may evoke a central concern or a peripheral one; it may help clarify the respondent's opinion or irreversibly shape it; it may even create an opinion where none existed before.

Listing a few specific effects may indicate the power an elicitor may deliberately, or inadvertently, wield in shaping expressed preferences. The desirability of possible outcomes is often evaluated in relation to some reference point. That point could be one's current (asset) position, or an expected level of wealth (what someone with my talents should be worth at time t), or that possessed by another person. Shifts in reference point are fairly easily effected, and can lead to appreciable shifts in judged desirability, even to reversals in the order of preference. Consider, for example, how one might think about the same safety program conceptualized in terms of lives saved or lives lost, with the respective reference points of the current situation or an ideal one. As one gets closer to an event with mixed consequences, the aversiveness of its negative aspects may increase more rapidly than the attractiveness of its positive aspects, making it appear, on the whole, less desirable than it did from a distance. People may have opposite orders of preference for gambles when asked which they prefer (which focuses their attention on how likely they are to win) and when asked how much they would pay to play each (which highlights the amount to win). People may prefer to take a chance at losing a large sum of money rather than absorb a smaller sure loss, but change their mind when the sure loss is called an insurance premium. A relatively unimportant attribute may become the decisive factor in choosing between a set of options if they are presented in such a way that the attribute affords the easiest comparison between them (Fischhoff, Slovic, and Lichtenstein in press; Kahneman and Tversky 1979).

Three important features of these shifting judgments are (1) people are typically unaware of the potency of such shifts in their perspective, (2) they often have no guidelines as to which perspective is the appropriate one, and (3) even when there are guidelines, people may not want to give up their own inconsistency, creating an impasse.

LIMITS TO SETTING LIMITS

The bottom line of a cost-benefit analysis is the analyst's best guess at the relative preponderance of costs or benefits. Before action can be taken, one must know how good that best guess is. Depending upon the breadth of the confidence intervals on the "best-guess" cost-benefit ratio, one might want to collect more data, install backup systems to reduce some of the uncertainties, or abandon the project for one whose consequences are better known.

The analysts' standard practice for acknowledging and accommodating uncertainty in their inputs is through the judicious use of sensitivity analyses. The final calculations are repeated, each time using an alternate value of one troublesome probability or utility. If each reanalysis produces similar results, then the case is made that these particular errors do not matter. One way of viewing the research on judgmental biases described in the previous section is that it merely points to additional sources of error, calling for sensitivity analysis.

Unfortunately, however, there are no firm guidelines as to which inputs might be in error or what is the appropriate range of possible values to be tested. The possibility of judgmental biases would, for example, be considered only if the analyst were aware of the relevant research and took it seriously. A further problem with sensitivity analysis is that it typically tells us little about how the uncertainty from different sources of error is compounded or about what happens when different inputs are subject to a common bias. The untested assumption is that errors in different inputs will cancel one another out, rather than compound in some pernicious way (Fischhoff in press).

The reasonableness of such an independence assumption seems weak when a set of judgments is elicited with the same procedure, inducing the same perspective. For example, asking about preferences in a mode that incorporates a reference to dollar values might persistently deflate the expressed importance of environmental or other less tangible values. To take an example from the elicitation of judgments of fact, the U.S. Reactor Safety Study called upon its experts to assess unknown failure rates by the "extreme fractiles" method, choosing one number so extreme that there was only a 5 percent chance of the true failure rate being higher and a second number so low that there was only a 5 percent chance of the true rate being lower. Research conducted with a variety of other tasks and subjects has shown that this technique routinely produces too narrow confidence intervals, so that the precision of these estimates is systematically exaggerated (Lichtenstein, Fischhoff, and Phillips 1977).

Even if sensitivity analysis could handle the compounding of uncertainty, in some contexts, it completely misses the point. Many of the effects discussed under the rubric of the lability of values reflect the introduction of new, possibly foreign, possibly distorted perspectives into a decision-making process. Invocation of sensitivity analysis will not excuse the imposition of an elicitor's perspective on the respondent. Nor will it handle shifts in perspective that lead to reversals of preference.

In the end, determining the quality of an analysis is a matter of judgment. Someone must intuit which inputs are dubious and which alternate values should be incorporated in sensitivity analyses. Essentially, that someone must decide how good his or her own best judgment is. Unfortunately, an extensive body of research suggests that people are overconfident in the quality of their own judgment. Indeed, people have been found to be so overconfident in their degree of general knowledge that they will accept highly disadvantageous bets based on their confidence judgments. Furthermore, this bias seems to be impervious to instructions, familiarity with the task, question format, and various forms of exhortation toward modesty (Lichtenstein, Fischhoff, and Phillips 1977; Fischhoff, Slovic, and Lichtenstein 1977).*

A particularly relevant version of this overconfidence emerges when people are asked to judge the completeness of the representation of a problem. Research here has shown a persistent tendency to underestimate what is left out and overestimate what is known. As before, while most of this psychological evidence is derived from work with laypeople, there is some systematic and considerable anecdotal evidence of similar processes at work with experts. Among the generic kinds of issues whose omission might not be adequately noted by technical experts are: (1) the imaginative ways in which human error can mess up a system (for example, Three Mile Island); (2) the range and rate of possible changes in people's values and behavior (for example, regarding energy consumption); (3) the number of unknown or undetected physical, biological, or psychological effects of a new system; and (4) the interrelation between system components (for example, common mode failures or the possibility of a system failing because a backup component has been removed for routine maintenance) (Fischhoff, Slovic, and Lichtenstein 1978).

No analysis, performed in real time and with finite resources, claims to be complete or error free. Indeed, all responsible analysts include sensitivity analyses with their reports. The preceding discussion suggests, however, that it is hard to assess the adequacy of

---

*One recent piece of convergent anecdotal evidence is the conclusion of the review committee chaired by H. W. Lewis that the Reactor Safety Study had greatly overstated the precision with which it had been able to assess the probability of a core melt-down (U.S. Nuclear Regulatory Commission 1978).

these analyses. We have an urgent need for a better understanding of what errors may enter into an analysis, how virulent they are, how they are propagated and compounded through the analysis, what can be done to reduce their impact, how we can assess their total impact, and what that assessment means in terms of action. In a sense, what we need is an error theory for cost-benefit analysis, supplemented by some empirical study of the fallibility of analyses conducted in the past.

The qualifications accompanying many (or most) analyses include reference to what could have been done with greater time and resources. These two commodities are, however, always going to be limited, and we must know how well cost-benefit analysis serves us under realistic constraints. One conclusion of such an assessment might be that cost-benefit analysis is useless unless X percent of the total budget can be invested in it; another might be that virtually all the value of a cost-benefit analysis comes from structuring the problem and conducting a few back-of-the-envelope calculations within that structure. A third possible conclusion is that in most situations, the judgmental components of cost-benefit analysis are so essential and so deeply buried that conducting a formal analysis merely creates an aura of solvability around problems that are quite dimly understood.

LIMITS OF SCOPE

Like all other policy-making procedures, cost-benefit analysis deals with only a portion of an entire problem. The crucial question here is whether that segment can stand alone and is able to contribute to the rest of the process or whether the internal logic of the model disintegrates when confronted with broader realities.

The segment addressed by cost-benefit analysis is that most amenable to formal analysis and least accessible to individuals without technical expertise. This is most certainly true in variants that rely heavily on tools like shadow pricing or revealed preferences to deduce what people want without asking them. Some variants, like decision analysis, try to overcome this bias by incorporating elicitation procedures that can, in principle, be used with corporate executives, government regulators, or people off the street. Despite such efforts, however, the very sophistication and centralization of the analysis gives added weight to the opinions of those who are articulate and close to the analyst.

When analytic resources are limited, the analyst must take cues from someone about how to restrict the alternatives and consequences considered. That someone is likely to be the one who commissioned the study. If commissioners all come from one sector of society and consistently prefer (or reject out of hand) particular kinds of solutions or consequences, a persistent bias may be produced. Such bias would determine what issues are never analyzed and how results are presented. If the commissioners are public officials, there may be a strong predisposition toward reports that bury uncertainties and delicate assumptions in sophisticated technical machinations or in masses of undigested data.

If one examines the public criticisms to which cost-benefit analyses are subjected, a number of themes emerge. One is that there is usually a population of experts who are angered because the sensitivity analysis did not include what they believe to be appropriate alternative values for some inputs. When these experts view themselves as having qualifications rivaling those of those experts who conducted the study, the obvious implication is that even the elite community involved is somewhat restricted, perhaps for reasons of political or academic power.

A second group of critics views the segmentation of participants as a more serious issue than the substantive topic at hand. Their main concern is that the use of analysis transfers power for societal decision-making to a technical elite, in effect disenfranchising the lay citizenry.

One might argue that given the vagaries of lay judgment described above, such a transfer of power is in the best interests of even that lay public. Let someone competent do the job; we'll all be better off. The counterargument has several facets. One is that every analysis requires a variety of judgments that might just as well be performed by laypeople. Regarding questions of fact, when they are forced to go beyond their tools and data and rely on intuition, experts may be little better than nonexperts. Regarding questions of value, being close to the action should not confer superiority on experts' beliefs. The second part of the argument is that there are higher goals than maximizing the efficiency of a particular project. These include developing an informed citizenry and preserving democratic institutions. The process may be more important than the product, making it important to devote the resources needed to make meaningful public participation possible.

Such participation requires new tools for communicating with the public, both for presenting technical issues to laypeople and for eliciting values from them. It may also require new social and legal forms, such as hiring representative citizens to participate in the analytic process, thereby acquiring the expertise needed to confer the informed consent of the governed on whatever decision is eventually reached. Such a format might be considered a science court with a lay jury. It would consider cost-benefit analysis as one input to its proceedings. It would also place the logic of jurisprudence above the logic of economic analysis, acknowledging that there is no formal way to summarize the issues at hand.

A third group of critics objects to the segmentation of the particular problem from the broader context of social issues. The critics often fight dirty or irrationally (from the perspective of the formal analyst) because they view the cost-benefit analysis as one arena in which political struggles are waged. Those struggles have a different logic than that of economic analysis. In them, it may be fair to engage in unconstructive criticism, viciously poking holes in analyses if the results do not support one's position. It may even be legitimate to ridicule or chastise analysts for ignoring issues (like income distribution) that were outside their analytic mandate.

Some representatives of this position would argue that the very reasonableness of formal analysis involves a political-ideological assumption, namely, that society is sufficiently cohesive and common-goaled that its problems can be resolved by reason and without struggle. Although such a "get on with business" orientation will be pleasing to many, it will not satisfy all. For those who do not believe that society is in a fine-tuning stage, a technique that fails to mobilize public consciousness and involvement has little to recommend it.

Thus, there are logics other than that of cost-benefit analysis, coming from legal, political, and even revolutionary theory. Like the various ways of implementing the basic cost-benefit framework, each embodies both ideological predispositions and notions of how society operates. Considering these perspectives and the impact that problem formulation can have on people's judgments of their own values and the tendency for such analysis to create an aura of solvability, cost-benefit analysis no longer appears as a value-neutral procedure. This does not mean that it is not or cannot be made into the one technique most compatible with or capable of incorporating the broadest range of values in a particular society. It does mean that a political position of sorts is being taken when one adopts the procedure.

Like most choices involving ideologies, questions of taste are somewhat disciplined by questions of reality. Those who oppose cost-benefit analysis are responding in part at least to social concerns and facts to which the analysis is relatively or totally deaf. Attention to these concerns can strengthen an analysis and heighten its impact. For example, an analysis that ignores questions of equity will often be overturned by those who come out in the short end of the project in question. Rather than let their work become a number game with no real effect, some analysts have attempted to exploit the kernel of truth in their critics' arguments and incorporate equity considerations. A more political perspective might also help one realize that formal analyses deal with ideal types often having no representation in reality. It is fairly easy to become enamored of abstractions and analyze projects that are never implemented in the way or at the time they are proposed (Majone 1975). Although the method may be tricky, one could respond to this challenge by considering ensembles of possible representations of the proposed project (that is, ways in which it might be carried out) or by requiring periodic updates of an analysis as the facts change. A broader perspective could motivate analysts to specify the assumptions about society upon which their analyses are predicated and heighten their sensitivity to the tenuousness of those assumptions. In the extreme, it might even lead them to reject analytical mandates that separate projects from their social context in ways that are not meaningful.

CONCLUSION

How well does cost-benefit analysis fare according to the various criteria listed in Table 8.1? What work is needed to make it fare better? Even though the preceding discussion has focused on some of these topics at the expense of others, a few words about each will give a flavor of what a fuller consideration might reveal.

Conceptually Sound

The cost-benefit family of analytic procedures has a logical foundation that is both carefully thought out and widely accepted in both political and academic circles. As a result, both its failings and its assets are better documented than those of its competitors. Although there are still important technical and conceptual problems to work out within the cost-benefit framework (Pearce 1979), a useful investment of energy might be trying to clarify the relationship between that framework and the logic (or ostensible logic) of other approaches. Are they really incompatible? Can cost-benefit analysis be elaborated to incorporate the elements of truth embodied by the alternatives? Perhaps the weakest competition is provided by the "logic" uncovered in studies of people's intuitive decision-making. Yet, even here, it is worth asking whether there is not a method in people's apparent madness. Are there not decision-making criteria overlooked by formal analysis, yet essential for human welfare or psychological well-being (Slovic, Fischhoff, and Lichtenstein 1979)?

Implementability

Like other computational enterprises, cost-benefit analysis rises or falls on the strength of its inputs. While enormous strides have been made to develop a cumulative data base on various topics, all too often, the analyst is forced to rely on intuitive judgments. Judgments of fact tend to be subject to persistent biases that are only now beginning to be understood. Further work is needed here, particularly in studying the judgments of experts. Judgments of value tend to be highly labile and subject to complex and subtle manipulation by the questioning procedure used. Research is needed to produce techniques and settings that enable respondents to elucidate their own opinions.

Politically Acceptable

In contrast to the political objections to cost-benefit analysis raised earlier, one may cite a number of fundamental assets. The most important of these is the explicit expression of its structure and inputs, all of which are in principle open to question and revision. To realize this potential advantage, several developments are needed. One is procedures for communicating technical issues to laypeople (including regulators and legislators without a technical background) so that they can offer reasoned critiques. A second need is to develop some way for critics to perform their own sensitivity analyses, incorporating their own alternative values for various inputs. Such an opportunity might produce some surprising results, showing the conclusions of analyses to be much more (or less) robust than they initially appeared. It could also help allay fears that these conclusions represent the result of ingenious number-fudging by the analysts. In the back of many cynical critics' minds must lurk the thought that the experts have played around until they found a constellation most favorable to a particular point of view.

Respects Institutional Constraints

The initial popularity of cost-benefit analysis probably was due to its fitting well into the way in which business was done in various seats of government. Its continued success may be due to the ability of proponents to shape legal and government proceedings to accommodate this tool further. Its future prospects may depend on the successful resolution of several persistent problems. One is that it assumes a single decision maker; difficulties arise when there are many hands involved and many views to be incorporated. A second problem is that it is a one-time analysis; as a result, it is not as responsive to changing contingencies, preferences, and scientific data as are the bureaucracies it is designed to serve. A third problem is that it requires a level of analytical expertise not possessed by many of the individuals involved in its use, producing aberrations and frustrations.

Open to Evaluation

As mentioned, cost-benefit analysis claims to be, if nothing else, open to inspection. To realize the promise of this claim, several developments are needed. Psychological research must find ways to help people appraise the limits of their own knowledge or, failing that, ways to assess how confident they should be given how confident they say they are. Theoretical efforts are needed so that analyses produce better assessments of their own limits and derive the action implications of that cumulative uncertainty. Since such efforts have their own inherent limits, empirical work is needed to review past analyses to explore their foibles and contribution (or lack of it) to the management process.

Creates No Side Effect

Disenfranchising the lay public is one possible side effect of the wide-scale adoption of cost-benefit analysis, about which some segments of the public are quite agitated. Denigrating the importance of consequences that cannot readily be expressed in dollar or other quantitative terms (for example, extinction and aesthetic degradation) is another. Making a fetish out of currently enjoyed benefits is a third (Mishan 1972). In general, though, the implications of having a cost-benefit society are poorly understood.

Promotes Long-Term Effective Management

Cost-benefit analysis, particularly its sensitivity analysis component, has been instrumental in setting the research agendas of those concerned with understanding the effects of technological projects. To the extent that the priorities of such analyses are correct, this is a major contribution to creating a base of data relevant to sound management. It has also provided a framework within which talented economists could apply themselves to these problems.

Finally, although it is criticized for emphasizing product over process, the cost-benefit analysis framework has probably raised the level of debate in many settings and broadened the understanding of even its harshest critics.

There is no verdict on cost-benefit analysis per se. One must consider it in the light of alternative approaches (Fischhoff, Slovic, and Lichtenstein 1979) and in the context of particular situations that might accentuate its strengths or weaknesses. One must consider not only cost-benefit as it is today, but as it can be improved. One must consider not only the nice idea and the sparkling theory, but the integrity with which it will be applied.

Given the limits to human judgment and consensus described here, it is unlikely that cost-benefit analysis in a pure form will ever be practiced or followed anywhere. The critical question then becomes, Does it degrade gracefully?

REFERENCES

Fischhoff, B. 1975. "Hindsight ≠ Foresight: The Effect of Outcome Knowledge on Judgment under Uncertainty." Journal of Experimental Psychology: Human Perception and Performance 1 (August): 288-99.

_____. 1977. "Cost Benefit Analysis and the Art of Motorcycle Maintenance." Policy Sciences 8 (June): 177-202.

_____. In press. "Clinical Decision Analysis." Operations Research.

Fischhoff, B.; Slovic, P.; and Lichtenstein, S. 1977. "Knowing with Certainty: The Appropriateness of Extreme Confidence." Journal of Experimental Psychology: Human Perception and Performance 3: 552-64.

_____. "Fault Trees: Sensitivity of Estimated Failure Probabilities to Problem Representation." Journal of Experimental Psychology: Human Perception and Performance 4 (May): 342-55.

_____. 1979. "Weighing the Risks." Environment 21: 17-20, 32-38.

_____. In press. "Knowing What You Want: Measuring Labile Values." In Cognitive Processes in Choice and Decision Behavior, edited by T. Wallsten. Hillsdale, N.J.: Lawrence Erlbaum.

Harriss, R.; Hohenemser, C.; and Kates, R. 1978. "The Burden of Technological Hazards." Environment 8 (September): 6-15, 38-41.

Kahneman, D., and Tversky, A. 1976. "Prospect Theory." Econometrica 47 (March): 263-92.

Keeney, R. L., and Raiffa, H. 1976. Decisions with Multiple Objectives. New York: Wiley.

Layard, R., ed. 1974. Cost Benefit Analysis. Harmondsworth: Penguin.

Lichtenstein, S.; Fischhoff, B.; and Phillips, L. D. 1977. "Calibration of Probabilities: The State of the Art." In Decision Making and Change in Human Affairs, edited by H. Jungerman and G. de Zeeuw. Amsterdam: D. Reidel.

Majone, G. 1975. "The Feasibility of Social Policies." Policy Sciences 6 (March): 49-69.

Mishan, E. J. 1972. "What Is Wrong with Roskill?" In Cost-Benefit Analysis, edited by R. Layard, pp. 452-72. New York: Penguin.

Pearce, D. W. In press. "Social Cost Benefit Analysis and Nuclear Futures." In Energy Risk Management, edited by G. Goodman and W. Rowe. London: Academic Press.

Raiffa, H. 1968. Decision Analysis. Reading, Mass.: Addison Wesley.

Ross, L. "The Intuitive Psychologist and His Shortcomings." In Advances in Social Psychology, edited by L. Berkowitz, pp. 173-220. New York: Academic Press.

Slovic, P.; Fischhoff, B.; and Lichtenstein, S. 1977. "Behavioral Decision Theory." Annual Review of Psychology 28: 1-39.

_____. 1979. "Rating the Risks." Environment 21 (April): 14-20, 36-39.

Stokey, E., and Zeckhauser, R. 1978. A Primer for Policy Analysis. New York: Norton.

Tversky, A., and Kahneman, D. 1974. "Judgment under Uncertainty: Heuristics and Biases." *Science* 185 (September): 1124-31.

U.S. Nuclear Regulatory Commission. 1978. *Risk Assessment Review Group Report to the U.S. Nuclear Regulatory Commission.* NUREG/CR-0400.

9
UNCERTAINTY
Emmanuel Demby

The distance between the researcher and the decision maker is often the distance between certainty and uncertainty in research. This distance is compounded by such nice-sounding sentences as, "Let's take an interdisciplinary approach." To what?

That is the first aspect of uncertainty—unpredictability—to which we have to pay attention. The predictability of data—their certainty—is knowing what they are to predict. The same data may predict any number of phenomena. Thus, the operational closeness of the researcher and the decision maker is essential. The basic question which the decision maker is asking the researcher (though s/he may ask him/her many questions), is whether or not success is predicted if s/he takes certain actions.

But the researcher, besides delivering certainty, is also delivering answers to specific questions, and we should ask ourselves how a multidisciplinary approach may be achieved.

The only chances of developing an interdisciplinary approach are in the following: (1) handling qualitative research; (2) the wording of questions; (3) the technique of quantitative analysis; and (4) the communication of the report. Neither a unidisciplinary or multidisciplinary approach makes the researcher feel more or less secure about his/her findings, more or less certain that s/he has come upon the "truth," certainty of the data's predictive powers. Data, without knowing what the decision maker will do with information, has little predictive power because one never has the whole story. For some decision makers, just knowing what people did before, may be enough to predict that what people did once, they will do again. Other decision makers, knowing about the psychographics of respondents, might take the same "did before" data as a cue that those involved are ready for a change. The predictive model has to take into consideration the point of view already in the decision maker's mind prior to the research. This has to be accomplished in a meeting between the researcher and the decision maker. It will not be learned from accumulation of data.

The problem of the researcher and the question of an interdisciplinary approach ought to be put this way: The decision maker, who may be a bureaucrat, a marketing manager, a political candidate's manager, a public relations or an advertising person, prior to the start of any research should sit with the researcher and explain what would be done "if only the following were known." It is at this point that the main researcher—the project leader—could decide what kind of "profit" might be possible if an interdisciplinary approach would be used on how the research might contribute to the certainty of the decision maker. Perhaps this is very unacademic of me. It is about 20 years since my research has been confined only to academic circles. I see two requirements of the research to answer the questions posed in this symposium: (1) What will contribute to the decision maker's feeling of "certainty" about the data; and (2) How can the multidisciplinary approach increase the decision maker's level of certainty?

What is required is a definition of <u>certainty</u>—who and what is meant by the researcher when discussing certainty and what is meant by a <u>multidisciplinary</u> approach and how it is achieved.

Let us start with the word <u>certainty</u>. If we ask the respondent to tell us about the behavior s/he has just practiced—for example, the purchase of a magazine—the chances are good, as researchers, that we shall achieve a high level of certainty. Past behavior is a good predictor of future behavior. Thus, such information has great predictability value. However, if the respondent conforms to the demographic and socioeconomic profiles of readers of the magazine, the inference that the respondent is a reader of that magazine—because of the matching of the demographic and socioeconomic profiles—and the psychographic profiles (psychographic being defined as the attitude, self-concept, and the benefits sought by the respondent) from reading the magazine—are similar, then we are dealing with the kind of inferential approach that social scientists believe will be correct most of the time. Respondents who conform to the profile of magazine readers are assumed—without asking if they are readers—to be that magazine's readers.

In evolving a multidisciplinary approach for the example cited, the use of psychology (in determining behavior) and a combination of psychology (self-description and nonsocietal benefit) and sociology (how the person feels or is looked upon because of reading the magazine) and, to go further, adding a touch of anthropology (the meaning of the magazine's readership as a factor in modern society), finally makes the probing complete.

In truth, the multidisciplinary approach does not reside in numbers of people but in that single person directing the research effort. The splitting of the effort into different segments to satisfy the appealing and self-justifying label of interdisciplinary can produce competitiveness and destruction of a project; whereas, the natural division of a project into tasks better handled by one person, rather than the other—a division based on ability rather than possession of a social science discipline—is probably the more correct way of going about things.

In 30 years of commercial work, I have developed a "certainty-uncertainty" yardstick. This yardstick is expressed in a number of ways. First, there are various forms of regressions. By splitting our sample in half, we can see how well each half is willing to (or does) take certain actions related to certain profiles or attitudes. Another way of expressing this yardstick is by using "common sense." Common sense is sometimes hard to use because one cannot assign such logic to any one discipline. It is simply being aware that one and one are two, that salespeople work not just for money but, also, for recognition. Perhaps I should not call common sense a second way of testing data for predictability (certainty). I have found that good predictability in a regression usually makes common sense.

It is possible in academic research to use the "yardstick" approach if one realizes this very simple and obvious relationship. The yardstick I would recommend for both unidiscipline and multidiscipline approaches would utilize this combination—high-powered statistics and common sense. The predictability of data from surveys can easily be tested with almost any grandmother (preferably with a foreign accent). You should be able to explain what you are predicting—and why and how—to her. If she disagrees or cannot understand you, review your data and predictions. The more the decision maker tells us of his/her plans (if research supports him/her) and his/her desire to change his/her plans (if research so indicates), the closer we come to certainty—because the research not only gathers data (with selective reporting possible by the decision maker) but it also tests the decision maker's hypothesis. As a matter of fact, the discussion between the researcher and the decision maker may not only modify the latter's plans, but it may also affect the multidisciplinary aspects of the planned research.

The following steps may indicate how we have been affected. First, the discussion with the decision maker should include each of the social sciences. Each representative may refer to past findings in that particular discipline which may affect how the research may be designed. Second, if qualitative research is to precede a quantitative study, and it should—both the psychologist and the sociologist should collaborate in writing the protocol; actual qualitative probing should be under the direction of the psychologist. Analysis, on the other hand, should involve both the psychologist and sociologist. There should be a number of qualitative reports—one should merely be a summary of what has been said; there should also be two analytical reports, one prepared by the sociologist and the other by the psychologist.

Third, the qualitative findings—both the summary reports and the analytical reports—should be presented to the decision maker by the psychologist and the sociologist. This is one step toward certainty. As a result of the joint conference between the three: (1) the decision maker should review his/her plans and present to the researchers plans that have been modified by the qualitative research; and (2) both the psychologist and sociologist should modify their plans for the quantitative research based both on the findings of the qualitative phase and the modifications of the decision maker's plans. Fourth, the quantitative questionnaire requires both the psychologist and the sociologist who took part in the discussions with the decision maker, and possibly an economist (or some other specialist whose area might be affected by the results of the research), so that the quantitative questionnaire reflects each of the areas that ought to be considered by the decision maker. Fifth, the analysis of the quantitative research should be multidisciplinary, with either (but not both) the psychologist or sociologist in charge. Finally, the one in charge of the research ought to present the quantitative findings to the decision maker, with emphasis (using an appropriate multivariate technique) on market targets and possible results of these segments on various possibilities of action.

The critical variable is not how many disciplines are involved in the research, as long as the researchers operate closely with the decision makers, the potential for certainty increases.

2
THEORETICAL ANALYSIS IN SPECIFIC SUBJECT AREAS

10
HEALTH, UNCERTAINTY, AND THE ACTION SITUATION
Talcott Parsons

Exposure to uncertainty is perhaps the most important negative aspect of what many have considered to be the central feature of human life and action as distinguished from lower forms of living systems. The more general feature has often been summed up in the concepts of human freedom and responsibility. In relatively simple terms, it concerns the capacity of human beings as individuals to exercise some kind and degree of freedom of choice. Humans are not fully constrained by the conditions of the situation in which they act; what in fact occurs, and may be described as their action or behavior, is not a simple resultant of the operation of situational conditions (compare Parsons 1949, chap. 2). A good analogy is the much used example of the set of billiard balls caused by a player to move about the table according to purely deterministic physical laws. I think few these days would accept this conceptual model as adequate for description and analysis of human action systems.

If there is freedom, there must also be uncertainty on two levels at least. To define these levels, however, it is probably best to go back to the deeper evolutionary roots of our problem, which reach far back in the evolutionary scale of organic life. A useful reference is the concept of teleonomy, introduced by the biologist Ernst Mayr (1970) to characterize what in common sense

---

This work was edited by Victor Lidz after Talcott Parsons' sudden death. A copy of the original draft will be placed in the Talcott Parsons Papers at the Harvard University Archives.

terms may be called the goal-directedness of organisms in relation to their environment. As Mayr uses this concept, it does not imply subjectively conscious choice among alternatives, but does imply that the organism behaves selectively within an environment. The environment is conceived to provide not a single possible mode of behavior, but a manifold of plural possibilities. The most obvious case is that of physical movement. In evolutionary terms, movement goes as far back as the unicellular organisms. Even a very simple organism may approach various objects in its situation (for example, potential food objects), may withdraw from an approach, or may move to one side or the other, thereby deviating from a straight line.

As we advance in the evolutionary course, the scope of "maneuverability" steadily widens. Since man is a descendant of other members of the mammalian order, we can perhaps briefly consider the mammalian situation. Most mammals not closely related to the human development have been quadrupeds. As such, they have had high capacity for spatial mobility. They have been able to move rapidly over the earth's surface, advancing and retreating, turning around, or deviating to the left or right of any initially determined course of motion.

It should be noted that only the phenotypical individual organism possesses these capacities of mobility. The genetic constitution, through a necessary condition of the development of such organisms, has by itself no such capacity.

Any highly developed version of maneuverability clearly requires some kind of central nervous system appraisal of the situation in which the organism behaves (Mayr 1970). This capacity is not simply given in an instinctive, inherited pattern but is importantly modifiable through learning. Edward Tolman (1932) may serve as prototypal student of these matters. He postulated that his favorite experimental animals, rats, came, through learning, to establish what he called "cognitive maps" of the situation in which they might pursue, for example, the famous quest for food. The cognitive map in Tolman's sense clearly implied that the animal might develop alternative orientations to the environment in which it behaves. The rat following a maze could, on arriving at a choice point, turn either to the right or the left and might be faced with a series of choice points before the end of its run. Whether the trial resulted in successful attainment of a food object or failure to eat might depend upon the rat's cognitive map of how to turn at each of the choice points.

Thus, the outcome of a course of behavior from the point of view of the behaving animal is contingent on the choices made at the choice points. In the classical learning experiments, the situation was structured by the experimenter in advance. In real life, even that of rats, it may not be so prestructured. There may be contingencies in the situation that the behaving animal cannot foresee. Once the rat has learned the laboratory maze, no such contingencies exist unless the experimenter alters the structure. The rat, therefore, can make all the correct turns without hesitation and arrive at the food reward with great certainty. In real life, however, a rat on its way to a food goal might encounter a cat and immediately become absorbed in evading the cat rather than pursuing the food reward.

The possibility that a cat might appear in the situation is prototypical of the contingency aspect of behavior situations. In any particular case, neither the rat nor the experimenter could positively predict that a cat would appear, unless the experimenter deliberately introduced the cat. However, the behavioral capacities of the rat include the possibility of coping with the situation presented by the appearance of a cat, even though this appearance is not predicted with any high degree of certainty by rat or observer.*

Little is known about the senses, if any, in which a rat has "conscious" assessments of the future development of its behavioral situation. When we reach the human level, however, we have a quite different order of evidence, namely, what the behaving subject can tell us about how he views the situation of action. At this level, individuals not only predict future developments in the situation in which they act—for example, preparing in summer for colder weather in winter—but they also make allowances for contingencies. Here, I would define a contingency as a possible alteration in the situation that cannot be positively predicted in a given period in advance, but which also cannot be ruled out on the basis of prior knowledge. Thus, to continue with the example of weather, in the northern temperate regions, it can be confidently predicted that heavy snowfalls will not occur at low altitudes in July. When specific long-range plans depend on weather, however, it cannot be accurately

---

*Ethologists have found a large instinctual or inborn component in the mapping behavior of rats. When placed in new environments, rats will roam around to map the setting until they have learned where, for each position they encounter, they can find the nearest cover to hide from predators. Thus, their ability to learn the mazes of laboratory psychologists seems to derive in considerable part from a specialized "instinctive" ability of important adaptive significance to the species. (See Etkin 1964, esp. pp. 185-86.)

predicted a considerable period in advance whether there will be sunshine or rain. Therefore, the planning of an outdoor program will normally take account of a contingency of rain by including alternative arrangements.

My general argument is that orientation to uncertainty, the contingency of unpredictable changes in the situation of action, is a built-in feature of the behavioral and action processes of living organisms, but one which grows in relative importance with the evolution of living systems. There seem to be no very sharp lines of division along the evolutionary scale, and the nature of behaving systems is such as to include various kinds of provision for coping with uncertainty and contingencies. However, in the process by which human individuals have become increasingly self-conscious and increasingly concerned to apply consciously formulated knowledge, the capacity to cope with uncertain contingency has very substantially increased (see Parsons 1978, Chapter 5, for a more comprehensive discussion of these matters).

The human level of evolution involves, besides the vast increase in awareness of uncertainties and in capacities to cope with them, another factor which, though hardly peculiar to the human species, is also greatly accentuated. Thus, the situation in which any given individual acts is more complex and extensive a <u>social</u> situation. The human actor not only faces situations in the physical environment—for example, the weather and the possible intervention of other species, as when a farmer has predators attacking his flocks or herds—but the situation is composed of the action of other human individuals in some state of interdependence with his own.

Coping with uncertainty or contingencies implies a capacity to decide among alternatives. If one actor's situation calls for such decision, however, the contingencies with which he may have to cope include unexpected decisions on the part of other actors in his situation. Since a social situation is composed of a plurality of interacting individuals, each is subject to a <u>double</u> contingency: first, the contingency dependent on the environment in general and, second, the ways of coping with the contingencies of the environment adopted by the several participants to the interaction (see Parsons 1951, Chapter 7, for systematic attention to the consequences of contingencies in social interaction). The social environment, therefore, imposes a set of conditions that are extremely important in defining both the kinds of contingencies with which actors have to cope and the mechanisms by which their capacities to cope are determined. Indeed, that there is an element of uncertainty and contingency on <u>both</u> sides of any behavior-to-situation relationship is one of the cardinal facts with which I am trying to deal. Even at levels of evolution far short of self-conscious choice or intention, there is no certainty in the nature either of the organism or its relation to its environment that enables us to predict exactly what kind of behavior it will engage in. Alternatives of selective directionality in behavior must be connected with the state of the organism, which must somehow provide for more than one possible outcome. I would regard the double contingency of self-conscious human social interaction as an extension of a more general state of affairs based on some ingredients that go very far back in the evolutionary scale.

I will now discuss the implications of the foregoing considerations for the understanding of certain mechanisms of human social organization and of health. Health will be treated primarily at the organic level, but with special reference to human individuals.

The existential facts about human freedom and human capacity to choose among courses of action open in the situation may be illustrated in many different fields. In passing, let me comment upon the case of linguistic action. Command of a language on the part of a competent speaker in Chomsky's sense is not a predetermined intention to say any particular thing (compare Chomsky 1972). It is a generalized capacity, through use of a medium of communication, to say many different things—indeed, an indefinite range of things. Moreover, it is a capacity to say them in an ordered, rule-governed way that enables their meaning to be communicated to an indefinite range of auditors (Chomsky 1972, 1979). It is not necessary here to analyze the conditions under which such processes are possible, but their existence and enormous importance seem to be as well-established as any of the "facts of life."

Linguistic communication, however, does not stand by itself in this respect. At ordinary levels of social interaction, there are several sets of "mechanisms" by which freedom on the part of individual actors can be exercised as a way of attaining certain types of goals and, also, the advantages that accrue from their attainment. A particularly familiar example is the use of money in economic market behavior. A society like ours is characterized by an immensely ramified network of markets. By and large, the markets have certain common features. One that bears on our present theme is that sellers of ordinary commodities and of many services do not know in advance who will make the particular purchases. They even do not know how much will be purchased in given time periods or, sometimes, at what prices (the theory of market exchanges and their symbolic mediation involved here was developed in Parsons and Smelser 1956 and Parsons 1961, pp. 60-70 and 1969, Chapters 13-17.) But with relatively few and minor exceptions, whoever approaches the sellers with an appropriate money offer can expect to consummate the purchase. On both sides of an ordinary market, therefore, there is great uncertainty with respect to specific transactions, for example, who will buy what, how much, and at what price. Yet, there may be a much greater approach to certainty with respect to aggregate and longer-term questions of what goods and services and, broadly, what quantities will be produced and offered for sale, on the one hand, and purchased by consumers, on the other hand.

Money, as a medium of exchange, is a mechanism that operates, usually to an approximation without complete precision, to "cancel out" the uncertainty factors working on both sides of the market relationship.* Thus, even though no one can predict (or even wants to predict, we might say) exactly who will buy what on what terms or on what occasion, the consumer is able, given adequate income, to purchase what he needs, and the producer is able to dispose, generally at reasonably satisfactory prices, of what he offers for sale on the market. Producers may continually change their plans about what and how much to produce, whether to introduce quality or style changes, whether to enter different markets, and so on. Consumers, however, are also generally advantaged by not being bound in advance to spend their money in very specific ways, that is, they retain options to decide what and how much they will purchase in the light of how their situations develop.

In these situations, anxiety about the functioning of markets tends to be transferred to a new level. It generally does not come to focus upon questions of what precisely is going to be available, on what terms, at what particular times, to what particular individual purchasers, or upon questions of what and how much will be produced and offered on particular markets by particular producing units. Concern is transferred cybernetically upward to problems of the functioning of the economy as a whole or large sectors of it (Parsons and Smelser 1956). In the current situation, we worry primarily about such matters as the national balance of trade, the rate of unemployment, the rate of inflation, and the like. These are certainly economic problems, but not at the level of the individual income-receiver being able to buy what he or she wants or of the individual producer being able to market his product.

To the common sense of most educated people, I would suppose, money appears to be a unique phenomenon in this connection.

---

*The notion of canceling out factors of uncertainty should be compared with the idea of complexity reduction discussed in "Generalized Media and the Problem of Contingency," by Niklas Luhmann, and in "Communication and Media," by Rainer C. Baum, in Explorations in General Theory in Social Science, ed. J. Loubser et al. (New York: Free Press, 1976).

Even its resemblance to language is seldom pointed out. However, I would not only emphasize its kinship with language, but also suggest that for sociological analysis, money is by no means an isolated phenomenon. It is a member of a larger family of symbolic media of interchange (see Parsons 1961, pp. 60-70, and 1969, Chapters 14, 15, and 16, and Parsons and Platt 1973, Chapter 2 and Appendix, for treatment of the "family" of media). In that family, I would also include—in senses deriving from rather technical analysis—the phenomena of political power and social influence (Parsons 1969, Chapters 14 and 15).

It is not possible to pursue analysis of these related mechanisms within the limits of this chapter. Let us return briefly to the case of money. Money is not a commodity. It is not an object one can use. Nor is it a form of human service. It is a symbolic medium constituting only a claim of access to useful commodities and services. The access is gained, however, through certain institutionalized channels that we call markets (on this conception of economic markets, see Parsons and Smelser 1956, esp. Chapter 3). If one has control of money funds, one may enter market situations and offer to exchange the control of one's money holdings for control of desired goods or services. On the other side of the market situation, one may offer control of goods or services in exchange for money.

Whatever the potential for instability in market systems—and it is certainly substantial—the satisfaction of individual interests in social environments characterized by division of labor and contingency in detailed situations is ordinarily much facilitated by operations of the monetary medium. Money functions as a stabilizing mechanism, enabling actors who are uncertain about what their decisions will be in particular cases to hold a generalized expectation that they can cope with their uncertainties at some point in the future operation of the relevant market systems.

Most students of the phenomena of health and illness would find very strange an effort to treat the problem of health in theoretical terms resembling the ones I have been sketching. However, I would like to suggest that health may be treated as a generalized medium, comparable in certain respects to money.*

---

*I have put forward this suggestion in an essay published in the Encyclopedia of Bioethics (New York: Macmillan, 1978) under the title, "Health and Disease." The original draft, which had to be substantially condensed for the Encyclopedia, appears as Chapter 3 of my recent collection of essays, Action Theory and the Human Condition (1978).

First, let us try to locate the phenomena we call health and its obverse, illness or disease. These concepts are, of course, freely applied to parts of organisms. One might say that "X has a diseased lung" or, in the absence of that judgment, "His lungs are healthy." However, the concept health is also applied to a state of the individual organism as a whole, rather than to parts of it. By contrast, it is seldom applied to aggregates of many organisms, as, for example, to flocks of sheep. Of course, the metaphor of illness or sickness has also been applied to societies.* However, these collective usages are generally understood to be metaphorical in a sense not true of the term's application to individual organisms.

My own interest in the concept of health has concerned especially the relation between the organic aspect of health and what is ordinarily called mental health or illness. Starting with the organic (or physical) aspect of health, however, I would like to link it with a crucial concept of modern physiology, namely, the "internal environment" of the organism. This concept, first introduced by the French physiologist, Claude Bernard, stresses the relative stability of the organism's functioning, as compared to the state of the environment external to the organism (see Bernard 1957 [first published in 1865]; Bernard's ideas were later extended by Cannon 1932). It is the environment of the internal parts—the cells, tissues, and organs—that comprise the organism. Three aspects of its relative constancy may be mentioned. For mammals and birds, a conspicuous one is the constancy of body temperature in the face of substantial fluctuations in the environmental temperature. Probably, the most important aspect is the existence of a relatively uniform liquid medium, namely, the blood, circulating throughout the whole body. Though the composition of the blood changes within narrow limits— for example, there will be more hemoglobin in arterial blood than in venous blood—the mechanisms of the circulation of the blood work to assure a general adequacy in its effects upon the physiological processes of exceedingly diverse cells, tissues, and organs (see Bernard 1957; Henderson 1928). The third point is that there are certain much subtler, quantitatively less conspicuous biochemical mechanisms associated with the blood stream that affect the maintenance of a relatively stable state of affairs very powerfully. Best known of these are the hormones, such as insulin, adrenalin, and the like.

---

*In the tradition of modern sociological theory, the metaphor was developed most notably by Emile Durkheim in his <u>Suicide</u> (New York: Free Press, 1951).

I would suggest that at the organic level, health can be thought of in relation to the effective stabilization of the internal environment of the organism and the maintenance of its distinctiveness, as compared with the external environment. When a particular organ becomes "diseased," only if its malfunctioning in some way produces effects that become generalized and harm the organism as a whole would we speak of the organism or the body as unhealthy. Unhealthy states, of course, may proliferate into fatal ones.

The organism, the more so the more advanced in evolutionary terms, is not merely a physiologically functioning, but also a behaving, entity. As I have noted, behavior goes very far back in the scale of organic evolution. What we call <u>action at symbolic levels</u>, however, is distinctively human. It is characterized above all by the use of symbolism and the special capacities that requires. The development of language and language-capacities is the key criterion of the attainment of what I would call a <u>level of action</u> as distinguished from <u>behavior</u> (compare Lidz 1976, pp. 124-50).

Relatively little is yet known in a really technical sense about the ways in which organic functioning, even its behavioral aspects, are articulated with action functioning, especially with the more highly developed symbolic levels of actions. That there must be definitely structured articulations between the organic and action levels, however, is a major reason why I have felt that the concept of health should not be treated so as to preclude its extension beyond the organic domain to the mental, or, more technically, action, domain. Here and there, bits of evidence on these articulations have appeared, but unfortunately, I am not competent to appraise them in any general sense.

As part of a theoretical strategy for approaching these exceedingly important articulations, I would like to suggest use of the concept of the internal environment. From my amateurish level of knowledge, I think it can be maintained that the internal environment concept is now firmly established in the discipline of the physiology of the phenotypical organism. Specifically, I believe it is firmly established for the case of human physiology.

In the study of systems of human action, it has become increasingly clear that we need a parallel concept of internal environment. There remains one substantial difference: at the physiological level, the internal environment is best established for the individual organism, whereas at the action level it is best established for the social system (see Parsons 1973). It is not completely clear what significance this difference implies, assuming it is a real difference. Although I have my own ideas, I think they should not occupy space in the present work.

The most important origin of the idea of an internal environment for action systems came from the French sociologist, Emile Durkheim, who wrote on this topic early in the present century. In his writings, Durkheim (1951) referred frequently to what he called the <u>milieu sociale</u>. By this, he meant the environment in which human individuals act and in which, there being indefinite numbers of them, they <u>interact</u>. For each of the participants, the structured situation of the interaction system constitutes an environment of his action. It seems to me that the generalized symbolic media of interchange should be placed in this theoretical context, so far as they concern the social system level. The media are features of the environment in which individual acting units must act. They enable individual units in the social system to articulate their actions interpersonally in the face of the uncertainties compounded at the human level of complexity, as compared, for example, to the behavioral situation of Tolman's rats.

From one point of view, the process of the development of the human individual, which sociologists are inclined to call <u>socialization</u>, is one of engagement in broader internal environments. These environments have the function, among other things, of controlling factors of uncertainty in individual lives. However, such control can be both negative, in the sense of preventing or lessening any disturbing contingencies, and positive, in the sense of capacity to cope with uncertainty and contingencies.

The human individual is both a living phenotypical organism and a participant in a social order, as some of us have put it. If the individual is to be a stable system, he/she must have a relatively stable internal environment in both respects. Moreover, this internal environment must be articulated with the broader internal environment of the action system, the core of which is the milieu of social interaction. A few things can be said about the nature of the articulations by which the series of interconnected environments has been built up (this idea is spelled out somewhat more fully in Parsons 1978, Chapter 15).

Though conditioned by many environmental circumstances, the health of the organism is basically internal in the spatial sense. I have stressed the importance of the blood stream in this connection. In the behavioral context, the central nervous system has a comparable importance for stabilizing the organism's relations to its external environment. Thus, memory in general, for example, as the basis for Tolman's cognitive maps, provides relatively stable modes of the orientation of behavior toward the environment. It should be remembered, then, that what is external environment for the individual organism comprises internal environment for systems of social interaction.

Considerable evidence indicates that at least two main points of articulation between the organism and its external environment take on special importance in the transition from the "pure" organism of the neonate to the socialized human individual. These two are, first, the erogenous zones, and beyond them, the whole erotic complex, as first seriously analyzed by Freud (1938), and second, the food complex, which has only recently been subjected to serious analytical study (the most important work pertaining to the food complex and its intricate significance for the human condition has been Levi-Strauss's Mythologiques [1969, 1973, 1979]).

The erotic complex can be said to be the underlying template for the organization of motivational energy for human actors. It is the framework within which organic energy is transformed to levels utilizable in action.

It must be noted that the erogenous zones, though organs of human bodies, are not conceivably organs of only one body. The four that seem important to single out are the genital organs of the two sexes, the mouth, which is common to all ages and both sexes, and the woman's breasts. Freud also treated the anus as an erogenous zone, but I would categorize it with the mouth under the more general heading of the termini of the alimentary canal. All of the erogenous zones are orifices of the body, and, therefore, mediate relations of the phenotypical organism to its environment. All of them also relate functionally to the transindividual level of human organic life. The genital organs of the two sexes are essential to the process of organic reproduction. The human infant, far more than the young of most species, is virtually helpless at birth and requires, among various kinds of care, feeding. The female breast is an organ of food supply for infants. Of course, infants receive food through the highly erogenous organ of the mouth.

Therefore, the framework of erogenous zones has built into it the two socially fateful axes of the differentiation of phenotypical organism by sex, on the one hand, by generation, on the other hand. Of course, these relations make sense only given the fact that the phenotypical organism is mortal and that, if a species is to persist, its individual members must be replaced through reproduction (see Parsons 1978, Chapter 15).

As constituents of the erotic complex, the erogenous zones are important less as functioning parts of the organism than as objects endowed with symbolic meaning through human experience. As symbols, they are a part of the culturally patterned system of action, which is an emergent feature of human life built on organic foundations. Most actual births in human societies occur within a framework of the type of social organization usually called kinship. Though its status has been controversial, especially in the anthropological literature, I would contend for present purposes that the nuclear family comprises the core of kinship systems, the more so the more differentiated the society. The nuclear family consists of four primary role types, differentiated from each other by sex and by generation. These are, of course, father, mother, son, and daughter. There is good reason to believe that the nuclear family provides a kind of compact paradigm of the more extensive and complex forms of social organization (see Parsons 1978, Chapter 15 and Turner 1976, pp. 431-41).

However this may be, the functional significance of the four familial role types is articulated with biological status at the level of species reproduction. We have reason to believe that all four role types become internalized in the personalities of maturing children of both sexes. The children internalize not only a paradigm of their own sex role, but also that of the opposite sex. Similarly, they internalize not only the role of child in a family, but the roles of the parental generation as well (Parsons and Bales 1955). Freud (1962) stated the last point in his famous formula about the superego as constituent of the personality, that it represents the "parental function."

There is every reason to believe that the state of health of the individual is intimately interdependent with the erotic complex that Freud, in his structural paradigm of the personality, located in the id. A substantial part of psychopathology certainly involves malfunctioning of these "unconscious constituents" of the personality. Furthermore, the field of so-called psychosomatic medicine has revealed much evidence of subtle interconnections between phenomena of strain at the unconscious erotic level of the personality and organic malfunctioning of various sorts.

It may be helpful to call attention to a striking resemblance between conceptions of health in primarily organic references and in this aspect of psychological well-being. Freud (1938, 1959) stressed the concept of erotic pleasure and spoke of the id as primarily dominated by what he called the "pleasure principle." Views of human motivation as pleasure oriented have had a long history in Western civilization, to say nothing of other cultural traditions. Sex has been, from some points of view, the very epitome of sensations of pleasure. In the organic context, however, we speak of a healthy state as one of "feeling well" subjectively. Erotic pleasure is associated with stimulation of the erogenous zones, while "feeling well" is a more diffuse sense of well-being. Yet, surely the two have a similar emotional quality. This consideration seems to me to ground a strong argument in favor of postulating interdependencies between the organic and the action levels.

Closely interdependent with the erotic complex is the food complex. All living human organisms are subject to the imperative of frequent intake and ingestion of nutritional material. Typically, and above all symbolically, the experiential side of nutrition begins in the life cycle with nursing by the mother. Even if the child is bottle fed from birth on, the agent will probably be an adult woman, usually the actual mother. Turner (1976, pp. 427-46) has contended that the mother-infant relationship is a true cross-cultural universal, institutionalized as the original matrix of the experience of intimacy and security in every known human society.

As the child matures, its food intake becomes more varied, approximating more closely that of adults in the child's surroundings. Some time about the end of the first year of life, the child begins to learn the use of spoken language. It is a striking fact of human socialization that often this development nearly coincides with the institutionalized limit of nursing and a predominantly liquid diet. It is also striking that the primary early teacher of language tends to be the child's own mother. I would suggest that language-learning is connected with a crucial early differentiation between the erotic complex, on the one hand, and the cybernetically higher orders of action meaning, on the other hand. Of course, the food complex stands far closer to the erotic complex, providing another very prominent source of pleasure. Moreover, the fact that in all societies it is structured about an axis of discrimination between enjoyment of particular foods and revulsion against others directly parallels a conspicuous characteristic of the organization of the erotic complex.

The relation of experience with food to the health of the organism is scarcely open to question. That ill health may be connected with lack of food, improper food, and poorly prepared food is a universal of human experience. To "eat well" is surely a major aspect of feeling well and of well-being more generally, which, again, is closely articulated with pleasure. The pleasure of eating and erotic pleasure are not the same, but they do have common genetic roots in the individual life history and do remain in close kinship with each other.

Another relationship may also be noted. In Freud's (1962) view, a primary significance of the Oedipal transition is the repression of the childhood erotic complex. Children, by virtue of this transition, renounce above all their erotic attachments to their parents, especially their mothers—regardless of the sex of the child. From then on, sharing of the ingestment of food takes on an enhanced primacy in the symbolization of the solidarity of the family. The food complex does not have a differentiation between the feeding of children and the feeding of adults comparable to the difference between stimulation of childhood erotic feelings and the genital sexual relations of adults. In most societies, the common table or locus of eating becomes a primary symbol of family solidarity shared by both generations and both sexes.

What I have said about the erotic complex and the food complex suggests that there is a continuous series, on the one hand, of distinctions between internal and external environments and, on the other hand, of involvements of generalized media of interchange, as we move in the domain of human organization from the level of the purely organic to the level of action, with specific reference to its social aspect. The age-generation framework is the organic reference of the primary mechanism of transition from the organic to the action levels. The family is the primary framework of social organization that becomes involved in this transition, which we call <u>socialization</u> as it occurs in the life-cycle of the individual person.

The course of socialization transforms the individual from being purely an organism increasingly into being a participant in a broad system that includes many organisms which have developed personalities. From the beginning of the individual's experience in the mother-child relationship, his or her participation involves action-level relationships with acquired symbolic meanings.

I have earlier referred to the problem of the relations between organic health and mental health. I have no doubt that exceedingly fundamental organic factors are involved in what we ordinarily consider to be mental health and pathology. However, I consider the action level to be an essential component of any more generalized conception of health or illness. A model for my thinking here was presented by Freud, who insisted that the organic references of the erogenous zones are an indispensable ingredient of the development of personality, and, therefore, any pathology, as well as health, of a particular personality. In a similar way, Levi-Strauss (1969, 1973, 1979) has recently stressed that the food complex, though having fundamental organic references, also acquires cultural meanings that are essential ingredients of human cultures. On these models, the concept of health must be considered a bridge between the organic level and the phenomena of action. I am not in a position to detail all the elements in the series running from the internal environment of the organism, as exemplified by the bloodstream, to the internal environments of action systems. They do, however, interpenetrate complexly with one another, as illustrated by the cases of the erotic and food complexes.

Earlier in this work, I used the example of economic markets and money to illustrate the concept of a generalized medium of exchange. The phenomena of markets stand well beyond the cases that I have just been discussing in the series leading up to the total society and the total culture. However, it is my conviction that they do belong in the same series. I do not think that the internal environments of highly complex systems can be effectively understood unless they are conceived to be stabilized by the functioning of at least one generalized medium, and usually more. Money can be considered prototypical of generalized media and, being so common a phenomenon of the everyday experience of modern human beings, should be rather readily understandable.

Perhaps I can conclude by returning to the problems of uncertainty and contingency. It seems to be essential when we try to analyze some features of the human condition to keep clear that we are always dealing with a dual conception. We are dealing with some kind of living system and with an environment in which it functions, but which is not a part of it. I have suggested that the concept of the internal environment is particularly useful in relating these two reference points to each other. As a general principle, the internal environment is more stable than the external environment in a number of respects that are functionally essential to the living system of reference. Capacity to cope with changing conditions in the external environment, then, is enhanced by the evolution of internal environments, in which the constituent units are protected in their relations with one another against certain variabilities and contingencies.

What we think of as illness or disease seems to me particularly to refer to processes that have undermined some aspect of the greater stability of the internal environment. Where the internal stability becomes precarious, the capacity of the system to cope with the instabilities and contingencies of its external environment is in turn undermined. This is the context in which ill health is appropriately conceived as involving impairment of capacities. In principle, however, the same holds true for the whole series I have alluded to. The series extends from organic health to mental health, from mental health to capacity to participate in many types of social functioning, and from performance in routine social contexts all the way to the highest levels of cultural creativity.

The kinds of considerations I have discussed seem to me to be fundamental to a fruitful conception of the relation between freedom and exposure to uncertainty. There is an important sense in which the argument I have presented constitutes a way of relativizing the stark either/or dilemma of freedom versus determinism, freedom versus constraint. By the mere fact that it reduces the impact of instability and contingency, an internal environment imposes constraints on the units that act within it. However, the stability of an internal environment also provides the <u>conditions</u> under which capacity to cope with exigencies in the external environment, and therefore the effectuve use of freedom, become possible. The present analysis of ways in which systemic constraints may positively stabilize the exercise of human freedoms contrasts fundamentally with views propounded by a number of currently popular ideologists. They feel that they must be absolutely free or must regard themselves as absolutely constrained. To my mind, this is one of the great false dilemmas that is played up in much ideological discussion of our time.

REFERENCES

Bernard, Claude. 1957. An Introduction to the Study of Experimental Medicine. New York: Dover; first published in France in 1865.

Cannon, W. B. 1932. The Wisdom of the Body. New York: Norton.

Chomsky, Noam. 1972. Language and Mind. New York: Harcourt Brace Jovanovich.

──── . 1979. Language and Responsibility. New York: Pantheon Books.

Durkheim, Emile. 1951. Suicide. New York: Free Press.

Etkin, William. 1964. "Theories of Animal Socialization and Communication." In Social Behavior and Organization among Vertebrates, edited by William Etkin, pp. 167-205. Chicago: University of Chicago Press.

Freud, Sigmund. 1938. Three Contributions to the Theory of Sex in Basic Writings of Sigmund Freud, edited by A. A. Brill. New York: Modern Library.

──── . 1959. Beyond the Pleasure Principle. New York: Bantam.

──── . 1962. The Ego and the Id. New York: Norton.

Henderson, L. J. 1928. Blood: A Study in General Physiology. New Haven, Conn.: Yale University Press.

Levi-Strauss, Claude. 1969-79. Mythologiques. New York: Harper & Row. Vol. 1, The Raw and the Cooked, 1969. Vol. 2, From Honey to Ashes, 1973. Vol. 3, The Origin of Table Manners, 1979.

Lidz, Victor. 1976. "Introduction to General Action Analysis." In Explorations in General Theory in Social Science, edited by J. Louber et al. pp. 124-50. New York: Free Press.

Loubser, J., et al., eds. 1976. Explorations in General Theory in Social Science. New York: Free Press.

Mayr, Ernst. 1970. Populations, Species, and Evolution. Cambridge, Mass.: Harvard University Press.

———. 1974. "Theoeological and Teleonomic: A New Analysis." In Method and Metaphysics: Methodological and Historical Essays in the Natural and Social Sciences, edited by Marx Wartovsky, pp. 78-104. Leiden: Brill.

Parsons, Talcott. 1949. The Structure of Social Action. New York: Free Press.

———. 1951. The Social System. New York: Free Press.

———. 1961. "An Outline of the Social System." In Theories of Society, edited by T. Parsons et al. pp. 20-79. New York: Free Press.

———. 1969. Politics and Social Structure. New York: Free Press.

———. 1973. "Durkheim on Religion Revisited." In Beyond the Classics, edited by C. Y. Glock and P. A. Hammond. pp. 156-190. New York: Harper Torchbooks.

———. 1978. Action Theory and the Human Condition. New York: Free Press.

Parsons, Talcott, and Bales, Robert F. 1955. Family Socialization and Interaction Process. New York: Free Press.

Parsons, Talcott, and Platt, Gerald M. 1973. The American University. Cambridge, Mass.: Harvard University Press.

Parsons, Talcott, and Smelser, Neil J. 1956. Economy and Society. New York: Free Press.

Tolman, Edward C. 1932. Purposive Behavior in Animals and Men. New York: Appleton-Century.

Turner, Terrence S. 1976. "Family Structure and Socialization." In Explorations in General Theory in Social Science, pp. 419-46. Edited by J. Loubser et al. New York: Free Press.

11
MACRO AND MICRO UNCERTAINTY
George Katona

For a long time, uncertainty has been a topic of interest to economists. Economic theorists, recognizing that the most important business decisions are future oriented and that the future is uncertain, developed probability models about how businessmen cope with uncertainty.

This author, in his studies of the psychological determinants of economic processes, approached the problem of uncertainty from a different angle. In his endeavors to forecast economic trends through collecting survey data on changes in attitudes and expectations, he was impressed by the fact that the survey approach to forecasting was successful on the aggregate or macro level, while on the micro level, it was impossible or very difficult to produce evidence for the influence of the attitudes of individuals on their subsequent actions. The Index of Consumer Sentiment, developed by the Survey Research Center of the University of Michigan in 1952 and published at quarterly or monthly intervals ever since, represents a macro measure reflecting the changes in the attitudes and expectations of all Americans. When the index was contrasted with another macro measure reflecting the changes in the economic activities in the entire country (for example, changes in the gross national product), it was found that the index declined substantially prior to the beginning of periods of economic recovery (see Katona

---

The following pages are reproduced with the permission of the American Psychological Association, from George Katona, "Toward a Macropsychology," American Psychologist 39 (1979): 118-26.

1975). In contrast, such actions of individuals as their major expenditures or additions to savings could not be predicted by the changes in their attitudes and expectations.

After describing these findings in an article published recently, the author turned to a study of the differences between macro and micro processes and used the problem of uncertainty as a major example in his attempt to clarify the problem.

Many years before the predictive value of consumer attitudes could be tested by comparing survey findings with subsequent economic developments in the manner illustrated in Figure 11.1, the question of the relation of attitudes to behavior was raised in a form that threatened the continuation of the financial backing of the surveys. In the late 1940s and early 1950s, the survey expenses were borne by the Federal Reserve Board, which also provided a prompt and influential outlet for publication of the survey findings in the Federal Reserve Bulletin. In 1954, the board appointed a committee of experts to scrutinize the operations of the Survey Research Center. The committee was very helpful in calling the survey studies "indispensable" and "unique," by acknowledging the predictive value of buying intentions and even referring to data on attitudes collected in 1949 and 1951 as "a major predictive success." But in view of the few observations available at that time, it was not possible to test the predictive value of expectations by means of regression equations on the aggregative level. The committee was restricted to analyzing studies on the relation of attitudes and behavior on the individual level and failed to find evidence that optimists had bought more durable goods than pessimists had. The eminent economists on the committee therefore assumed the role of behavioral theorists and concluded:

> It would surely be very difficult to construct a plausible model of human behavior, even allowing for much purely random and idiosyncratic differences among individuals, on which attitudes could influence subsequent behavior of large groups without influencing the behavior of those who observed to hold them (Consultant Committee on Consumer Survey Statistics 1955, p. 61).

This quotation points to a major problem: Is it possible to have predictive success on the aggregate level—as shown in Figure 11.1, which indicates recessions representing the performance of the entire economy—in the face of failure of predictions on the individual level? Before studying this question systematically, it may be mentioned that several tests conducted over the last several years have disclosed some impact of attitudes on the behavior of

FIGURE 11.1

Index of Consumer Sentiment

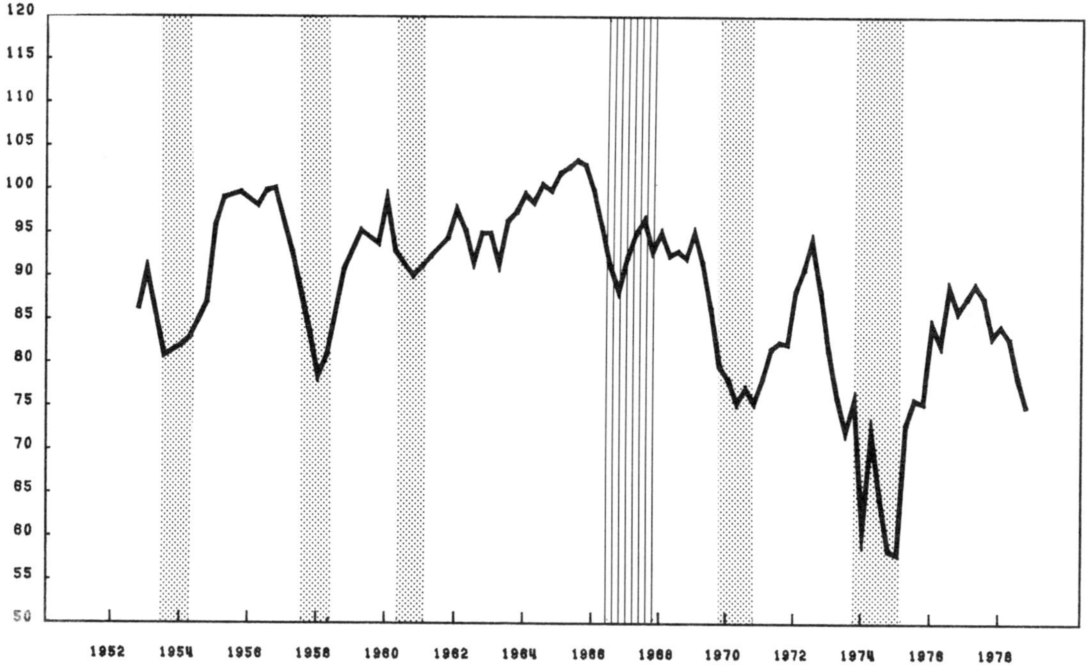

Shaded areas indicate recessions.

Note: Shaded portions indicate recessions.

individuals as well. The discretionary purchases of individuals who have become optimistic in the recent past were found to be larger than the purchases of individuals who have become pessimistic (Dunkelberg 1972; Katona 1975, p. 194). It was also shown that difficulties of measurement were responsible for much of the failure of individual tests (Katona 1960, pp. 254ff.; Maynes 1967, p. 121). Nevertheless, there is no doubt on the basis of experience with the Index of Consumer Sentiment over 25 years that the predictive value of attitudes and expectations is much stronger and may be demonstrated much more easily and strikingly in aggregative tests than in tests with individuals.

It is important to distinguish what has just been said from the well-known implications of the law of large numbers, known since Bernouilli's time. That law has occasionally been expressed in a way which may appear to be a suitable formulation of the experience with the Index of Consumer Sentiment, namely, that what individuals will do is not equally uncertain (see Katona 1951, pp. 20ff., for a discussion of this aspect of the law of large numbers). If I toss a coin 1,000 times, I can make several well-justified predictions. Obviously, the law of large numbers applies only when nothing but random factors prevail, so that each toss is independent of the next one. When this is not the case or when the dice are loaded, it may be possible to predict even a single throw with certainty. The findings about the differences in the outcome of aggregate and individual tests on the impact of expectations differ from what the law of large numbers postulates. Such attitudes and expectations as waves of optimism or pessimism spread like a contagious disease rather than in a random manner. Nevertheless, the determination of the influence of attitudes on action is much simpler when actions of thousands of people rather than those of a few people are studied.

UNCERTAINTY ON THE MICRO AND MACRO LEVELS

In economics, the distinction between macro and micro processes is well established, and it is well-known that there are macro regularities that do not apply on the micro level. Perhaps the best known among these is that investment and saving must be equal for the economy as a whole, but that the two differ for practically all individual persons and firms. Psychology is overwhelmingly micro because it is only the individual who reacts, learns, thinks, and has emotions. Social psychology also analyzes mostly how individual behavior is influenced by belonging to groups, although group norms and social forces are occasionally discussed.

Does macro psychology therefore belong in sociology, or is it something hazy and unnecessary?

The proposition that psychologists ought to be involved in the study of macro processes is developed below by studying specific examples of economic behavior. The first example to be used to clarify the meaning of macro psychology is the study and measurement of uncertainty.

In the fall of 1977, a news magazine featured the following statement: "A pervasive sense of uncertainty grips businessmen and investors." What is meant by this journalistic observation? Perhaps simply that there were in 1977 very many businessmen and investors who felt uncertain about forthcoming economic trends. Alternatively, what was meant may have been that uncertainty was "in the air," so most if not all businessmen and investors were affected by it.

In the past, psychologists have used the term <u>uncertainty</u> primarily to mean a psychological state of individuals. Most recently, the term was also meant to refer (for instance, in information theory) to characteristics of stimuli in a sense closely related to ambiguity. Insufficiency of clues, whether in perception or in a detective story, may create uncertainty, so that additional stimuli or clues are needed to provide clarity. In this sense, the uncertainty prevailing in the economy may be identified with insufficient information or conflicting signals about forthcoming trends. Uncertainty in the sense of a puzzling situation in which contradictory outcomes are possible may also be viewed as an early and transitional phase of the problem-solving process. When a problem is solved or when full understanding is achieved in a learning situation, uncertainty is dispelled.

The economic literature on uncertainty is so voluminous that only brief references can be included here. Econometricians tended to replace uncertain expectations with "certainty equivalents." The practice of disregarding uncertainty may have been based on Keynes's (1936) proposition that "it would be foolish in forming one's expectations to attach great weight to matters which are very uncertain" (p. 148). This may be justified if uncertainty means that the probability assigned to an expectation is very low. Uncertainty, however, may also mean great concern with future contingencies, fear of adverse developments, and lack of confidence, which should not be neglected. When the Index of Consumer Sentiment was constructed, it was thought that it indicated not only the optimism-pessimism dimension but, also, the dimension from confidence to uncertainty. This was emphasized by Juster (1972), who wrote, "When the consumer sentiment index is improving optimism is growing and uncertainty is being dispelled, and vice versa when the index is deteriorating" (p. 323).

A major task on hand is the measurement of uncertainty, so as to clarify its meaning and, also, to confirm or reject the journalistic notion about uncertainty being pervasive in 1977. The author's first attempt to measure uncertainty was stimulated by Paul Lazarsfeld, who, in studies of the panel method, distinguished between individual respondents answering the same question at different times in the same way or in a different way (turnover). He wrote: "If the turnover is large, it indicates that the opinion or behavior is unstable. We know that people feel uncertain" (Lazarsfeld, Berelson, and Gaudet 1948, p. x).

In a paper published 20 years ago (Katona 1958), I called attention to the fact that change of response from a first to a second interview might be caused by the acquisition of new information rather than by uncertainty about the answer. Distinguishing between the two was possible by contrasting the individual or micro measure of "proportion of changers" with an aggregate or trend measure indicating the extent of change from the first to the second interview. When the answers of the entire sample, representing all Americans, revealed that optimism had been growing or declining (see Table 11.1) substantially, a large proportion of changers appeared to indicate a change in attitudes resulting from new information. Alternately, the changers may be divided into two groups: those who moved in the same direction as the aggregate change and those who "swam against the current." This is done in Table 11.1. We see there that in 1955, for instance, the number of changers were fairly high, but indicated a sizable trend (toward optimism) that occurred at that time. In 1976, on the other hand, a substantially greater proportion of changers (and a smaller proportion of consistent answers) was obtained, with changes in both directions being about equal. (Thirty-six percent of the sample shifted from pessimistic to optimistic and 28 percent from optimistic to pessimistic answers). A large proportion of those swimming against the current—in 1976, and to a lesser extent in 1971 and 1977—point toward a great volatility of response (see Katona and Strumpel 1978, chap. 4). Yet, it is far from assured that volatility is identical with uncertainty. Therefore, the search for other measures of uncertainty has continued.

A volatility measure based on the extent of changes in the Index of Consumer Sentiment, and therefore on changes in the aggregate response of the entire sample, was used next. As is shown in Figure 11.2, suggested by Richard Curtin, this measure indicates little volatility from 1965 to 1972 and great volatility from 1972 to 1978. Again, the observed volatility may be interpreted in different ways; it may or may not reflect uncertainty.

FIGURE 11.2

Volatility of Consumer Sentiment

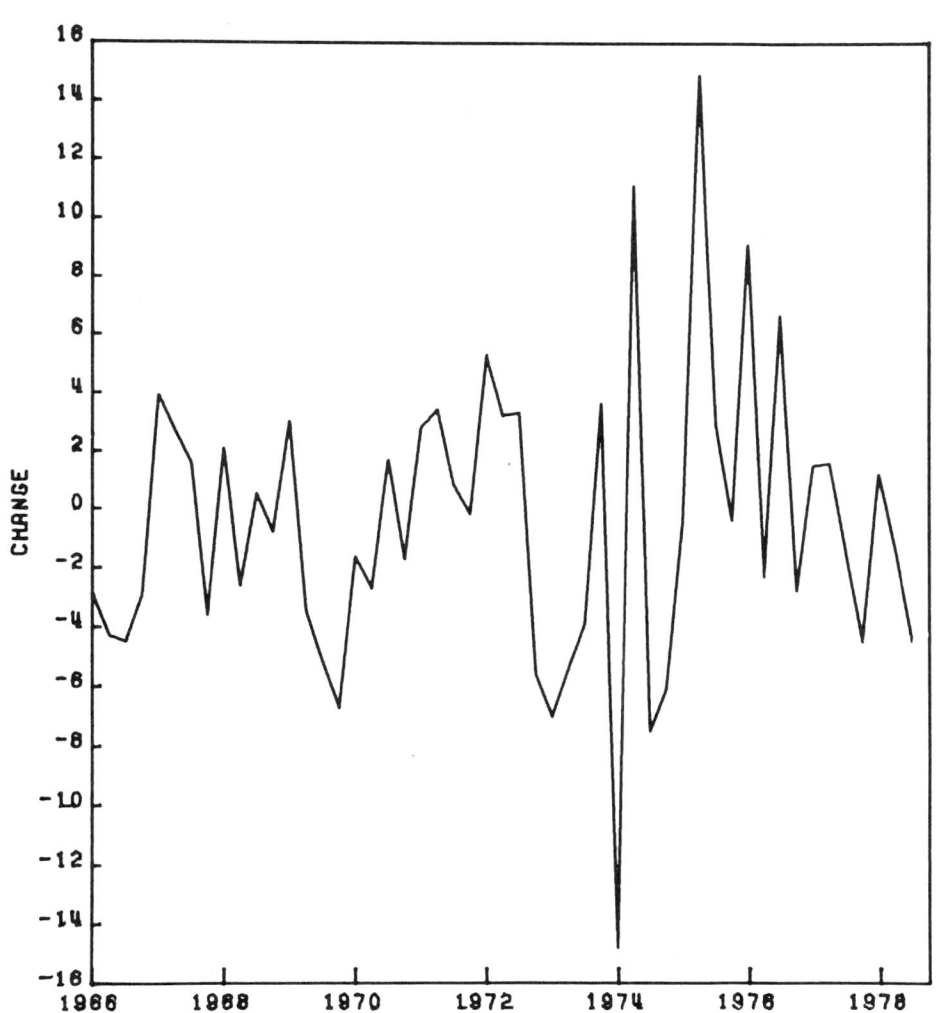

Change in index points from quarter to quarter.

Note: Change in index points from quarter to quarter.

TABLE 11.1

Measures of Volatility on the Micro Level
in Two Consecutive Interviews

Date of Second Interview	Percent Consistent	Percent of Changers	
		Trend	Swimming against Current
June 1955	56	30	14
September 1964	69	17	14
September 1971	57	23	20
October 1973	57	27	16
May 1975	47	37	16
October 1976	36	36	28
May 1977	57	23	19
September 1977	58	24	18

Note: Two interviews were conducted with identical respondents at six-month intervals. The answers to three questions—personal financial expectations during the next year, and general economic outlook for the next year and for the next five years—were averaged. The three questions are parts of the Index of Consumer Sentiment. The sample sizes were between 600 and 1,600.

Therefore, a third measure was constructed, based on the dispersion of responses. At a time when almost everybody in a representative sample expresses optimistic expectations, or almost everybody expresses pessimistic expectations, we may say that the people are optimistic or pessimistic. On the other hand, when a substantial proportion is optimistic and a similar substantial proportion is pessimistic, the people as a whole may be viewed as uncertain in their expectations about future developments. Thus, the smaller the difference between expecting good or better times and expecting bad or worse times, the greater the uncertainty on the aggregate or macro level. This measure, constructed irrespective of whether optimists or pessimists are more frequent (that is, by disregarding signs), is shown in Figure 11.3. It indicated not only, as Juster proposed, that growing optimism dispels uncertainty (say, in 1965) but, also, that growing pessimism dispels uncertainty (say, in 1974). Figure 11.3 differs greatly from Figure 11.1. It shows that from 1969 to 1977, uncertainty was substantially greater than

FIGURE 11.3

Index of Uncertainty on the Macro Level

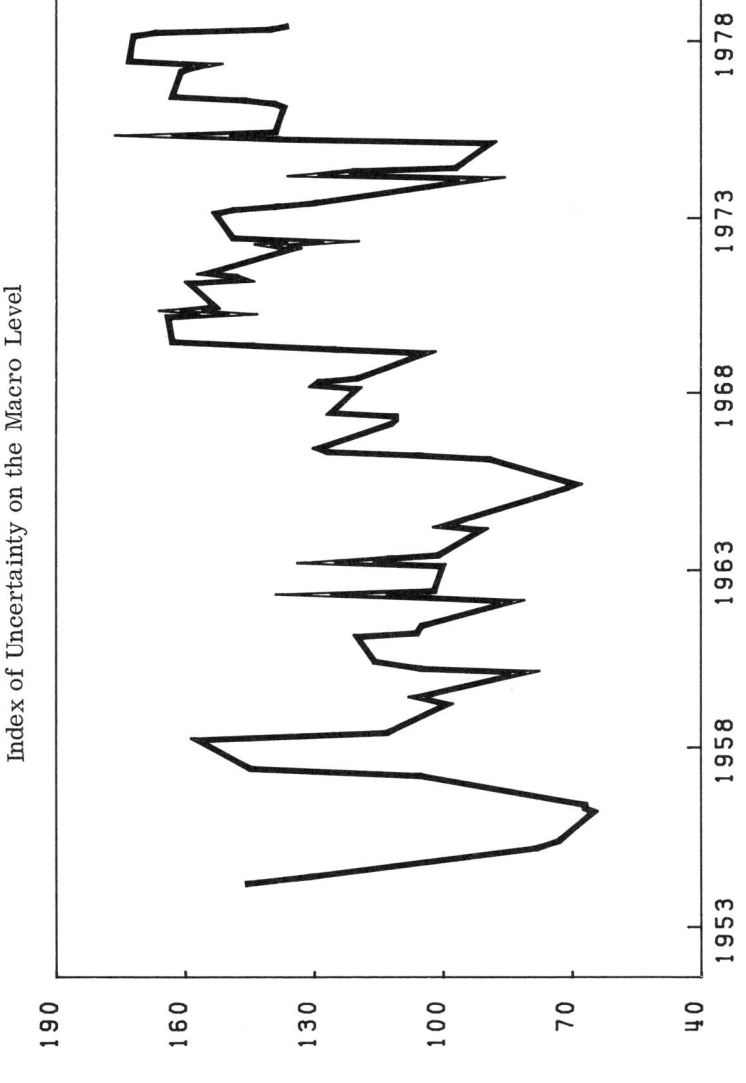

Note: Aggregate dispersion—favorable minus unfavorable expectations with sign disregarded—of the forward-looking components of the Index of Consumer Sentiment.

in the preceding 20 years. In spite of the high level of uncertainty in 1957, prior to the 1958 recession, and the low level of uncertainty in 1974, during the deepest postwar recession, we find great differences between the earlier decades and the 1970s.

An additional measure of uncertainty was constructed by F. Thomas Juster of the Survey Research Center, University of Michigan. He argued that during the last few years, uncertainty about the level of money income may have been less pronounced than uncertainty about the level of real income (shown here as Figure 11.3), that is, about the purchasing power of income received in the future, dependent on the extent of inflation. Using survey data on price expectations, Juster measured the variance of expected price changes in the population—in other words, the dispersion of people's best guesses about future price increases. A time series of this macro measure of uncertainty served as a predictor of the rate of private saving in the United States over several years (see Juster 1975).

The question of how to measure uncertainty is rather complex. So are the consequences of uncertainty. Zajonc and Burnstein (1961) concluded from an experimental study that "the likelihood of cognitive changes increases with increasing uncertainty" (p. 115). This conclusion is in accord with our linking uncertainty with the volatility and instability of attitudes and behavior. Weighty arguments have also been marshaled for another consequence of uncertainty: when in doubt, do nothing, goes an old adage. Economists frequently argue that uncertainty retards or even inhibits spending and investing because people, feeling uncertain about the future, tend to abstain from committing large funds. The two assumptions about the consequences of uncertainty are not necessarily contradictory, yet they call for further investigation, for which, probably, a study of economic behavior may be most suitable.

To clarify the meaning of macro in contrast with micro data, a comparison of the methods used in Table 11.1 and Figure 11.3 may be helpful. Though Table 11.1 indicates that it is possible to measure the extent of the uncertainty and volatility of attitudes of individuals, Figure 11.3 does not reflect individual attitudes or behavior. Data obtained from a large number of people are characterized in Figure 11.3 either by uniformity, by consensus (and fit in a normal curve), or by dispersion-divergence (and fit in a U curve). The macro psychological data appear to add something to the usual micro psychological data.

FORECASTING ON THE MACRO LEVEL

The meaning of macro psychology will be illustrated by discussing further examples. The processes of learning may be mentioned first. The psychology of learning represents a clear instance of micro psychology. It deals with the acquisition of knowledge, experience, or skills by individuals, irrespective of whether learning is due to association, conditioned reflex, or insight. I have argued in the past that we must also recognize learning by masses of people. I can illustrate this by recounting what repeated surveys have disclosed about the American people's opinions and beliefs regarding a substantial tax reduction in the years 1962-64. When President John Kennedy first proposed the reduction of income taxes in 1962, the majority of Americans thought it was a bad idea for the country as a whole and was impractical or even impossible. Many people believed that the government could not reduce its revenues at a time of deficits and the need for substantial additional expenditures. In the following 18 months, masses of people acquired new information. After the enactment of the tax cut law early in 1964, most survey respondents said that the tax cut was a good thing for the country. They had learned that because of the tax cut, people would spend more and, thereby, raise the level of economic activity. Thus, not only the taxpayers but the entire economy would profit from the tax cut.

What we have just described as the starting point and the end point of a macro learning process are rather different from what individual people have apparently learned. The macro learning process is much less elaborate than the learning process by individuals, so it could be described in simple terms. Analysis of individual answers disclosed that in addition to the common core presented above, individual learning encompassed a variety of further arguments that were far from identical from person to person. Nevertheless, mass behavior in 1964-65, not just in the form of expressed attitudes but also in spending and incurring installment debt, was in line with the macro learning process. The optimism generated by the newly acquired understanding stimulated expenditures and the incurrence of installment debt.

Acquisition of information occurred among the American masses also with respect to inflation. In the mid-1970s, practically all people thought that inflation was inevitable. Surveys disclosed that they expected that prices would be higher.

What must be added to these considerations reproduced from an earlier article is a plea for further research. We need to know much more than we do both about micro uncertainty—individuals displaying uncertainty—and about macro uncertainty—high frequency of uncertainty among the members of a given universe, for instance, all Americans. How uncertainty spreads among people and how people cope with it represents crucial problems that may be studied by analyzing economic attitudes and various forms of economic behavior.

At this time, the author will restrict himself to advancing the following hypothesis about coping with uncertainty: Belief and trust in continuity and stability are common. Uncertainty of the future is disregarded unless strong motivational forces intervene. Confusion and disorientation then lead to either of three forms of behavior: to continue to do what one had done before, or to do nothing, or to shift from one response to the opposite one and back again (vacillation or volatility).

An important question arises beyond that of the ways of responding to, or coping with, uncertainty. Under which conditions are we aware of uncertainty and confronted with the necessity to choose and make genuine decisions?

Psychological studies of decision-making often presuppose the presence of definite expectations about the future. For instance, valuable experiments have been carried out by A. Tversky and D. Kahneman (published in several articles) in which such questions were asked of the subjects in the experiments as whether they preferred a "25 percent chance to gain $300" or a "20 percent chance to gain $400." Such alternatives, perhaps present in some cases of gambling, are not typical of economic behavior. Neither businessmen nor investors in stocks know in advance the exact probabilities of chance or the specific amounts of expected gain. Their expectations are typically vague and uncertain. True, it was found that expecting to make either a gain or loss was infrequent; but when people expected to make a gain, they were highly uncertain about its extent and its probability. At best, they expected a small gain or, in other cases, a sizable gain. The elimination of uncertainty through "certainty equivalents," represented by assuming knowledge of the probability of future events, is not realistic and does not contribute to an understanding of either the psychological or the economic processes as they usually occur.

Studies of decision making must go beyond studies of choice between exact probabilities given. A similar requirement confronts the usual experiments in problem-solving. When subjects are presented with problems, as is done in practically all experiments, the first phase of problem-solving is eliminated from the study. This phase consists of recognizing that there is a problem. We just go on and do what we did before or do nothing, rather than perceiving that a problem and a choice exist. Uncertainty in the sense of hesitation or the notion that we better "stop and look" before we act are not always present, as the first part of the hypothesis advanced before suggests. The circumstances under which awareness of uncertainty arises must be studied.

REFERENCES

Consultant Committee on Consumer Survey Statistics. 1955.

Juster, F. T. 1975. "Inflation and Consumer Savings Behavior." Mimeographed. Ann Arbor: University of Michigan, Survey Research Center.

Juster, F. T., and Wachtel, P. 1972. "Uncertainty, Expectations, and Durable Goods Demand Models." In Human Behavior in Economic Affairs, edited by B. Strumpel, J. N. Morgan, and E. Zahn. New York: Elsevier.

Katona, G. 1958. "Attitude Change: Instability of Response and Acquisition of Experience." Psychological Monographs 72: 1-38.

_____. 1975. Psychological Economics. New York: Elsevier.

Katona, G., and Strumpel, B. 1978. A New Economic Era. New York: Elsevier.

Keynes, J. M. 1936. The General Theory of Employment, Interest, and Money. New York: Harcourt, Brace.

Lazarsfeld, P. F.; Berelson, B.; and Gaudet, H. 1948. The People's Choice. 2d ed. New York: Columbia University Press.

Zajonc, R. G., and Bernstein, E. 1961. "The Resolution of Cog- Conflict under Uncertainty." Human Relations 14: 113-19.

12
UNCERTAINTY AND MODELS OF URBAN TRAVEL BEHAVIOR
Vincent B. Robinson

INTRODUCTION

Typically, models of urban travel behavior fulfill two functions. They are often used in planning to provide predictions of behavior and to provide theoretical or conceptual explanations of travel behavior in urban areas. Depending upon the modeling paradigm, these two functions may be seen as mutually exclusive. In efforts to provide more accurate predictions and/or to add to the behavioral realism of urban travel models, modelers have sought to maximize uncertainty, minimize uncertainty, and incorporate uncertainty. The concept of uncertainty has therefore been important in development of contemporary models of urban travel behavior. Hence its definition and role in the various modeling efforts may vary substantially. This chapter presents a critical review of three contemporary modeling efforts in which a concept of uncertainty plays a major role. It is shown that uncertainty has been treated primarily as a characteristic of the observer. Thus, concern with the handling of uncertainty in a model of urban travel behavior does not necessarily add to its behavioral realism. In fact, one approach very much concerned with uncertainty is barren of any particular theory with behavioral content. Finally, this chapter does present an emerging modeling perspective that emphasizes uncertainty as a characteristic of individual urban travelers.

MAXIMIZING UNCERTAINTY

Maximizing uncertainty models are more commonly known as entropy-maximizing models. This approach is largely based on the seminal work of Wilson (1967, 1970). Entropy is a measure of uncertainty; therefore, it is more correct to speak of maximizing uncertainty. This method of modeling urban travel behavior has become popular within the past few years. Its popularity is said to evolve from the method's capacity to provide accurate estimates of the interaction between places (Webber 1977). This section explains the basis of uncertainty-maximizing models of urban travel behavior. Explanation of the basis of such models provides justification for maintaining that like the gravity model, these models are barren of any intrinsic behavioral theory.

Uncertainty is a common phenomenon in everyday life. But how is it to be measured and operationalized for use in modeling travel behavior? Consider the situation where the transportation planner knows that 10 percent of the social trips attracted to zone j had their origin in zone i; the planner is still uncertain about the origin of a given trip-maker. The probabilities of travelers' origin-destination flows are known and can be used to measure the transport planner's uncertainty. This approach relies on the use of probabilities. However, to use Jaynes's (1957) terminology, it consists of using subjective probabilities, for

> to the subjectivist, the purpose of probability theory is to help us in forming plausible conclusions in cases where there is not enough information available to lead to certain conclusions; thus detailed verification is not expected. The test of a good subjective probability distribution is: does it correctly represent our state of knowledge as to the value of x? (Jaynes 1957).

This is the underlying rationale of the uncertainty-maximizing paradigm, which contributes to its flexibility both theoretically and in application.

It has been argued that entropy is a reasonable measure of uncertainty. Entropy is formally defined as the quantity

$$H = - \sum_{i=1}^{N} P_i \log P_i \qquad (1)$$

where P_i is, the probability of an individual making a trip to zone i. Several researchers have shown that H satisfies the conditions for a quantity that would represent the uncertainty associated with a probability distribution (Jaynes 1957; Shannon and Weaver 1949; Khinchin 1957). In addition, when the behavior of an individual is known with certainty, then one of the probabilities equals 1, the others equal 0, and the measure of uncertainty equals 0. In other words, the observer has no uncertainty regarding the choice of trip destination. However, if the probabilities are all of equal value, the measure of uncertainty is at its maximum; hence, the observer is as uncertain as possible about the travel behavior of an individual.

A model in which entropy is maximized is one in which the model builder is maximizing his/her uncertainty about the actual choice made by an individual subject to constraints. This may seem a strange concept, since model builders in the field of urban transportation are used to trying to draw sure conclusions, that is, minimizing their uncertainty.

In an attempt to reduce the strangeness of the concept, consider the following problems. Some facts are known about people in the aggregate, but the known information is not sufficient to predict surely at the level of detail desired. It is a research problem to bridge this information gap. Traditionally, this gap has been filled by making assumptions about individual behavior. In this situation, a relationship exists between data, assumed behavior, and predictions. In other words, the traditional approach has been to construct models of choice. Using the uncertainty-maximizing approach, the research task is to try to infer detailed patterns from known aggregate data without intermediary assumptions—that is, the relationship is between the data and the prediction only.

If uncertainty-maximizing methods are applied to a transport problem, the answer is a set of probabilities, which is used to predict choice patterns. Associated with this set of probabilities is a measure of uncertainty, say, H, which is the maximum possible uncertainty attainable given the constraints. It is, as argued by Jaynes (1957), the least biased assignments of probabilities. The bias eliminated is that of the observer. Hence, the observer is legitimately entitled to conclude that the probability distribution generated is one in which no private bias has entered. Thus, it is nonsensical to question whether or not the world maximizes uncertainty subject to constraints.

Constraints play an important role in the uncertainty-maximizing approach. The builder of such models confronts a research problem that consists of identifying the set of constraints which yields sufficiently accurate estimates of the probability distribution giving rise to the measure of uncertainty. In essence, the data contained in the constraints represent information available to the modeler or forecaster. Also, the more information is available, the less the uncertainty about the prediction of behavior. The interesting research problem is then to explain the origin of the constraints—that is, What are the social processes which explain the constraints?

It has been said that the most successful planning applications of the uncertainty-maximizing technique have been with models of spatial interaction (Webber 1977). This class of models was originally formulated by Wilson (1967). The elementary event is a trip from some origin to some destination. The urban spatial structure—that is, the pattern of location of people, jobs, and shops—is typically assumed to be given. The output of a simple formulation is commonly of the form

$$T_{ij} = a_i O_i \gamma_j D_j (\exp - \beta c_{ij}) \qquad (2)$$

when T_{ij} is the number of trips generated in origin i that end in destination j, D_i is the total number of trips having origin i, D_j is total number of trips having destination j, and c_{ij} is the generalized cost of a trip from i to j. The constraints are

$$\sum_j T_{ij} = O_i \text{ for all i} \qquad (3a)$$

$$\sum_i T_{ij} = D_j \text{ for all j} \qquad (3b)$$

$$\sum_i \sum_j T_{ij} c_{ij} = C \qquad (3c)$$

In the constraints, D_i is the number of trips that begin in origin i; D_j is the number of trips ending at destination k; and C is some fixed total expenditure on transport in the region. The parameters a_i, γ_j, and β ensure that the constraint equations hold (see Appendix 2).

This interaction equation (2) was known to exist before the application of the method of maximizing uncertainty. It is equivalent to the gravity model formulation of spatial interaction associated with the school of social physics (see Appendix 1). Due to this result, the derivation of the gravity model via the maximizing of uncertainty has been considered one of the greatest theoretical successes of this approach. What becomes clear is that the gravity model form of the interaction model is shown to be the most probable if the cost of travel is constrained so as not to exceed a total for the whole region, if there is a constraint on the number of trips beginning and ending in each zone of an urban region, and if <u>no other</u> constraints operate upon the individuals of the system. Thus, it shows that if these conditions are met, then this conclusion is most probable.

The maximizing-uncertainty approach is based on the use of an analogy—the uncertainty of a probability distribution. As such, it has provided for the development of new models of modal-split and route-split. It has introduced the concept of generalized cost, C_{ij}, into transportation modeling. The use of the generalized cost term has led to an improved definition of the friction factor term of the gravity model (Stopher and Meyburg 1975). This approach has proved useful in an applied situation (Selnec 1969).

The major criticism of this approach is that it does not contribute much in the way of conceptual or behavioral development of an explanatory theory of urban travel behavior. It is a logical construct approach, lacking any particular theoretical statements on the behavior of travel consumers. It does provide, in the way of constraints, a means of hypothesis generation.

The major research tasks facing those working this area are (1) identification of the constraints that operate on the urban transportation system, particularly behavioral constraints; and (2) construction of a body of theory that explains the origin of those constraints.

Finally, this perspective asserts that although the study of individual behavior may be of interest, it is not necessary for the study of aggregate social relations. This is, of course, at odds with an economic/behavioral perspective, which asserts that the central concern of consumers of transportation is with making optimal (in some sense) choices with scarce resources. Furthermore, it contends that the characteristics of aggregate social relations may be deduced from choices made by individuals. Thus, these perspectives are at odds, and yet, contemporary thought in both fields is concerned with the reduction of observer uncertainty. To develop this assertion further, we consider the economic/behavioral theory of travel demand.

ERROR, UNCERTAINTY, AND TRAVEL DEMAND

In the articulation of a behavioral, yet economic, theory of urban travel behavior, the trip-maker is considered to be a consumer of transport goods. It is assumed that the transport goods (that is, services) can be characterized by their attributes and that the consumer desires to maximize a utility function. This utility function has commodity attributes as its arguments rather than quantities of the goods consumed (Quandt 1976). In this framework, it is assumed that a set of characteristics exist where the amounts of them are given by the compounds of vector Z and the amounts of a set of commodities are given by the components of vector C. It is then posited that U(z) is the utility function and that D(c) describes the manner in which amounts of attributes are produced by different amounts of the various commodities. Furthermore, let p be the vector of commodity prices and y the consumer's (that is, tripmaker's) income. Thus, assuming maximizing behavior, the consumer's rational travel consumption decisions are arrived at by solving the programming problem

$$\text{Maximizes} \quad U(z) \tag{4}$$

$$\text{Subject to} \quad z = D(c) \tag{5a}$$

$$pc \leq y \tag{5b}$$

$$c > o$$

(Lancaster 1966).

In practice, function $D(c)$ is assumed to be linear. Nevertheless, a noted result of this approach is that the individual tends to consume only one type or only a few types of commodities. This accords with the observation that a person traveling from i to j at a particular time normally employs a single travel mode for the principal part of the journey (Quandt 1976).

The preceding framework assumed not only a maximizing, rational consumer but, also, a homogenous population in every respect. Consider a situation where (1) all individuals with the same sociodemographic characteristics are living in the same place (for example, neighborhood) and (2) possess identical utility functions, since (3) they all have the same travel alternatives. The outcome of conditions (1), (2), and (3) is that all such individuals should make identical decisions. This, however, is not the case. Therefore, it is reasonable to posit that utility functions differ from individual to individual because of idiosyncrasies and some inherently random factors (Domenich and McFadden 1975; Quandt 1976). This argument suggests that a stochastic utility function may be more realistic in light of the social scientist's uncertainty regarding the correspondence between the predicted and observed behavior of individuals. Such a utility function is specified by

$$U_i = F(X^i, s) + E_i \tag{6}$$

where U_i is the utility of travel mode i and $F(X^i, s)$ is the representative utility function where X^i is a set of attributes of travel mode i and s is a set of sociodemographic characteristics. Then E_i represents the error in estimating U_i (Levin 1978). In other words, E_i represents the random factors and idiosyncrasies of people that contribute to the social scientist's uncertainty regarding the estimate of U_i. Domenich and McFadden (1975) argue that the rate at which an urban population takes a particular trip can indeed be treated as a continuous variable. However, the individual's decision to make a trip or choose a mode to make that trip is discrete. Formulation (6), extended to a probabilistic formulation, is for discrete outcomes of the choice process in which the effects of individual differences in tastes or idiosyncrasies are a part of the error structure (E_i) in (6). Thus, the probability of alternative i being chosen (P_i) is

$$P_i = \{P \ U_i > U_j, \text{ for all } i \neq j \} \quad (7a)$$

$$= P\{(E_j - E_i) < F(X^i, s) - F(X^j, s), \quad (7b)$$

$$\text{for all } i \neq j\}$$

$$= G(F(X^i, s) - F(X^j, s)) \quad (7c)$$

where G is the cumulative distribution function of ($E_j - E_i$) (Levin 1978; Quandt 1976). For ease of operationalization, $F(X,s)$ is usually assumed to be linear. Of more importance in the operationalization of this approach are assumptions concerning the nature of E_i, E_j. Under certain assumptions, one may obtain the probit model, or if E_i, E_j are assumed to have independent Weibull distributions, one obtains the logit model.

The logit model is widely used (for example, Recker and Stevens 1976; Train 1978), and its applications have produced satisfactory results that include reasonable economic interpretations (Quandt 1976). Perhaps one of the more attractive aspects of this approach, from a behavioral scientist's perspective, is that the most suitable data consist of disaggregate data that contain attitudinal measurements. Thus, if abstract characteristics of yet nonexisting modes are known and consumer attitudes concerning those characteristics are gathered, then it is theoretically possible to predict the demand for future travel modes. This is of course dependent on the clarity of consumer attitudes or perceptions with regard to attributes of the abstract mode. It is therefore suggested by Quandt (1976) that a problem in need of resolution is the determination of the informational content that can be extracted from a trip-maker's perceptions of the relative desirability of using different modes as opposed to their actual behavior.

Although the probabilistic behavioral model of urban travel behavior has provided a rich and useful addition to both the theory and method of studying urban travel behavior, it represents the sophisticated articulation of an effort in minimizing the social scientist's uncertainty regarding the prediction of urban travel behavior. Very little has been done concerning the incorporation of uncertainty in the choice decision of the transport consumer.

UNCERTAINTY AND INDIVIDUAL CHOICE

Recent work on a behavioral theory of travel behavior relies heavily on assumptions regarding the (1) existence and constructability of opportunity or preference sets, and (2) the integration of these concepts with postulates on utility and choice. The basis for direction in this field lies in the uncritical acceptance of the relevance of set theory—that is, that the principle of the excluded middle holds. For example, mode-choice is a set partitioned neatly into a set of urban subspaces. These become operationalized as choice sets. In addition, these principles govern the attributes assigned to modes, destinations, or trips. Thus, the notable assumption of set theory is that set assignments are unambiguous and that, therefore, all universes of entities can be partitioned into exhaustive and mutually exclusive sets.

Several problems commonly encountered in the operationalization of urban travel behavior theory reflect the problems of a theory of behavior based on set-theoretic principles. There is frequently difficulty in establishing classes of destinations, as well as making their attributes discrete. Crediting consumers with unambiguous set assignments in perceived choice sets and subjective preference relations is also a very difficult task (Pipkin 1978). Zadeh has extended the concept of sets to provide an account of the vagueness and ambiguity, which is the basis for objections to reliance on the principle of the excluded middle. As a simple example, consider that a fuzzy set S in a space Z is defined as a membership function f_S whose values are restricted to 0 or 1 (the principle of excluded middle). Continuous, rather than discrete, functions are then used to describe membership. Thus, the value of f_S (z) is taken as a measure of the degree of membership of Z in S (Zadeh 1965, 1968). Pipkin (1978) has shown that this approach can, theoretically, be applied to the study of urban travel behavior. This approach suggests that there is inexactness in the individual's choice decision that has not been previously considered in a formal manner.

To some, the concepts of inexactness, ambiguity, and vagueness are synonymous with uncertainty. The most obvious contemporary framework for the analysis of uncertainty is probability theory. However, Goguen (1968-69) argues that

> a probability distribution might be thought of as representing an inexact concept. But the manipulations

allowed in probability theory are different from those our example suggests for fuzzy sets. In fact, the theory is a calculus of vagueness, ambiguity, and ambivalence rather than likelihood.

Thus, it is argued that fuzzy set theory is capable of capturing many kinds of ambiguity in the modeling of urban travel behavior. More specifically, at the individual level, it provides an appealing description of (1) ambiguity in class membership, such as destinations in general choice-opportunity sets, or possession of specific predicates describing site and distance attributes of destinations in urban space; and (2) inexactness in the subjective values or preferences attached to modes, destinations, or trips.

As an example, consider the fuzzy modeling of distance. Inexactness in the perception of distance is a well-studied phenomenon. Subjective estimates of physical distance or travel time (often correlated with cost) are typically rounded to simple cognitive units of mile or minutes (or dollars and cents). This imprecision can be formalized by defining fuzzy sets in a space of points, X. The description "fairly close to" is made more precise as a fuzzy set $C \subset X \times X$. Where d is actual distance (travel time or travel cost), we can specify

$$f_c(x, y) = aC^{-B(x,y)} \qquad a, B > 0$$

From a fixed point, such as home, fuzzy distance minimization may be formulated as a fuzzy set $D \subset X$, which can be interpreted as "approximately the shortest." It is interesting to note that Kochin (1975) found that about half of his sample population interpreted "far distances" as a fuzzy set with a membership function that was monotonic and continuous. Thus, there is some evidence of the efficacy of this approach. Other relevant contributions include a study by Tanaka and Mizumoto (1975), which provides an explicit fuzzy formulation of an urban auto trip from the driver's perspective, and Pipkin's (1974) derivation of a general class of probabilistic destination choice models.

Implementation of the ideas contained in the fuzzy set literature await specification of appropriate mathematical forms for membership functions and development of appropriate estimation procedures. Pipkin (1978) provides a discussion of possible approaches, intuitive and otherwise. Kochen's (1975) study suggests the use of a series of behavioral assumptions on subjective "degree of agreement" to deduce a specific characteristic membership function.

The study of urban travel behavior seeks to understand the behavior of people moving through urban space. The workings of the mind in this complex area invariably encounter vagueness and ambiguity in cognition and ambivalence and inconsistency in evaluation. These ambiguities in human cognition have typically been handled essentially by attributing them to a statistical error structure. The use of fuzzy set theory is based on an assertion that many difficulties in handling the ambiguities of human cognition can be attributed to the persistent use of traditional set theory, which partitions the universe into discrete sets.

The concept of a compound fuzzy choice set propounded by Pipkin (1978) permits integration of the cognitive and affective aspects of destination choice, mode choice, or, more generally, spatial choice. Formulations of urban cognitive space (for example, Wolpert 1965; Horton and Reynolds 1971) have emphasized a dichotomy between information and preference. Evidence has accumulated that information and preference are not independent; in fact, their relationship appears to be very complex (Thompson 1965; Tardiff 1977). Thus, the fuzzy model provides a conceptually more natural account of subjective inexactness in the specification of choice sets and the formation of preferences. A major problem remains, since few estimation frameworks exist to operationalize this intuitively attractive approach. Estimation is one of the primary research tasks of researchers seeking to establish the utility of fuzzy set theory.

CONCLUDING REMARKS

This chapter has shown that consideration of uncertainty in the formulation of models of urban trend behavior does not necessarily contribute to either the applicability or behavioral realism of that model. Three approaches to modeling urban travel behavior were reviewed in a sequence that led from uncertainty maximizing to an economic/behavioral formulation to a personal cognitive application of fuzzy set theory. This progression led from a model barren of explicit behavioral tenets to an economic model incorporating individual idiosyncrasies to a new modeling approach that is largely cognitive-psychological. One might suggest that this only follows logically, since we progressed from an aggregate model to a disaggregate model. Although both disaggregate models allowed for "individual" idiosyncrasies, the economic/behavioral model fails to admit that people are uncertain about the exact definition of the concepts to be operationalized in application. Failure to recognize such an intuitively obvious phenomenon has resulted in contradictory results. For example, Hartgen (1977) argues that attitudinal variables only minimally improve mode-choice models, while Recker and Golob (1977) conclude just the opposite. Further confusing the issue is evidence that travel behavior may precede the formation of attitudes rather than the assumed antecedent relationship. These contradictory results are based on the assumption that attributes are unambiguously defined in the mind of any individual.

The conception of uncertainty varies substantially from model to model. This variation illustrates that there does not exist a uniform, rigorous definition of uncertainty. On the other hand, this does not necessarily indicate that the concept of uncertainty is impotent; rather, its power as a concept is due to the many contexts in which it is useful. It is an intuitively appealing concept, since, as human beings, we all have had some experience with one or more forms of uncertainty. This is one reason that in order to enrich the theoretical content of models of urban travel behavior, an approach such as that of fuzzy set theory is advocated. Its importance in prediction and application must await development of appropriate empirical work and estimation methods. It has, however, already enriched the theory of urban travel behavior through its ability to present a kind of uncertainty common to urban trip-makers regardless of socioeconomic status.

APPENDIX 1

The gravity model is developed by analogy with Newton's law of gravitational force, F_{ij}, between two masses m_i and m_j separated by distance d_{ij}. It is formally defined as

$$F_{ij} = \lambda \left(\frac{m_i m_j}{d_{ij}^2} \right) \qquad (A1.1)$$

where λ = a constant. The transport model developed from the above equation is

$$T_{ij} = k \left(O_i D_j / C_{ij}^2 \right) \qquad (A1.2)$$

where k is a constant; T_{ij} is the number of trips between zones i and j; O_i is the total number of trips originating from zone i; D_j is the total number of trips ending in zone j; and C_{ij} is a travel cost term analogous to the distance term. The following constraints should, however, be satisfied by (A1)

$$O_i = \sum_j T_{ij} \quad \text{constraint (1)}$$

$$D_j = \sum_i T_{ij} \quad \text{constraint (2)}$$

Constraints (1) and (2) can be satisfied if sets of constraints describing trip-production zones, A_i, and trip-attracting zones, B_j, are introduced. Wilson (1970) calls them "balancing factors."

The gravity model modified to satisfy the constraints (1) and (2) becomes

$$T_{ij} = A_i B_j O_i D_j f(c_{ij}) \quad (A1.3)$$

where
$$A_i = \left[\sum_j B_j D_j f(C_{ij}) \right]^{-1} \quad (A1.3a)$$

and
$$B_j = \left[\sum_i A_i O_i f(C_{ij}) \right]^{-1} \quad (A1.3b)$$

APPENDIX 2

To generate a good estimate of T_{ij}, the following variables must be defined:

T_{ij} = the number of trips originating in zone i and ending in zone j

O_i = the total number of trips originating in zone i

D_j = the total number of trips ending in zone j

C_{ij} = the cost of traveling from zone i to zone j

C = the total expenditure of trip-making

The constraints on T_{ij} that restrict the number of assignments giving rise to the trip distribution are:

$$\sum_j T_{ij} = O_i \quad (A2.1)$$

$$\sum_i T_{ij} = D_j \quad (A2.2)$$

$$\sum_i \sum_j T_{ij} C_{ij} = C \quad (A2.3)$$

Suppose T is the total number of trips (that is, $T = \sum_i \sum_j T_{ij}$). How many assignments give rise to the most probable matrix T_{ij}? Let the assignment function be $G(\{T_{ij}\})$.

T_{11} can be selected from T, T_{12} from $T-T_{11}$, and so forth. Therefore, the number of possible assignments is the number of ways of selecting T_{11} from T, multiplied by the number of ways of selecting T_{12} from $T-T_{11}$, multiplied by the number of ways of selecting T_{13} from $T-T_{11}-T_{12}$, and so forth. Thus,

$$W(\{T_{ij}\}) = \frac{T!}{T_{11}!(T-T_{11})!} \cdot \frac{(T-T_{11})!}{T_{12}!(T-T_{11}-T_{12})!} \cdot \ldots \frac{T!}{\prod_{ij} T_{ij}!} \quad (A2.4)$$

$W(\{T_{ij}\})$ is now maximized subject to constraints (1), (2), and (3) in order to find the most probable T_{ij}.

To obtain the set of T_{ij}s that maximizes $W(\{T_{ij}\})$ as previously defined with the noted constraints, the Lagrangian L has to be maximized, where

$$L = \ln W + \sum_i \lambda_i^{(1)} (O_i - \sum_j T_{ij}) + \sum_j \lambda_j^{(2)}$$

$$(b_i - \sum_i T_{ij}) + \beta (C - \sum_i \sum_j T_{ij} c_{ij}) \quad (A2.5)$$

where $\lambda_i^{(1)}$, $\lambda_j^{(2)}$, and β are Lagrangian multipliers. (Note: it is more convenient to maximize lnW than W; then, it is possible to use Sterling's approximation $\ln N! = N\ln N - N$ to estimate the factorial terms.)

The T_{ij}s that maximize L and that therefore constitute the most probable distribution of trips are the solutions of

$$\frac{\delta L}{\delta T_{ij}} = 0 \text{ and the constraints.}$$

Using Sterling's approximation

$$\frac{\delta \ln N!}{\delta N} = \ln N \quad (A2.6)$$

therefore

$$\frac{\delta L}{\delta T_{ij}} = -\ln T_{ij} - \lambda_i^{(1)} - \lambda_j^{(2)} - \beta C_{ij} \quad (A2.7)$$

and the variables, when

$$T_{ij} = \exp(-\lambda_i^{(1)} - \lambda_j^{(2)} - \beta C_{ij}). \quad (A2.8)$$

Substituting constraints (1) and (2)

$$\exp(-\lambda_i^{(1)}) = O_i \left[\sum_j \exp(-\lambda_i^{(2)} - \beta C_{ij}) \right]^{-1} \quad \text{(A2.9a)}$$

$$\exp(-\lambda_j^{(2)}) = D_j \left[\sum_i \exp(-\lambda_i^{(1)} - \beta C_{ij}) \right]^{-1} \quad \text{(A2.9b)}$$

To obtain the final result in more familiar form, let

$$A_i = \exp(-\lambda_i^{(1)}) / O_i \quad \text{(A2.10a)}$$

$$B_j = \exp(-\lambda_j^{(2)}) / D_j \quad \text{(A2.10b)}$$

which then yields

$$T_{ij} = A_i B_j O_i D_j \exp(-\beta C_{ij}) \quad \text{(A2.11a)}$$

where

$$A_i = \left[\sum_j B_j D_j \exp(-\beta C_{ij}) \right]^{-1} \quad \text{(A2.11b)}$$

$$B_j = \left[\sum_i A_i O_i \exp(-\beta C_{ij}) \right]^{-1} \quad \text{(A2.11c)}$$

REFERENCES

Domenich, T. A., and McFadden, D. 1975. Urban Travel Behavior: A Behavioral Analysis. Amsterdam: North-Holland.

Goguen, J. A. 1968-69. "The Logic of Inexact Concepts." Synthese 9: 325-73.

Hartgen, D. T. 1974. "Attitudinal and Situational Variables Influencing Urban Mode Choice: Some Empirical Findings." Transportation Research 3: 377-92.

Horton, F. E., and Reynolds, D. R. 1971. "Effects of Urban Spatial Structure on Individual Behavior." Economic Geography 47: 36-48.

Jaynes, E. T. 1957. "Information Theory and Statistical Mechanics." Physical Review 106: 620-30.

Johnson, M. A. 1975. Psychological Variables and Choices Between Auto and Transit Travel: A Critical Research Review. Travel Demand Forecasting Project Working Paper No. 7509, University of California at Berkeley.

Khinchin, A. E. 1957. Mathematical Foundations of Information Theory. New York: Dover.

Kochen, M. 1975. "Applications of Fuzzy Sets in Psychology." In Fuzzy Sets and Their Applications to Cognitive and Decision Processes, edited by L. Zadeh, et al., pp. 395-408. New York: Academic Press.

Lancaster, K. J. 1966. "A New Approach to Consumer Theory." Journal of Political Economy 84: 132-57.

Levin, R. C. 1978. "Allocation in Surface Transportation: Does Rate Regulation Matter?" Bell Journal of Economics 9: 18-45.

Pipkin, J. S. 1974. "Two Probabilistic Revealed Preference Models of Choice Process in Recurrent Urban Travel." Ph.D. dissertation, Northwestern University, Chicago.

──────. 1978. "Fuzzy Sets and Spatial Choice." Annals of the Association of American Geographers 68: 196-204.

Quandt, R. E. 1976. "The Theory of Travel Demand." Transportation Research 10: 411-13.

Recker, W. W., and Golob, T. F. 1976. "An Attitudinal Mode Choice Model." Transportation Research 10: 299-310.

Recker, W. W., and Stevens, R. F. 1977. "An Attitudinal Travel Demand Model for Non-Work Trips of Homogenously Constrained Segments of a Population." Transportation Research 11: 167-76.

Shannon, C., and Weaver, W. 1949. The Mathematical Theory of Communication. Urbana: University of Illinois Press.

Stopher, R. R., and Meyburg, A. H. 1975. Urban Transportation Modeling and Planning. Lexington, Mass.: Lexington Books.

Tanaka, K., and Mizumato, M. 1975. "Fuzzy Programs and Their Execution." In Fuzzy Sets and Their Applications to Cognitive and Decision Processes, edited by L. Zadeh, et al., pp. 41-76. New York: Academic Press.

Tardiff, T. J. 1977. "Causal Inferences Involving Transportation Attitudes and Behavior." Transportation Research 11: 399-404.

Thompson, D. L. 1965. "New Concept: Subjective Distance." Journal of Retailing 39: 1-6.

Train, K. 1978. "A Validation Test of a Disaggregate Mode Choice Model." Transportation Research 12: 167-74.

Webber, M. J. 1977. "Pedagogy, Again: What Is Entropy?" Annals of the Association of American Geographers 67: 254-66.

Wilson, A. G. 1967. "A Statistical Theory of Spatial Distribution Models." Transportation Research 1: 253-69.

_____. 1970. Entropy in Urban and Regional Modelling. London: Pion.

Wilson, A.G.; Hawkins, A. F.; Hill, G. H.; and Wagon, D. J. 1969. "Calibrating and Testing the SELNEC Transport Model." Regional Studies 3: 337-50.

Wolpert, J. 1965. "Behavioral Aspects of the Decision to Migrate." Papers and Proceedings of the Regional Science Association.

Zadeh, L. 1965. "Fuzzy Sets." Information and Control 8: 338-53.

_____. 1968. "Fuzzy Algorithms." Information and Control 12: 94-102.

Zadeh, L.; Fu, K.; Tonaka, K.; and Shimura, M. 1975. Fuzzy Sets and Their Applications to Cognitive and Decision Processes. New York: Academic Press.

13
UNCERTAINTY IN PUBLIC OPINION ASSESSMENT
Robert Mason
G. David Faulkenberry

Uncertainty in public opinion assessment stems from two sources. First is the difference between public opinion, as defined by such classical theorists as John Locke and James Madison and, more recently, A. Lawrence Lowell and Walter Lippmann, and what is measured as public opinion by present-day pollsters. Second is the neglect, both conceptually and operationally, of the role of equivocal responses in public opinion research. The thesis of this chapter is that attention to the second source of uncertainty may well contribute to reducing uncertainty from the first.

Uncertainty from the first source—use of the term <u>public opinion</u> by political theorists and pollsters alike—is a fundamental one that obscures much of the relevance for assessing the importance of survey results in political decision making. Nisbet (1975) recently formulated the distinction most clearly: the term <u>public opinion</u> should be confined to the public as people organized by convention and tradition into a community in which opinion is rooted in experience and knowledge and generated by deeply held convictions and sentiments. He argues that the term <u>popular opinion</u> should describe what pollsters report: the public as a mere aggregate and opinion as a transitory collective that is summarized from a random sample who will respond "yes," "no," or "maybe" to any opinion question asked.

There is no question that responsible pollsters are aware of this distinction. Forty years ago, Gallup and Rae (1940) laid down the justification for what was then a new approach for ascertaining mass interests of the general public. They noted then that "polls of public opinion command interest because they articulate what the mass of the common people thinks about the headline issues of everyday life" (p. 91). Scientific sampling and face-to-face interviews were new on the U.S. scene then, a time when democracy as a viable political system was threatened from many quarters. Scientific polling was proffered as a procedure by which much of the intuition and uncertainty concerning public opinion could be assessed more accurately. Gallup and Rae viewed the country as an enormous community that had changed greatly from the agrarian economy of the founding fathers, where public opinion had been confined to a small and exclusive minority of educated persons, who enjoyed a monopoly of economic and political power. They contended that a new kind of public opinion had appeared on the land, developed from the impetus of growing industrialism and urbanism, mass education, and revolutions in transportation and in development of the mass media. The business of politics was no longer confined to the old-fashioned face-to-face relationships of a small governing class. Political power had been diffused, according to these authors, so that many voices claimed to speak for the people. The problem of building a methodology to ascertain this mass opinion of people was apparent to them. Infrequent elections often were not clear expressions of public opinion, and political leaders depended on all sorts of impressionistic ways to monitor the public will. Scientific polling was advocated as a methodology by which ordinary citizens could find self-expression on important public issues.

The approach was not without its problems, however. Gallup and Rae, for instance, recognized that poll results reflect answers that may be inconsistent and confused—the stereotypic responses of propaganda rather than the results of thinking through an issue carefully. They still interpreted this effect as an important contribution of surveys, for they identified the deficiencies in public thinking and the educational needs concerning public issues.

Moreover, the danger of oversimplifying the description of opinion by reducing various points of view to simple "yes" or "no" responses was recognized. As a way of widening the sphere of response choices, increasing attention was paid to those who expressed "no opinion," and rudimentary modeling of people who held this equivocal opinion position was undertaken. Surveys came to be viewed as providing more than simple measures of referendum-type situations, where only "yes" or "no" options were available. More attention was paid to diagnosing the stability of opinion states and their antecedents; the importance of equivocal opinion positions was recognized as well.

Early on, in the late 1940s, schemas were developed that specified more precisely if opinions expressed were informed ones. Respondents were asked, for example, to report their awareness of an issue so their knowledge about the topic could be measured.

Reasons for one's views could be asked and the intensity of opinions ascertained. Complex public issues could be broken apart, specific views asked about specific aspects of a problem, and responses aggregated to describe an overall opinion position. Gallup's (1947) quintamensional approach is an example of this schema.

Statistical modeling often was confined to simple two-way comparisons; this rudimentary approach allowed one to learn if opinion responses were informed or uninformed and the depth to which opinion states were held. What the results showed was that the uninformed frequently held equivocal opinions and that these persons tended to be in lower socioeconomic groupings. As an issue developed, continuing surveys were thought to reflect changes in public understanding of issues and a commensurate crystallization in public thinking. Little conceptual work concentrated on the nature of equivocal opinion positions, however. Their importance was recognized primarily as a residual response alternative to opinion questions.

THE IMPORTANCE OF THINKING ABOUT AN ISSUE

Up to now, equivocal responses have been considered of the simple "no opinion" type. This response may conceal an important distinction, one which unfortunately has received only passing attention in the survey community. Converse (1970), one of the few who has discussed the issue, has recommended that "no opinion" scores identify those who are truly ambivalent and represent a zero point in the attitude or opinion continuum. A "don't know" response should identify holders of nonopinions and be located off the opinion continuum in recognition of a state not on the opinion continuum. Converse formulated his recommendation after analyzing his own panel turnover data and from examination of the literature on attitude change. His own analysis suggested that less than 20 percent of the total sample were holders of real and stable substantive opinions; the remaining 80 percent represented confessions of "no opinion" or random responses. Only a minority—some 35 percent of the total sample—had accepted the interviewer's invitation to proffer a "no opinion" response when asked. Even in this setting, where equivocal opinions were sought, people were remarkably obliging in giving substantive responses. Moreover, research of experimental psychologists underscore the fact that formation and change of substantive opinions do take work and practice. Converse (1970) reached this conclusion after reviewing much of this research; subsequent experiments point to the same conclusion. The level of information a person holds about important issues probably can be measured more reliably than one's true opinion; therefore, the role of information level in opinion formation may become an important variable in modeling the true opinion states of people. The assumption here is that people who hold considerable well-organized and internally consistent information about an issue are likely to believe that the issue is centrally important to them as well. An analysis of the _fit_ between information level and organization and issue importance seems a reasonable first step in assessing the true opinion responses of people.

The amount of thinking a person does about an issue also may have a powerful effect on the establishment of substantive opinions. One piece of recent evidence supporting this assertion is a series of papers by Tesser and his associates. Formation of favorable or unfavorable opinions may come about, according to Tesser and Cowan (1977), as a person thinks about information that is consistent with his/her opinion or reinterprets inconsistent information. Opinion polarization, however, is not always related to mere thought. Tesser and Leone (1977) report that polarization depends on the involvement of salient or important beliefs a person holds about an issue and on the rules of inference s/he employs in organizing this information. Cognitive schemas control the information that is selected for thought, and since different schemas can be relevant, an opinion may become polarized, depending on which schema is employed. Cognitive schemas, according to Tesser and Leone (1977), are naive theories and function much like scientific theories. An event can be defined or characterized on a number of dimensions, but a formal theory or schema prescribes which dimensions are relevant and which can be ignored. Schemas contain rules for making inferences about an issue—and just as scientists may use different theories for explaining the same phenomenon, people can formulate different schemas for thinking about the same issue. The use of different schemas, according to these authors, would bring into use a different set of beliefs and information and lead to different inferences. A change in schema would mean a change in opinion, and thinking would accentuate these changes. Thus, opinions are not static entities, but function as dynamic cognitive processes that undergo reformulation as new information about events is processed.

Thought may be considered cognitive work under rules of a schema. If a person has only a poorly developed or no schema for thinking about an issue, one would expect him/her to have a non-opinion in the Converse sense. This stems from the fact that there would be no mechanism for selecting which information about the issue is important. The individual would focus on any of his/her beliefs with equal probability. There would be no rules for making inferences; therefore, any thinking would result in few cognitive changes. Substantive opinions proffered in response to the typical closed opinion item would not always represent a true opinion because some would not be based on thinking about an issue. They might well be in response to perceived interviewer expectations, to well-established acquiescent sets, or to a plethora of other influences. The task of the survey analyst is to separate opinion responses that are based on thinking from "noise" or other confounding influences.

The importance of distinguishing accurately between "no opinion" and "don't know" responses can now be spelled out. "No opinion" responses, according to our formulation, are based on thinking from a schema. "Don't know" responses, however, are not based on thought. Suppose, for example, one can accurately classify responses to an opinion item as 30 percent "agree," 30 percent "disagree," and 40 percent "no opinion"/"don't know." The modal response is important for the "no opinion" group is likely to differ greatly from the "don't knows." According to our formulation, the "no opinion" group is processing information, and the response may well reflect an inability to develop consistent cognitions for a number of reasons, for example, events or new information have produced inconsistent cognitions. Thought may well alter cognitions that will lead to greater consistency and, hence, to opinion polarization. Therefore, a "no opinion" response suggests a group that is likely to change opinions by thinking about an issue.*
A "don't know" response, however, suggests that no schema has been developed for processing information and, hence, an opinion state has not been formed. More work is required for the individual to develop the necessary schema for this to occur.

THE PROBLEM OF NONSAMPLING ERRORS

Opinion items in public opinion surveys contain an evaluative response alternative (for example, "favor" or "oppose," "agree" or "disagree"), as well as an equivocal response category (that is, "no opinion" or "don't know") for those who refuse or cannot select a substantive opinion response. Some employ a Likert-type item that offers opinion-intensity alternatives, such as "agree strongly,"

---

*Using survey data, however, Converse (1970), among others, has noted that "no opinion" responses may be intense and well-thought-out and would require new information and well-informed arguments before they would change.

"agree," "no opinion," "disagree," or "disagree strongly," in an effort to measure intensity or strength of conviction, as well as direction.

If we consider only opinion direction and assume that each respondent has a "true" classification at the time of a survey, we have 16 possibilities:

Observed Classification

		Favor	Ambivalent	Oppose	Nonopinion
True Classification	Favor	X			
	Ambivalent		X		
	Oppose			X	
	Nonopinion				X

If we had perfect operational methods for classification, all observations would be along the diagonal, shown as "Xs." Nonsampling errors are the reasons this is not the case. The nonsampling errors occur in what seem to be even the most straightforward of observations (Faulkenberry and Tortora 1978). We will concentrate on the particular problem of misclassification of ambivalent and nonopinion response groups.

First, there is the misclassification due to respondents giving a substantive opinion response who should be classified as a nonopinion. Converse (1970), for instance, felt he had evidence in his panel study that a high percent of respondents belonging in the nonopinion group gave substantive opinion responses rather than a "don't know" response. Second, there is the difficulty of separating ambivalence from nonopinions. Users of Likert-scale items with "neutral" or "no opinion" alternatives consider this a low-intensity response; however, a true ambivalent respondent may be well informed on the subject, which is quite different from a nonopinion. DuBois and Burns (1975), for example, have noted:

> Operationally, it therefore may be possible to separate ambivalent from indifferent respondents if one has data concerning the respondents' level of involvement. It is hypothesized that the ambivalent respondent should

EFFECT OF MISCLASSIFICATION ON STATISTICAL ANALYSIS

We will first consider some implications of true nonopinion respondents giving substantive opinion responses. Then, we will discuss the problem of operationally separating ambivalent and nonopinion response groups.*

Let p_F, p_O, p_A, and p_N equal the true proportions in the population who favor, oppose, are ambivalent, and have nonopinions on a particular opinion issue measured by a single item. To illustrate misclassification of nonopinions, let the F, O, and A groups be classified without error and denote the probabilities for misclassification of a nonopinion respondent by $\hat{p}_{F\,N}$, $p_{O\,N}$, and $p_{A\,N}$. If $\hat{p}_F$ is the observed proportion who favor the issue in a simple random sample of size n, then the expected value of $\hat{p}_F$ is given in equation (1):

$$E(\hat{p}_F) = p_F + \text{Prob (N and F)}$$
$$= p_F + p_N p_{F\,N} \qquad (1)$$

and the variance of $\hat{p}_f$ is given in equation (2):

$$V(\hat{p}_F) = \frac{E(\hat{p}_F)\,[1 - E(\hat{p}_F)]}{n} \qquad (2)$$

The bias in the estimate is $p_N p_{F|N}$. Similar results hold for the O and A groups.

For example, if $p_F = .3$, $p_N = .3$, and $p_{F|N} = .5$ (that is, a nonopinion respondent is equally likely to express favor or oppose), then

$$E(\hat{p}_F) = .3 + (.3)(.5) = .45$$

and

$$V(\hat{p}_F) = \frac{1}{n}\,(.45)(.55)$$

---

*The terms <u>no opinion</u> and <u>ambivalence</u> are used interchangeably.

Note that in this example, if $n \geq 44$, the expected value of p_F is two or more standard deviations away from the true value.

Suppose we are estimating opinion change for the population based on independent samples at two points in time. If there has actually been no change in the population, then $\hat{p}_{F1} - \hat{p}_{F2}$ gives an unbiased estimate of change, that is, $E(\hat{p}_{F1} - \hat{p}_{F2}$ no change) = 0. In fact, the chi-square statistic for testing $H_o : p_{F1} = p_{F2}$ has (for large samples) the correct null distribution. However, if a change in opinion in the population has occurred, that is, $P_{F1} \neq P_{F2}$, then the estimated change is given in equation (3):

$$E(\hat{p}_{F1} - \hat{p}_{F2}) = p_{F1} - p_{F2} + P_{N1}P_{F1\ N1} - P_{N2}P_{F2\ N2} \qquad (3)$$

Therefore, the change in P_F is not estimated unbiasedly by the difference in sample proportions. The previous paragraph shows one effect of misclassification on estimating overall population proportions. On an individual basis, the model proposed by Rasch (1961) has received considerable attention. The model can be formulated as follows:

$$p(x_{\nu i}) = \frac{\exp(T_\nu - a_i)x_{\nu i}}{1 + \exp(T_\nu - a_i)} \qquad (4)$$

where $x_{\nu i}$ is the response of respondent ν to item i; T_ν is the opinion measure of respondent ν; and a_i is the affective value of item i.

Now suppose that some respondents are in the nonopinion class, N. Let $\bar{N}$ denote the complement of N, and assume respondents belonging to $\bar{N}$ are not misclassified. Then, for this group we have

$$p(x_{\nu i}|\bar{N}) = \frac{\exp(T_\nu - a_i)x_{\nu i}}{1 + \exp(T_\nu - a_i)} \qquad (5)$$

This results in the model

$$p(x_{\nu i}) = p(x_{\nu i}|\bar{N})p_{\bar{N}} + p(x_{\nu i}|N)p_N$$

$$= (1 - p_N)\left[\frac{\exp(T_\nu - a_i)x_{\nu i}}{1 + \exp(T_\nu - a_i)}\right] + p(x_{\nu i}|N)p_N \qquad (6)$$

The proportion of the population who are nonopinions is p_N and $p(X_{vi}|N)$ is the probability that a person with a nonopinion gives a substantive opinion response X_{vi}. It can be shown that in general, the maximum likelihood estimates are different when the nonopinion group is allowed in the model and the asymptotic variances of the estimates of T_vs and a_is are increased.

These examples by no means provide extensive coverage of the effect that a nonopinion group has on the statistical analysis. We have considered only the simplest case of nonopinions being misclassified in the substantive opinion groups. However, it does illustrate how the nonopinion group can be included in models for statistical analysis, and it shows some of the effects this group has on the analysis. As well, the case of nonopinions reported in the opinion groups is possibly the most common misclassification because of the stigma of ignorance attached to a "don't know" response; as Schuman and Presser (1979) point out, many polls discourage this response.

SEPARATING AMBIVALENT AND NONOPINION RESPONSE GROUPS

Two considerations are involved in distinguishing between ambivalent and nonopinion responses. First, one must recognize that there will be a substantial number of nonopinions associated with many social issues, and these nonopinions should be considered as separate and different in analysis and interpretation of survey results. Second, there is a legitimate ambivalent state on many issues (especially complex ones), and this group belongs in the "middle" position on an attitude or opinion continuum. Nonopinions should not be included with ambivalent opinions. Although many will agree with these ideas, there is much difficulty in distinguishing operationally between these two states. Our review of the literature and consideration of alternative approaches suggest the following:

Related Knowledge or Involvement Items

Stored information or knowledge about the topic appears to be a necessary precondition for the formation of truly substantive and ambivalent opinions. Measurement of level of information, as Converse (1970) has noted, is likely to be far easier and more reliable than measurement of true opinion states. Inclusion in opinion models of variables, such as the knowledge one has about the topic or the individual's level of involvement concerning the issue, may well enhance the ability of survey researchers to evaluate more precisely the meaning of responses to opinion items. One should expect, for example, holders of nonopinions to be less informed and less involved than those with truly substantive opinions.

Use of Filter Questions

Two items might be asked prior to the opinion question. One, based on our review of the work of Tesser and his colleagues, would ask if the respondent has thought much about the issue. The second, employed by both Converse (1970) and Schuman and Presser (1979) invites the respondent to proffer an equivocal response. Assuming respondents can be grouped into a fourfold table (below) from responses to these two items, one would expect that those who had thought about an issue and who said they had an opinion would have true substantive opinions. Those who had not thought about the issue and who said they did not have an opinion would be true nonopinions. Those who had thought about the issue and who said they did not have an opinion probably have true ambivalent opinions, and those who had not thought about the issue but who said they had an opinion are probable nonopinions. By the use of these two filters, one may be able to measure true favor, oppose, ambivalent, and nonopinion responses more accurately.

	Respondent Reported Substantive Opinion	Respondent Reported No Opinion
Respondent Had Thought about the Issue	True Substantive Opinion	True Ambivalence
Respondent Had Not Thought about the Issue	Probable Nonopinions	True Nonopinion

Interviewer Decisions concerning Ambivalent and Nonopinion States

Faulkenberry and Mason (1978) used judgments of interviewers to distinguish between ambivalent and nonopinion states. While an effort was made to check for confounding effects of responses to items asked early in the interview (none was found), the possibility remains that subtle cues proffered by respondents affected or biased interviewer judgments. In their study, interviewers were instructed to score those who did not understand the opinion item as nonopinion, while those who understood the question but could not select a substantive (favor or oppose) alternative as ambivalent. A discriminant analysis showed major group differences between the ambivalent and nonopinion groups.

Internal Analysis of Opinion Items

Internal analysis of item responses may measure true ambivalent and nonopinion states more accurately. DuBois and Burns (1975), report that users of the question mark (?) alternative in self-administered attitude instruments hold an intermediate or ambivalent position on the attitude continuum. They base their conclusion on a comparison of variances of average total scores for each response alternative. (They had hypothesized that larger variance of the "?" response would have been evidence of motivation rather than showing an ambivalent attitudinal position.) No difference was found. They also found that means of average total scores for each response category were on a straight line with the "?" means in the "middle" position. They noted, however, that additional understanding of the meaning of the "?" response can be achieved by analysis of responses across different formats and by a comparison of the average total score of items with response category variability. Additional insight may be achieved, according to these authors, by allowing respondents to state their reasons for selecting the "?" response, thereby permitting one to differentiate between ambivalent and other response states.

These four approaches are by no means exhaustive, but are only suggested lines for further inquiry.

THE IMPORTANCE OF UNCERTAINTY IN
PUBLIC OPINION ASSESSMENT

We have argued that one source of uncertainty in public opinion assessment stems from the inability to distinguish among substantive, ambivalent and nonopinion states and that errors associated with this measurement problem are likely to affect the accuracy of many opinion polls. We have illustrated how failure to distinguish accurately between opinion and nonopinion states can affect the statistical analysis and we have reviewed possible operational approaches to better make this distinction.

We don't know if the proportion of true "no opinion" and "don't know" responses is grossly underestimated with conventional methods employed in contemporary sample surveys. However, the evidence points to the possibility of underestimation and to the need for additional work. Confusion over the measurement of true opinion states remains at the root of criticism concerning the efficacy of much contemporary polling, and the claimed accuracy of public opinion assessments may well be strengthened by further consideration of equivocal responses to opinion items.

REFERENCES

Converse, Philip E. 1970. "Attitudes and Non-attitudes. Continuation of a Dialogue." In The Quantitative Analysis of Social Problems, edited by Edward R. Tufte. Reading, Mass.: Addison-Wesley.

DuBois, Bernard, and Burns, John A. 1975. "An Analysis of the Meaning of the Question Mark Response Category in Attitude Scales." Educational and Psychological Measurement 35 (Winter): 869-84.

Faulkenberry, G. David, and Mason, Robert. 1978. "Characteristics of Nonopinion and No Opinion Response Groups." Public Opinion Quarterly 42: 533-43.

Faulkenberry, G. David, and Tortora, R. D. 1979. "A Study of Measurement Error Suitable for a Classroom Example." The American Statistician 33 (February): 19-22.

Gallup, George. 1947. "The Quintamensional Plan of Question Design." Public Opinion Quarterly 11 (Fall, 1975): 385-93.

Gallup, George, and Rae, Saul Forbes. 1940. The Pulse of Democracy. New York: Simon & Schuster.

Nisbet, Robert. 1975. "Public Opinion Versus Popular Opinion." The Public Interest 41: 166-92.

Rasch, G. 1961. "On General Laws and the Meaning of Measurement in Psychology." Proceedings of the Fourth Berkeley Symposium on Mathematical Statistics and Probability Theory 4: 321-33.

Schuman, Howard, and Presser, Stanley. 1979. "The Assessment of 'No Opinion' in Attitude Surveys." In <u>Sociological Methodology 1979</u>, edited by Karl F. Schuessler, pp. 241-75. San Francisco: Josey-Bass.

Tesser, Abraham, and Cowan, Claudia L. 1977. "Some Attitudinal and Cognitive Consequences of Thought." <u>Journal of Research in Personality</u> 11: 216-26.

Tesser, Abraham, and Leone, Christopher. 1977. "Cognitive Schemas and Thought as Determinants of Attitude Change." <u>Journal of Experimental Social Psychology</u> 13 (July): 340-56.

14
RISK AND UNCERTAINTY IN POLITICAL CHOICE
Eugene J. Alpert

INTRODUCTION

"What are Jimmy Carter's chances of winning reelection to the Presidency in 1980?" is a question that many potential candidates need to consider before deciding upon a course of action (or inaction). Since even a year or less can be considered a political lifetime, it is extremely difficult for one to estimate what those chances will be so many months ahead, yet to run an effective campaign these days, planning must often begin years ahead of an election. Unfortunately, political strategists are unable to rely upon repeated trials of past events to estimate the chances of winning an election. Instead, they must rely upon their experience, intuition, and perhaps some sample data, such as public opinion polls or personal contacts. In other words, subjective estimates of the chances or probabilities of events must be relied upon to chart appropriate strategies when complete information about the consequences of one's actions is unavailable.

Since political decision-making involves the selection of alternatives under uncertain conditions, the use of Bayesian decision theory (Schmitt 1969; Winkler 1972; Phillips 1973) as a framework for analyzing political choice behavior is most appropriate. The Bayesian approach to decision-making involves the selection of a decision rule that minimizes expected losses under uncertainty. Uncertainty is a situation in which the probability relationship between alternatives and their consequences is unknown. A particular advantage of this method is that it allows for the use of subjective probabilities, which can be revised at any point on the basis of new information to identify an alternative that can be chosen to minimize expected loss. When these probabilities are estimated by the use of subjective probabilities, decision-making under uncertainty becomes decision-making under risk.

Consideration of the effects of uncertainty and risk on decision-making has not been widespread in the political science field. Attention has been focused either on the empirical effects of these factors (that is, Kingdon 1968; Hershey 1974) without a theoretical perspective or on the theory of subjective decision-making without a strong empirical linkage (that is, Shepsle 1972a, 1972b, 1972c; Ferejohn and Noll 1978). A few studies have attempted to bridge the gap (Black 1972; Rabushka and Shepsle 1972, Ben-Dak and Finsterbusch 1974; Ferejohn and Fiorina 1974; Fiorina 1974; Rohde 1974; Alpert 1976), but greater specification and operationalization of these models are required before more progress can be made in this area. Some researchers have been successful in applying the Bayesian method for analyzing and comparing estimates (McGowan 1974; Budge and Farlie 1975, 1976, 1977), but the use of subjective probabilities has not been fully integrated into their analyses.

Although the research in this area is not as bountiful as it is in other disciplines, such as psychology (Edwards and Tversky 1967), economics (Mansfield 1970), sociology (Iversen 1970), and business (Tummala and Henshaw 1976), it is growing and attracting more interest. This is the result of not only increased interest in the study of perceptions in political decision-making but partly as a reaction to the restrictive assumption of perfect information found in many formal models of electoral competition that have appeared over the last 15 years or so. These are often highly complex, mathematical representations of political behavior under ideal conditions, which seek to identify and describe equilibrium positions of candidates' public policies on spatial dimensions (Riker and Ordeshook 1973). Although the formal models have had considerable heuristic value and have led the way toward the development of systematic theory in political science, their empirical relevance, especially when perfect information is a basic assumption, has been questioned. Political scientists are therefore looking at alternative formulations that can relax this assumption and describe choices as a function of one's subjective perceptions of the political environment.

The analysis of the effects of risk and uncertainty has thus become an important avenue of research in the study of political decision-making. However, it is significant that such research has not yet been fully compared nor well integrated so that important generalizations deduced from the research can be systematically related to build theories of decision-making. Part of the problem is that risk and uncertainty have various interpretations and uses, some of which imply that the terms are interchangeable, while others clearly consider them to represent quite different and distinct circumstances.

It is the purpose of this study to analyze the interpretations of risk and uncertainty in political decision-making in order to identify important independent and dependent variables that have been or could be of concern to researchers. This will help reveal not only gaps in present research but, also, indicate paths of future inquiries. This has particular significance, since the limitations of frequentist (objective probability) models can be clarified, and the value of Bayesian decision models to analyze dynamic situations in which decisions can be revised according to newly received sample information can be shown. Therefore, by illustrating the utility and versatility of considering risk and uncertainty in subjective decision-making, it is hoped that this will serve as an impetus for future research to be applied to other decision-making situations.

THE MEANING OF RISK AND UNCERTAINTY

The Bayesian approach to decision-making starts with the assumption that certain characteristics of the decision problem can be identified. These include the unit of analysis, the states of the world, a set of actions or alternative choices, and a set of payoffs.

The individual is usually the basic unit of analysis and is charged with making the decision. S/he is presumed to be uncertain about which value or condition of a parameter is the true one to occur. These values are the <u>states of the world</u> or <u>states of nature</u>, which are assumed to be mutually exclusive and collectively exhaustive. Empirically, one could envision the states of the world as representing possible policy positions (Shepsle 1972a, 1972c), voter turnout (Ferejohn and Fiorina 1975), the level of salience of an issue to groups in a constituency (Fiorina 1974), or the possible reactions of a country in response to a buildup of arms by another country (Alpert 1976). A political actor must choose an action, such as adopting or emphasizing a policy position, for which the net benefit or payoff would be determined by the extent to which his/her estimate of majority opinion fell short of the true majority position (that is, true state of the world). The decision problem would be to choose the best alternative action to achieve the highest payoff possible.

When the true state of the world, say θ_j (see Figure 14.1), is known, the probability of the true state of the world, $P(\theta_j)$, equals 1 and 0 for all other possible states. This is called decision-making under <u>certainty</u>. The outcome is deterministic, since the optimum choice can be made simply by selecting the alternative, A_j, that maximizes the payoff, E_{ij}, or, in more complex decision problems, one may employ linear or dynamic programming to select the optimum decision.

FIGURE 14.1

The Decision Problem

States of the World

Actions	Θ_1	Θ_2	Θ_3	*	*	Θ_n
A_1	E_{11}	*	*	*	*	E_{1n}
A_2	*	E_{22}	*	*	*	*
A_3	*	*	E_{33}	*	*	*
*	*	*	*	*	*	*
*	*	*	*	*	*	*
A_m	E_{m1}	*	*	*	*	E_{mn}

Under <u>uncertainty</u>, the individual does not know the probabilities of the states of the world, nor can probabilities be assigned. In this situation, game-theoretic procedures (Luce and Raiffa 1957) may be selected to maximize expected utility or, perhaps, maximize minimum regret (loss).

Decision-making under <u>risk</u> occurs when the probabilities of the states of the world are known or can be estimated. Once this has been done, a decision rule can be used to select the appropriate alternative, which, depending upon the true state of the world, determines the outcome.

It is at this point where the distinction between risk and uncertainty is significant, since there is no complete agreement on whether decision-making under certainty is a separate category or actually a special case of decision-making under risk (Borch and Mossin 1968). The difference in interpretation is primarily based on the contrast between objective and subjective probabilities and because not every theorist is willing to consider subjective probabilities in an analysis, for many believe that personal opinions are often too vague and are incapable of being quantified. This, however, may be more of a reflection of the relative complexity of events rather than an inability to quantify judgments (see Kyburg and Smokler 1964; Hampton 1976; Tummala and Henshaw 1976).

Although an excellent discussion of the controversy is presented by Palumbo (1975), it is worthwhile to emphasize the difference between the use of subjective and objective probabilities in political science, as well as to consider how the distinction between risk and uncertainty, first noted by Knight (1921), has been interpreted in the literature and has affected research possibilities. To some extent, the transformation of situations under uncertainty through the use of subjective probabilities to those of risk have opened new areas of investigation, but, as we shall see, have posed some difficult questions as well.

One of the reasons for the confusion between the meaning of risk and uncertainty has been the increasing interest in the subjective, or "personalistic," theory of probability, which was first introduced by Ramsay (1926), but not widely accepted until after publication of Savage (1954). The basic thesis of the subjective theory of probability is that the probability of an event is the "degree of belief or degree of confidence placed in the occurrence of an event by a particular individual based on the evidence available to him" (Hamburg 1970, p. 20).

This definition contrasts with the more traditional view, in which a probability of an event is seen in terms of a relative frequency:

> Non-Bayesians argue that the only legitimate types of probabilities are "objective" or relative frequency of occurrence probabilities. They find it difficult to accept the idea that subjective or personalistic probabilities should be processed together with relative frequencies, as in the Bayesian's use of Bayes' theorem, to arrive at posterior probabilities (Hamburg 1970, p. 766).

The occurrence of some events, however, cannot validly be assigned an objective probability. For example, the statement, "The Democrats will probably win the election tomorrow," appears to be a probability statement, but it is very difficult to see how it could describe long-run relative frequencies of outcomes of repeated experiments. The problem is that this event is unique and cannot be duplicated, as is the case for most political events. Information regarding past events in similar situations is not available, and no information in the form of observed frequencies exists as repeated trials under identical conditions. Instead, the statement describes one's degree of belief or subjective judgment about a situation that will occur only once. Long-run objective frequencies are thus incapable of being used for interpreting many of the kinds of events that are of concern to those studying political behavior, and if we maintain that only objective probabilities have meaning, "we prevent ourselves from handling some of the most important uncertainties in problems of decision making," (Hamburg 1970, p. 766).

Subjective probabilities have the same properties as objective probabilities* and may be chosen in any manner prior to the occurrence of an event and may be based in part on objective evidence. Thereafter, the change in subjective probability as a result of experience or sampling is governed by Bayes's theorem. The simplest version of Bayes's theorem can be stated as follows: For two events, A and B,

$$P(A/B) = \frac{P(B/A)P(A)}{P(B/A)P(A) + P(B/\overline{A})P(\overline{A})}$$

where $\overline{A}$ represents the complement of the event A ("not A").

The equation consists of two basic components: a <u>prior probability</u>, $P(A)$, and a <u>likelihood</u>, $P(B/A)$. The prior probability is the subjective probability held at the beginning of the investigation. The likelihood is the probability of B conditional on the occurrence of A. When the probabilities are combined in the manner specified by Bayes's theorem, they form a <u>posterior probability</u>, $P(A/B)$, which summarizes the state of knowledge after taking into account the new information from observing B. The equation can thus be restated as follows:

Posterior Probability =

$$\frac{\text{Likelihood x Prior Probability}}{\text{Likelihood x Prior Probability} + (1-\text{Likelihood}) \times (1-\text{Prior})}$$

As more information becomes available, the first posterior probability may be combined with the new information to form a revised posterior probability. These new posterior probabilities can then be used to select an alternative within a Bayesian decision-making model.

---

*This may be true by definition, but researchers have often found that this is not true experimentally. See Hampton (1976) and Edwards and Tversky (1967).

Under this interpretation, it is always possible to assign a subjective probability to a state of the world, even if one has no idea (at least at first) what the likelihood of an event is. Consequently, as Shepsle (1970) has argued, uncertainty becomes a degenerate case of risk (that is, a known probability distribution collapsed on a single point). The risk versus uncertainty dichotomy is therefore one of degree and becomes an artificial distinction according to the subjective interpretation of probability. In this manner, decision-making under uncertainty can be defined as any situation in which the probability of an event is not equal to 1.

The distinction between uncertainty and risk can also be diminished by acceptance of the validity of the principle of insufficient reason (Borch 1968), which states that when the probability of a series of events is unknown, the events should be treated as equally likely. Thus, any uncertain conditions could be characterized as risk, since the probabilities can be defined and agreed upon by even a diverse group of people without any subjective biases. However, the use of equal probabilities of events arising from ignorance or uncertainty may have different implications for political decision-making compared with the use of equal probabilities based on knowledge (Shepsle 1970; Lee 1971).

Savage (1972, p. 66) argues that while holders of objectivistic views may hold the principle of insufficient reason to be meaningless, they may regard it as an experimental fact, such as the existence of a fair coin. Holders of personalistic views agree that experiences determine to a large extent when people employ the idea of insufficient reason. For example, the contrast can be shown by considering a situation in which a subject is given two urns, A and B, with urn A containing five red and five black balls, and urn B containing ten balls of unknown color, but either red or black. If asked to select a ball from one of the urns and predict the color of the ball, which urn would the subject choose—urn A or urn B?

Since the subject would have no knowledge of the distribution of the balls in urn B, the subject could apply the principle of insufficient reason and assume the selection of either a red or black ball is equally likely. The selection of either color ball is also equally likely if a ball is selected from urn A, so there is actually no reason to select one urn over the other in order to improve the prediction of what ball would be selected. There is, however, reasonable evidence to believe that urn A will be chosen, since the subject was told what the true distribution of balls was in urn A (Ellsberg 1961).

In this case, the subject was more "certain" or "confident" that s/he knew the true distribution of balls in urn A. This phenomenon underlies the notion of <u>ambiguity</u> in terms of a probability distribution of probabilities, or, as Savage (1972, p. 58) calls it, a <u>second-order distribution</u> of probabilities.

This notion of a probability distribution of probabilities has much significance for the study of political phenomena, since the nature of the second-order distribution can help determine the extent to which political strategies result in patterned or randomized behavior. Consider the following example of a candidate in an election who must decide on a public policy position to take on an issue of salience to his/her constituency.

A candidate may have one of an infinite number of probability distributions about the state of the world, but we can identify two diverse kinds of distributions: one that is uniform, indicating equal probabilities among all states of the world, and a second, in which the probabilities of all states of the world are zero, except one. The former distribution has maximum variance, and the latter has minimum variance (see Figures 14.2 and 14.3).

With a uniform distribution, minimum information is available, therefore, ceteris paribus, the selection of a policy position would be totally unbiased and could be any position along the issue continuum. Given a number of trials, a candidate would choose a policy position, but in this situation, the positions would appear to be random, since no policy position would be preferred to any other.

On the other hand, a candidate whose probability distribution showed minimum variance would be likely to choose the position with the highest probability most often, if not exclusively, ceteris paribus. Thus, the variance of the distribution could indicate the extent of a candidate's confidence in his/her subjective probability distribution of the states of the world. It follows that the greater the variance of the subjective probability distribution, the more likely the candidate would vary in the selection of a public policy position. However, since elections are unique events and nature does not always allow second chances, we can operationalize the situation by considering the extent to which candidates are likely to adopt policy positions they believe are representative of the majority of the constituents in their district. For example, it can be hypothesized that the more uncertainty perceived by a candidate, the less likely s/he will adopt a policy position close to that perceived by the majority of the voters in his/her district. Thus, the confident candidate will appear to be more representative by following his/her perceptions of district opinion (although, in reality, s/he may be far off the mark), while the less confident, uncertain candidate will adopt policy positions that are less likely to follow his/her perceptions of district opinion. The former exhibits systematic behavior, while the latter adopts a randomized strategy based on the equal probability of events.

The consideration of second-order probabilities could have important implications for the study of political behavior in such

FIGURE 14.2

A Uniform Probability Distribution of a Parameter

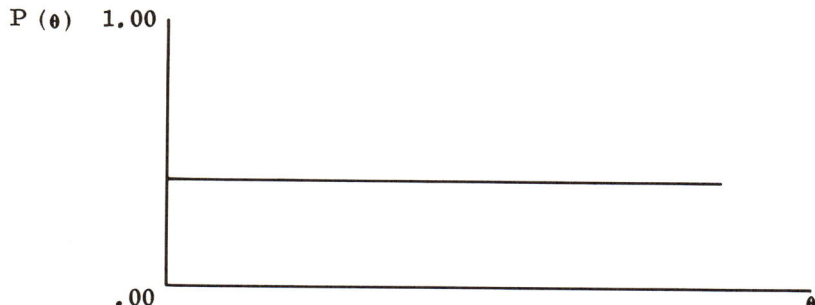

FIGURE 14.3

A Spiked Probability Distribution of a Parameter

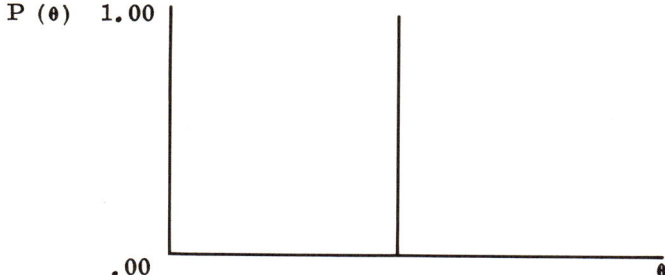

areas as the study of representational role in legislatures, the effect of electoral marginality on representation, and the choice of strategies in an election (Alpert 1978a, 1978b, 1979). Its impact would be relevant in the redirection of research toward consideration of the perceptions of political actors, rather than reliance upon objective, aggregate data. These studies have often found contradictory evidence, but consideration of subjective perceptions of legislators, candidates, and other decision makers may enable political scientists to reorganize their previous findings within a subjective decision-making framework, which should indicate new paths of investigation.

The significance of treating events as equally likely is also illustrated by the exchange of Whitely (1976) with Farlie and Budge (1976) over the proper use of the principle of insufficient reason as a prior distribution in the calculation of new posterior probabilities. Depending upon one's perspective, the use of the principle can be considered either "naive," by eliminating consideration of other distributions of probabilities, or "unprejudiced," by attempting to use a neutral, uniform prior distribution. Actually, Budge and Farlie (1976, p. 110) do not consider their probability assignment to be Bayesian, since they reject other possible probability distributions of finding Labour and Conservative supporters in favor of an equiprobable distribution. This allows them to base their results exclusively on the data, rather than on any preconceptions imposed upon the data. Thus, the Bayesian method may be used, but incorporation of subjective probabilities can be applied whenever it suits an analytic purpose. However, if the sample size is sufficiently large, the choice of an initial prior may not matter significantly, since different priors can converge rapidly to about the same posterior distribution (Iversen 1970, p. 191).

To summarize, we have defined Bayesian decision-making, which implies the use of subjective personal probabilities, as decision-making under uncertainty. The distinction between risk and uncertainty is unnecessary, since under the subjective theory of probability, all events can be assigned a probability. If no knowledge is available to formulate such probabilities, each event may be treated as equally likely until new information is available and combined with the uniform prior distribution to form a new posterior distribution.

THE RISK ENVIRONMENT

The term *risk* has also been used to describe the expected loss from choosing an alternative given the possible states of the world that may obtain. The expected loss is determined by some loss function, $L(A,\Theta)$, which reflects the loss in taking action A_i when Θ_i is the true value of the parameter. The loss is smallest when A is the "best" action for Θ (Mood and Graybill 1963). The risk is the expected value of the loss function given an action and each of the values of the states of the world. The task of the decision maker is thus to adopt a decision rule to maximize expected loss under uncertainty.

The calculation of the risk depends upon the value of the loss (the payoff matrix is transformed into a loss matrix), which can be either positive, negative, or zero, which results from the selection of an action given the state of the world. Since the value of the loss is determined by the individual's utility function, the shape of the curve could have a profound effect on the choice of an alternative. For example, Shepsle (1972a, 1972c) has shown that in political situations, individuals with concave, convex, or linear utility functions vary to the extent to which they prefer particular policies, despite identical preference orderings of alternatives. Voters with concave, convex, and linear utility functions were found to be <u>risk-averse</u>, <u>risk-acceptant</u>, and <u>risk-neutral</u>, respectively (see Arrow 1951).

Shepsle's work has involved the use of a formal examination of what policy positions a candidate should take to maximize his/her appeal to obtain the support of as many voters as possible, considering even cases when voters' preferences are cyclical. He shows (Shepsle 1972b), for example, that candidates who adopt a risky strategy, which establishes a probability distribution over a set of possible positions, will benefit by being vague and ambiguous on critical, salient issues in a campaign. This would of course be more likely to work for nonincumbent candidates, who are able to be more flexible in establishing a degree of ambiguity about their positions than incumbents, who must stand on their record.

Brams (1976, pp. 60-65) points out the possibility of an "ambiguity paradox," which can occur when there is a conflict between candidate and voter rationality, as a result of candidates adopting a probability distribution over a set of possible policy positions on an issue, with voters thus being unable to maximize their own expected utility. Thus, voters must try to determine their own strategy for coping with the uncertainty about candidates' issue positions. This may be accomplished by examining their utility curves to determine the choice between a candidate who will choose a position with certainty and another who will take a position with a certain probability. Voters who are risk-averse will prefer the former, and those who are risk-acceptant will prefer the latter. Risk-neutral voters will be indifferent between the two. Thus, the more voters who are risk-acceptant, the more likely candidates who present ambiguous policy positions will be elected. It follows that the increased intensity of an issue among voters will also increase the appeal of this strategy of ambiguity to the candidates.

The net result of ambiguity is that the candidates' best strategy is one that best reflects the interests of the voters, since candidates try to maximize support of the electorate. Thus, by considering the effect of uncertainty on voters' strategies, Downs's (1957) warning that ambiguity in the presentation of issue positions to the electorate will foster irrational voting is not accurate. Instead, it fosters the adoption of an ambiguous strategy, which works on behalf of the voters to maximize support and minimize loss of voters.

This points out the narrowness of Downs's definition of rationality, since it does not take into account the uncertainty that exists. If uncertainty (ambiguity) prevents rational decisions by voters, then voters can never act rationally. Instead of eliminating the notion of rationality, Shepsle (1972a, pp. 367-68) redefines rationality as "the efficient use of contextual information so as to produce actions consistent (a priori) with preferences."

As Shepsle refers to the way in which uncertainty is handled in spatial models of electoral competition:

> The particular way . . . may be inadequate and is certainly incomplete. Not included, for example, are any manifestations of uncertainty in candidate decision making except as they arise in the game context of strategy selection. Thus it was supposed that there is no uncertainty in candidate information about voter preference or strategy constraints. It would be of great interest to incorporate questions of this sort (Shepsle 1972a, p. 568).

Ferejohn and Fiorina (1974, 1975) introduce risk and uncertainty into an analysis of whether a citizen should consider voting or abstaining; depending upon his/her estimate of the value of his/her vote, in terms of making a difference in the election outcome, this choice is determined in part by what s/he expects his/her fellow citizens to do. By comparing the decision rules of expected maximum utility and minimax regret (Luce and Raiffa 1957; White, 1969), Ferejohn and Fiorina show, for example, that under the former rule, which employs subjective probability distributions of what other citizens are likely to do, citizens are not likely to vote except under very restrictive conditions (that is, when voting costs are considerably low). In contrast, the minimax regret criterion shows it is rational for the citizen to vote, while under a criterion such as maximin, citizens would never vote.

The significant difference in these results occurs because under expected maximum utility, a probability distribution of the states of the world is formulated to choose the appropriate alternative. However, under minimax regret, one state of the world is chosen, and the citizen selects a strategy given that one state of the world. The question for researchers is which rule should be applied and when. Ferejohn and Fiorina (1974, p. 535) suggest studying the association between different rationality criteria and various socioeconomic groups. This could lead to an identification of what groups in society are expected utility maximizers, minimax regret decision makers, or maximin decision makers. This would obviously have value for studying the behavior of these groups under other choice situations.

Mayer and Good (1975) have taken issue with Ferejohn and Fiorina over the appropriateness of the minimax regret principle, since they claim that voters do take at least rough estimates of probabilities of events into consideration. Decision-making is thus made under risk, not uncertainty, which precludes the use of minimax regret. Ferejohn and Fiorina (1975) argue against this and other concerns (Beck 1975; Stephens 1975; Strom 1975; Tullock, 1975) with an analysis of public opinion data, which provide "no empirical basis for rejecting the minimax regret model as a descriptive model of the turnout decision" (Ferejohn and Fiorina 1975, p. 925).

The question that remains is why the minimax regret model, which does not consider subjective probabilities, works so much better than the expected utility model. The answer may still lie within the realm of subjective probability estimation. By not specifying the probabilities over each state of the world, but choosing the alternative that minimizes maximum regret (loss), the citizen in effect assumes each state of the world has equal probability. This implies that Ferejohn and Fiorina invoked the law of insufficient reason, so that instead of decision-making under uncertainty, they considered it to be a risky situation. If this assumption is made, then the minimax regret criterion could be appropriately applied. An interesting result would be that if voters act as if they assume the states of the world (the number of votes a candidate will receive) to be equally likely, then this could imply that the voters are completely ignorant of the probabilities of a candidate winning. Although equal probabilities in this case do not seem too plausible, since polls or previous election results could be used to form a prior distribution, "good feelings in one's tummy are not considered persuasive empirical evidence" (Ferejohn and Fiorina 1975, p. 925). Actually, this illustrates well the ability of formal models to explain and predict behavior despite the use of "unrealistic" assumptions. Nevertheless, as Mayer and Good (1975) suggest, an empirical study of the conditions under which citizens would be likely to vote on the basis of their subjective estimates would be very useful.

Although this analysis attempts to bridge the relationship between the use of maximum expected utility and the minimax regret criteria by showing that the two situations are compatible when the states of the world are believed equally likely (reducing decision-making under uncertainty to decision-making under risk), the use of the principle of insufficient reason does have its limitations. For example, since one must identify the possible states of nature, some states may be (consciously or otherwise) excluded as possibilities or they may be thought of as discrete, rather than as continuous values. Therefore, specification of the model itself involves a separate choice. Also, the choice of a decision rule, as well as the model, may be a value judgment, for as Milnor (1964) indicates, each decision rule is based on mutually incompatible assumptions. Yet, if decision-making can be reduced to decision-making under risk through the use of subjective probabilities, then the principle of the maximizing expected utility is a universal decision criterion (Shepsle 1970, p. 55).

A major follow-up to Shepsle's (1972a, 1972c) work in developing a framework for introducing uncertainty into candidate decision-making is Ferejohn and Noll (1978). In their model, candidates tackled uncertainty regarding the majority rule outcome by estimating the likely outcome of the election based on the set of policy positions each candidate presents before the voters. Since each candidate may differ in the level of accurate information and the way in which it may be processed, the personal assessments can result in each candidate believing himself/herself to be the likely winner. Therefore, under certainty, the contest is zero-sum, but under uncertainty, with each candidate possibly believing that s/he will win, the game becomes nonzero-sum, as perceived by the candidates.

The implications are that electoral strategies exist in which candidates adopt different, rather than matching or mixed, positions indicated by models of perfect information. Also, candidates may not choose to increase the amount of information on voter reaction to their campaign activities, depending upon the belief that a poll (either public or private) will either help or hurt their chances of election. The results are significant because they add another dimension to the meaning of uncertainty and the effects of estimating subjective probabilities in order to select a set of public policy positions. However, as the authors recognized, their model was not directly operational in empirical terms, since, for example, no cost is assumed to be associated with candidates switching positions or informing the electorate of their positions.

RISK, UNCERTAINTY, AND REPRESENTATION

While these studies have been rich in theoretical constructs, there has been a considerable lack of evidence on the empirical relevance of this research. Although part of the problem is operationalization, as well as measurement, further insights can be gained by applying the framework to new areas and studying the relevant variables that can influence the decision-making process. In this way, the empirical components can be made more explicit, and the models can be reformulated to generate new hypotheses, some of which may prove to be nonobvious.

Two empirical studies are of particular significance in terms of their potential for generating new hypotheses and promoting further research. Fiorina's (1974) model of legislative decision-making is based on an analysis of legislators' perceptions of their constituency support and how uncertainty influences representatives' voting behavior. Black's (1972) study of the ambitions of city councilmen employs a calculation of the potential utility of running for higher office to determine the impact of risk (defined as the expected loss of investment) of a politician's decision to run for higher office. In both cases, the establishment of empirical linkages to concepts of subjective decision-making have strengthened the potential for more significant research into the effects of uncertainty and risk on political choice. Nevertheless, greater specification of the components of these models needs to be accomplished before the true significance of the research can be shown.

Basically, Fiorina (1974) presented a unique approach to the problem of an elected representative choosing an optimal strategy of roll call voting to assure himself of a certain minimally acceptable level of the probability of reelection. A set of hypotheses were deduced from the model that incorporated the parameter of a representative's perceptions about the state of the world and was able to reorganize much of the seemingly contradictory evidence about representative-constituency relationships found in the literature into a coherent framework. Although the connection between the formal model and the testing of its hypotheses was not entirely a direct one, Fiorina offered several convincing arguments and additional data that helped support the hypotheses.

In the model, the states of the world were represented by a parameter, C, the degree to which a representative believed that a group in his/her constituency "cared" about the representative's vote on an issue, and might be drawn into the campaign, either in support or in opposition to the legislator.

Two kinds of goals were postulated: (1) to maximize the probability of winning, or (2) to maintain a minimum acceptable level of the probability of winning. A "maximizer" would then choose an alternative that yielded the largest expected increase in the probability of winning. A "maintainer" would adopt an optimal voting strategy that is a discrete probability distribution over the set of alternatives, such that the expected value of voting over time would equal zero. This would result in a "break even" situation, in which the legislator's personal probability of election would remain at an acceptable constant level.

From these and other assumptions, hypotheses were deduced to indicate the best strategies for either kind of representative. The concern is what effect the subjective estimate, C, of drawing a group into the next election campaign had upon these strategies. Once this was determined, one could begin to see the importance that the estimation of this parameter has upon other types of political choices, including those outside of the legislative environment.

The parameter C was described as a function of group organization, group cohesion, intensity of preference, and a representative's past voting record. Just as we showed how candidates could estimate the probability of Θ, the majority opinion on an issue, these legislators could be shown to estimate C in the same way, by employing Bayes's theorem. If the data were available to operationalize Bayes's theorem, one could estimate the value of C, which could be revised after each vote cast by the legislator. As a result, the difficulty that Fiorina discussed in regard to measuring C (and also the parameter S, the strength of the group) may not be as burdensome as he proposed:

> Enough has been written in this section to indicate the dimensions of the problem we face, and why we began by taking estimates of $\underline{S}$ and $\underline{C}$ as givens. The questions raised will be topics of future research for a rather lengthy future. Isolating the major variables affecting group strength and concern should not be terribly difficult. But theorizing about the relationships among them and carrying out the measurements necessary for empirical estimation pose no easy task. Yet if the $\underline{S}_j$ and $\underline{C}_j$ are important variables in a representative's voting decision problem, then eventually we must face up to these problems (Fiorina 1974, p. 86).

Our point is that it may be possible to estimate $\underline{S}_j$ (group strength) and C_j (the degree to which a group cares), not by necessarily considering the above four factors but, instead, by reconceptualizing this problem also in terms of subjective probabilities and by using Bayes's theorem. Even if the law of insufficient reason could be employed, this would be useful, since the probabilities can still be revised as new information becomes available.

Fiorina's model, however, was concerned only with legislative decision-making, and no clues were given as to how legislators formulated their estimates of the states of the world or how various levels of risk and uncertainty were likely to affect their decisions. It would be just as appropriate to apply the Bayesian framework to the study of campaign decision-making (Alpert 1978a, 1978b) and the kinds of policy decisions candidates are likely to make in a situation involving risk and uncertainty. It is conceivable that in order to describe the complete process of constituency influence, it is necessary to develop a two-stage model, with the first stage linking the constituents with the candidates in the campaign environment and the second, as described by Miller and Stokes (1963), linking the constituents to their representatives, the winners of the election campaign (see Figure 14.4).

FIGURE 14.4

Paths of Constituency Influence

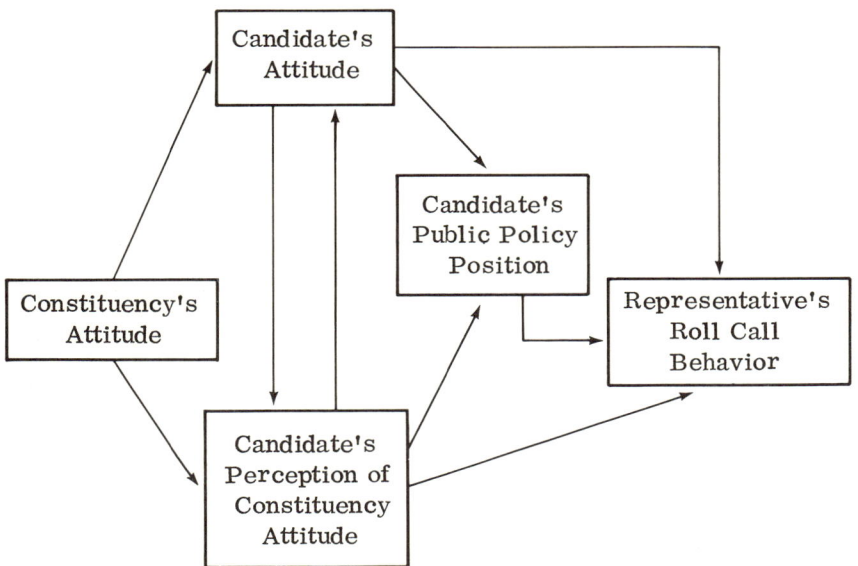

For example, in the legislature, a representative's only opponent is himself/herself; his/her own actions will help raise or lower his/her probability of reelection. A political campaign, however, introduces additional factors over which the candidate may have little control, including the activities of his/her opponent. In addition, a bad decision or a mistake in judgment during the campaign can have a very critical effect on the outcome, perhaps more so than anything the representative had done during his/her entire tenure in office. No matter how careful or cautious one may be, just one error could possibly deflate the candidate's probability of reelection to a totally unacceptable level.

During the campaign, public awareness of the candidates is likely to be relatively high, and it is a time when a candidate's actions are more closely scrutinized by a wider set of groups and individuals in the district. It is therefore essential that the candidate not only have a good perception of which groups care or do not care but, also, a good estimate of the probability that other parameters important to the campaign will attain certain critical values necessary for winning the election. Fiorina's model may be important in explaining legislative voting influences, but it does not consider the important variables related to campaigning and how they may affect the candidates' policy positions, which may be carried over in some form to the legislative arena. There are constraints in legislative decision-making, but the constraints in a campaign may be even more serious, especially if they affect the spatial mobility of the candidates and their ability to meet the challenges of their opponents. The problem then becomes one of reconciling the difference between what is promised during a campaign and what limited policy options are available in the legislature. Since occasionally a legislator must vote for a bill that does not represent his/her most preferred policy position rather than face the prospect of no bill at all, it is important for him/her to estimate the risk involved in voting and to what extent that risk can be transferred to the forthcoming campaign.

It is therefore important to study the perceptions of the candidates in an election campaign in order to gain some empirical knowledge about candidate choices that can provide the basis for the development of a model of campaign decision-making and a more complete explanation of the process of representation. As Kingdon (1968, p. 7) states:

> A full account of representation, therefore, must include representatives' perceptions of the constituents as a variable intervening between the constituents and the behavior of the elected policy maker. These perceptions may or may not be accurate, but it is

necessary to take them into account in order to explain the behavior of politicians.

Since nonincumbent challengers occasionally defeat an incumbent seeking reelection, it would also be worthwhile to study the changes in risk and uncertainty perceived by the newcomers as they begin their political careers. In this way, representation can be seen more as a process rather than as a product of the electoral system. To do this, we must study how politicians develop their attitudes and formulate their perceptions of constituency opinion. Since the process is dynamic, there is also an opportunity for a politician to revise his/her perceptions and, thus, his/her policy positions. If we can identify the important independent variables that alter decision makers' perceptions, then we will not only be closer to explaining and predicting the kinds of public policy choices that are made, but also closer to influencing these decisions according to the normative values of society.

RISK AND AMBITION THEORY

Although risk has more than one interpretation in the decision-making literature, one of the areas that offers a good opportunity for more empirical research is in the study of political ambition. As Schlesinger (1966) states in his book, Ambition and Politics:

> Any elective system of opportunities is full of risks for the politician. But if we look at the American system from the standpoint of ambitions we can see that the risks tend to foster some ambitions and reduce others. The risks for those with progressive ambitions are not equally distributed among officeholders. Career risks are maximized in a situation in which, in order to seek a higher office, a man must give up his current office. The congressman who reaches for the Senate and fails loses everything (p. 17).

The loss involved in such decisions would include the possible loss of the office presently held, unless a candidate was fortunate enough to be able to hold on to one office while running for a higher one.

Black (1972) has extended this interpretation of risk by defining it in terms of the investment that would be lost if a candidate were to lose an election. Black (1972, p. 148) described an election as "a risk taking venture in which candidates are forced to wage a portion of their resources in the pursuit of office." The magnitude of the risk is determined by the structural characteristics of the electoral system, such as the size of the unit and the competitiveness of its elections. He hypothesized that the risk of running for office is an increasing function of the size and the degree of electoral competition in the unit. Thus, as the size of the investment (risk) increases, the less committed individuals would be the ones most likely to drop out of the race.

Besides indicating who is likely to run for office, Black's conceptual scheme could be applied to an officeholder who must decide whether to run for reelection or a higher office (see Rohde 1979; Kritzer 1978). Black (1972, p. 156) hypothesized that "the greater the cumulative investment of the individual in political office seeking, the greater will be the value placed on the offices to which the individual might aspire." The investments made while holding office were presumed to be transferable to other offices. The data collected from interviewing city councilmen in the San Francisco Bay area seemed to confirm this hypothesis.

Also of interest was that he found that uncertainty played a role in councilmen's aspirations. Those who were certain of winning their reelection bids were also the ones more likely to aspire to higher office. The logic behind this presumes that the subjective probabilities of obtaining various offices are interdependent and that winning one election increases the probability of winning a race for another office.

CONCLUSION

The study of risk and uncertainty in political science is not broadly based in the literature, but current research efforts are increasing the number of hypotheses that need to be operationalized and tested by more empirical research. Part of the problem of why more research has not been conducted is methodological, since a simple decision problem with discrete events can quickly increase in complexity. Also, computer routines that provide for Bayesian iterations are not as widely available to social scientists as are other statistical procedures.

The collection of data is a particular problem, since the measurement of citizens' perceptions over a continuous period of time is burdensome, and individuals are not always able to specify the components of a decision problem in terms that can be transformed into intercomparable utility units. The studies of international conflict provide an encouraging avenue for research (Alpert 1976; Ben-Dak and Finsterbusch 1974; McGowan 1974), since large amounts of data are available concerning the capabilities, resources, and activities of nations. In this regard, the analysis of events data would be a worthwhile area to pursue for the empirical testing of subjective decision-making models.

Another problem is the choice of a prior distribution and the acceptance of the personal probability approach of considering decision-making under uncertainty as a special case of risk. Clearly, there are some events whose probabilities are unknowable, such as the probability of reincarnation. Consequently, the appropriateness of the law of insufficient reason continues to be debated.

Despite these concerns, there remains a strong potential for the growth of Bayesian analysis in political science. The incentives for relaxation of the perfect information assumption are becoming more attractive, for political scientists are searching for more realistic models with which to study political choice. By pursuing the course of subjective decision-making, we can learn more about the nature of information-processing by investigating the revisions of subjective estimates. As a result, simulation models can be developed to provide information on how to explain and predict the kinds of decisions that will be made, as well as, for example, to describe the nature of political representation. If we become aware of what sources of information are more likely to be used by decision makers and how information is interpreted to provide a set of acceptable alternatives for action, then we shall be well on the way toward the development of a theory of political choice.

REFERENCES

Aitchison, John. 1972. Choice Against Chance: An Introduction to Statistical Decision Making. Reading, Mass.: Addison-Wesley.

Alpert, Eugene J. 1976. "Capabilities, Perceptions and Risks: A Bayesian Model of International Behavior." International Studies Quarterly 20: 415-40.

_____. 1978a. "Incumbency and Election Outcomes: Candidates' Policy Positions in Congressional Elections." Paper presented at Annual Meeting of the Southwestern Political Science Association, Houston, Texas.

_____. 1978b. "Marginality and Responsiveness: A Subjective Decision Making Analysis." Paper presented at Annual Meeting of the Midwest Political Science Association, Chicago, Illinois.

_____. 1979. "A Reconceptualization of Representational Role." Legislative Studies Quarterly 4.

Arrow, Kenneth J. 1951. "Alternative Approaches to the Theory of Choice in Risk-Taking Situations." Econometrica 19: 404-37.

Beck, Nathaniel. 1975. "The Paradox of Minimax Regret." American Political Science Review 69: 918.

Ben-Dak, J. D., and Finsterbusch, K. 1974. "Bayesian Analysis: Applications for the Study of Foreign Behavior." In International Yearbook of Foreign Policy, edited by Patrick McGowan, pp. 296-306. Beverly Hills, Calif.: Sage.

Black, Gordon S. 1972. "A Theory of Political Ambition: Career Choices and the Role of Structural Incentives." American Political Science Review 66: 144-59.

Borch, Karl. 1968. The Economics of Uncertainty. Princeton, N.J.: Princeton University Press.

Borch, Karl, and Mossin, Jan. 1968. Risk and Uncertainty. New York: St. Martin's Press.

Brams, Steven J. 1976. Paradoxes in Politics. New York: Free Press.

Budge, Ian, and Farlie, Dennis. 1975. "Political Recruitment and Dropout: Predictive Success of Background Characteristics over Five British Localities." British Journal of Political Science 5: 33-68.

_____. 1976. "A Comparative Analysis of Factors Correlated with Turnout and Voting Choice." In Party Identification and Beyond, edited by I. Budge, I. Crewe, and D. Farlie. New York: Wiley.

_____. 1977. Voting and Party Competition. New York: Wiley.

Downs, Anthony. 1957. An Economic Theory of Democracy. New York: Harper & Row.

Edwards, Ward, and Tversky, Amos, eds. 1967. Decision Making: Selected Readings. Baltimore: Penguin Books.

Ellsberg, Daniel. 1961. "Risk, Ambiguity and the Savage Axioms." Quarterly Journal of Economics 75: 643-69.

Farlie, Dennis, and Budge, Ian. 1976. "A Rejoinder." British Journal of Political Science 6: 126-27.

Ferejohn, John A., and Fiorina, Morris P. 1974. "The Paradox of Not Voting: A Decision-Theoretic Analysis." American Political Science Review 68: 525-36.

Ferejohn, John A., and Noll, Roger G. 1978. "Uncertainty and the Formal Theory of Political Campaigns." American Political Science Review 72: 492-505.

Fiorina, Morris P. 1974. Representatives, Roll Calls and Constituencies. Lexington, Mass.: Lexington Books.

Goodin, R. E., and Roberts, K. W. S. 1975. "The Ethical Voter." American Political Science Review 69: 926-28.

Hamburg, Morris. 1970. Statistical Analysis for Decision Making. New York: Harcourt Brace & World.

Hampton, J. M.; Moore, P. G.; and Thomas, H. 1976. "Subjective Probability and Its Measurement." In Concepts and Applications of Modern Decision Models, edited by V. M. R. Tummala and R. C. Henshaw, pp. 65-86. East Lansing: Graduate School of Business Administration, Michigan State University.

Hershey, Marjorie Randon. 1974. The Making of Campaign Strategy. Lexington, Mass.: Lexington Books.

Iversen, Gudmund. 1970. "Statistics According to Bayes." In Sociological Methodology 1970, edited by E. F. Borgatta, pp. 185-99.

Kingdon, John W. 1968. Candidates for Office: Beliefs and Strategies. New York: Random House.

Knight, Frank H. 1921. Risk, Uncertainty, and Profit. New York: Houghton-Mifflin.

Kritzer, Herbert M. 1978. "The Senatorial Ambitions of U.S. Representatives: The Decision to Run." Paper presented at Annual Meeting of the Southern Political Science Association, Atlanta, Georgia.

Kyburg, Henry E., Jr., and Smokler, Howard E., eds. 1965. Studies in Subjective Probability. New York: Wiley.

Lee, Wayne. 1971. Decision Theory and Human Behavior. New York: Wiley.

Luce, Duncan, and Raiffa, Howard. 1957. *Games and Decisions.* New York: Wiley.

McGowan, Patrick. 1974. "A Bayesian Approach to the Problem of Events Data Validity in Comparative and International Political Research." In *Comparative Foreign Policy*, edited by James N. Rosenau, pp. 407-33. Beverly Hills, Calif.: Sage.

Mansfield, Edwin, ed. 1970. *Elementary Statistics for Economics and Business.* New York: Norton.

Matthews, Donald R., and Stimson, James A. 1975. *Yeas and Nays: Normal Decision Making in the U.S. House of Representatives.* New York: Wiley.

Mayer, Lawrence, and Good, I. J. 1975. "Is Minimax-Regret Applicable to Voting Decisions?" *American Political Science Review* 69: 916-17.

Miller, Warren E., and Stokes, Donald E. 1963. "Constituency Influence in Congress." *American Political Science Review* 57: 45-56.

Milnor, John. 1964. "Games Against Nature." 1964. In *Game Theory and Related Approaches to Social Behavior*, edited by Martin Shubik, pp. 120-31. New York: Wiley.

Mood, Alexander M., and Graybill, Franklin A. 1963. *Introduction to the Theory of Statistics.* New York: McGraw-Hill.

Palumbo, Dennis J. 1975. "Organization Theory and Political Science." In *Handbook of Political Science: Micropolitical Theory*, edited by Fred Greenstein and Nelson W. Polsby, pp. 319-69. Reading, Mass.: Addison-Wesley.

Phillips, Lawrence D. 1973. *Bayesian Statistics for Social Scientists.* New York: Crowell.

Rabushka, Alvin, and Shepsle, Kenneth A. 1972. *Politics in Plural Societies: A Theory of Democratic Instability.* Columbus, Ohio: Merrill.

Ramsay, F. P. 1926. *The Foundations of Mathematics and Other Logical Essays.* London: Kegan Paul.

Riker, William H., and Ordeshook, Peter C. 1973. <u>Introduction to Positive Political Theory</u>. Englewood Cliffs, N.J.: Prentice-Hall.

Rohde, David W. 1979. "Risk-Bearing and Progressive Ambition: The Case of Members of the United States House of Representatives." <u>American Journal of Political Science</u> 23: 1-26.

Savage, Leonard J. 1954. <u>The Foundations of Statistics</u>. New York: Wiley; republished New York: Dover Press, 1970.

Schlesinger, Joseph A. 1966. <u>Ambition and Politics: Political Careers in the United States</u>. Chicago: Rand McNally.

Schmitt, Samuel. 1969. <u>Measuring Uncertainty: An Elementary Introduction to Bayesian Statistics</u>. Reading, Mass.: Addison-Wesley.

Shepsle, Kenneth A. 1970. "Essays in the Theory of Risk-Taking." Ph.D. dissertation, University of Rochester.

──────. 1972a. "The Strategy of Ambiguity: Uncertainty and Electoral Competition." <u>American Political Science Review</u> 66: 555-68.

──────. 1972b. "The Paradox of Voting and Uncertainty." In <u>Probability Models of Collective Decision Making</u>, edited by Richard G. Niemi and Herbert F. Weisberg, pp. 252-70. Columbus, Ohio: Merrill.

──────. 1972c. "Parties, Voters and the Risk Environment: A Mathematical Treatment of Electoral Competition Under Uncertainty." In <u>Probability Models of Collective Decision Making</u>, edited by Richard G. Niemi and Herbert F. Weisberg, pp. 272-97. Columbus, Ohio: Merrill.

Stephens, Stephen V. 1975. "The Paradox of Not Voting: Comment." <u>American Political Science Review</u> 69: 914-15.

Strom, Gerald S. 1975. "On the Apparent Paradox of Participation: A New Proposal." <u>American Political Science Review</u> 69: 908-13.

Taylor, Michael. 1971. "Review Article: Mathematical Political Theory." <u>British Journal of Political Science</u> 1: 339-82.

Tullock, Gordon. 1975. "The Paradox of Not Voting for Oneself." American Political Science Review 69: 919.

Tummala, V. M. Rao, and Henshaw, Richard C. 1975. Concepts and Applications of Modern Decision Models. East Lansing: Graduate School of Business, Michigan State University.

White, D. J. 1969. Decision Theory. Chicago: Aldine.

Whitely, Paul. 1976. "Bayesian Statistics and Political Recruitment: A Comment." British Journal of Political Science 6: 124-25.

Winkler, Robert L. 1972. An Introduction to Bayesian Inference and Decision. New York: Holt, Rinehart & Winston.

15
UNCERTAINTY IN FAMILY LIFE
Andrew Cherlin

When social scientists hear the term <u>uncertainty theory</u>, they tend to think of the large technical literature on rational choice and decision-making developed for the most part by economists. This literature stems from a concern with the ability of organizations—and particularly firms—to function effectively. Beginning with the now-classic work of Simon (1955, 1956, 1957), many writers have argued that the ability of people in organizations to make rational decisions is limited. "Rational choice," wrote March (1978), "involves two kinds of guesses: guesses about future consequences of current actions and guesses about future preferences for those consequences."

In this chapter, I will attempt to demonstrate that the concept of uncertainty, which has been so useful in organizational analysis, also is useful in analyzing family life. Several recent studies by sociologists and economists suggest that levels of uncertainty can have important effects on the everyday functioning of families. To some extent, the same theoretical framework developed for organizations can be applied to the study of uncertainty in family life. But families are not firms, and as a result, our way of thinking about uncertainty must be modified in order to study families. In this chapter, I will describe the similarities and differences between the standard approach to uncertainty and the approach that is most fruitful for research on the family. In addition, I will review some of the historical trends that have affected the types of uncertainties family members face, and I will conclude with some suggestions for future research. I will draw most of my examples from studies of divorce and remarriage, where research findings suggest that uncertainty has a number of influences, but I also will discuss the effects of uncertainty on other aspects of family life.

Consider first the relationship between income and divorce. Sociologists have known for at least 20 years that husbands with the lowest earnings are the most likely to become divorced, other things being equal (Goode 1956; Glick and Norton 1971). Most sociologists in the 1950s and 1960s assumed that this association was due to a simple lack of funds: families with less money had fewer resources, which led to more separations and divorces. Recently, however, evidence from two independent national surveys of families, each of which extended over several years, suggests another explanation. The surveys are the Michigan Panel Study of Income Dynamics, which was studied by Ross and Sawhill (1975), and the National Longitudinal Survey of Mature Women, which I analyzed (Cherlin 1979). In these studies, the researchers distinguished between the <u>level</u> of the husband's earnings—as measured by his hourly wage or his annual earnings—and the <u>stability</u> of the husband's earnings—as measured by recent unemployment or by a recent drop or rise in earnings from the usual level. The researchers isolated several thousand couples whose marriages were intact at the beginning of the study and followed them for a four-year period. In both studies, couples in which the husband's earnings were less stable were more likely to divorce or separate in the next several years, other things being equal, but the level of the husband's earnings seemed not to affect the probability of dissolution once the stability of his earnings was considered.

This pattern of results implies that unstable earnings can be a greater source of tension in family life than a low but steady level of earnings. In other words, it is uncertainty about the husband's earnings that appears to impair family functioning. We can interpret this finding in two ways—in terms of decision-making theory and in terms of role theory. As for the former explanation, we can infer that a husband who provides a stable source of income allows his family to develop a stable set of expectations about available resources. These expectations aid family members in evaluating the consequences of alternative actions, and therefore, these expectations assist them in making rational decisions. When earnings are unstable, on the other hand, families cannot anticipate as well the situation they will face in the future, and they therefore are less able to decide on appropriate activities. Even if earnings <u>increase</u> suddenly, these difficulties may appear; Becker, Landes, and Michael (1977) found that unexpectedly high, as well as unexpectedly low, earnings increased a husband's probability of divorce in a 1967 national sample. A stable source of earnings—such as a steady job at a given wage level—structures the family's environment; it increases the ability of family members to make rational decisions in the same way that a formal organization structures what Simon (1957) called the <u>psychological environment</u> of its members. When this structure is lacking, family unity often suffers, and the probability of divorce or separation rises.

There is, however, a second interpretation of these findings, which emphasizes the social role of the husband, and this interpretation applies particularly to unexpected <u>loss</u> of income. When we examine case histories of unemployed men and their families, we find that the consequences of the uncertainty about earnings go beyond economic matters; in fact, they affect almost every aspect of husband-wife and parent-child relations. This point was illustrated by Komarovsky (1940) in a well-known study of Depression families in which the father had been unemployed for at least a year. She noticed a general breakdown of the husband's status in many of the families: "Loss of earning ability has lowered the prestige of the man in the eyes of his wife" (p. 42). This loss of prestige meant that the husband's authority was lowered even in decisions unconnected with money. One Catholic wife, for example, had been attempting to persuade her Protestant husband to let their children attend Catholic schools. She succeeded only after he became chronically unemployed. "After two years of unemployment," said the husband, "I just could not fight her any more" (p. 29).

This pervasive loss of status and authority seemed due as much to the man's failure to live up to the role of a good provider as to the actual loss of income. A major component of the social role of a husband is providing money: it appears from Komarovsky's study and the more recent national surveys that the stability and uncertainty of the husband's financial contribution is a more important criterion of successful performance than the amount of money he brings home. A married man who fails to be a steady provider also fails, to a large extent, in his performance in the role of husband. He often loses the respect of his family, and he often loses the basis of his authority as well. Consequently, he may be unable to hold his family together, and divorce or separation may become more likely.

Thus, sociologists often explain the effects of financial uncertainty by reference to the performance of social roles, while economists tend to stress constraints on rational decision-making. In the abstract, one could attempt to reconcile these views by arguing that a social role consists of nothing more than a framework for decision-making—in fact, this argument was advanced by Simon (1957). But in practice, such reductionist arguments seem neither very conclusive nor very fruitful. The important point is that the consequences of financial uncertainty—however one conceives of them—are diffuse. Uncertainty often causes a pervasive erosion of the husband's authority: this erosion is due not only to the husband's failure to provide an adequate amount of money but, also, to his inability to provide his family with a set of stable expectations about the future.

This first example, then, shows how uncertainty can affect the performance of social roles. A second example may make clearer how social institutions affect the amount of uncertainty that family members face. Until the 1930s, most remarriages in the United States followed the death of a husband or wife. But with the rise in divorce in recent decades, most remarriages now follow a divorce. This change means that the families of remarried adults often have a complicated structure: each partner in a remarriage may have children from a previous marriage, as well as from the current marriage, and the children from the first marriage may have a custodial parent, a noncustodial parent living elsewhere, and a stepparent. If the noncustodial parent remarries, another set of adults and children will interact with the original family members.

While this structure may seem complex to Americans, many other societies have existed with even more complex family structures (Bohannan 1963). But as several authors have observed recently (Walker, Rogers, and Messinger 1977; Cherlin 1978a; Furstenberg 1978), what distinguishes the contemporary U.S. situation is the lack of established guidelines for proper behavior in remarried life. Adults and children in a remarriage—who form the so-called reconstituted family—do not know how they are expected to behave in a large number of everyday situations. Stepparents, for instance, are unsure of how firmly they can discipline their stepchildren; ex-spouses do not know how civil their relationships with each other are supposed to be; and no one knows what term a stepchild who still has a living father should use in addressing the stepfather. The support provided to these individuals by the social institution of the family—the set of norms and values that define appropriate behavior—is inadequate. Remarriage after divorce is what I have called elsewhere an <u>incomplete institution</u> (Cherlin 1978a).

The result of this lack of institutional support is increased uncertainty among members of reconstituted families about how they should behave in common situations. By way of contrast, we can see that the institution of the family provides a large number of guidelines to families of first marriages, guidelines that are taken for granted until their absence—as in remarriages—causes difficulties. People in first marriages know, without stopping to think, what types of discipline are appropriate for their children and what terms to use in addressing each other. Adults in first marriages and their children, then, are able to rely on habit to guide them in most aspects of everyday life. Habitual behavior, as writers as diverse as Berger and Luckmann (1966) and Simon (1957) have pointed out, assists people by narrowing choices. Members of reconstituted families, however, face too many choices too often, and since different family members frequently have competing interests (Bernard 1956), conflict can result over what decision to take. Therefore, just as steady employment structures the environment of family members, so too does the set of norms that forms the institution of the family. Commonly accepted rules about behavior influence a family's activities and decisions in a way that furthers the values of the institution—in this case, the value of a stable and harmonious family life. All this occurs in the same manner that the rules of a bureaucracy guide the actions of a bureaucrat so as to further the values of the organization.

The consequences of a lack of guidelines, however, may differ between families and formal organizations. The goals of family life—such as family unity—are intrinsically rewarding, and they become central to a person's sense of well-being. For example, when Campbell, Converse, and Rodgers (1976) asked a national sample of adults to rank a number of aspects of their lives according to their overall importance, a happy marriage was ranked second (after good health), and a good family life was ranked third. Because marriage and family life are so important to personal satisfaction, conflicts over appropriate behavior in remarriages are likely to lead to psychological distress, especially increased anxiety and depression. Yet in a formal organization, the rewards for achieving the goals of the organization are primarily extrinsic— such as a raise in salary—and successful performance of these goals, while still important to individuals, is less central to feelings of well-being. Thus, in the Campbell, Converse, and Rodgers study, an interesting job ranked seventh in importance and a large bank account ranked eleventh. Under these circumstances, I would suggest, it is less likely that increased anxiety and depression will follow from uncertainty about appropriate behavior in a formal organization. For members of reconstituted families, however, the heightened levels of conflict and anxiety that incomplete institutionalization produces are, presumably, one reason why the divorce rate is even higher in remarriages than in first marriages (U.S., Bureau of the Census 1976).

THE RATIONALIZATION OF FAMILY LIFE

These examples illustrate some of the ways in which uncertainty affects family life. In order to better understand the role of uncertainty, it may be useful to examine briefly some of the historical trends in family life that have shaped the current situation. This analysis may enlighten us as to whether the effects of uncertainty have been a constant element in family life or whether these effects have changed in recent decades. If there has been a change, a look at historical developments may suggest whether uncertainty currently plays a larger role in some aspects of family life and a smaller role in others than in the past.

Much of the uncertainty family members face currently is a result of the long-term trend toward the rationalization of family life. People are said to be acting rationally when they act with a specific goal in mind and when they choose the most appropriate means of attaining that goal from among those known and available to them. Thus, rational action presupposes both a goal and the possibility of choosing among alternative ways of achieving it. Irrational action, in contrast, may involve unthinking obedience to norms or customs. Max Weber (1968) is the most prominent of a long line of scholars who have argued that social life became increasingly rational with the rise of capitalism. According to Weber, the pervasiveness of rationality, especially in the quintessential form of the bureaucracy, is one of the central characteristics of modern life.

Weber also emphasized the connection between the growth of rationality and the growth of the state, and it is the state that has influenced most strongly the changing nature of family life. The influence of the state, however, was ignored by most students of family life until recently. Sociologists tended to study the family as if it were isolated, as if it were merely a "unity of interacting personalities," in the famous phrase of Burgess (1926). Societal controls on family life had diminished, according to Burgess, so that the family had changed "from an institution to a companionship" (Burgess and Locke 1945, p. 7). Consequently, most students of marriage limited their studies to the personal characteristics of husbands and wives: their adaptability, sociability, and so forth.

But in reality, the growth of the modern state has had much to do with defining the nature of family life. In precapitalist societies, the institution of the family often was the basis of social organization. Yet today, many of the functions that families used to perform have been taken over by the state, as Ogburn (1938) observed. Modern states established schools, armies, police forces, prisons, and a host of public welfare institutions to perform tasks previously left to family members. Even the criterion of membership in society changed. Formerly, a person's status in a society was determined at birth by his or her links to kin through the father and mother—what Malinowski (1930) called the <u>principle of legitimacy</u>. Now, a person's status is determined at birth by the principle of citizenship: all children are guaranteed full status by the state.

The state left to the family those tasks that were less central to the state's interests. The family remained the setting for emotional gratification; it became the primary place where personal needs were met. As functions were transferred to the state, many of the customs and norms that had regulated family behavior in the interest of society lost their force. No longer was the patriarch the unchallenged head of the home, and no longer did parents choose marriage partners for their children. Nor was divorce necessarily seen as a personal tragedy, or out-of-wedlock births universally abhorred. Consequently, family members have become freer to pursue their own interests and to choose the most appropriate means for doing so; in other words, they have become freer to act rationally. The rise of the state, then, created the conditions that made widespread rational action possible in family life. This change was not complete; we saw from the contrasting situations of first marriages and remarriages that institutional guidelines still regulate much of everyday behavior in first marriages. But the latitude for rational action has widened.

The change means that instead of the solidarity of the larger kinship group taking precedence, the satisfaction of the individual and the family unit has become paramount. In some respects, this emphasis on personal satisfaction is liberating. People need not obey all-encompassing traditions about marriage, childbearing, and childraising. Instead, individuals can make rational choices about many aspects of their personal lives, choices that presumably maximize their satisfaction within the constraints of their situation. But rational behavior has its limits, no less in families than in large-scale organizations. Family members cannot anticpate fully the consequences of their actions; they do not know what values to place on those consequences; and they often fail to consider all the relevant courses of action. As a result, the extension of rational choice to family life brings with it the potential for frustration, anxiety, and conflict.

Consider, for example, a wife and husband who are unhappy with their marriage. A few generations ago they might have remained together and attempted to resolve their problems because of community pressure or because of concern about the effects of a divorce on their children. Today, there is much less sentiment against divorce, and some widely cited research seems to show that children are better off living with a divorced parent than living in an "unhappy, unbroken home" (Nye 1957). But no study and no social norms tell married persons how unhappy they must be before separation is the preferable alternative for themselves and their children. The spouse who takes custody of the children after a divorce—usually the wife—faces an uncertain financial situation and an ambiguous social situation. Many, perhaps most, husbands do not pay alimony and child support regularly, so the economic position of mothers often declines after a divorce (Hoffman 1977). As Goode (1956) noted, the social role of the divorced person and the relationship of others to her or him is ill-defined. Thus, parents who contemplate divorce face an agonizing decision, which, while it can result in a long-term increase in personal satisfaction, also can result in a short-term rise in distress for all concerned (Weiss 1975).

Although there has been a trend toward greater rationality in family life, the amount of uncertainty that family members face has decreased in some respects due to medical and technological improvements. Perhaps the most notable example is the regulation of fertility. Even in preindustrial societies, there were attempts to regulate births (Wrigley 1969), but fertility control was far from adequate until recently. Only in the last few decades have major advances in contraceptive technology made a high degree of control attainable. Now the so-called medical methods of contraception— the pill, the IUD, and surgical sterilization—along with the widespread use of abortion, allow couples (and single women) to plan the births of their children with a high degree of certainty. Less than 10 percent of all U.S. couples in 1960 who were not trying to have children were using a medical method of contraception; but by 1970, more than 50 percent were using one of these methods (Westoff and Ryder 1977). This new capability has had profound effects on family life. In the United States, there has been a sharp decline in unwanted births (Westoff and Ryder 1977). One result of this decline should be better child-care; parents are presumably better prepared, economically and psychologically, to raise children who are planned. The decline in unwanted births also has made it easier for both parents to work outside the home, because there are fewer years in which preschool children, who need a great deal of care, are present in the home. Young wives with career aspirations can postpone childbearing until their careers are well under way, and there is evidence that some are doing so (Cherlin 1978b). Others may decide to remain childless; the decline in fertility has lengthened the average duration of the "empty-nest" stage of marriage, which occurs after all children leave home.

In addition, another type of uncertainty has declined: the possibility that a husband, wife, or child will die. The decline in child mortality may have led parents to develop stronger emotional ties with their children (Aries 1962); it also may have led parents to have fewer children, since they could be more confident that a child would survive to adulthood. As for adult mortality, as late as 1920, more than a fifth of all children in the United States lost either their father or mother by age 18. Today, the corresponding proportion is much lower—probably less than a tenth (Bane 1979). Family members now can expect that the family unit will not be broken involuntarily. But although there was much uncertainty about the survival of parents in past time, the consequences of a death were quite different from the consequences of a divorce today. In most preindustrial societies, where early death was common, standard procedures existed for responding to a death in the family. Often, remarriage occurred quickly, out of necessity; in Plymouth Colony, many widows and widowers remarried within a year (Demos 1970). In some societies, it was the custom for widows to marry the dead husband's brother (Fox 1967). In these and other ways, the surviving family members were reintegrated into the community in an established way. Norms about how family members should act following a death may have been institutionalized to a greater extent than are norms today about how to act following a divorce.

Overall, then, rational calculation has replaced obedience to tradition as the dominant mode of behavior in family life. Many of the norms governing the actions of family members have lost their authority. This is especially true in those aspects of family life, such as divorce, cohabitation, and fertility control, which have changed so rapidly as to make existing norms out of date. The rise of the state, and its intrusion into family matters, appears to have played a large part in undermining the force of tradition. Free of the restrictions of custom, family members can act so as to increase their individual satisfaction, but they often find that deciding on the most appropriate course of action to do so is a difficult and anxiety-producing task.

THE CONSEQUENCES OF UNCERTAINTY

How, then, should we study the nature and consequences of uncertainty in family life today? One way is to study the responses of family members to uncertainty. There are a number of plausible responses to an uncertain situation. The first is anticipatory behavior: individuals may pursue a course of action to protect themselves and their families against the possibility of an undesirable event occurring in the future. There is evidence, for instance, that for some unhappy wives, labor force participation is an anticipatory response to the possibility of a divorce. In an analysis of the National Longitudinal Survey of Young Women, Mott and Moore (1977) found that white married women were more likely to be in the labor force if their marriages were to break up in the following year than if they were to remain married in the following year, other things being equal. The implication that Mott and Moore drew is that many women in troubled marriages entered the labor force so that they would have a source of income in the event that they became divorced. This implication, however, could not be tested directly with the survey data, and it is open to the opposite assumption of causal ordering.

Similarly, we know that labor force participation rates are higher for women in remarriages than for women in first marriages (Cain 1966). Having lived alone or with relatives for a time, women in remarriages are likely to have faced the problem of supporting themselves and their cildren. They may be more likely, therefore, to maintain an independent economic position in case they face a second—or third—divorce. Some support for this conjecture comes from evidence that a couple's economic situation appears to be a more important determinant of divorce and separation in remarriages than in first marriages (Cherlin 1979). But the research findings on anticipatory behavior are far from definitive.

Family members may also respond to uncertainty by attempting to change the social institution of the family. They may attempt to restructure their kinship network or to modify existing norms so as to compensate for the uncertainties of their situation. Ethnographic studies, for instance, have shown how some low-income black families have constructed networks of kin and friends based on the exchange of goods and services (Stack 1974). By providing assistance to members of this network, an individual obligates others to assist him or her at some unspecified time in the future. Thus, if a mother who has loaned furniture to others is unable to buy clothes for her children, she can turn to her network for help. Stack suggested that this system is a response to the marginal position of many poor blacks in the U.S. economy—a rational adaptation to high unemployment. Future research must determine how widespread this adaptation is among blacks and other groups in the United States and abroad and how it has developed historically.

Remarried adults and their children also try to modify the institution of the family to meet their needs. Their problem, as I mentioned previously, is less a lack of resources than a lack of behavioral guidelines. Consequently, many remarried individuals spend a great deal of time trying to develop a consensus on proper behavior. In the past few years, a number of organizations, newsletters, and other means of communication have been established by remarried adults. Their attempts to construct a consensus are continuing at this time; their efforts provide an opportunity for social researchers to observe how the norms of a fundamental social institution are restructured.

Another response to uncertainty is conflict within the family. Given unstable expectations about employment or fertility or stepparent-stepchild relations, family members may argue more frequently about what behavior is appropriate. This seems especially likely in families of remarriages, where the members often have different interests, as Bernard (1956) noted. But uncertainty also could have the opposite effect: it could promote solidarity among family members. Whether, for example, family members rally around an unemployed male parent or blame him for failing to provide a stable income is an empirical question. Komarovsky (1940) suggested that much depends on the state of family relations before the onset of unemployment, but there has been little further research since her study.

The last response to uncertainty that I will consider is fatalism, or resignation. Given a high degree of uncertainty, family members may decide that there is no use in attempting to combat the effects of instability with the meager level of resources available to them. Instead, they may resign themselves to an unpleasant situation; they may accept their inability to control fertility, or they may withdraw from participation in the labor market. Fatalism is one of the characteristics that Lewis (1966) and others have ascribed to the more general "culture of poverty." Whether such a culture exists has been a topic of much debate (Valentine 1968). The possibility still remains that some families resign themselves to an uncertain future, but this response has not been demonstrated convincingly.

One might investigate, moreover, the conditions under which each of the responses mentioned above is more likely to occur. One hypothesis might be that the type of response varies according to access to resources. Anticipatory behavior and attempts to modify institutional norms should be more probable when resources such as marketable skills or support groups exist; conversely, conflict and resignation may be more probable when there is a lack of resources to change the situation. In addition, at least two of the responses I have mentioned are similar to "exit" and "voice," the general responses to decline in organizations noted by Hirschman (1970): anticipatory behavior is a form of _exit_ (as is a marital separation), and attempts to change norms or create new norms about family life are similar to _voice_. Following Hirschman, then, we might hypothesize that variations in "loyalty" to the organization—in this case commitment to the family unit—would affect the likelihood of choosing exit or voice; where commitment is lower, anticipatory behavior would be more likely and attempts to modify the institution less likely, and the opposite should be true where commitment is higher. Yet, it would be a mistake to suppose that the responses mentioned here are mutually exclusive; rather, some combination is likely to occur.

In addition to studying responses to uncertainty, future researchers also should be concerned with monitoring changes in the amounts and types of uncertainty family members face. An implicit hypothesis of this chapter has been that changes in economic and technological circumstances affect the level of uncertainty in family life. Thus, widespread unemployment causes widespread income instability, and better birth control methods reduce the uncertainties of planning births. It is possible that the causal sequence works the other way—that uncertainties, in turn, influence the economy and, the level of technology—but the impact of the economy and technology on uncertainty seems to be large and worthy of further study.

I have already discussed how, in some respects, uncertainty has declined. But in other respects, uncertainty may have increased in recent years due to a number of major changes in family life. Consider, for example, the large-scale movement of wives into the labor force. On the one hand, the income earned by wives reduces the overall instability of the family's income and provides a buffer against the unemployment of one spouse. Furthermore, in the event of divorce, the wife's employment experience should increase her economic security and that of her children; she should be able to find a better job than if she had not worked previously, and she should be less dependent on alimony and child-support payments. On the other hand, however, the new type of family in which both spouses have life-long careers can lead to uncertainties about proper behavior. The dual-career family, first studied extensively by Rapoport and Rapoport (1969), became visible in the mid-1960s, but at that time, there were no established norms about how these families should resolve the often conflicting demands of work life and home life. Much of the Rapoports' research describes the attempts of husbands and wives to develop new norms about appropriate family behavior. Thus, the changes in women's roles may have increased uncertainty in some aspects of family life and decreased uncertainty in other aspects. The precise effects of these changes only can be determined by further study.

Other recent changes in family life also may affect the level of uncertainty. Persons living in single-parent families face ambiguities in their roles and responsibilities; for instance, as more single women decide to have children, legal issues, such as support by the father and the child's inheritance rights, need to be resolved. Also, declining fertility and mortality may create a large, older, dependent population for whom support is uncertain—witness the current concern about the social security fund. Similar kinds of ambiguities may confront individuals in other alternative family forms, such as communes.

Yet by the end of the 1970s, many of the nontraditional forms of family—single-parent families, reconstituted families, and dual-career families—became much more common. It is possible that with this rise in numbers, the ambiguities that nontraditional families face will be reduced by the cumulative efforts of the family members. By exerting pressure on government and industry to meet their needs, as well as by creating accepted solutions to their common dilemmas, these family members may act to reduce uncertainties. Noting the struggle of remarried adults to create new norms, an eminent anthropologist wrote in 1970, "It is my opinion that nothing short of a presidental blue-ribbon committee . . . can lead to new and approved patterns of family organization" (Bohannan 1970). I would suggest, however, that these patterns may be emerging already among remarried adults, as well as among people in other nontraditional families. If so, then instead of awaiting the report of a presidential committee, social scientists interested in uncertainty and family life might be better advised to study the current efforts of family members themselves.

REFERENCES

Aries, P. 1962. Centuries of Childhood. New York: Random House.

Bane, M. J. 1979. "Marital Disruption and the Lives of Children." In Divorce and Separation: A Survey of Causes and Consequences, edited by G. Levinger and O. C. Moles, pp. 276-86. New York: Basic.

Becker, G. S.; Landes, E. M.; and Michael, R. T. 1977. "An Economic Analysis of Marital Instability." Journal of Political Economy 85 (November/December): 1141-87.

Berger, P. L., and T. Luckmann. 1966. The Social Construction of Reality. New York: Doubleday.

Bernard, J. 1956. Remarriage. New York: Dryden.

Bohannan, P. Social Anthropology. 1963. New York: Holt, Rinehart & Winston.

———. 1970. "Divorce Chains, Households of Remarriage, and Multiple Divorces." In *Divorce and After*, edited by P. Bohannan, pp. 127-39. New York: Doubleday.

Burgess, E. W. 1926. "The Family as a Unity of Interacting Personalities." *The Family* 7: 3-9.

Burgess, E. W., and Locke, H. J. 1945. *The Family: From Institution to Companionship*. New York: American.

Cain, G. 1966. *Married Women in the Labor Force: An Economic Analysis*. Chicago: University of Chicago Press.

Campbell, A.; Converse, P. E.; and Rodgers, W. L. 1976. *The Quality of American Life*. New York: Russell Sage Foundation.

Cherlin, A. "The Effects of Children on Marital Dissolution." *Demography* 14 (August) 265-72.

———. 1978a. "Remarriage as an Incomplete Institution." *American Journal of Sociology* 84: (November): 634-50.

———. 1978b. *Postponing Marriage: The Influence of Schooling, Working, and Work Plans for Young Women*. Paper presented at Annual Meeting of the American Sociological Association, San Francisco, September.

———. 1979. "Work Life and Marital Dissolution." In *Divorce and Separation: A Survey of Causes and Consequences*, edited by G. Levinger and O. C. Moles, pp. 151-66. New York: Basic.

Demos, J. 1970. *A Little Commonwealth: Family Life in Plymouth Colony*. London: Oxford University Press.

Fox, R. 1967. *Kinship and Marriage*. Baltimore: Penguin.

Furstenberg, F. F., Jr. 1978. *Recycling the Family: Perspectives for Researching a Neglected Family Form*. Paper presented at Meeting of the American Sociological Association, San Francisco, September.

Glick, P. C., and Norton, A. J. 1971. "Frequency, Duration, and Probability of Marriage and Divorce." *Journal of Marriage and the Family* 33 (May): 307-17.

Goode, W. J. 1956. *Women in Divorce.* New York: Free Press.

Hirschman, A. O. 1970. *Exit, Voice, and Loyalty.* Cambridge, Mass.: Harvard University Press.

Hoffman, S. 1977. "Marital Instability and the Economic Status of Women." *Demography* 14 (February): 67-76.

Komarovsky, M. 1940. *The Unemployed Man and His Family.* New York: Dryden.

Lewis, O. 1966. *La Vida.* New York: Random House.

McKeown, T. 1976. *The Modern Rise of Population.* New York: Academic Press.

Malinowski, B. 1930. "Parenthood, the Basis of Social Structure." In *The New Generation,* edited by V. F. Calverton and S. D. Schmalhausen, pp. 113-68. New York: Macauley.

March, J. G. 1978. "Bounded Rationality, Ambiguity, and the Engineering of Choice." *Bell Journal of Economics* 9: 587-608.

Mott, Frank L., and Moore, Sylvia F. 1977. "Marital Disruption: Causes and Consequences." In *Years to Decision* 4, edited by Frank L. Mott, Steven H. Sandell, David Shapiro, Patricia K. Brito, Timothy J. Carr, Rex C. Johnson, Carol L. Jusenius, Peter J. Kuenig, and Sylvia F. Moore, pp. 207-56. Columbus: Center for Human Resource Research, Ohio State University.

Nye, F. I. 1957. "Child Adjustment in Broken and Unhappy Unbroken Homes." *Marriage and Family Living* 19: 356-60.

Ogburn, W. F. 1938. "The Changing Family." *The Family* 19: 139-43.

Rapoport, R., and Rapoport, R. N. 1969. "The Dual-Career Family: A Variant Pattern and Social Change." *Human Relations* 22: 3-30.

Ross, H. L., and Sawhill, I. V. 1975. *Time of Transition: The Growth of Families Headed by Women.* Washington, D.C.: The Urban Institute.

Simon, H. A. 1955. "A Behavioral Model of Rational Choice." *Quarterly Journal of Economics* 69: 99-118.

———. 1956. "Rational Choice and the Structure of the Environment." *Psychological Review* 63: 129-38.

———. 1957. *Administrative Behavior*. 2d ed. New York: Macmillan.

Stack, C. B. 1974. *All Our Kin: Strategies for Survival in a Black Community*. New York: Harper & Row.

U.S., Bureau of the Census. 1976. *Number, Timing, and Duration of Marriages and Divorces in the United States: June 1975*. Current Population Reports, Series P-20, no. 297. Washington, D.C.: Government Printing Office.

Valentine, C. A. 1968. *Culture and Poverty*. Chicago: University of Chicago Press.

Walker, K. N.; Rogers, J.; and Messinger, L. 1977. "Remarriage after Divorce: A Review." *Social Casework* 58 (May): 276-85.

Weber, M. 1968. *Economy and Society*. New York: Bedminster.

Weiss, R. S. 1975. *Marital Separation*. New York: Basic.

Westoff, C. F., and Ryder, N. B. 1977. *The Contraceptive Revolution*. Princeton, N.J.: Princeton University Press.

Wrigley, E. A. 1969. *Population and History*. New York: McGraw-Hill.

16
CLINICAL CHOICE UNDER UNCERTAINTY: ITS SIGNIFICANCE FOR REGULATING HOSPITALIZATION RATES
C. E. Brian Frost

Observed differences in hospitalization rates, particularly for surgery, have been blamed on physicians' professional discretion. Hospitalization rates can also vary because of variation in morbidity patterns and payment systems. These two elements, along with the physician's technical knowledge, are identified as the determining factors of a simple model of physician behavior. Fee-splitting and referral arrangements are interpreted in the light of the model and assessed in terms of their likely effect on consultation rates. Three types of regulatory activity in the United States (Professional Standards Review Organization [PSRO], Certificate of Need [CON] programs, and rates regulation) are discussed, with special reference to their significance for clinical choice under uncertainty. PSRO and CON are found not to be mutually supportive, and it is suggested that rates regulation is a more flexible instrument for regulating hospitalization rates in accordance with patients' and community values.

Over the next few years, it is likely that the clinical freedom of medical practitioners will diminish as a result of government regulation of hospitals. The concept of clinical choice is clearly fundamental to an understanding of the issues raised by such regulatory action, and one of the main themes of this contribution is that if the concept of choice between alternative treatments is related to uncertainty of diagnosis, the interaction between the physician and his/her patient will be better understood. Further, if the effect of regulation by external agencies on clinical choice is to be fully appreciated, more needs to be known about the medical allocative system and its interface with conventional competitive markets.

Considerable interest has been displayed recently in the idea of the hospital as an economic institution in its own right. Behavioral models have been developed to explain the determination of hospital outputs and costs, and a survey of this literature is provided by Jacobs (1974). A novel approach to assessing the effect of regulation on clinical choice involves abandoning traditional models of the hospital in favor of a model of the physician. Before developing these ideas, it might be useful to consider certain aspects of the delivery of medical care.

THE MEDICAL ALLOCATIVE SYSTEM

A number of observations regarding the delivery of medical care can be condensed into three stylized facts. The first fact is the substantial variation in surgery, which Bunker and others have noted (for example, Bunker 1970). Typically, this variation has been measured in terms of number of operations (with or without complications) performed per head of the population of a region or country. Hospitalization for nonsurgical conditions has also been observed to vary (Cullis, Forster, and Frost 1978). Clearly, available capacity is an important factor determining the hospitalization rate observed in practice. There is widespread agreement that an increase in hospital beds will lead to an increase in the hospitalization rate. This phenomenon, which has been termed Say's law of hospital beds by some, or Roemer's law, after its discoverer, by others, will constitute the second stylized fact. Finally, it is usually observed that there is a positive association between the density of hospital physicians and consultation rates. Further, this phenomenon appears to be independent of the payment system in force for hospital physicians. It might also be claimed that closely related stylized facts hold for other branches of clinical medicine.

Physicians accept that some variations in medical practice are difficult to account for. Differences in hospitalization rates might have gone unheeded, particularly when the efficacy of some treatments is disputed within the medical profession (Cochrane 1972). The fact that these differences have attracted unfavorable comment must be due in part to the rising cost of medical care and public concern over its quality and availability.

Contrary to normal expectations, technological change has made medical care more rather than less expensive (Scitovsky 1967). A demand-and-supply-type explanation of this phenomenon would stress the possibility that the growth in demand has outstripped any cost-conditioning improvements. The trend toward wider insurance coverage and the increasing reliance of patients on third-party payments might well be quoted in support of this view.

The market model works well when the demand-determining factors are fully independent of the supply-determining factors. In the view of some, this condition is not satisfied for medical care because, to an exceptional degree, the physician determines price, quality, and quantity of treatment (Culyer and Cullis 1976). In addition, the patient, through a combination of ignorance and uncertainty, is frequently restricted to making all-or-nothing choices when deciding to seek a consultation or to continue with treatment. This does not mean that there is no demand curve or that it does not have the conventional downward slope. The current concern with hospital-cost inflation surely stems from a belief that there are diminishing returns to medical care. What these considerations suggest, however, is that the layman and the physician have different perceptions of the demand-determining factors.

Uncertainty and Clinical Choice

Uncertainty affects clinical choice in a way that is only just beginning to be understood. The recognition of its significance represents another point of departure from traditional models of the hospital. The work of von Neumann, Morgenstern, Edwards, and Savage has greatly enhanced contemporary understanding of the expected utility hypothesis. Uncertainty characterizes medical treatment almost as much as it does gambling, statistical inference, and insurance, to name but a few areas where the expected utility hypothesis has found an application. To understand its relevance for modeling physician behavior, some aspects of the physician-patient relationship can usefully be considered.

An individual presents himself to a physician with a view to seeking advice, reassurance, or action initiated by the physician. The one outcome that the patient can be sure of is that his/her treatment will be determined by the physician's knowledge. In return for accepting someone as a patient, the physician may receive a fee for item of service, a capitation payment, or nothing at all. However experienced or talented the physician may be, s/he cannot normally guarantee the effectiveness of treatment. This is because of the presence of uncertainty that is inherent in the diagnosis or the outcome of treatment.

Summary

The medical allocative system needs to be discussed in relation to the concept of clinical choice. Traditional demand and supply analysis is not helpful because of its focus on aggregate measures of output rather than on individual patients. The physician's decision process as it relates to one patient will be considered next, and this discussion will be of assistance in developing a model of physician behavior, which will be used to explain the three stylized facts. This chapter will conclude with a discussion of various forms of regulatory activity and their implications for clinical choice.

A MODEL OF THE MEDICAL CONSULTATION

During the consultation, the physician will be looking for information that will help him/her to select the most appropriate treatment for the patient. It is convenient to assume that the physician is seeing the patient for the first time, thus ruling out prior knowledge of the patient's morbidity. From the medical point of view, there is substantial agreement that diagnosis precedes treatment (Feinstein 1967, p. 73). This implies that the search for information is designed to slot the patient into a disease category, which, once determined, may be used to select the most appropriate treatment. At this stage, the possibility cannot be excluded that the physician will decide that nothing shall be done either because the patient is not ill or because there is no known cure or palliative.

Feedback during the course of treatment may lead the physician to revise his/her initial diagnosis. In other words, when the physician takes his/her initial decision on treatment, s/he may have at his/her command less information than s/he requires for a definitive diagnosis. The behavior of the physician in the presence of uncertainty can be modeled by making two assumptions: first, that the uncertainty of diagnosis can be measured in terms of probability, and, second, that the physician chooses between outcomes according to their relative desirability. When these two assumptions hold true, the expected utility hypothesis is appropriate. The interested reader is referred to Luce and Raiffa (1957) for further information about the hypothesis and to Lusted (1968) for a summary of its previous applications to clinical decision-making. A previous work has shown that it is possible, using the expected utility hypothesis, to model a salaried physician's induced demand for medical resources, and this model has been successfully tested using National Health Service (NHS) data for selected hospital specialties (Frost 1979). It is now intended to amend the model to cover the case of a profit-orientated physician whose fees or rates are regulated by an external agency—that is, the third assumption will be that physicians' maximum fees are unalterable. In view of this modification, it is appropriate to reconsider the position regarding the scarcity of medical resources.

In most countries before World War II, the physician's willingness to pay determined his/her command over medical resources. The position is very different today. In England, NHS hospitals are financed by taxes, and hospital physicians, in general, do not exercise budgetary responsibilities. In the United States, the regulation of investment in hospital beds and other major items of expenditure through CON programs now extends to a number of states, and in the view of some commentators (for example, Cain and Darling 1979), this development represents a significant departure from previous attempts to regulate the hospital sector through rates regulation and indicative planning. For the present, however, all regulation of the hospital sector apart from rates regulation will be assumed to be absent.

An example first introduced to illustrate a model of the salaried physician will now be adapted to illustrate the model of the profit-oriented physician. Consider a physician who is being consulted by a patient with jaundice. The causes of jaundice are various, but let them, in this instance, be artificially restricted to just two, which would be: acute viral hepatitis (condition 1), and tumor of the biliary tree (condition 2). Suppose also that the physician's prior probabilities are .4 for condition 1 and .6 for condition 2. The physician's immediate decision is whether to withhold surgery (action 1) or to operate (action 2). The physician is paid according to the following payoff matrix:

		Condition	
		1	2
Action	1	$R(1,1)$	$R(1,2)$
	2	$R(2,1)$	$(R(2,2)$

The possibility that the physician's fee depends not only on the treatment but, also, on the underlying condition will be kept open at this stage. The expected value of not operating will be

$0.4R(1,1) + 0.6R(1,2)$

whereas the expected value of operating will be

$0.4R(2,1) + 0.6R(2.2)$

The expected value of an action is not necessarily the most frequently occurring value or even a possible value. For some statisticians, the expected value is the mean value in repeated sampling, while others define the term as the probability of each condition times the resulting fee, summed over all conditions. Both definitions have their advocates. Fortunately, both lead to much the same results, and whichever definition is favored, it will be assumed that the physician chooses the action that yields the greatest expected monetary value.

As a description of the physician's decision process, the model is unrealistic because it appears to overlook several important considerations, such as the cost of treatment, the relevance of clinical findings, and the structure of incentives.

The physician's out-of-pocket expenses need to be deducted from the fee actually paid. This means that a profit-oriented physician will not wish to maximize the expected value of the gross fee, but, rather, the expected value of the fee net of costs paid by the physician and directly attributable to the treatment of the patient. Even under the fee for service system, the net fee may depend on the patient's condition, as well as the treatment, because the cost of treatment may be affected by the patient's true condition.

The physician's diagnosis is based on clinical findings, which do not appear to feature in the model. Arguably, no intelligible model can possibly encompass the variety of clinical tests and findings that are available to the contemporary physician. Another complicating feature is that the interpretation of a symptom or test result can owe just as much to the physician's experience as it does to modern science. A useful solution to this problem would be one that covers both possibilities. In addition, the solution should explain why the physician changes his/her beliefs in response to clinical findings.

Suppose the physician is reviewing his/her decision to operate in the light of the serum alkaline phosphatase test. From reading the medical literature or from past experience, the physician knows that a given test value, s, occurs two and two-thirds more often for condition 1 than it does for condition 2. In technical language, the ratio of the probabilities of the test result s arising from condition 1 rather than condition 2 (that is, the likelihood ratio of condition 1 to condition 2) is eight to three. By a straightforward application of Bayes's theorem, it can be deduced that the probability of condition 1 given the test result s (usually referred to as the <u>posterior probability</u> of condition 1) is .64, implying that the equivalent posterior probability of condition 2 is .36. In reality, the physician may call for a whole battery of tests. As a result, additional evidence may be obtained confirming the physician's view that the correct diagnosis is almost certainly condition 1. The principle of the calculation is substantially the same regardless of the number of the test results considered. Depending on the actual value of the net fees, the physician may now decide that an operation is no longer required. However, the more surprising possibility that the physician may still go ahead with an operation has not been entirely eliminated. The expected value, it must be remembered, depends not only on the probability set but, also, on the set of values appearing in the payoff matrix. This matter will now be considered in more detail.

For a particular patient, any number of incentive structures are consistent with one or other of the two actions. It may appear, therefore, that the choice of incentive structure is of secondary importance for clinicians and their patients, but, it will be argued, the opposite is really the case. To understand why this is so, consider the position of the physician who is paid $1,000 for a correct diagnosis, but nothing at all for an incorrect diagnosis (that is, $R(1,1) = R(2,2) = 1,000; R(1,2) = R(2,1) = 0$). Such a fee schedule may be called <u>neutral between diagnoses</u> because the physician is not predisposed to one diagnosis rather than another. Before the results of the phosphatase test were known, the physician would have operated, but on receipt of the test results, surgery is abandoned. If the value of correct treatment to the patient is at least $1,000 and the expected value of not operating (.64. 1000 + .36. 0 = 640) exceeds the treatment costs to third parties (charities, governments, and so forth), then it is safe to assume that the most appropriate treatment has been prescribed and that both the patient and the community will benefit from the treatment.

By way of contrast, consider a fee schedule that is neutral between treatments (that is, each entry in the payoff matrix is $x). In this case, the physician will receive the same net fee regardless of his/her action, and the choice of treatment, for a profit-maximizing physician, will be arbitrary. Considered from the perspective of a patient who values correct diagnosis only, the situation is even worse when the fee schedule is biased toward treatments. For example, if payment is only made for surgery and the net fee for the operation is $x, surgery will always be preferred by a profit-maximizing physician as long as x is positive. Clearly, this situation is not desirable, particularly for life-threatening diseases, such as hepatitis. There is a fourth assumption implicit in the foregoing, which is that the physician maximizes his/her total net income (or "profit") for the number of hours that s/he works. Of course, if the physician's preferences for leisure do not affect his/her clinical activities, this is equivalent to assuming that the physician is a straightforward profit maximizer. Many, if not all, physicians do ignore the dictates of imperfect incentive structures: a fact that we all have every reason to be grateful for. Why they do so is a matter that deserves further study.

One possibility is that physicians derive from their work a satisfaction that does not depend on their fees. One source for this job satisfaction could be the pleasure derived from making a correct diagnosis. In other words, over and above the net fee appearing in the payoff matrix, there may be a psychic satisfaction. In particular, the psychic incentive structure may be neutral between diagnoses; to the extent that this incentive structure is present, physicians will themselves be correcting the deficiencies in fee schedules that are neutral or even biased toward treatments.

Yet another possibility derives from the reciprocity that seems to characterize physician referral networks. The case of the patient with jaundice may be used to illustrate this idea. Suppose that the patient was seen initially by a surgeon who, after inspecting the results of the phosphatase test, decides to refer the patient to a specialist in medicine. The proper explanation for the surgeon's referral, in the absence of a direct financial inducement, may be that s/he is participating in a referral network. Several such arrangements have been identified (Freidson 1970, pp. 92-98). In this connection, the important feature is that the surgeon is counting on his/her referrals being reciprocated by his/her colleagues. The surgeon's behavior is easier to understand if it is seen in the context of decisions taken on a group of patients rather than on a single patient. Even if there is no immediate increase in his/her consultations, the referral arrangement can still be advantageous for the surgeon because s/he will now be treating patients whose diagnoses s/he is more sure of. As a result, less litigation will arise, and the surgeon's practice will grow along with his/her reputation. Of course, if the surgeon also obtains a psychic satisfaction from making the correct diagnosis, the incentive to join a referral network will be even stronger. However, in the discussion that follows, such psychic satisfaction will be assumed to be absent from the physician's calculus. In particular, it will be assumed that the physician is a straightforward profit maximizer. Despite its lack of realism, this assumption simplifies the exposition without affecting the substance of the analysis.

A BEHAVIORAL MODEL OF THE PHYSICIAN

Many authors have blamed physicians' professional discretion for the observed differences in consultation and hospitalization rates. An alternative approach adopts the strategy of looking first at morbidity patterns and payment systems. Any variation that is unaccounted for is then attributed to professional discretion. A different method proceeds by examining the factors that contribute to clinical choice; for this purpose, a model of the medical consultation was briefly introduced. The model will now be extended to include decisions taken on a number of patients.

The possibility that each patient can be distinguished from any other in terms of symptoms and clinical findings is fundamental to the explanation of professional discretion. All that is necessary by way of modification of the illustrative example is the recognition that the phosphatase test result can take on any value over a certain range, the limits of which are determined by factors outside the physician's control. As before, the physician will prefer the treatment that maximizes the expected value of his/her fees. In general, there will be a value of the phosphatase test on either side of which different actions will be taken. This particular test value will be called a switch point, and it may be used to identify a patient whose expected value for the two actions is equal. Such a patient will be called a marginal patient.

The value of the phosphatase test identifying a marginal patient depends on the set of values in the payoff matrix and on the set of prior probabilities (which may be identified with the physician's local knowledge) and likelihood functions (which are an essential part of the physician's technical knowledge). It follows that if there is a change in the identity of the marginal patient, it is because of a change in one or other of these determining factors.

Observed differences in consultation rates can to some extent be explained either in terms of physicians educating their patients as to the proper use of the consultation or as a consumer response to price differences. In respect of the latter factor, it is the price perceived by the consumer that is relevant, and this price may be a money or a time price or both. The model of physician behavior, however, is best suited to explain differences in consultation rates attributable to variations in referral practice. Clearly, as each referral leads to an additional consultation, the practice of referral is worth considering in its own right as a factor contributing to the overall consultation rate.

It has long been held that the incentive to refer is irresistable when fee-splitting is practiced. Referrals from a general practitioner to a hospital physician seems to be most conducive to fee-splitting, and it was this practice that attracted the unfavorable reaction of the Committee on the Costs of Medical Care (1932, p. 24, cited by Harris 1964, p. 123). The feature that they criticized was the scope for unnecessary referrals and surgery. We should recognize that the specialization of physicians would not be viable if it were not for the referral system, and patients' well-being owes a great deal to the type of referral system that is permitted. No conceivable system can entirely eliminate unnecessary referrals.

It seems just, therefore, that outright condemnation of fee-splitting should give way to a more pragmatic approach.

The impact of different morbidity patterns and incentive structures on consultation rates requires careful consideration. The morbidity factor will be dealt with first (for the moment, it will be supposed that referrals to hospital physicians are solely in the control of a separate group of physicians, the general practitioners, as in Great Britain). An upward revision by these physicians of the prior probability of hospital treatable conditions will lead to an increase in both the specialists' consultation rate and the overall consultation rate (which is the sum of the consultation rates for both general practitioners and hospital physicians). In the case of self-referrals by patients to hospital physicians, however, it is quite likely that the patient's choice of physician will be an arbitrary one. If this is so, an upward revision by hospital physicians of the prior probability, say, of medical conditions (at the expense of the prior probability of surgical conditions) will affect the consultation rate for individual specialists, but leave the overall consultation rate unchanged. This is because, following the revision of prior probabilities, the direction of referrals will change, but their overall number will remain unaffected. From this brief discussion, it can be seen that whether perceived differences in morbidity do account for variations in the overall consultation rate depends critically on the type of referral. If the referral is from a general practitioner to a hospital physician, then the overall consultation rate will be affected. In the United States, where physicians practicing in the community frequently have access to hospital beds for their private patients, it is to be expected that perceived differences in morbidity will not have such a noticeable impact on the overall consultation rate as in Great Britain, where physicians work either in the hospital or in general practice.

Such considerations are helpful in understanding the implications of different incentive structures. For example, if hospital physicians are in more intense competition with one another than is normal and, as a result, give general practitioners a share of the fee (that is, engage in fee-splitting), it is probable that the overall consultation rate will increase. Hence, wherever fee-splitting is practiced, we should expect to observe a positive association between the overall consultation rate and physician density. On the other hand, even a radical change in hospital physicians' propensity to refer is unlikely to affect the overall consultation rate. There is an important exception to this rule, which almost certainly explains why the positive association between the overall consultation rate and physician density can be independent of the type of payment system in force. This is because higher physician densities permit an increase in the specialization of hospital physicians. At a given time, the specialization of hospital physicians can vary even within one country. In addition, over a period of time, there can be an increase in the specialization of physicians; the changes that have occurred in this respect since 1945 have probably contributed to the observed increases in consultation rates. Whether fee-splitting is more conducive to unnecessary referrals than less formal referral arrangements is a question that deserves reexamination. Suffice it to say that the practices which should be condemned are those which bias the incentive structure of physicians toward treatments, particularly treatments of unproven value.

It may be thought that a direct and positive association between consultation and hospitalization rates is inevitable, because the hospitalization of nonemergency patients is invariably preceded by a consultation. This may be so in many situations, in which case the positive association between consultation rates and physician density can be extended to explain the positive association between hospitalization rates and physician density. However, in other circumstances, it is possible that the association between consultation and hospitalization rates may be tenuous, if not nonexistent. For this reason, it is necessary to understand why hospitalization rates may differ. Consider the case of two physicians, A and B, serving the same community, whose fee schedules are neutral between diagnoses, but who disagree over morbidity. If physician A believes conditions 1 and 2 to be equally probable a priori, then his/her switch point will occur where the likelihood ratio is equal to 1. Physician B, who believes that condition 1 occurs twice as frequently as condition 2, will have a different switch point, which will be identified by the test value associated with a likelihood ratio equal to 2. The variation in switch points is important, because as long as the two physicians are using the same likelihood functions, fewer patients will be given surgery by one physician compared with the other physician's practice.

A plausible explanation of the disagreement over the prior probabilities is that one of the physicians is wrong. Physician A may have held that the two conditions were equally probable in the absence of information to the contrary. If physician B is correctly informed, then it is to be expected that as physician A accumulates more experience, the feedback s/he receives will enable him/her to revise his/her estimates and bring them more into line with physician B's. Alternatively, it is possible that both physicians were correct, the apparent inconsistency being resolved by noting that each was serving a different subpopulation. In the second case, unlike the first, each physician will continue to use a different switch point. In such cases, clinical choice will lead to unresolvable differences in the definition of the marginal patient and in hospitalization rates.

Disagreements over the definition of the marginal patient may be due to differing interpretations being given by physicians to clinical findings. On purely theoretical grounds, it seems reasonable not to overemphasize this possibility, given that physicians can learn from their experience. In particular, as the number of observations increases, the probability that the likelihood ratio will approach a limiting value for a given test will tend to 1. The dissemination through medical schools and the learned journals of the results of diagnostic trials will speed up this process. Therefore, it is likely that this explanation of differences in medical practice will not be as fruitful as others.

The final explanation for the observed variations in hospitalization rates fastens on variations in incentive structure. Even imposing a uniform fee schedule on physicians, who subscribe to a common set of prior probabilities and likelihood functions, may not exclude variations in switch points. Both fee-splitting and referral arrangements can alter the structure of incentives. Therefore physicians, when attending the same patient, can arrive at different actions.

NHS dentists probably come close to sharing a common incentive structure. There is a uniform fee schedule for NHS treatment, and referral to nonhospital-based dentists is rare. The Dental Estimates Board probably tries to satisfy itself that observable variations in NHS dental practice are solely attributable to differences in morbidity. If it cannot, the board can refuse to pay practitioners for individual treatments.

By way of contrast, when private health insurance schemes compete for custom, it is likely that the occurrence of substantial variations in fee schedules will lead to similar variations in switch points. The difficulty here is that as patients from different schemes may be attracted to the same physician, it is quite likely that s/he will not be internally consistent in his/her treatment strategies, because s/he may adopt a different strategy for each scheme. The implied differences in hospitalization rates will not be observable unless the physician has to make an all-or-nothing choice with respect to "contracting into" a particular insurance scheme. Some evidence arising from prepaid group practice supports the view that hospitalization rates are affected by variations in payment method (Donabedian 1969; also Pineault 1976).

It has been suggested that the factors affecting the hospitalization rate of an individual physician are morbidity, technical knowledge, and incentive structure. Of these, the first and last are probably of some importance when it comes to explaining differences in hospitalization practice. As far as a particular physician is concerned, as long as there are spare beds and morbidity and incentive structures are unchanging, an increase in consultations will lead to a similar increase in the number of hospital admissions. This particular combination of circumstances, however, may not often prevail in practice. Nevertheless, when observations are available for areas serving, say, 1 million residents, the relationship between consultation and hospitalization rates may be found to be statistically significant and positive. In this case, there should be a positive association between hospitalization rates and physician density.

REGULATING HOSPITALIZATION RATES

The post-World War II era has been marked by several attempts to regulate hospitalization rates on both sides of the Atlantic. In Great Britain, a national plan for hospitals has been in existence for some time, and on a year-to-year basis, the expenditure of Regional Health authorities is now tightly controlled. In the United States, there have been the PSRO, the CON programs, and the more traditional rates regulation, to mention but three forms of postwar regulatory activity, and each of them will now be assessed in terms of their effect on clinical choice.

In the previous section, it was argued that physicians need not agree on what constitutes a marginal patient. It follows that professional discretion will become apparent in the application of different switch points or professional standards. Even when all physicians face the same incentive structure and subscribe to the same likelihood functions, different switch points will persist as long as physicians have conflicting assessments of prior probabilities. Those who contend that there will be no observable differences in the best professional practice are really saying that uniform switch points should be applied, which means that every physician should be applying the same set of prior probabilities. Even if this were possible, it is hardly desirable, because morbidity does vary across regions and even within narrowly defined areas. In addition, physicians' lists may not be representative of the area they are serving. For these reasons, it has to be recognized that no single mind can possibly be informed of the manner in which physicians adjust to the real differences in their environment. Accepting this point means that the quality of care cannot be regulated on the basis of a uniform set of switch points. At best, all that an external agency can hope to do by way of standardizing switch points is to set ranges within which "normal" practice should fall. These ranges will have to be quite broad if the intention is to apply them nationally or even regionally. Nevertheless, peer review will always be required as an essential adjunct to any such regulatory system. It seems reasonable to conclude that that part of PSRO which is directed toward monitoring switch points may be too expensive in terms of what it can hope to achieve.

Rates regulation based on fee for service will typically show some bias toward either diagnoses or treatments. In fact, as long as fee schedules are not biased toward patients' valuations of outcome, there will be criticism of existing schedules—and the more schedules are biased toward treatments, the louder the criticism will be. If the current concern over professional standards and excessive hospitalization arises from inappropriate fee schedules, then the obvious and sensible remedy is to attend to the disease rather than to the symptom. Excepting fees charged for office consultations and for hospital care (rather than cure) of the dying and the handicapped, both physicians and patients might welcome a move to fee-schedules that are more outcome and less process orientated. Such a schedule should not be confused with one that is everywhere neutral between diagnoses. The fee actually paid could depend on both the diagnosis and the prognosis: it could range from high values for life-threatening conditions that are curable to possibly nothing at all for conditions that do not affect the patient's quality of life. Given that fees will only be paid for correct diagnosis and treatment, physicians would have every incentive to improve on their diagnostic performance, and there might be fewer unnecessary referrals and hospital admissions. Of course, recognition should be given to the fact that the information required for auditing the reformed rates structure is not a free good, but has a cost of acquisition that may not be worth paying.

Several obstacles will have to be overcome before such a fee schedule will be feasible. For example, a physician may be able to reduce his/her audited score of unnecessary treatments by bringing forward the normal time for discharge, and for some patients, at least, reduced lengths of stay may be undesirable. In addition, most physicians would want the fee paid for correctly prescribed treatment to take into account the length and cost of the process by which the diagnosis or discharge had been reached. Hence, fee for service might be reintroduced surreptitiously. These and other difficulties will have to be looked into very carefully. One possible solution might be to pay the physician more when there are complications. An extension of the role played by tissue committees, which are there to protect the patient against unnecessary surgery, may provide one way of taking care of these matters.

The NHS has apparently solved the problem of finding an appropriate incentive structure by abolishing all hospital fees. The difficulty with this solution is that little is known about physicians' psychic incentive structure. To the extent that this incentive structure is not uniform and not regulable, the remaining instrument for controlling hospitalization rates will be the supply of hospital beds.

Regulating the provision of hospital beds and other key hospital facilities has been a feature of the British NHS since its inception. In the United States, an important factor contributing to the spread of such regulation has been the CON program. For a discussion of the background to CON and an early assessment of its effects, see Havighurst (1974, particularly pt. 2) and Cain and Darling (1979). A comparison of the two countries' policies is illuminating. In another work, it has been shown that changes in the provision of NHS hospital beds will affect both the switch point applied by hospital physicians and the demand for bed-days (Frost 1977). The demand for bed-days is the product of the number of admissions and the mean duration of stay. Although this result was obtained for physicians who were utility maximizers, an identical result obtains for profit-maximizing physicians subject to arbitrary capacity constraints. In other words, Roemer's law may be expected to apply whenever the availability of hospital beds is not determined only by market forces. Further, the switch points actually applied by hospital physicians can be affected through the regulation of hospital beds. Hence, switch points will vary either because of variations in hospital bed provision or because of differences in morbidity or incentive structures. This means that regulation of hospital beds will exacerbate the difficulties of reviewing professional standards, but a more substantial criticism of bed regulation as a policy instrument stems from its artlessness. Unless the licensing agencies are well-informed about the configuration of physicians' switch points over all possible conditions, it is unlikely that this type of regulation will achieve its own goals. It is conceivable that hospitalization rates may be equalized by area, while, at the same time, the quality of care will be adversely affected in unpredictable ways. Almost inevitably, hospital physicians will have greater discretionary power than before and yet be even more frustrated by arbitrary capacity constraints. The fact that CON has the tacit support of the medical profession is not paradoxical if the regulation preserves the monopoly position of hospitals.

FINAL REMARKS AND CONCLUSION

A frequent response to the claim that hospitalization rates are excessive and that physicians exercise their discretionary power incorrectly is a call for further regulation, if need be to be supported by legislation. Although many, including physicians themselves, have favored this approach, it seems worthwhile taking stock of what such regulation can hope to achieve. A successful model of physician behavior should help us in this respect because it will give us an appreciation of the factors determining hospitalization rates. The important factors were: prior probabilities (which have been identified with the physician's local knowledge); likelihood ratios (which were viewed as an essential part of the physician's technical knowledge); the structure of incentives, particularly the fee schedule; and the supply of beds.

The regulation of professional standards by, for example, PSRO, has to be weighed against the need for fine-tuning by physicians to real differences in morbidity. The model presented explains why audit according to switch points (that is, audit of outcome according to explicit criteria) will have to be supplemented by peer review (that is, audit of outcome according to implicit criteria). The study of Brook and Appel (1973) is particularly valuable for exploring the degree of conflict that can arise from different types of audit for common medical conditions, even in the best run hospitals. Regardless of the cost of reviewing professional standards, it has been suggested that rates regulation provides a more direct method of control.

In Great Britain, there has been a long history of providing beds to meet observed demand; hence, hospitalization rates have had ample opportunity to adjust to local differences in the supply of beds. Even so, the feeling has grown that the differences that are observed cannot be justified (Logan 1972). The model put forward here and elsewhere attempts to show how clinical choice will be affected by hospital licensure or other arbitrary capacity constraints. Again, the indications are that rates regulation will prove to be more flexible and more responsive to patients' demands.

One strength of the model presented is that it gives due consideration to the experience, as well as the training, of the individual physician. It attempts to show why efforts to regulate hospitalization rates by CON, PSRO, and the like are likely to achieve some goals (for example, the containment of hospitalization rates) at the expense of robbing the person-on-the-spot of some of his/her clinical freedom. To my mind, the relationship of trust between physician and patient will be impaired if it becomes general knowledge that the choice of treatment should conform on average to externally imposed norms. A possible remedy is not to replace one set of arbitrary rules by another set, but, rather, to reexamine the main source of existing incentives: the fee schedule. By revising the schedule so that it is less biased toward treatments and more biased toward conditions, physicians should be given a greater incentive to improve their diagnostic skills. This new arrangement should be to the advantage of the patient and the community given that diagnosis does precede treatment.

POSTSCRIPT

The abundance and regional diversity of institutions and regulatory instruments involved in the delivery of medical care in the United States is well-known; nevertheless, this chapter contains no detailed institutional analysis. The omission is intentional. I have tried to draw attention to the existence of three polar regulatory types, but in practice, a regulatory body may be a composite of more than one of these types. PSRO is a case in point. To see its activities solely in terms of monitoring switch points is a caricature of real life. For example, the prepayment review sanction applied by state PSROs could be even more important for the rates regulatory system.

REFERENCES

Bunker, J. P. 1970. "Surgical Manpower: A Comparison of Operations and Surgeons in the United States and in England and Wales." New England Journal of Medicine 282: 135-43.

Brook, R. H., and Appel, F. A. 1973. "Quality-of-Care Assessment: Choosing a Method for Peer Review." New England Journal of Medicine 288: 1323-29.

Cain, H. P., II, and Darling, H. N. 1979. "Health Planning in the United States: Where We Stand Today." Health Policy and Education 1: 5-25.

Cochrane, A. J. 1972. Effectiveness and Efficiency: Random Reflections on Health Services. London: Nuffield Provincial Hospitals Trust.

Committee on the Costs of Medical Care. 1932. Medical Care for the American People: The Final Report of the Committee on the Costs of Medical Care, adopted October 31st, 1932. Chicago: University of Chicago Press.

Cullis, J. G.; Forster, D. P.; and Frost, C. E. B. 1978. "The Demand for Inpatient Treatment: Some Recent Evidence." Discussion paper 78.5. Sheffield, England: Division of Economic Studies, University of Sheffield.

Culyer, A. J., and Cullis, J. G. 1976. "Some Economics of Hospital Waiting Lists in the NHS." Journal of Social Policy 5: 239-64.

Donabedian, A. 1969. "An Evaluation of Pre-paid Group Practice." Inquiry 6: 3-27.

Feinstein, A. R. 1967. Clinical Judgement. Baltimore, Md.: Williams and Wilkins.

Freidson, E. 1970. Profession of Medicine: A Study of the Sociology of Applied Knowledge. New York: Dodd, Mead.

Frost, C. E. B. 1977. "Clinical Decision-making and the Utilization of Medical Resources." Social Science and Medicine 11: 793-99.

Frost, C. E. B., and Francis, B. J. 1979. "Clinical Decision-making: A Study of General Surgery in Trent RHA." Social Science and Medicine 13A: 193-98.

Harris, S. E. 1964. The Economics of American Medicine. New York: Macmillan.

Havighurst, C. C., ed. 1974. Regulating Health Facilities Construction: Proceedings of a Conference on Health Planning, Certificates of Need, and Market Entry. Washington, D.C.: American Institute for Public Policy Research.

Jacobs, P. 1974. "A Survey of Economic Models of Hospitals." Inquiry 11: 83-97.

Logan, R. F. L., et al. 1972. Dynamics of Medical Care: The Liverpool Study into the use of Hospital Resources. London: London School of Hygiene and Tropical Medicine.

Luce, R. D., and Raiffa, H. 1957. Games and Decisions. New York: Wiley.

Lusted, L. B. 1968. Introduction to Medical Decision Making. Springfield, Mass.: Thomas.

Pineault, R. 1976. "The Effect of Prepaid Group Practice on Physicians' Utilization Behaviour." Medical Care 14: 121-36.

Scitovsky, A. A. 1967. "Changes in the Costs of Treatment of Selected Illnesses, 1951-1965." American Economic Review 57: 1182-95.

3
SPECIFICALLY EMPIRICAL STUDIES IN PERSONAL OR ORGANIZATIONAL UNCERTAINTY

17
UNCERTAIN TIMETABLES: A CASE OF SPARE-PART SURGERY
Daniel J. Klenow
Fabio B. Dasilva

INTRODUCTION

Temporal or time-oriented concepts, such as crisis and recovery (Davis 1963), timetables (Roth 1963), and sociological calendar (Light 1975) have frequently provided an important analytic focus for research in medical sociology. Such long-term conditions as tuberculosis (Roth 1963), polio (Davis 1963), and rheumatoid arthritis (Wiener 1975) have allowed fruitful applications of these concepts. Recent developments in biomedical technology have increased the life span of many patients with other types of chronic medical conditions. However, these medical innovations have often required patient dependency upon a mechanical device (for example, pacemaker, dialysis machine, and so forth) or extraordinary surgical intervention, such as heart or kidney transplantation. Such innovations provide new areas for applying and extending a temporal analytic frame. Accordingly, this chapter draws upon Roth's concept of timetables to characterize the situation of dialysis patients awaiting cadaver kidney transplants. Data are also presented on the social organization of cadaver kidney procurement, as well as physician ideologies used to influence patient perceptions of appropriate treatment options.

KIDNEY DISEASE, DIALYSIS,
AND TRANSPLANTATION

End-stage kidney failure is a disease condition that results in death. The patient's life may be saved and sustained, however, if hemodialysis treatment is initiated. This therapy requires the use of an artificial kidney machine, which is hooked up to the patient three times a week for roughly four to eight hours. During the treatment process, the patient remains immobile in a reclining chair or bed, while the blood is pumped from the patient's body through a clear plastic tubing system to a filter that cleanses it (that is, removes waste products, controls levels of electrolytes, maintains proper pH, and eliminates excess fluid). Access to the patient's blood is usually facilitated through the use of a surgically placed entry device (that is, a shunt, fistula, or bovine graft) in the nondominant forearm. This treatment must be maintained for the duration of the patient's life or until a kidney transplant is performed.

There are two types of kidney transplant, the living-related and the cadaver. A living-related kidney comes from a healthy relative (most frequently a parent or sibling) who decides to donate and who is determined to be a good genetic match. The success rate for this operation varies from one transplant center to the next, but is generally in the 80 to 90 percent range. A cadaver kidney comes from a deceased nonrelated person. These kidneys lack the genetic similarities that the living-related organs have for the recipient. Cadaver kidney transplants have a success rate in the vicinity of 50 percent. The patients included in this study are all awaiting a cadaver kidney transplant.

Patients in this study receive their treatment at hemodialysis facilities administered by a hospital and under the codirectorship of two physicians who are board certified in both internal medicine and nephrology. The staff includes four registered nurses, four licensed practical nurses, one chief technician, and six dialysis technicians. At the time of the study, the unit served 74 patients. Thirty-two of these patients were dialyzed at the chronic maintenance unit, linked with the hospital, while the remaining 42 were dialyzed with the help of a trained partner (usually a spouse or parent) at home.

The transplant center that serves this program is located in a major university medical center in the state and serves three other dialysis units as well. As of August 1, 1976, the end of the fieldwork and interviewing phase of this research, 25 transplants had been performed. Twelve of these were cadaver and 13 involved living-related donors.

METHODS

This study is an intensive case analysis of one hemodialysis unit and its involvement with a major university transplant center.

Case material was gathered by employing the field method described by Schatzman and Strauss (1973). A wide range of quantitative and qualitative data were gathered over a 14-month span. Observations and interviews were conducted at the hemodialysis unit, as well as the transplant center. Official dialysis unit and transplant center publications, statistical reports, organizational handbooks, consent forms, medical education lectures, medical records, and occasional letters of correspondence with the transplant center provided other important sources of data. In addition, semistructured intensive interviews were conducted with a complete sample of patients in the city who were eligible for a cadaver kidney transplant. This includes eight patients, with an age range of 17 to 45. Three patients are female, and five are male. Their time on dialysis ranges from one year to seven years, with a mean of three years. Similar interviews were conducted with all staff members, including two nephrologists, working in this hemodialysis facility.

SOCIAL ORGANIZATIONAL FEATURES OF CADAVER KIDNEY PROCUREMENT

The social organization of cadaver kidney procurement is depicted in Figure 17.1. Block A denotes the patient who is desiring a transplant but is placed in an uncertain time frame regarding such surgery. These patients have been (B) tissue typed and placed on (C) the waiting list. At the time of this research, there were 73 patients on the list. To illustrate the problem of waiting, we only have to point out that nine cadaver transplants have been performed (E) during the first half of the year in which this study was completed. Again, the cadaver kidneys that become available must be closely matched (D) to the patient. This is why seniority, that is, time on the waiting list, is not the most important denominator in determining who will receive a cadaver kidney. A patient at the top of the waiting list will not be transplanted if the tissue match is not considered acceptable by the physicians.

Other social organizational contingencies that affect a patient's transplant possibilities include (F) the number of card-carrying and driver's-license-designated donors who happen to die.* In addition,

---

*The National Kidney Foundation distributes organ donor cards that may be carried in a purse or wallet. Many states now provide a place for such a notification, that is, intent to donate organs at death, on the driver's license.

FIGURE 17.1

The Social Organization of Cadaver Kidney Procurement

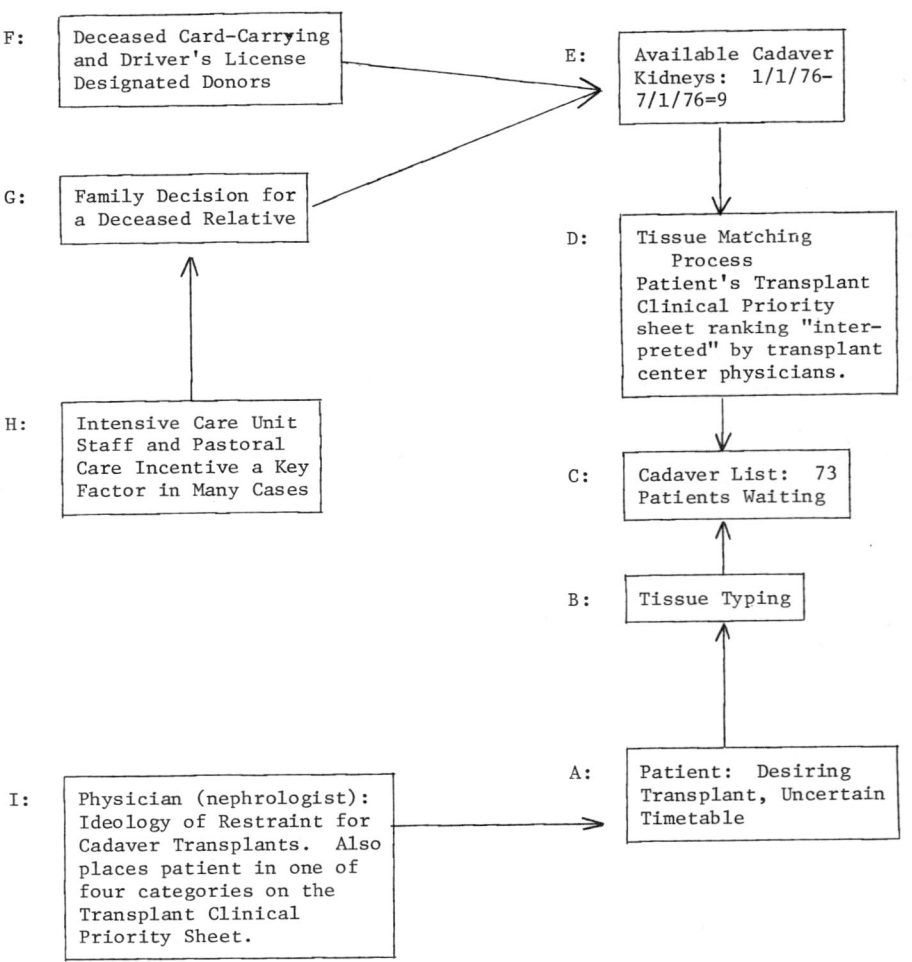

Source: Constructed by the author.

it is not sufficient that a designated donor die, it is necessary that the type of death not harm the function of the internal organs (for example, head injury deaths provide good sources of cadaver kidneys). Another source of cadaver kidneys includes family decisions for a deceased relative (G), unrelated to the ultimate recipient, who is not a card- or license-designated donor. Although this type of donation may come from the initiative of the family, the nursing staff and pastoral care personnel (H) are often key factors in suggesting this option to the family.*

Another input into the social structure of cadaver kidney procurement includes the transplant clinical priority sheet, which the nephrologists fill out and review monthly on each of their cadaver kidney eligible patients. This sheet contains a ranking system that allows each patient placement in one of four categories. These categories are: (1) deteriorating on dialysis—because of medical or physiological reasons—transplantation urgent; (2) doing poorly on dialysis—transplantation highly desirous; (3) handling dialysis well—but transplantation still indicated; (4) fully rehabilitated on dialysis—transplant only with superior match and superior cadaver organ.

No additional information is provided on the form to make these categories more explicit. The classification system on this transplant clinical priority sheet does present problems in interpretation for the transplant facility physicians. One of these physicians stated:

> We, so far, have only used the priority as far as helping us when people of equal match are available. I, personally, have some doubts as far as the clinical significance of this as in dealing with 14 different nephrologists, I find I have to make a value on the priority in relation to that particular nephrologist. For example, there is one nephrologist in our program who currently has seven people on the cadaver list, six of these he rates as priority 1 and one as priority 2. Another nephrologist with over a dozen on the list has no priority 1s or 2s, all his patients are 3s and 4s. So I must personally look at the priority and keep in mind the particular nephrologist and how he grades them.

---

*This process has been performed quite successfully by intensive care nurses and those in pastoral care at a hospital in a city near the present research site.

This material indicates that a patient's actual passage from dialysis to cadaver kidney transplantation depends upon the medical decisions and reinterpretations of those initial decisions on more than one level of the medical system involved in transplantation.

Another important input into the social organization of cadaver kidney procurement and transplantation is the ideology of patient care (Mauksch 1973; Klenow 1979) held by the nephrologist directing the hemodialysis unit. The orientation in this unit is primarily to transplant those persons having a good potential family source (living-related donor) for a kidney. The contrasting ideologies regarding cadaver and living-related transplants are typified in the following statement by one of the dialysis unit's nephrologists:

> I don't think cadaver transplants are a proven method. I think there is an awful lot wrong with cadaver transplants. There's still a significant mortality, 10 to 15 percent in cadaver transplants. The success rate is still low. So what I tell my patients is, that if they are young and they have a family, I start, . . . I talk transplant from the beginning. I get them tissue-typed, the whole works and look into it. If it works out that they can get a related donor transplant, that should be done as soon as possible.

The treatment ideology varies considerably for those who do not fall into the living-related donor category. This nephrologist continued:

> If it doesn't work out that they have someone in the family and they fall into the theoretical category of cadaver transplants, then I think those people ought to learn to see what dialysis is like for awhile. If they tolerate dialysis then I think they should hang in there with dialysis.* If they don't tolerate dialysis, depending upon how badly they tolerate it, then I start to introduce the idea of cadaver transplants. I introduce it in a, not negative, but in a much less positive way than I introduce the related donor transplant.

---

*In this context, the term tolerate refers to the degree of mental and physical adjustment that a patient is able to make in regard to dialysis treatment.

This restrained perspective on cadaver transplantation is also supplemented with speculations that the technology of dialysis may improve (reducing the time spent on the machine) and that breakthroughs in immunosuppressive therapy may make the cadaver transplant a more viable option in the future.*

In reviewing the inputs in Figure 17.1, it seems that a large increase in the number of cadaver organs would not necessarily revolutionize the status passage from dialysis patient to transplanted person. It would appear that the gatekeepers (nephrologists) would look at a large increase in cadaver kidneys as a mixed blessing, unless progress was also made in the improvement of immunosuppressive drugs. Since few cadaver organs are available at the present time, it is possible that the ideology of patient care that looks with restraint upon cadaver transplants performs a latent function (Merton 1968) of providing patients with some solace, given their transplant hopes and the current underdeveloped social structure of cadaver kidney procurement and transplantation.

Although uncertainty is a central category in relation to this type of medical treatment, it is clear that the social construction of hope is also an important social process for staff and patients. Indeed, it is the uncertainty of obtaining cadaver kidneys that allows one nephrologist to use the cadaver waiting list to provide hope to some types of patients. He indicated having patients on the cadaver list that are "closed transplant candidates." Specifically,

> There are a few patients who I have who can only live from one day to the next, thinking that there's a possibility that someone may call that night and they're going to get a transplant. Now I have put them at the very lowest priority list and if the call came through . . . to get in touch with the patient because they have a kidney available I would turn it away for that particular patient because they're not medically suited for a transplant. The risk of death is just overwhelming. But I have not told them that. Because I have nothing to gain by doing that. They're holding on to this one

---

*Immunosuppressive drugs retard the body's negative reaction to the foreign tissue (cadaver kidney). Rejection of a cadaver organ due to this natural mechanism is the major threat to the success of cadaver transplants. Improved immunosuppressive measures would make the cadaver transplant a more desirable option by increasing the low success rate.

concept because there are some people who just hate
dialysis and are using it as only a means to an end.
And that end is staying alive long enough to get a
transplant. And I have a few patients in their late
fifties, for example, who have had major medical
complications along the way from other disease
processes or from the total loss of kidney function
who are by no way a transplant candidate but who I
still keep in the computer for transplant purposes
because it offers that little glimmer of hope.

This nephrologist indicated that there are only two or three patients in this facility allowed to think that they are transplant eligible when they are, in fact, not actual candidates for such surgery.

PATIENT PERCEPTIONS OF TRANSPLANTATION: CONSTRUCTING UNCERTAIN TIMETABLES

Occupying a position on the cadaver kidney transplant list is an exercise in waiting. As indicated in Figure 17.1, there are 73 patients on the list, and only nine cadaver transplants were performed at the transplant center during the first six months of 1976. Cadaver grafts, as pointed out earlier, are performed on the basis of tissue-typing data rather than seniority. Consequently, those who have waited the longest have no assurance that they will come up next or even in the near future. The transplant chances of these patients are contingent upon the number and genetic characteristics of the cadaver organs that are donated or "harvested."

A dialysis patient has no concrete norms or cues that might give any indication of the amount of time that s/he must wait to receive a cadaver kidney transplant.* This is in contrast to the treatment expectations that developed among the tuberculosis

---

*An exception to this rule involves the dialysis patient who is also diabetic. The mortality statistics for these patients are high if they remain on dialysis, so they are given priority for cadaver transplants. However, they are transplanted at another medical center and do not occupy positions on the cadaver waiting list described in this study. Since these patients presumably develop timetables that are characterized by temporal immediacy and a greater sense of certainty, future researchers should focus on this category.

patients studied by Roth (1963). The latter patients could develop group norms approximating their length of stay in the sanitorium, and in turn, these group norms could be converted into timetables in order to give some order and predictability to their movement through the patient career. As Roth indicates, these norms are constructed in a limited and unsystematic fashion and yield a group consensus regarding temporal expectations for various treatment phases of the tuberculosis patient career.

The case of the dialysis patient waiting for a "spare part," or cadaver kidney, is characterized by temporal uncertainty. A transplant is viewed as something in the vague and nebulous future. Three patients provided the following representative statements:

> I hope some day I won't be sick and that I'll have a transplant and I'll be fine. I hope someday to see that day. I used to fret about it. I don't no more. I get out and go shopping and I enjoy life from day to day now, taking things in stride. I figure when that call comes I'm gonna put my trust in God.

> I think about it, you know. I have to wait till that time come, you know. I just have a lot of patience, you know, wait till that time come. But, ahh, first I couldn't accept it, you know, the waiting. I just accept in my mind to stay on the machine until the time come, whenever it is. If it's a year, two years, five years. Whatever it is, you know.

> I try in the midst of that to still have the hope that it might happen today, it can happen tomorrow, it could happen twenty-five years from now.

This material indicates that only the first condition for existence of a timetable appears for cadaver transplantation. Roth (1963, p. 94) describes the first condition as specifying the presence of a "group definition of success or attainment of a goal." These patients clearly define the cadaver transplant as the desired goal. Roth (1963, p. 65) indicates that the second condition requires "an interacting (not necessarily face to face) group of people with access to the same body of clues for constructing the norms of the timetable." Although there is an interacting group, this condition is not totally fulfilled, as the nephrologists and social organization of cadaver kidney procurement generate no concrete norms or cues for constructing predictable cadaver transplant timetables.

One patient believed that a transplant could be obtained more quickly if he lived near the transplant center. This suggests the social psychological importance of contiguity or geographical closeness as a hopeful factor for possibly reducing uncertainty. As this patient stated:

> But I think I can get transplanted quicker down there than I kin here. . . . Well, you have to be in [city where the transplant center is located]. But, I don't know. I believe the doctors work faster. Maybe more concerned about it. That's what I believe now. That's my belief about it. I haven't heard anything. I went down there in June last year. A doctor should come up and tell you what's going on, you know. But I don't want to bug no doctor. . . . But I believe I can get a transplant quicker down there because . . . I would be there where everything is, you know. I would go around the corner and ask, be nosey about it, you know. You know, I can't do that 100 and something miles away from there, you know.

This patient may be reacting against the restrained cadaver perspective of these nephrologists when he feels that living near the transplant center would speed up his eventual transplantation. Although it is impossible to determine whether this would occur should the patient move, Simmons, Klein, and Simmons (1977) indicate that there is tension between transplant and dialysis physicians because patients are influenced by the physician they see first. In this unit, it is clear that cadaver transplantation is not highly regarded by the physicians that these patients see.*

The status of the transplant center for potentially reducing transplant uncertainty, at least in the mind of the patient, is further exemplified in the case of a patient called for a transplant that was canceled at the last moment. This patient was flown to the transplant center and worked-up for surgery. An infection was discovered

---

*An acknowledgment of the differences between dialysis unit nephrologists and transplant surgeons was indicated in the following quote taken from an interview with one of two nephrologists in this study. He stated: "Some dialysis units are run by surgeons and some by nephrologists. There are many dialysis units that are strictly there to support the transplant facility. If that's the case, obviously everybody's very interested in the transplants because that's what the whole indoctrination of the place is."

near the end of the work-up, and the transplant operation was canceled. In an interview two weeks after the canceled attempt, he indicated: "I feel a little disappointment but I can honestly say I have not felt terribly disappointed as a big depressing low thing. I felt, you may say, a lot more hopeful for the second call. It made me feel better about the eventual possibility of getting a transplant." Although the experience of having an actual chance at a transplant, in itself, yields no concrete cues as to when another transplant opportunity might develop, it does raise the hope of another chance based on the "logic of emotion" that if I was called once, then it should happen again. Part of the cognitive and emotional basis for such thinking stems from the fact that the patient realizes that after all these years of waiting, they really did call me. Something is happening. The possibility of a transplant becomes infused with reality due to such an experience. It is difficult for patients to trust or believe in the reality of a social system (the social organization of cadaver kidney procurement, the transplant team, and so forth) that they cannot see or come into contact with any of its activities.

Consequently, this patient's timetable construction was transformed. In this instance, it was changed from one of pessimism and uncertainty to one of hope, possibility, and temporal immediacy. The trip for the transplant provided the basis for constructing a timetable that was more certain. The main thread decreasing this uncertainty was the view that a transplant possibility has emerged once and such a possibility will develop again; he will have another chance.

Face-to-face interaction with the transplant team also provided a basis for increased hope. The experience of actually being at the transplant center infused a degree of vivid personalism into what had previously been a vague and invisible process. The patient tried to sort out his feelings in the following manner:

> Another thing, trying to sort all of this out, a lot of it is mixed reactions, but ahh, one thing I think it is really important, at least to me it is; that is, the rapport that was really improved between the transplant team and myself, as a patient. In talking to the doctor just before I left he said, "I'm going to be seeing you again." And I said, "Doctor I feel it's going to be quite soon." He said, "I agree with you." But there was this idea there, I had been there. They were aware, not just of X number of kidney patients but here's so and so in a given situation.

This patient recommended that transplant-eligible patients not be simply told about the dynamics of cadaver transplantation but, also,

280 / UNCERTAINTY

go down and tour the transplant center and actually get acquainted with those who will be working with them in the eventuality of a transplant.

This patient provided additional comments on his construction of a hopeful outlook. He continued:

> And I have this feeling, maybe this is just me, maybe this is a hope that I've built. That is, that I feel this doctor, after having talked to him, and his team, they went through the disappointment of having to shut-off an operation they thought was going to be another success. And I feel this all is going to make them work more in a directive way towards getting me a kidney. Not just getting a kidney for the next patient, but getting me a kidney. I feel they are going to be more individualized, perhaps, in their approach.

The face-to-face encounter with the transplant team led the patient to a realization of the sense of "we" that characterizes the common goals of the transplant team and the hopeful patient. However, as this patient indicated, his hope for individualized treatment and a shorter timetable may be a purely personal construction. In addition, the social structure of cadaver kidney procurement has a number of inputs that can constrain the treatment intentions of the patient and the transplant team. The number of cadaver kidneys coming into the system provides one of the main constraints.

DISCUSSION

This case study material has provided a rich source of data on patients and staff in one hemodialysis unit and their interaction with a major medical facility providing transplantation capabilities. These data, gathered as part of a larger study, are quite valuable, since such a range of information is difficult to obtain except through a long-term field study, such as the present. A shortcoming includes the possible lack of generalizability of the data due to the focus on only one hemodialysis and transplant facility, as well as the small number of patients and physicians interviewed. Accordingly, a primary contribution of this research is the reestablishment—or, in a sense, replication—of several important conceptual categories of analysis in medical settings. Specifically, this analysis reaffirms and/or modifies and extends the work of Roth (1963), Fox and Swazey (1978), Davis (1960), and Simmons, Klein, and Simmons (1977). In addition, this research sensitizes us to the existence of several ideologies of patient care similar to those previously analyzed by Kauksch (1973) and Klenow (1979).

The material in this chapter utilizes and modifies Roth's concept of timetable. Specifically, the data indicate that the structural aspects of cadaver kidney procurement and transplantation produce an uncertain timetable. However, Roth's (1963) categories of <u>optimistic doctor</u> and <u>pessimistic doctor</u> also find partial expression in this study. Roth's optimistic doctor tries to make things easier for his tuberculosis patients by not indicating the long period that the patient must tolerate in the hospital. Similarly, one nephrologist used placement on the transplant list for nontransplant candidates as a strategy for giving them hope and, consequently, making it easier to live with dialysis, so he theorized. A pessimistic stance is taken regarding cadaver kidney transplantation. Future research might focus on the impact of such strategies on patients. Do dialysis patients lose trust in optimistic doctors after they have waited years for a cadaver transplant that they will never receive? Do patients believe and internalize the ideology of pessimistic doctors who want their patients to stay on dialysis until cadaver transplants have a higher success rate?

This research extends the work of Fox and Swazey (1978), who focus on the biomedical aspects of uncertainty stemming from the transplant operation itself; they state (p. 42) that "rejection is the central problem of uncertainty in transplantation." Specifically, they indicate three primary sets of uncertainty problems associated with rejection and its control in the transplant recipient. These include (p. 43): (1) the indeterminate role that donor-recipient tissue typing plays in decreasing the likelihood and the magnitude of a rejection reaction; (2) the many unresolved questions about the properties and value of the various medical regimens that have been tried to forestall or control such a reaction; and (3) those of the often unanticipated and intractable side effects of immunosuppressive therapy. The data in this study supplement and extend the characterization of uncertainty in transplantation by examining its temporal dimension in the social structure of cadaver kidney procurement.

The data from nephrologists indicating that they sometimes put a patient on the transplant list even though he or she is a closed or nontransplant candidate exemplifies a strategy similar to that used by the staff dealing with paralytic poliomyelitis patients and families described by Davis (1960). He differentiated between <u>real</u> uncertainty, that is, scientific or medically grounded uncertainty, and <u>functional</u> uncertainty, which refers to the use of real or pretended uncertainty so as to control or manage patients in ways desired by the staff. However, there is a critical difference between the polio patients and their families and the closed cadaver transplant patients described in this study. The polio patients and their families were given an uncertain prognosis, when the prognosis was indeed clear and certain, because the treatment staff felt it better if they found the prognosis out for themselves in "a natural sort of way." In short, these patients and their families would gradually discover the limitations imposed by the polio over a long period of time through their own observation. The situation with cadaver kidney patients is radically different, as the passage of time will provide no additional information to the patient about the transplant chances. This disease condition is a discrete condition and will only change through radical external intervention (cadaver kidney transplantation) and not through a self-contained personal healing process or rehabilitation regimen. The psychological condition of these few "closed" cadaver kidney transplant candidates is also apparently quite different from the polio patients. Davis indicated psychological and self-image problems for these patients, in contrast with the nephrologist, who stated that a couple of patients needed the functional uncertainty of false transplant hopes to live from one day to the next. It appears that at least one nephrologist perceives functional uncertainty as an extremely important strategy in unusual cases. Future researchers might greatly enhance our understanding of the value of functional uncertainty by employing longitudinal designs and comparing the social and psychological adjustment of patients receiving complete prognostic information with those managed by functional uncertainty. However, the strategy of functional uncertainty must also be thoroughly analyzed from the perspective of ethical theory (see Veatch 1976) to further clarify its appropriateness.

The present study also complements the analysis of normative and ethical uncertainty in kidney transplantation provided by Simmons, Klein, and Simmons (1977). These researchers describe the normative uncertainty that characterized the selection of patients for dialysis and kidney transplantation when these therapeutic resources were extremely scarce. No norms were available to guide physicians in their selection of patients for such therapies. In addition, Simmons, Klein, and Simmons (1977) describe the ethical uncertainties involved in the use of cadaver and living-related kidney donors.

Finally, this research elaborates the ideology of patient care (a restrained view of cadaver kidney transplantation) that these nephrologists employ. Future researchers might analyze the possible conflict in ideology between transplant and dialysis physicians mentioned by Simmons, Klein, and Simmons (1977). Such analysis might reveal a primarily curative ideology (see Mauksch 1973; Klenow 1979) for transplant staff, as opposed to a long-term care ideology for dialysis physicians. It may well be that the basic ideologies of these two groups are similar, but the assessment and use of available medical resources and technologies may vary.

REFERENCES

Davis, Fred. 1960. "Uncertainty in Medical Prognosis: Clinical and Functional." American Journal of Sociology 66: 41-47.

———. 1963. Passage Through Crisis: Polio Victims and Their Families. Indianapolis, Ind.: Bobbs-Merrill.

Fox, Renee C., and Swazey, Judith P. 1978. The Courage to Fail: A Social View of Organ Transplants and Dialysis. 2d ed. Chicago: University of Chicago Press.

Klenow, Daniel J. 1979. "Staff Based Ideologies in a Hemodialysis Unit." Social Science and Medicine 13A (November): 699-705.

Light, Donald. 1975. "The Sociological Calendar: An Analytic Tool." American Journal of Sociology 80 (March): 1145-64.

Mauksch, Hans. 1973. "Ideology, Interaction and Patient Care in Hospitals." Social Science and Medicine 7 (October): 817-30.

Merton, Robert K. 1968. Social Theory and Social Structure. New York: Free Press.

Roth, Julius A. 1963. Timetables. Indianapolis, Ind.: Bobbs-Merrill.

Schatzman, Leonard L., and Strauss, Anselm L. 1973. Field Research: Strategies for a Natural Sociology. Englewood Cliffs, N.J.: Prentice-Hall.

Simmons, Roberta G.; Klein, Susan D.; and Simmons, Richard L. 1977. Gift of Life: The Social and Psychological Impact of Organ Transplantation. New York: Wiley-Interscience.

Veatch, Robert M. 1976. Death, Dying, and the Biological Revolution. New Haven, Conn.: Yale University Press.

Wiener, Carolyn. 1975. "The Burden of Rheumatoid Arthritis: Tolerating the Uncertainty." Social Science and Medicine 9 (February): 97-104.

18
APPLIED BEHAVIOR UNDER UNCERTAINTY
Peter Lorenzi

APPLIED BEHAVIOR UNDER UNCERTAINTY

The concept of uncertainty—a general lack of predictability or precision in estimation—is fundamental not only to the physical sciences but, also, to the social sciences. The purpose of this chapter is to explore the role of uncertainty in the behavioral sciences, with particular attention to the effect of uncertainty on applied or goal-directed behavior in organizational situations.

Measurement and Prediction in Science
and the Social Sciences

A fundamental difference between the physical and the social sciences lies in the nature and measurement of their constructs. In the physical sciences, the properties are generally concrete and immutable. Theories are rejected on the basis of relatively precise, reliable measurement of these properties. In the social sciences, the constructs themselves are regularly the subject of argument. Conceptual and operational definitions are in dispute, primarily due to the contrived nature of the science itself. For example, it is simpler to agree to a definition of gravity than to one of motivation, and the measurement and demonstration of the former is easier still.

Heisenberg's uncertainty principle states that the measurements of the mass and the velocity of a molecular particle can not both be optimally precise. Increased precision in the measurement of one can only be achieved at the expense of the precision in the measurement of the other. A very appropriate analogy for the social sciences is the trade off between internal and external validity. Increased internal validity, generally attained in controlled, laboratory experiments, usually is achieved at the expense of the external validity or generalizability typically attained in more realistic field settings. However, for this chapter, the more relevant aspect of uncertainty for the social sciences concerns unpredictability. Uncertainty regularly confronts the social scientist in the dynamic, complex nature of the social environment. Rapidly changing social systems create problems not only for the individual or organizational decision maker, who must make numerous decisions concerning highly uncertain future conditions, but also for the scientist's theories, which were often drawn from more stable environments. Uncertainty, therefore, inhibits a basic need of the social scientist—the need to predict events, behaviors, and the like.

Uncertainty poses both a threat and a challenge for the social scientist. While uncertainty threatens established theories, patterns, and predictions of human behavior, it also provides new opportunities for more vigorous and flexible approaches to the study of human behavior.

Uncertainty and Applied Behavior

The focus of this chapter is the effect of uncertainty on applied behavior. Why applied behavior? Consider Lewis Carroll's explanation from Alice in Wonderland:

> "Would you tell me, please, which way I ought to go from here," asked Alice. "That depends a good deal on where you want to go," said the Cat. "I don't much care where," said Alice. "Then it doesn't matter which way you go," said the Cat.

In brief, uncertainty does not create a problem for the decision maker unless s/he possesses (a set of) preferences concerning particular "paths" or subsequent outcomes. The identification of a preferred path or a desired future state is necessary; otherwise, an unpredictable future is of little consequence to the decision maker. The dichotomizations of the means versus ends continuum and preference versus no-preference continuum are illustrative oversimplifications. A portion of this chapter will address those areas between the extreme points of the continua.

Uncertainty

March and Simon (1958) described the factors influencing uncertainty and the outcome associated with uncertainty, as follows: "In the case of uncertainty, the individual does not know the probability distributions connecting behavior choices and environmental outcomes" (p. 113). This description involves knowledge of a cause-effect relationship, stated in terms of a quantitative, decision-making terminology. Uncertainty represents the opposite of certainty. Risk is the state lying between these two extremes, where the individual has a knowledge of the probability distribution of outcomes associated with his/her choices.

Performance

In the field of organizational behavior, performance is synonymous with what has been referred to here as applied behavior. In the study of the behavior of people in organizations and the behavior of organizations, performance is a paramount criterion. Performance can be expressed in terms of individual, group, or organizational achievement. The individual may be acting on his/her own or in an organizational context. The organization may be public or private, profit or not-for-profit, or large or small. The fundamental assumption is that performance or effectiveness can be ranked in terms of a relevant scale or dimension(s). The application of this standard may be made internally by the individual decision maker or an external source, the latter of which is a typical management control function and the cause of another set of psychological ramifications not to be discussed here. The key element is the need for effective decisions that result in the desired level of performance.

UNCERTAINTY AND PERFORMANCE

Perceived Environmental Uncertainty

The psychological importance of uncertainty lies in the individual's perception of his/her external environment: perceived environmental uncertainty (PEU). Dill (1958) recognized the distinction between perceptual and objective definitions of this environment. Perception of the organizational environment or suprasystem by members of the dominant coalition is essential to understanding organizational goals. Furthermore, although PEU is generally studied as an organizational variable, organizations do not perceive and adjust—individuals perceive and adjust. Concurrently, individuals create or enact their relevant environments by a process of attention (Weick 1969). In sum, the perceptual process mediates a transaction between the individual and the external environment. The outcomes of this dynamic process influence the behavior of the individual and, subsequently, the organization (see Figure 18.1).

FIGURE 18.1

Model of Environmental Uncertainty
and Applied Behavior

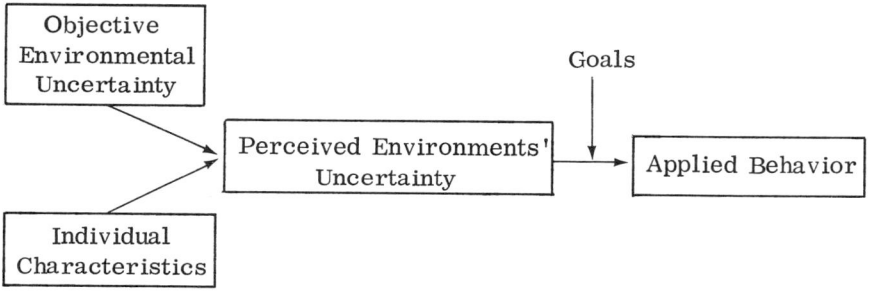

Source: Compiled by the author.

Uncertainty refers to events that cannot be forecasted. It is not merely change or the rate of change, but the unpredictable change, in variables that affect critical dependent relationships. According to Thompson (1967, p. 159), "Uncertainty appears as the fundamental problem for complex organizations"; he states (p. 162) that the process of administration is "a process of coping with uncertainty." The accurate perception of uncertainty emanating from the environment—or at least perceived to be emanating from the environment—has been regarded as critical to organizational performance (Duncan 1972; Miles, Snow, and Pfeffer 1974; Osborn and Hunt 1974).

Duncan (1972) and Downey and Slocum (1975) have emphasized the distinction between the perception of uncertainty resulting from an environmental characteristic versus that resulting from personality attributes of the respondent. Downey, Hellriegel, and Slocum (1977) found that cognitive process variables were more consistently related to perceived uncertainty than were perceived environmental variables. Tosi, Aldag, and Storey (1973) discussed the environmental influence issue indirectly, interpreting uncertainty as "the degree of accuracy with which one can predict the future. Where there is less variance, there is more certainty" (p. 30).

In literature reviews of the organization-environment issue, Ford and Slocum (1977) and Starbuck (1976) concurred with the Tosi, Aldag, and Storey (1973) interpretation of environmental uncertainty. Starbuck (1976) stated:

> There is a fairly strong case for saying that uncertainty is inevitably a characteristic of a perceiver . . . even if organizational properties are measured in some objective fashion, it can be argued that the realism of the environmental perceptions is irrelevant; organizational members should adapt their organizations to the environments which they believe exist, whether their perceptions would be objectively confirmed or not.

Although the reality of the environmental perception is likely to be of extreme importance for the long-run survival of the individual or the organization, the dilemma left unresolved concerns the source of the particular perception, regardless of its congruence with objective measures of "reality." In identifying the source of perception, it is equally important to develop a reasonably objective measure of both the individual and the environment.

Measurement of Perceptions

In any perceptual method, difficulty may arise because of error induced in the measurement by attributes of the individual, rather than the attributes of the external environment. In essence, different people may tend to perceive the same environment in a different manner.

In perceptual scale development, it is nevertheless important for the measurement technique to have a reasonable degree of correspondence to objective attributes of the environment to be able to discriminate between different environments. This discriminatory power is necessary if the perceptual measurement technique is to be regarded as valid for the purpose of deriving useful conclusions regarding the relationship of the environment and individual perceptions. Therefore, a perceptual measurement shown to possess acceptable reliability and validity can be useful in deriving generalizable conclusions about how environmental characteristics relate to individual perceptions or performance. The perceptual method has the distinct advantage of being usable and generalizable across many different environments and organizational settings.

Perceived Environmental Uncertainty in
Organizational Research

An attempt to operationalize PEU was made by Lawrence and Lorsch (1967). They identified organizational uncertainty as (1) a lack of clarity of information, (2) a general uncertainty of causal relationships, and (3) a long intervening time span between events and the feedback of results. These factors, in turn, were thought to lead to the perception of environmental uncertainty. Using a sample of ten firms from three industries, they found that each organizational subunit in the more successful organizations met the demands of its subenvironment by various administrative methods. Duncan (1972) described uncertainty with three different attributes: (1) a lack of information concerning the environment, (2) a lack of knowledge regarding the consequences of a specific decision, and (3) an inability to assign probabilities to the effects of an environmental factor. He proposed two environmental dimensions: First, the static-dynamic dimension indicates the degree to which "the factors of the decision unit's internal and external environment remain basically the same over time" (p. 316). A decision maker in a dynamic environment perceives the internal and external environments as changing. Second, the simple-complex dimension refers to the "degree to which the factors in the environment are few in number and similar to one another" (p. 315). In a simple environment, decisions are thought to be influenced by few factors. Duncan found that dynamic-complex environments resulted in the highest uncertainty in decision making for managers. His data showed that the static-dynamic dimension contributed more to uncertainty perceptions than the simple-complex dimension.

In their study of 51 divisional managers of a major conglomerate, Downey and Slocum (1979) reported a negative relationship between performance and perceived uncertainty. This relationship was moderated by the individual's cognitive structure. Those managers who were cognitively complex and who perceived little uncertainty were the highest performers. Their conclusion was that PEU is primarily an individual rather than environmental attribute.

A difficulty with these studies was that these researchers were not able to objectively measure environmental influences. Indices of objective environmental uncertainty have proven elusive; their conceptual and operational definitions have been problematic. The critical issue concerns the source of the particular perception, whether it pertains to a characteristic of the individual and/or the objective environment.

A thorough investigation of a perceptual measurement technique that separates individual and environmental influences is difficult to implement in field settings due to the difficulties of accurately describing and controlling objective attributes of the environment. Therefore, three laboratory experiments were conducted to (1) isolate relevant variables and (2) achieve experimental control. Experiment I represents a preliminary attempt to isolate and measure environmental and individual attributes. Experiments II and III represent constructive extensions of their predecessors.

Experiment I

Procedure

Ninety undergraduates enrolled in introductory management courses participated in the experiment. Subjects individually reported to a computer terminal to participate in an interactive decision-making simulation. They were told to assume the post of regional sales manager for a large firm, where they were asked to (1) employ salesmen, (2) forecast a profit, and (3) state a degree of confidence about their forecast. Their job was to maximize profits and minimize forecast error. The simulation consisted of a baseline period and an experimental period. The baseline period was used to acclimate subjects to the simulation and to serve as a period in which all subjects were exposed to a relatively identical environment. The actual baseline experience was partially determined by the interaction of subject decisions and learning.

The number of salesmen was the sole determinant of profit. The maximum profit came from employing 27 salesmen. Variations from this number resulted in increasing decreases in the amount of profit. By informing the subjects in the instructions that the previous hypothetical period had 22 salesmen and $19,600 in profit, subjects had a point from which to commence their own experimentation.

At the end of the baseline period, perceptions of the environment were collected. These were labeled baseline measures of PEU. Since all subjects had been operating in ostensibly similar task environments, variance in these measures represent a pure individual difference, although the exact antecedents of these measures are unknown.

The only difference between the baseline and the subsequent experimental periods was that the model used in the experimental period included a stochastic error term (objective environmental uncertainty [OEU]) created by a random generating routine. Depending on the size of the stochastic term, the potential range in variation about the deterministic model was from $330 to $13,524. The actual profit was a function of the subject's decision and the value of the stochastic term within each time period. At the end of the 20 experimental periods, the subject was informed that the simulation was complete and the experimental measures of PEU were collected.

Measures

Measures of individual characteristics, speculated to be related to performance and PEU, were collected prior to the experiment and are summarized below.

Locus of Control. Anderson, Hellriegel, and Slocum (1977) used the measure of internal-external locus of control developed by Rotter (1966) to measure managers' reactions to the environment. They found locus of control to be related to individual decision-making behavior. The external locus of control individual perceives himself/herself to be controlled by the environment. The "internal" perceives himself/herself to be controlling the environment.

Cognitive Complexity-Simplicity. This instrument measures the subject's degree of cognitive differentiation. A person who differentiates highly among persons is considered to be cognitively complex. Cognitive simplicity reflects an incomplete differentiation of the boundaries between self and the environment.

General Incongruity Adaptation Level (GIAL). This instrument was developed by Driver and Struefert (1965) to measure individual response to ambiguous and dissonant situations. According to the authors, individuals develop adaptation levels concerning the amount of incongruity they can tolerate in their environments. Individuals with a high GIAL score will desire more risk in their environment and will engage in more risk-taking behavior than individuals with a low GIAL. Low GIAL individuals would be expected to perceive more uncertainty in any given situation than high GIAL individuals.

Need Achievement. A scale developed by Hermans (1970) was used to assess an individual's psychological need for achievement. Individuals scoring high on this instrument would be expected to strive for higher performance because of a stronger drive for achievement than low-scoring individuals, and they may also perceive their environment differently.

Mathematical Aptitude. The mathematics portion of the Scholastic Aptitude Test (SAT) was used as a predictor of ability at the task and as a possible determinant of the perception of environmental uncertainty.

During the simulation, performance and perceived environmental uncertainty measures were collected; they are summarized below.

Performance. The assigned objectives—(maximize) profit and (minimize) profit forecast error—were summed over both that baseline and experimental decisions to constitute measures of performance.

Perceptions of Environmental Uncertainty. Items designed to measure various dimensions of the environment were used, ranging from general to more task-specific measures of the environment. The items were as follows: (1) environmental dynamism, (2) environmental complexity, (3) environmental dominance (environmental dominance of individual actions), (4) need for information (need for more information to improve decision-making), (5) environmental unpredictability, (7) decreasing probability 05 (probability attached to a 5 percent forecast error range), and (8) decreasing probability 10 (probability attached to a 10 percent forecast error range).

The first five items were eventually classified as general; the last three were classified as task-specific because they referred to unique aspects of the simulation's environment. This full set of items was collected twice, at the conclusion of (1) the baseline period, and (2) the experimental period. Under the baseline deterministic model, the variance in the items was considered to be entirely attributable to individual differences.

Factor Analysis A factor analysis was undertaken to evaluate whether the instrument represented a unidimensional or multidimensional construct. No simple factor structures consistent across both baseline and experimental periods were obtained. However, a consistent clustering of the last three items was present in the first factor of all of the factor structures. These three items formed a factor labeled specific PEU index. The remaining five (general) items were retained as single items.

Results

Determinants of Perceived Environmental Uncertainty. Comparing the preexperimental individual attributes and the baseline PEU measures provides clear distinction between the general and specific measures of PEU (see Table 18.1). In brief, individual

TABLE 18.1

Correlation of Individual Attributes and Baseline Perceptions
of Environmental Uncertainty
(Experiment I)

	Baseline Perceptions of Environment Uncertainty					
Individual Attribute	Environmental Dynamism	Environmental Complexity	Environmental Dominance	Need for Information	Difficulty of Assigning Confidence	Specific PEU Index
Scholastic Aptitude Test (mathematics)	-.41[a]	-.21[b]	-.12	-.23[b]	-.22[b]	-.16
Need achievement	-.01	.05	.09	-.09	-.03	-.03
Locus of control	.20	.10	.36[a]	-.02	.04	.03
Goal incongruity adaptation level	-.34[a]	-.24[b]	-.19	-.02	-.05	-.17
Cognitive complexity-simplicity	.09	-.03	.12	.20	-.09	.00

[a] $p < .001$.
[b] $p < .05$.

Source: Compiled by the author.

attributes are (1) regularly related to general PEU dimensions, and (2) clearly unrelated to the specific PEU index, in an environment that is objectively identical for each individual.

The experimental period provides an opportunity to further isolate these individual influences from the objective environmental uncertainty, as shown in Table 18.2. In most cases, the objective environmental influence dominates the baseline, individual influence. The strong exception is environmental dominance, seen in Table 18.1 to be affected by the personality construct, locus of control. Again, the specific PEU index is different from the five general items as well: both individual and environmental influences are significant.

Two conclusions emerge: (1) the environmental influence generally dominates the individual influence, and (2) the absolute and relative influences are determined, in part, by the specificity of the measure.

Performance. Unlike global performance measures used in previous field studies (Downey and Slocum 1979; Osborn and Hunt 1974; Leifer and McDonough 1977), performance in this study was specified according to the instructions given to each subject: "Maximize your profits and minimize your forecast error." These performance criteria (experimental profit and profit forecast error) and their significant predictor variables are compared in Table 18.3. The five general PEU items were generally unrelated to the performance criteria.

The key observation is the difference between the performance criteria with respect to their relationships with the baseline and experimental measures. Experimental profit was strongly related to baseline profit ($r = .54$, $p < .001$) and negatively related to baseline specific PEU index ($r = -.40$, $p < .001$). Conversely, experimental forecast error was strongly related to objective uncertainty ($r = .80$, $p < .001$) and the experimental specific PEU index ($r = .47$, $p < .001$).

The evidence here suggests two preliminary conclusions. First, the inability of the general PEU items to correlate to a meaningful degree with performance measures illustrates the weak construct validity of global uncertainty measures used by previous researchers. Second, although the specific PEU index has been shown to be highly correlated with performance measures, it relates to the two aspects of performance in a distinctively different manner. The overall conclusion is that total experimental profit was primarily a function of ability and a priori beliefs about the environment. As Starbuck (1976) has noted: "A perceiver's ability to organize and interpret his observations depends very strongly on the theories and beliefs he holds a priori, and he tends to learn what he already believed" (p. 1080).

TABLE 18.2

Regression of Experimental Perceived Environmental
Uncertainty Measures with Baseline Perceived
Environmental Uncertainty Measures and
Objective Environmental Uncertainty
(Experiment I; n = 90)

	Beta Weights		
Experimental Measure	Baseline Measure	Objective Environmental Uncertainty	R^2_{adj}[d]
Environmental dynamism	.16	.22[a]	.050
Environmental complexity	.06	.23[a]	.029
Environmental dominance	.32[b]	-.04	.083
Need for information	.15	.09	.007
Difficulty of assigning confidence level	.16	.32[b]	.099
Specific PEU index	.23[a]	.47[c]	.225

[a] $p < .05$.
[b] $p < .01$.
[c] $p < .001$.
[d] adjusted R^2, where

$$R^2_{adj}) = R^2 - \frac{K-1}{N-K} \; 1-R^2$$

where K = number of independent variables in the equation
N = number of cases
R^2 = unadjusted R^2

Note: The left and center column statistics are standardized regression coefficients (β); the right column represents the proportion of explained variance of the equation adjusted for degrees of freedom.

Source: Compiled by the author.

TABLE 18.3

Summary of Key Predictor Variables Correlated
with Performance Measures
(Experiment I)

Key Predictor Variables	Experimental Profit		Experimental Forecast Error	
	Zero-Order	Partial[b]	Zero-Order	Partial
Baseline				
Baseline profit	.54[c]	.55[c]	-.05	-.16
Specific PEU index	-.40[c]	-.41[c]	.07	.29[d]
Experimentally Manipulated				
OEU	-.05	—	.80[c]	—
Experimental				
Specific PEU index	.06	.04	.47[c]	.22[e]
Experimental profit	—	—	-.21[e]	-.27[d]
Experimental forecast error	.21[e]	.27[d]	—	—

[a] Zero-order Pearson correlation coefficient.
[b] First-order Pearson correlation coefficient, controlling for objective environmental uncertainty.
[c] $p < .001$.
[d] $p < .01$.
[e] $p < .05$.
Source: Compiled by the author.

The results also show quite clearly that high variance in the environment leads to high variance in the forecast error. All other sources of explanation were minor compared to objective uncertainty.

In sum, the most important result is the confirmation that <u>perceived</u> environmental uncertainty is dominated by <u>objective</u> environmental uncertainty. In addition, the two performance measures demonstrate highly different patterns of antecedent variables.

Experiment II

Consistent with the line of reasoning argued in Experiment I, Experiment II was designed as a modified replication. Certain procedures and measures were adjusted to reflect the learning from Experiment I.

Procedure

Subjects for this study were 76 undergraduates in two introductory management courses. The procedure closely approximated Experiment I, with the following modifications: First, the monthly decision was made slightly more complex. The intent was to improve the generalizability of the task. The decision consisted of (1) hiring a salesman, (2) setting an advertising budget, and (3) forecasting a profit (the confidence measure was deleted). The decision involved an additional variable (advertising budget) that was simply added to the first variable (number of salesmen) to constitute the decision input. Subjects were not informed of this combinatorial rule. Second, in the baseline period, OEU was programmed to produce an error variance of approximately 0.5 percent to preclude trivial baseline results. In the experimental period, OEU was a dichotomous (vis-a-vis continuous in Experiment I), creating two distinct experimental treatments (high versus low OEU). Finally, the experimental period consisted of ten monthly decisions rather than 20.

Measures

Based on the results of Experiment I and the modified procedure in Experiment II, the items designed to measure PEU were revised to reflect the new experimental task. Two factors emerged from the factor analysis of the seven revised items. First, a general index was created by summing the items environmental dynamism and environmental complexity. A second, (task-) specific index was created by summing probability 1,000 (probability of actual forecast being within $1,000 of actual profit) and probability 500 (probability of being within $500).

Results

With a modified task, Experiment II addresses the fundamental research question posed in Experiment I: Is more of the variance in experimental PEU measures explained by baseline perceptions of environmental uncertainty or by objective environmental uncertainty? The results (Table 18.4) strongly reaffirm those of

Experiment I. Experimental general PEU index II is positively related to baseline general PEU index II ($r = .29$, $p < .01$) and OEU ($r = .31$, $p < .01$). In contrast, the stronger influence of OEU (including a larger increase in explained variance) is shown on the task-related PEU index II. Experimental task-related PEU II is positively correlated with baseline task-related PEU II measure ($r = .29$, $p < .001$), but once again, the <u>dominant</u> influence on the task-related PEU index was <u>objective</u> environmental uncertainty ($r = .66$, $p < .001$). The increase in adjusted explained variance with the task-specific index (from 15.7 percent to 55.9 percent) is substantial. It is fair to suggest that task-related uncertainty is more critical to our understanding of uncertainty than general measures of perceived uncertainty.

TABLE 18.4

Regression of Experimental Perceived Environmental Uncertainty with Baseline Perceived Environmental Uncertainty and Objective Environmental Uncertainty (Experiment II)

Experimental Measure	Beta Weights		R^2_{adj}[c]
	Baseline Measure	OEU	
General PEU index	.29[a]	.31[a]	.157
Task-specific PEU index	.29[b]	.66[b]	.559

[a] $p < .01$.
[b] $p < .001$.
[c] adjusted R^2, where

$$R^2_{adj} = R^2 - \left(\frac{K-1}{N-K}\right)(1-R^2)$$

where K = number of independent variables in the equation
N = number of cases
R^2 = unadjusted R^2

Source: Compiled by the author.

With regards to performance-related criteria, the OEU has only a moderate, negative effect on profit. The predominant determinant of the experimental profit improvement was baseline profit-making performance or skill. The evidence indicates that objective "noise" or variations in the external environment can be effectively filtered by some cognitive process or simply ignored to reduce the effect of OEU or PEU on performance.

Experiment III

Experiment III was a continuation of Experiment II. The difference in the third experiment was created by the experimenter's introduction of an overt goal. Subjects were: (1) asked to set a unilaterally <u>self-determined</u> goal, (2) given an externally-set <u>assigned</u> goal, (3) allowed to participate in a bilaterally determined <u>negotiated</u> goal, or (4) not given any goal-related information (a control group).

The results clearly indicated that the introduction of the assigned or negotiated goal had a positive effect on profit improvement. More important, those subjects in the high OEU condition (see Experiment II) showed the greatest progress—that is, subjects under high objective environmental uncertainty with an assigned or negotiated goal had a strong, positive profit improvement. The common element of these two important goal conditions is their external or "organizational" influence.

These performance results were obtained without significant changes in individual perceptions of environmental uncertainty. Any speculated influence of a goal in terms of a reduced level of individual uncertainty was not substantiated. The effect of the goal-uncertainty interaction was direct, not appearing to require a perceptual adjustment to environmental conditions.

DISCUSSION

The results of this research serve to clarify several important aspects of the study of applied behavior under environmental uncertainty. The environment→perception→performance model can be examined under new evidence.

Environment and Perception

In terms of the external environment's influence on individual perceptions, while individual characteristics have shown some antecedent relationships with perceptions of uncertainty when measured by general items, task-specific uncertainty measures are relatively free of these linkages. The presence of variance in the baseline measures of PEU, both general and task-specific, supports the presence of some individual differences. Nevertheless, the objective environment appears to have the major impact on experimental perceptions of uncertainty, especially when measured with task-specific items.

Performance and Perception

Correlational studies have attempted to relate PEU with performance. The results of the laboratory experiments allow speculation concerning a possible causal relationship between PEU and performance. In Experiment I, a shift in average subject confidence upon entering the experimental period and prior to receiving any experimental results suggests that some type of perceptual shift preceded performance effects. An alternative explanation of the cause of this shift is that in responding to PEU items, the subjects became sensitized to uncertainty, directly reducing their confidence. The position taken here is that since each subject was explicitly informed that the training period was over, like trainees leaving a classroom setting, the confidence in their ability to forecast profit in the "real" world declined accordingly. (Perceptual uncertainty appears to be open to the power of suggestion.) In the baseline period, individuals used simple operating rules and guidelines to make decisions. Much like other forms of avoidance, simple rules and procedures ignore uncertainty. Although the exigencies of the experimental period decreased the individual's ability to predict events, the individuals chose to ignore the richness of the environment and operate using noncontingent decision rules. Concomitantly, their confidence dropped.

The research cited here, along with additional studies (Yukl and Latham 1978; Lorenzi, Sims, and Slocum 1978), have provided theoretical and empirical evidence to suggest that objective influences may predominate performance, independent of perception—that is, objective reality appears to be more important in explaining task performance than mediating perceptual processes. The objective environment, goals, and rewards (Lorenzi 1980) are examples of these direct influences.

Uncertainty, Risk, and Ignorance

Thompson (1967) addressed the idea of decision-making along two dimensions: (1) knowledge of cause/effect relationships, and

(2) preferences for outcomes. Dichotomizing each dimension along an uncertainty/certainty scale produces four decision-making strategies (see Figure 18.2). The experiments described here entailed a baseline strategy of a judgmental or inspirational approach that evolved to a computational strategy as subjects become more familiar with, that is, learned about, their environment. The interjection of OEU reversed this process. Concurrently, boredom with the task and a lack of reinforcement of the desired (by the experimenter) outcomes produced compromise ("I was told to maximize profit but this is getting boring") or inspirational ("How can I be expected to maximize profit when the old formula doesn't work anymore?") decisions. Goals or rewards (Lorenzi 1980) provide the impetus for a shift to computational/judgmental decisions, independent of cognitive evaluations of environmental uncertainty. Finally, higher individual skill would provide an upward pressure (computational/compromise) on the decision strategy utilized.

FIGURE 18.2

Decision Strategies

		Preferences for Outcomes	
		Certainty	Uncertainty
Knowledge of Cause/Effect Relationships	Certain	computational	compromise
	Uncertainty	judgmental	inspirational

Source: Adopted from James D. Thompson, Organizations in Action (New York: McGraw-Hill, 1967), p. 134.

An inspirational strategy, created by the combined effects of uncertainty, constitute a state of ignorance and/or apathy. A decrease in uncertainty creates a state of risk; further decreases create a state of certainty.

Individual and Organizational Perception

The majority of research in the area of PEU has been set in an organizational context. The laboratory experiments shown here are basically removed from this organizational environment. Individual perceptions and performance in organizations are greatly influenced by organizational elements: reward systems, group influences, and corporate politics. The organization provides the immediate external environment for the individual decision maker, and this influence requires extensive research. The state-of-the-art does not provide the desired answers to plentiful questions.

Individual differences need more attention. Uncertainty is in the mind of the individual, but there is a need to know more about those individuals who not only cope with uncertainty, but thrive on it. The direct influence of the objective environment on performance may moderate this individual role, but lacking precise measures of environments and organizations, this role must be considered.

Applied Behavior under Uncertainty

Two important conclusions emerge from this study of applied behavior under uncertainty. First, current definitions of both objective and subjective (perceptual) uncertainty lack the reliability and validity necessary to make useful generalizations. Second, given this limitation, the slight evidence to date indicates that uncertainty—or at least its effects—can be dealt with in an effective manner. Applied behavior is demanded by the uncertainty of our social environment. The role of the social scientist is to continue to provide tools for decision makers to perform effectively under uncertainty.

REFERENCES

Anderson, Carl R.; Hellreigel, Don; and Slocum, John W., Jr. 1976. "Managerial Response to Environmentally Induced Stress." Academy of Management Journal 20: 260-72.

Dill, William R. 1958. "Environment as an Influence on Managerial Autonomy." Administrative Science Quarterly 2 (March): 404-43.

Downey, H. Kirk; Hellreigel, Don; and Slocum, John W., Jr. 1977. "Individual Characteristics as Sources of Perceived Uncertainty Variability." Human Relations 30: 161-74.

Downey, H. K., and Slocum, V. W., Jr. 1975. "Uncertainty: Measures, Research and Sources of Variation." Academy of Management Journal 18: 562-78.

———. 1979. "Uncertainty and Performance." Mimeographed. Norman: Oklahoma State University.

Driver, M. J., and Streufert, S. 1965. "The 'General Incongruity Adaptation Level (GIAL) Hypothesis': An Analysis and Integration of Cognitive Approaches to Motivation." Paper 114. West Lafayette, Ind.: Purdue University Institute for Research in the Behavioral, Economic, and Management Sciences.

Duncan, R. B. 1972. "Characteristics of Organizational Environments of Perceived Environmental Uncertainty." Administrative Science Quarterly 17: 313-27.

Ford, J., and Slocum, J. W., Jr. 1977. "Size, Technology, Environment and Structure." Academy of Management Review 2: 561-75.

Hermans, H. J. M. 1970. "A Questionnaire Measure of Achievement Motivation." Journal of Applied Psychology 54: 353-63.

Lawrence, Paul R., and Lorsch, Jay W. 1967. "Differentiation and Integration in Complex Organizations." Administrative Science Quarterly 12 (June): 1-47.

Leifer, R. M., and McDonough, E. F. 1977. "Relationships between Individual Performance and Personality, Perceived Environmental Uncertainty, and Organizational Structure." Proceedings: Eastern Academy of Management, pp. 41-45.

Lorenzi, P. 1980. "Validation of Measures of Leader Behaviors and Subordinate Responses." Paper presented at the Eastern Academy of Management.

Lorenzi, P.; Sims, H. P., Jr.; and Slocum, J. W., Jr. 1978. "Perceived Environmental Uncertainty: An Individual or Environmental Characteristic?" Paper presented at the 38th annual meetings of the Academy of Management.

March, James G., and Simon, Herbert. 1958. Organizations. New York: Wiley.

Miles, R. E.; Snow, C. C.; and Pfeffer, J. 1974. "Organization-Environment: Concepts and Issues." Industrial Relations 13: 244-64.

Osborn, R., and Hunt, J. 1974. "Environment and Organization Effectiveness." Administrative Science Quarterly 19: 231-46.

Starbuck, W. H. 1976. "Organizations and Their Environments." In Handbook of Industrial and Organizational Psychology, edited by M. Dunnette, pp. 1069-123. Chicago: Rand-McNally.

Thompson, James. 1967. Organizations in Action. New York: McGraw-Hill.

Tosi, Henry; Aldag, Ramon; and Storey, Ronald. 1973. "On the Measurement of the Environment: An Assessment of the Lawrence and Lorsch Environmental Uncertainty Subscale." Administrative Science Quarterly 18: 27-36.

Weick, Karl E. 1969. The Social Psychology of Organizing. Reading, Mass.: Addison-Wesley.

———. 1965. "Laboratory Experiments with Organizations." In Handbook of Organizations, edited by James G. March, pp. 194-260. Chicago: Rand-McNally.

Yukl, G. A., and Latham, G. P. 1978. "Interrelationships among Employee Participation, Individual Differences, Goal Difficulty, Goal Acceptance, Instrumentality, and Performance." Personnel Psychology 31: 305-24.

19
REDUCING UNCERTAINTY AND BUILDING TRUST: THE SPECIAL CASE OF AUCTIONS
Robert E. Clark
Larry Halford

INTRODUCTION

Most consumer purchases are made in the dyadic relationship between seller and buyer. While there may be buyer uncertainty in such purchases, it is minimized by such things as the reputation of the seller, the guarantee that s/he provides, the testimony of other buyers, and perhaps the past experience of the buyer. In addition, there is the reputation of the product being purchased and the warranty provided by the manufacturer, both of which increase buyer confidence in the purchase. All of these factors reduce the risk of buying a defective product.

But what about buyer uncertainty when purchasing an item in a different setting, such as an auction? Here the buyer-seller dyad becomes a triad with the addition of the auctioneer; the place of business is not the establishment of the seller, but varies from a permanent "auction barn" to the backyard of the seller. Lastly, the price of the goods is not fixed, but is determined by the highest bidder. These structural features are conducive to buyer uncertainty.

By its very design, the auction setting is especially conducive to buyer uncertainty. Several features and the buyer's accompanying response follow:

1. Limited quantity of a particular item for sale: there may be only one rolltop desk, for example, whereas at a retail outlet or antique shop, several would be available. (Consequently, the buyer's response is, "Will I get it?")

2. Increased competition: in addition to fewer numbers of a particular item, there are many competitors hoping to win the bid. ("Will someone outbid me?")

3. Public nature of the purchase: bidding on an item at an auction, especially if the competition is keen, is considerably different than making a purchase from a retail clerk. The buyer at auction is concerned about getting a "good deal" and avoiding "losing face" (Clark and Halford 1978). ("Will I pay too much?" "Will I make a fool of myself?")

4. Lack of warranty or guarantee on the item purchased. ("Even if I win the bid, will I buy a 'lemon'?")

5. Group pressure to bid and buy, including the influence of the auctioneer. ("Will I get carried away and buy items I don't need?" "Will I pay more than I should?")

In the course of this chapter, buyer uncertainty in the auction setting will be explored, with the role of the auctioneer, especially his attempts to reduce buyer uncertainty and build trust, as the central concern.* After a brief consideration of routine auctions that are held on a regular schedule in an established place, special auctions will be discussed in detail.†

If people who bid or sell at an auction feel they are entering into a situation of risk, how does the auctioneer minimize this feeling of uncertainty and maximize a feeling of fairness and honesty toward himself on their part? In other words, how does the auctioneer create a convincing impression?

---

*Data presented in this paper are from an earlier investigation of auctions and are the result of several years of attending auctions by the authors. During the major period of data collection, 132 auctions were attended by one or both authors. Included were weekly cattle sales, police department dispositions of accumulated property, art sales, estate sales, weekly consignment auctions, automobile auctions, and church-sponsored fund raisers—in short, almost every type of auction was observed. In addition to systematic participant observation, approximately 87 taped interviews were conducted with patrons of auctions and 19 with auctioneers (Clark 1973).

†Special auctions are "one-shot" dispositions of property, often held at the home of the seller. Routine auctions attract a more sophisticated, even professional, buyer. Buyer uncertainty is less of a problem at routine auctions.

To answer this question and to examine in general the element of trust in the auction as it is viewed by those who go and those who manage the occasion, Goffman's concept of the front is utilized (Goffman 1959).

According to Goffman, there are three parts to any front: (1) the setting (containing the backdrop and props) for the performance, (2) the performer's appearance (the part of the person, for example, clothing, and so forth) that tells the observers something about the performer's social status, and (3) the manner of the performer (the attributes of the person that tell the audience what to expect in terms of role performance or how the role will be played) (Goffman 1959).

ROUTINE AUCTIONS

Upon entering the places where routine auctions occur, one immediately encounters what appear to be overt attempts to promote trust in, and understanding of, the auction. For example, in livestock auction barns, signs are usually visible to the effect: "All livestock sold as is," "Pregnancy tested cows examined by a veterinarian are in his opinion with calf—the company guarantees nothing," or "New buyers—please establish financial responsibility at the office before purchasing livestock." There is an implied message in these signs that patrons can trust the owners of the auction barns to do their best for the buyer and that the buyers are not buying blind. These signs, in turn, become standard features of the setting. It should be mentioned at this point that in routine auctions, such as livestock sales, most of the buyers are professionals. For example, there are buyers present who buy for meat-packing companies and ranchers who buy to replenish their herds. In any event, it is taken for granted that these people understand the system of buying in this type of auction. Therefore, when the sale begins, the auctioneer does not have to explain any rules of operation such as he would do in most special auctions.

As one auctioneer stated: "You work on the attitude that the buyer comes here as a professional man, and he is supposed to keep himself posted on the market. He is expected to register with the office, and he is supposed to know the buying procedures here."

At the same time, there are reciprocal expectations on the part of the buyers, the auctioneer, and the sellers. In this respect, the auctioneer is expected to be well-versed in the product, for example, cattle, that he is selling. This expertise is to be reflected in soliciting opening bids, advancing them, and terminating them. One buyer commented:

> I get real suspicious if he [the auctioneer] opens the bidding too high. It makes me think he doesn't know the value of what he's selling, or he's trying to cheat someone. If he doesn't know the value then I have to watch and be extra careful when I bid. Otherwise, I might pay too much.

Buyers expect to be cued by the auctioneer to any defects in the animals being sold. Failure to do this, if a sale is consummated, can lead to distrust on the part of the buyers. In livestock auctions, someone always assists the auctioneer as a "spotter," that is, one who makes known any defects in the animals. When asked, he will examine a horse's teeth to determine age, or a cow to determine if sight is missing from an eye, or whatever. The role of the spotter never seems to be assigned, but falls naturally on one or more of the buyers who happen to be in the arena when such a need arises. Thus, it is only natural for trust or distrust in an auctioneer to be developed by professional buyers within the context of the routine auction. Once developed, this trust seems to serve the auctioneer for his career, unless behavior to the contrary is observed that calls this trust into question. Yet, even in cases where the trust is questioned, the response is apt to be written off as a mistake if the auctioneer has a longstanding reputation for being trustworthy.

Frequently, auctioneers will overlook defects in livestock, for example, a boil on the leg, a bad eye, and so forth. When the defect is called to his attention, the buyers then expect the auctioneer to ask if anyone would like to withdraw his/her bid. This reaction by the buyers can be explained by the fact that trust has been developed earlier, and only a reaffirmation is needed for continuation of that trust. Inherent in this situation is the notion that trust based on past experience becomes a basis for present action.

The auctioneer, the owner of the auction barn, and the seller also have a relationship built on mutual trust. One aspect of this is that the former two trust the seller to represent his/her stock honestly. This trust is to some extent manufactured, since veterinarians are normally employed to inspect all livestock, and a brand inspector makes sure the owner is indeed the legitimate one. If cattle are misrepresented, they will not be sold. This, in turn, raises doubts about the character of the seller and may hinder his/her selling stock at future sales. One auctioneer commented:

> We trust the sellers to represent their stock honestly. Of course, we take no responsibility after the animals are sold. But, if some fellow continually sells animals that are not what they are represented to be, and

as a result people feel cheated, then that hurts our business. So we have to watch and make sure that the animals we sell are honestly described.

At one particular horse auction, a bay horse came into the arena, and the auctioneer not knowing anything about the horse asked if anyone could provide some information. A man responded to the effect that the horse was a little strange in that some days anyone could ride him; however, on other days no one could stay in the saddle. The auctioneer thanked the man, who responded by saying that he wanted everyone to know about the horse because he did not want anyone getting hurt.

Of major concern at this point, then, is the trust the seller develops in the auctioneer.* This trust will normally manifest itself as a result of what may be called a <u>fair deal</u>. This refers to the price the auctioneer obtains for the seller's stock. This process has several dimensions in terms of the seller's expectations. For example, the seller, whether selling a large number or only a few head of stock, expects the auctioneer to be fair and work as hard for him/her as anyone else. This idea is illustrated in the following excerpt from a conversation with an auctioneer:

> Trust is built up by the owner of the auction barn. He keeps the buyers from stealing the cattle. He establishes the market for cows and protects them. He buys a lot of cattle to make sure the seller gets a good price for them, and then he will resell them. He builds trust in his market by buying the cattle. It's called market protection. If farmers and ranchers know this, they will trust you, and you have to do it. If a man comes in with five hundred head and you sell them, that's fine. But if another old boy comes in with ten head, you had better work just as hard to sell his ten as you did to sell that five hundred because that might be his [referring to the seller] check for the year. Now there're places that don't, and some auctioneers are too busy and what not. You gotta sell the little guys' cattle just like the big ones'. And if they know then they will keep coming—that's where you build your trust.

---

*Not only is the auctioneer presenting a performance for the buyer audience but, also, for the seller audience. Therefore, both clients must be satisfied in this kind of relationship if the auctioneer is to be successful.

310 / UNCERTAINTY

This may mean that the auction barn will buy the seller's stock if the auctioneer is not getting a price supportive to the market. For instance, a cattle buyer commenting on a particular auctioneer made the following observations:

> The thing that made _____ so great was that he could buy it all himself. If somebody tried to steal something he would put himself in; he would take them people just as far as they would go and if they quit him, and he got stuck with it, he would buy it. The consignor got his money. So the consignor would go through and he would say that _____ got such and such a price for this for him. Well, _____ owned the thing. This guy didn't know it. This is how he did it, support. And that guy would bring his cattle there again because he was certain of how he would be treated.

Trust, then, seems to be established on the part of the seller when s/he can be assured of getting a decent price at an auction. This, in turn, ensures that the seller will utilize the auction again, and the foundation of that auction business is thereby established. The following excerpt from a conversation with a rancher illustrates the seller's feelings:

> Researcher: Why do you bring your cattle to this particular auction?
> Subject: I guess because I have always been treated right.
> Researcher: What do you mean by that?
> Subject: Well, I never have over about twenty head to sell at any one time, but they [referring to auctioneer and the owner of the auction barn] always get good money for them. I've seen _____ sell cattle for years and he always gets the market price or close to it, no matter how many cattle you are selling. Like today, I noticed _____ from Ronan was selling over three hundred calves. Well, I only had fourteen, but _____ got the same money for my calves that he got for his. I noticed _____ had to work longer to sell mine, but I know he will always be fair.

In short, failure to consistently provide equal treatment promotes distrust.

SPECIAL AUCTIONS

The process of developing trust takes on somewhat different dimensions in the special auction. Special auctions do not normally occur in settings arranged for that purpose only. As a result, there are no standard features of the setting itself that might work to dispel uncertainty or suspicion and instill trust—for example, no signs. In addition, many special auctions do not have a fixed stage where all items are displayed in the process of being sold. The selling tends to be fluid, with the audience following the auctioneer from one item or group of items to another. There are no fixed features, then, that serve to promote trust, and, as a result, the responsibility to promote trust falls on the auctioneer.

Special auctions most generally represent the full spectrum of buyers. It appears that people attending an auction for the first time may be found more frequently at special auctions than at routine auctions. Those who attend an auction for the first time probably do so because they noticed a particular item in the auction advertisement that aroused their interest. These people are entering a strange setting. They are unfamiliar with auctions, yet are prospective buyers. In addition, there may be a number of buyers who are experienced auction-goers, even professionals, but who are encountering a particular auctioneer for the first time. Many go through a process of "testing" to determine if the auctioneer is to be trusted. Experienced auction-goers might be concerned with questions such as: "Will he (the auctioneer) point out any defects in the items before selling them?", or, "Will he run me on an item?" Novices, who by definition are attending an auction for the first time, are more concerned with questions of procedure, such as how and when to bid and how much to raise the bid. In any event, testing becomes a major concern. One person recalled his first experience at auctions in the following way:

> I was really confused. I couldn't understand what the auctioneer was saying, and I was afraid if I even scratched my nose or something he would think I was bidding. So I just stood there and watched. Things came up that I would have liked to have had but I was afraid to bid. I wasn't sure I could follow the auctioneer and would end up buying something and paying more than I wanted to. Well, you know, I didn't bid at all that day.

Much more risk-taking is involved in bidding for people unfamiliar with an auctioneer, since there are a number of "unknowns" promoting uncertainty. One person commented: "If I don't know the guy doing the auctioning, I usually will watch for awhile to see if I can determine his style. If he's a smart ass, then he may be trying to con people and I want to know that before I stick my neck out." In this particular situation, testing, then, becomes an important prelude to actual participation in the auction itself.* It must be understood too that there will be buyers present who do know and trust the auctioneer and will be engaged only in a reaffirmation of this trust in their continuing interaction with him.

Testing of the auctioneer begins as he makes his preliminary statements to the crowd concerning the procedure to be followed for that particular auction. Most auctioneers preface their sales with an announcement that all items are to be sold "as is" and that an attempt will be made to point out any defects in order to portray correctly the true character of each item. In most special auctions, there generally will be some comments about the seller as well. A typical example follows:

> Ladies and gentlemen, I'm _____, and I will be your auctioneer for this sale for _____. The clerk for the sale will be the _____ State Bank. The terms of the sale are cash. Please pay for your merchandise before you pick it up. We will take thirty minutes for lunch and it will be served by the ladies of the First Methodist Church. All of you know _____. He has lived here for sixty years but now has decided to retire. Our sale will start in five minutes. Everyone must have a number before you bid.

During this preauction period, the audience begins to develop its perspective of the auctioneer—that is, its acceptance or rejection of the front displayed. The auctioneer is saying, in effect, "I am an auctioneer," and the audience is asked to accept this definition. To quote one auctioneer: "You've got to convince those people that you're not only an auctioneer but a good auctioneer."

---

*In this situation, people who are testing will watch to see how the auctioneer handles himself, as well as those who are bidding. During these early stages of the sale, the auctioneer will make many impressions that are significant in terms of whether people will choose to bid or only watch, for example, how he solicits bids, whether he uses reasonable increases in price, whether he identifies the person who has the bid, and so forth.

People who attend auctions on a regular basis are likely to be exposed to many different fronts, as offered by different auctioneers. Therefore, they are likely to be sensitive to different cues that are or should be offered by the auctioneer. For example, an auctioneer who fails to provide an explanation of the conditions of the sale might be looked upon with suspicion. Likewise, one who uses what may be defined as unreasonable starting bids or bid increases may be viewed in a similar way. On many occasions, we have observed people entering an auction and watching from the "edge of the action" before deciding to get a number.

Important, too, is the fact that auctioneers are supposed to look like auctioneers. This "appearance" becomes a very nebulous idea when trying to describe an ideal typical auctioneer, but most people have an image of what they believe an auctioneer should look like; however, this expectation varies according to the type of sale.

For example, no one would venture a guess as to what an auctioneer who is selling cars is supposed to wear or one who is selling carpets. Yet, most auctioneers observed have a particular attire that they consistently wear, and this portion of the front in itself becomes taken for granted. Deviation from this might be reason for suspicion. One auctioneer made the following observation concerning appearance: "You really have to dress the part. Around here most auctioneers wear boots and cowboy hats, especially if they're selling livestock. If they didn't, people might think that they don't know what you're doing. So you don't see guys wearing fancy suits and ties. They would look like dudes to most people around here."

In another instance, one buyer, commenting on a particular auctioneer, said:

> When _____ sells, he looks like an auctioneer. You know, the Southern Colonel, stereotyped auctioneer. That's what he looks like, and he is a gentleman. You will never hear _____ swear. And he never says anything about a person who comes in. People trust him because he is a gentleman. There are very few auctioneers who are gentlemen.

Finally, the manner and the proffered definition of the person as an auctioneer are important. People expect the auctioneer to be in control of the situation so that he can protect them during times when they are engaged in the process of bidding. Thus, at the very start, when the man is seeking to define himself as an auctioneer, there necessarily must be an initial fit between the parts of the front in order to establish a basis for the development of trust. As can be seen in the excerpt above, it becomes difficult to separate appearance and manner, and in many accounts, they were talked about as one.

We attended a fur auction on one occasion in which a man from New York was attempting to sell various kinds of fur coats. He was dressed in a suit with a wide tie and had a distinctively eastern accent. Out of 50 furs, he was able to sell two, and the sale was a dismal failure. We discussed this particular auction with several informants, and they expressed the feeling that people did not buy because they did not know the fellow doing the selling. Also, the auctioneer, in whose establishment this sale was taking place, had a poor reputation because of several run-ins with the law. For many, it is this initial contact with the auctioneer that takes place during the preauction period which serves either to demonstrate a consistency or lack of consistency among the parts of the front. Any lack of fit at this point can be reason initially to distrust the auctioneer.

As Goffman has suggested, "If the individual's activity is to become significant to others, he must mobilize his activity so that it will express during the interaction what he wishes to convey" (Goffman 1959). In other words, the auctioneer establishes his identity in and through face-to-face interaction on the job.

The setting in which the auction is to take place also becomes an important concern in special auctions, whereas it is a taken-for-granted feature of routine auctions. The arrangement of the setting precludes its being defined as one in which an auction is to occur. Important in this respect is the arrangement of items to be sold. One auctioneer, commenting on the arrangement of the setting, stated:

> It's important that you set up your items so that they are accessible to your audience, that is, so they can see pieces. You line up all your power tools with drop cords available so you can show that they work. You put the odds and ends in boxes. Then you line up your machinery and make sure that, if it is in running order, it will start during the auction. If you are smart, and it's in the spring, you will put all of your machinery on a little slope so that if it rains, it won't get muddy.

In this sense, then, arrangement of the setting prior to a sale provides the audience with some initial information concerning the auctioneer that indicates whether or not he knows what he is doing. As Goffman has so aptly stated: "Information about the individual helps to define the situation, enabling others to know in advance

what he will expect of them and what they may expect of him"
(Goffman 1959).

Also, the written announcement that an auction is to take place
with its complete or partial list of items should agree with what one
is able to observe on the scene in order to establish these first
steps of trust. One irritated buyer at a country sale commented:
"I don't see half the stuff here they advertised. I bet they sold it to
some dealer or the auctioneer took it himself."

Up to this point in the processual development of trust, the
auction has not yet begun. If a preliminary basis for testing has
been established via the process discussed above, then the problem
for the auctioneer becomes one of developing trust further and holding it throughout the auction in order to facilitate the smooth functioning of the auction itself. One auctioneer noted:

> My main interest is to keep that auction moving along.
> Some of the sales I handle run for a couple of days because there's so much merchandise. If it bogs down
> and won't go because people don't want to bid for some
> reason or another, then I'm in trouble. To sell that
> stuff you've got to keep that sale moving. That's where
> your reputation counts. If people know you and respect
> what you're doing, then you can talk to them and usually
> get the bidding going because they know you're not trying to cheat them.

Auctioneers consequently develop techniques for increasing
trust on the part of their audience. Many of these techniques are
used in the initial phase of the auction to create interest and to
stimulate bidding, but they also function to build trust. For example, at most auctions, the items of lesser value are sold during the
first part of the sale, and the major items are sold last. There is
a practical reason for this in that if the major items are sold first,
the audience might lose interest and leave before everything is sold.
However, many auctioneers like to sell one or two items of interest
first and knock them down to the first person who bids. This not
only increases interest but provides an occasion for testing as well.

Another technique employed by several auctioneers is illustrated in the following statement:

> When I have a special sale I will invariably sell something to a lady who is sixty or seventy years old. Maybe it is a hand out item and after selling it to her I will
> make a point of saying, "Give it to the young lady in the
> front row." Even though the woman is old, I believe that

this will make her feel good. Also, at every auction there is always a toy of some kind, a doll or a teddy bear, something that nobody is going to give anything for. I will start it with a dollar or two and take it up. If I get somebody in, I tell them that I am in, and I will bid against them, and they know I am bidding against them, and if they get it, fine, and if I get it, fine. If I get it, I say, "Mark it on me." Usually, there is a kid in the front row, and I will give it to him. There are always people that look like they don't have a lot of money, and you give it to them instead of another kid. From then on, you can't do anything wrong.

As indicated earlier, buyers who are familiar with the auctioneer provide a service for those who are not, as well as for those who are not familiar with auctions at all. This service manifests itself in the experienced buyer's willingness to bid immediately rather than waiting to develop trust, since he will only be looking for a reaffirmation of trust: "I like to go to auctions where _____ is doing the selling. I've known him since he was a kid, and he's a good auctioneer. He's honest and doesn't try to take advantage of people. Not all these auctioneers are like that. With some, you have to be real careful when you bid." This type of action provides those who are still testing with an opportunity to view the auctioneer from a perspective of low risk in that they do not have to bid in order to test. Therefore, they are engaged in a period of observation in which they can make preliminary judgments about the auctioneers:

I went to an auction last Saturday with my husband. We went just for something to do. _____ [her husband] had never been to an auction, and I have only been to about four. . . . All the seats were taken, and we had to stand against the wall on one side. Anyway, we were able to watch all the people bidding. At first, I couldn't tell what the auctioneer was doing, but, then, I was able to tell who was bidding and could see the auctioneer take their bids. Finally, something came up that I wanted, and so I bid but I didn't get it.

For those who are experienced auction-goers, concern will be with how the auctioneer handles prospective buyers. There will be a concern with whether or not the auctioneer is using shills (one who offers a bid to stimulate further bidding), taking phantom bids, running the bidder, and how he handles bidders in general. At one particular auction, the auctioneer was trying to sell a small teapot and was having trouble getting anyone to bid. Finally, someone offered $.50. The auctioneer began to ridicule the girl for having raised the bid only a quarter, and eventually the girl got up and left. At that point a man next to me commented: "Boy, he's not much of an auctioneer. I was about to offer him seventy-five cents myself. Hell, if that's the way he operates I think I'll leave too!"

In addition, as mentioned earlier, most buyers will compare items listed in the auction advertisement with what they observe on the scene. An inconsistency at this point either in the existence of the item or its condition can be reason for distrust. A conversation was overheard at one auction in which the following comments were made:

> Person one: Do you see anything exciting?
> Person two: Not really, this advertisement is misleading. That rolltop desk he advertised is not what I expected. I sure didn't picture it to look like that. I wouldn't give him a penny for that thing!

Evidence indicating any of the above qualities would promote feelings of distrust, since there would be a feeling that a bid would be to run a greater risk than would be normal to take. Of special interest, too, is whether the auctioneer is describing the items, that is, pointing out defects, to the satisfaction of the buyers. Auctioneers will sometimes try to "gloss over" imperfections in items, such as cracks or breakage, in an attempt to get the buyers to define them as minimal problems or of no real concern. Most of the time, this is done in a joking manner: "Don't worry about this car [referring to a car that was smoking and leaking oil on the ground]. All it needs is a little work." It should be pointed out here that there is a perceived difference in terms of the risk factor between items with defects that can be hidden, for example, a sick horse, versus items in which defects cannot be hidden, for example, a tractor that will not run. This illustrates again the reliance on the auctioneer to describe and make known any defects.

On occasions such as estate sales, where many different items are being sold, it is not uncommon to find the auctioneer dealing with merchandise with which he has had no expertise. In these situations, it becomes extremely important for the auctioneer to make this fact publicly known. At a sale involving a number of different items, there were several paintings among the lots to be sold. When the paintings were put on the block, the auctioneer made the comment to the audience that he did not know the value of, or anything about, art work, but that he would work with the seller in terms of a starting bid.

The audience, however, still depends on the auctioneer for an honest appraisal of the items in terms of their condition, that is, whether they are broken, cracked, or whatever. Failure to call attention to an imperfection can easily give credence to the notion of dishonesty and, therefore, untrustworthiness. On one occasion, a professional buyer purchased a metronome at an auction from an auctioneer she knew well. Upon claiming the item at the end of the sale, she found it to be cracked. She immediately questioned the auctioneer about this, leaving the option up to the auctioneer as to what he would do. His response was to ask the woman if she would like her money back. Again, the woman left the option open to the auctioneer, indicating that he could do as he wished. Faced with this decision, the auctioneer returned her money. Some auctioneers add a "return your money" phrase to their preauction statement and then repeat it during the auction if necessary (especially when they get to a particularly mangled piece of merchandise).

Auctioneers are in particularly sensitive situations when they are selling to large audiences. As one auctioneer commented:

> A lot of people think auctioneers will say anything. That's not true. We look for the better parts of anything, but for an auctioneer to cover up anything, that's wrong; or cover up something that's decayed or broken—they don't do those kinds of things as much any more. If they do, they don't stay in the auction business very long . . . because everybody's looking and everybody's listening.

Most auctioneers observed during the course of this research attempted to rectify any mistakes on their part. We attended a special auction that was to run for two days because of the large amount of merchandise to be sold. During the early stages of the sale, a lot containing what was thought to be a set of tire chains was sold. Upon claiming the merchandise, the buyer discovered that the so-called tire chains were incomplete. He immediately called this to the auctioneer's attention. The auctioneer apologized, asked the clerk to remove the sale from the man's number, and then resold the chains, describing them as they actually were. This particular auctioneer had an excellent reputation in the area, and we were not able to observe any change in the bidding as a result of this incident. This serves to illustrate again the way in which the auctioneer's reputation and established trust contribute to a successful auction. Also, if an auctioneer failed to see a bid that resulted in knocking down the item to the wrong person, he might publicly apologize to the particular buyer. Some auctioneers went so far as to apologize in private again after the auction was completed. However, many auctioneers follow the pattern described by one auctioneer:

> When the sale is done depending on what the deal is, either go get paid, or whatever, and then get in your car and get out of there. Don't hang around after a sale. That's the worst thing you can do. You are going to have gotten in trouble two or three times during the day. Somebody wanted something, and you didn't see him or something. Everyone of those guys is going to come up to you. Just get in your car and get out of there. You are done.

TESTIMONIES AND STORIES

A feature that can be considered standard to most auctions, and indeed crucial to the selling of most goods, is the testimony or the story that accompanies the sale of individual items. Testimonies and stories are used not only as informative devices but, also, serve to reduce uncertainty and build trust. They occur in both routine and special auctions. However, their occurrence is usually dictated by the type of items being sold.

Testimonies are an expected feature of horse and cattle sales, especially those of registered stock. For example, there are many people attending a horse sale who are not versed in the buying of horses, and even if they were, they could tell nothing about the horse except its physical features. It is commonplace in these situations for the auctioneer to invite comments from the owner. This usually involves the owner extolling the virtues of the animal. An example follows:

> Auctioneer: Harry, tell us about your horse.
> Seller: Well, he's ten years old. I have raised him since he was a colt, and I's the only one who has ever rode him. He is an adult's horse. I wouldn't recommend him as a kid's horse. He is broke real good. I have used him in the mountains to pack elk, and he's been a good horse for me.

Testimonies in registered stock sales take the form of tracing the blood lines of the animal for sale. This may be done by the auctioneer; however, in special sales of registered stock, it is not uncommon for the owner of the auction barn to bring in an expert on the type of stock being sold, such as in the case of registered quarter horses or Hereford bulls. At one particular quarter horse auction, the auctioneer was selling a famous quarter horse stud. At one point, the person who was holding the top bid volunteered to give a testimony on the horse. During this testimony, he pleaded with the audience to bid more because the horse was not selling for what it was worth. When finished, he returned to his chair and eventually bid the top price. In these cases, the testimony provides information and also dispels uncertainty on the part of the buyer. In short, testimonies are used when the true nature of the object for sale is not readily discernible from simple observation. They lend credence to the notion that the object is indeed being represented honestly and fairly.

Another use of the testimony was observed at horse auctions, where the horses, if they are broken, will usually be reined around the auction arena. While this is taking place, the auctioneer will solicit information about the horse from the owner by asking questions such as: "Can he be packed?," "Can a child ride him?," and, "How well is your horse broke?" It is not uncommon for people selling horses to provide a guarantee to the effect that "if you buy him and don't like him, I will return your money." One person made the following statement when attempting to sell his horse: "This horse is good enough. If you take him out and can't ride him, you can have him. If you can ride him, then you pay me double."

Stories serve a different function, yet, by and large, see equal duty with the testimony. Auctioneers usually do not give testimonies because outside information or information from one who is closely associated with the item up for sale seems to carry a greater air of legitimacy. Auctioneers, however, do tell stories about certain items or lots of items, and, usually each story is a device used to impart background information about inanimate objects. In most instances, stories are very simple. For example, the auctioneer at an antique sale might tell something about the history of the items for sale, for example, who owned them, where they came from, and so forth. Stories are used not only to dispel uncertainty but to impart information or give character to the object as well; thus, the auctioneer hopes to increase bidder interest. Stories are usually utilized in the case of inanimate objects, where condition of the objects is readily discerned and is not questioned by the audience. Country or estate sales provide the auctioneer or the seller with ample opportunity for telling stories about objects, such as antiques, which may have been in a particular family for generations:

> Look here, look here! We have this clock to sell that belonged to _____'s greatgrandmother. It came all

the way to Montana from Kansas in a covered wagon. In fact, _____'s grandmother was born on that wagon on the way out here. So you know it's real old, but it still works and it's in real good condition. What will someone give to start the bidding?

People, then, look for cues that give them direction as to whether to trust or distrust an auctioneer. If negative cues are picked up, this might be reason enough to reexamine the front of the auctioneer and put the brakes on bidding for the time being. However, when trust has been established in the auction setting, the buyer has confidence that he will not be exploited.

CONCLUSION

As discussed throughout this chapter, the development of trust is relative to the type of person attending the auction. Inexperienced buyers are apt to engage in longer periods of testing than experienced buyers. Moreover, inexperienced buyers are more dependent on the auctioneer for guidance and fair treatment. Participation in the auction carries greater risk for them because they are not as experienced in controlling the situation to their benefit instead of their loss. In other words, participation puts them in the uncertain position of having to trust the auctioneer.

People who are experienced in auctions operate from a different perspective than those who are inexperienced. Trust in the auctioneer plays a minor role in the decision to interact. Consequently, experience in itself becomes the determining factor, since certain elements of trust can be waived when the person has a firm grasp of the situation. For example, people who are experienced auction-goers in most cases are able to tell if the auctioneer is using a phantom bidder or is selling to the house. One of our informants, who happened to be a professional buyer, was particularly adept at recognizing an auctioneer selling to the house. On numerous occasions, she pointed out the person she believed to be working with the auctioneer. When questioned, experienced people take this type of action for granted within certain limits, and because of their experience and ability to perceive these actions, the experienced auction-goer feels in control of the situation. One such auction-goer commented: "It doesn't bother me if the auctioneer uses a phantom bid occasionally. I can usually spot it, and if I am bidding and he uses it to try and raise my bid, I will usually drop out immediately depending on the size of the bid. If it's only a small increase, I might stick."

Uncertainty in an auction differs, then, depending on whether the buyer is experienced or inexperienced. Experienced buyers are more likely to know the value of items and how much they are willing to bid. In addition, their experience provides them with the ability to know when to abandon bidding; therefore, they can protect themselves. Inexperienced buyers must depend more on the auctioneer; he is the primary source for reducing their uncertainty.

REFERENCES

Clark, R. E. 1973. "On the Block: An Ethnography of Auctions." Ph.D. dissertation, University of Montana.

Clark, R. E., and Halford, L. J. 1978. "Going . . . Going . . . Gone: Some Preliminary Observations on 'Deals' at Auctions." Urban Life 7 (October): 285-307.

Goffman, E. 1959. The Presentation of Self in Everyday Life. New York: Doubleday.

20
BEHAVIORAL DETERMINANTS OF MARKET FAILURE: THE CASE OF DISASTER INSURANCE
Ralph B. Ginsberg
Howard Kunreuther

This chapter investigates consumer decision processes with respect to the purchase of insurance against low probability high-loss events, such as floods or earthquakes. To motivate the analysis, consider the following oversimplified example, which reflects problems posed by Arrow (1963) and Akerlof (1970) in their classic pieces. A flood-prone community is composed of homeowners, each of whom faces a different risk from potential overflowing of a nearby river. The insurance industry has refused to offer protection against flood losses because the efforts associated with determining customized rates for each homeowner are sufficiently costly that the resulting premiums would be unusually high. Furthermore, they fear problems of adverse selection if they set premiums on the basis of average risk characteristics of homes in the community. The industry has reasoned that only individuals closest to the river would purchase policies, thus generating inordinately large claims should the area suffer flooding. The industry is also concerned that following a severe disaster, insurance companies would suffer catastrophic losses in relation to premiums written.

Suppose we adopt the perspective of a policy maker who wishes to propose institutional remedies to cope with the market failure problems above. The policy maker wants to determine how to protect individuals so as to maximize an appropriate social welfare function. In order to develop alternative options, s/he makes the following assumptions about consumers: (1) they know the relevant probabilities of the risks facing them, the losses which they are likely to suffer, and federal aid associated with a flood disaster— they also would be knowledgeable about the insurance premium should coverage be made available to them; and (2) they utilize the above data to determine whether insurance is an attractive purchase relative to bearing the risk of possible loss by comparing the expected utilities of these two alternatives.

The above scenario suggests that the market has failed because the consumer has better information on his/her risk than the supplier does. If these informational asymmetries exist, as has been suggested by Akerlof (1970) and Williamson (1975), then the competitive outcome in markets for insurance may be nonoptimal (Pauly 1974). To remedy this situation without making insurance compulsory, the policy maker can follow one of two general courses of action. S/he can design some incentive scheme as part of a market mechanism to encourage individuals to reveal their true risk, or s/he can propose some form of public intervention. Solutions in line with the first option have been developed by Rothschild and Stiglitz (1976), Riley (1976), and Wilson (1977). These authors advocate presenting individuals with a system of premiums based on the amount of total coverage they demand. Those who want a large amount of insurance, presumably because they face potentially severe losses, would pay a higher rate than those who need less protection. As a second course of action, the policy maker may propose a social insurance program that enables the groups facing the highest risk to purchase coverage. This feature was at the core of the National Flood Insurance Act of 1968 and has also been proposed by Spence (1977) as a way of coping with the market's failure to optimally differentiate policies.

In this chapter, we shall take an empirical point of view and ask how successful the above remedies are likely to be. On the basis of evidence from a large-scale field survey and controlled laboratory experiments on insurance, we conclude that neither of the two general courses of action are likely to work well in practice because of faulty assumptions by the policy maker about the demand side of the market. Before turning to the empirical evidence and its implications for policy, we shall briefly summarize the institutional arrangements that have emerged historically to protect residents of flood- and earthquake-prone areas against the potentially severe financial consequences of these disasters. There has been a growing concern in recent years that the general taxpayer is bearing an undue burden of the financial costs of disasters through liberal relief in the form of low-interest loans and forgiveness grants to individuals who have not been protected with insurance. For example, tropical storm Agnes in June 1972 triggered over $1.2 billion in Small Business Administration (SBA) relief, of which over $440 million was in outright grants to uninsured victims. Hence, the search for effective remedies is a matter of serious concern.

HISTORICAL BACKGROUND: INSTITUTIONAL ARRANGEMENTS FOR COPING WITH FLOOD AND EARTHQUAKE LOSSES

Prior to 1897, homeowners residing in flood-prone areas were unable to purchase flood insurance protection and had to rely on charitable contributions and ad hoc congressional legislation for relief. Hence, there was no assurance on their part that they would be able to financially survive the consequences of severe flooding. In 1897, an insurance company in Illinois offered coverage against flood damage to houses, contents, and livestock along the Mississippi and Missouri rivers. The move was inspired by the extensive losses from the overflowing of these two rivers in 1895 and 1896. Since the insurance was voluntary, only homeowners and farmers with unusually high risks purchased policies. Although the rivers were peaceful in 1898, the following year, severe floods caused insured losses that were greater than the combination of premiums from this cataclysmic event. Another flood in the same year brought still greater insured losses. Even the home office of the company was washed away in the second flood (Manes 1938, p. 161).

A similar experience in the mid-1920s resulted in catastrophic losses to the industry, causing every responsible company to discontinue coverage. Few private insurance firms offered flood insurance on residential property again. Their rationale for discontinuing flood coverage suggests a case of market failure due to adverse selection. Specifically, in a report issued by the Insurance Executives Association (1952) one finds the following statement:

> Because of the virtual certainty of the loss, its catastrophic nature, and the impossibility of making this line of insurance self-supporting due to the refusal of the public to purchase such insurance at the rates which would have to be charged to pay annual losses, companies generally could not prudently engage in this field of underwriting.

Earthquake insurance, on the other hand, has been widely available since 1916 in California through the usual market mechanisms and remains so to this day. At the time it was first written by U.S.-based insurance companies, such coverage was considered a novelty. Little was purchased due largely to a misconception of earthquake damage rather than to an unattractive premium. Since over 80 percent of the losses from the 1906 San Francisco earthquake were caused by fire, the homeowners assumed that they would be covered by fire insurance for the bulk of the losses caused by future shocks. As the insurance industry shared this view, the result was low rates, small company reserves, and little reinsurance.

Today, premiums for wood frame homes in California, which comprise almost all residential structures in the state, average $.20 per $100 coverage (with a 5 percent deductible). Coverage can easily be written as an endorsement to comprehensive homeowners coverage. Nevertheless, today less than 3 percent of all homeowners in California are protected against earthquake damage. There is some evidence that the low subscription rate is due to the unwillingness of consumers to purchase coverage rather than to the unwillingness of the industry to market it aggressively. As an experiment following the San Fernando earthquake of February 1971, the Insurance Company of North America mounted a serious campaign to market earthquake insurance in California, by placing newspaper ads in the major dailies, advertising on TV, and enabling all their California agents to mail special brochures and announcements to their customers. The following month, only 61 policies were sold, and then sales dropped off during the next seven months to an average of seven per month (Syfert 1972). The Hartford Insurance group and Kemper Companies ran similar campaigns to market earthquake insurance. Their efforts also bore little fruit. Whether the unwillingness of the public to purchase earthquake insurance has been "rational" will be explored in later sections.

With the coming of the New Deal, the federal government began to take an active role in providing relief to uninsured victims of disasters, by making low-interest loans available to the private sector for rehabilitation and repair of damage. It thus assumed some of the risks that were previously borne by individuals affected and, hence, made insurance less attractive to them. The loan program proved particularly costly to taxpayers because monitoring cost made it practically impossible to exclude anyone suffering uninsured damage in a disaster area even if the damage was not disaster related.

The skyrocketing cost of federal assistance, together with demands by homeowners in flood-prone areas for insurance to cover losses not included in the loan programs, led to a series of legislative acts, whose two principal purposes were the following: (1) to redistribute the risk to those affected, and (2) to encourage private sector alternatives and remedies for the failure of the market. The National Flood Insurance Act of 1968 is typical. It attempted to reestablish the flood insurance market and encourage homeowners and businesses to purchase coverage through federal rate subsidies, while at the same time encouraging state and local governments to control unwise development of flood plains by instituting appropriate land-use adjustments. The program did not produce the anticipated effects. Communities were slow to participate in the program, even with the inducement of federal aid, and few individuals within the eligible communities purchased the highly subsidized coverage. By the end of 1973, fewer than 3,000 out of 21,000 flood-prone communities in the United States had entered the program, and only 274,000 policies had been sold to homeowners residing in these areas. George Bernstein, former administrator of the Federal Insurance Administration (FIA), alluded to possible shortcomings in the demand side assumptions of the program when he observed in congressional hearings in 1973 that "it is now becoming common knowledge that few people buy insurance . . . until they are forced to or are in imminent danger of sustaining a severe loss or have already suffered the loss. As we have said for some time, the total voluntary nature of the program is its major defect."

Revisions of the Flood Insurance Program reflect Bernstein's disenchantment with the previous assumptions. Legislation passed at the end of 1973 increased the financial incentives for flood-prone communities to participate in the program and imposed the requirement that residents of these areas purchase flood insurance as a precondition for loans and mortgages. The government and local financial institutions were thus forced to exert strong pressure to induce flood-prone communities and their residents to protect themselves. These actions appear to be well beyond what would be necessary were individuals and community officials acting according to the expectation built into the original legislation. Thus, today, the institutional arrangements reflect regulatory and administrative solutions rather than market mechanisms. We will have more to say about the impact of these changes in the concluding section.

TESTING ASSUMPTIONS ABOUT
INSURANCE PURCHASE

The recent changes in the Flood Insurance Program induced by Bernstein's comments were based on a set of assumptions that were no better corroborated by systematic evidence than the assumptions of our hypothetical policy maker. We turn now to a set of empirical studies designed to address these issues.

The results presented below are based on face-to-face interviews with 2,000 homeowners in flood-prone areas in the United States and 1,000 residents of earthquake-prone areas in California. By design, half of the respondents were insured and the other half were not, so we could examine their decision processes with respect to insurance purchase. The questionnaire probed their knowledge of the natural hazards affecting them, their knowledge of insurance, and their reasons for buying or not buying coverage. The details of the survey are discussed fully elsewhere (Kunreuther et al. 1978), so we will only summarize key results that directly bear on the two assumptions raised in the introduction.

Estimates of Relevant Data

One of the principal findings from the field survey is that homeowners inaccurately estimate both the damage from a severe future flood or earthquake in their area as well as the probability that such a disaster may occur. For example, on the damage side, a relatively large number of individuals in earthquake-prone areas (78 percent of the insured, 61 percent of the uninsured) feel that should a severe earthquake occur, it will cause more than $10,000 damage to their property. Since practically all of the houses in California are wood frame structures, the actual damage resulting from a severe quake is likely to be considerably less than these subjective estimates. On the other side of the coin, there are a large percentage of uninsured individuals in both flood- and earthquake-prone areas who estimate that they will receive no damage from a severe flood (29 percent) or earthquake (12 percent) in the area, even though our sample included only individuals residing in hazard-prone areas. Thus, knowledge of actual damage is rather imperfect.

On the probability side, uninsured individuals in flood-prone areas assess a much lower subjective probability of a severe flood next year than do insured individuals. In earthquake-prone areas, the difference between the two groups is much smaller. A large percentage of uninsured individuals in both flood-prone (31 percent) and earthquake-prone (17 percent) areas estimate the probability of a severe disaster in their areas to be almost impossible (that is, 1 in 100,000 or less), even though they are prime candidates for future loss. Some of these uninsured individuals may have provided such a low estimate as an ex post facto justification for their current uninsured status rather than because they really perceive the chance of a flood or earthquake to be so small. The same bias may be true in reverse for insured homeowners who estimate a high probability of a future flood or earthquake. There is no way to determine the actual rationale for estimates on the basis of our survey. This is one of the principal reasons for undertaking the controlled laboratory experiments discussed in the next section.

We must conclude that the subjective estimates of damage and probability of loss reflect considerable misinformation. The adverse selection argument requires people to estimate risks and damage more accurately than insurance companies, who must rely on aggregate data. The misinformation and vagueness of people's knowledge hardly support this view. Even though insured individuals expect more damage with a higher probability than uninsured individuals do, neither group has very accurate estimates of these figures.

Homeowners' knowledge of insurance was also rather imperfect. About 10 percent of the uninsured homeowners in the flood sample and about one-quarter of the uninsured in the earthquake sample were unaware that insurance existed as an option at all. These figures are significant because the vast majority of individuals in flood-prone areas are uninsured. Moreover, 60 percent of the uninsured homeowners aware of the existence of insurance did not know that they themselves were eligible for coverage. Those individuals aware of the availability of flood and earthquake coverage were asked to estimate the cost of a policy to them. The subsidized flood rate is between \$2.50 and \$3.50 per \$1,000 coverage, depending on the proportion of coverage devoted to structure and contents. The earthquake premium on wood frame homes in California averages \$2.00 per \$1,000. A homeowner who estimates the rates between \$2 and \$4 for flood coverage and \$1 and \$3 for earthquake insurance was classified as reasonably accurate. Figure 20.1 shows that most of the insured homeowners were accurate in their estimate, and those who were not within this range generally underestimated the amount. Uninsured individuals present quite a different picture. A much smaller percentage estimate premiums within \$1 of the actual rates, while approximately 36 percent of those in the flood sample and 45 percent in the earthquake sample overestimate the premium by more than \$1. Apparently, the uninsured group have not obtained rate information, on their own or through agent contact, even if they know coverage is available.

Data on the maximum amount that homeowners are willing to pay for their desired amount of flood or earthquake coverage are consistent with this hypothesis. Of the uninsured homeowners, about two-thirds could provide such a dollar estimate. Figure 20.2 plots percentage of nonpolicyholders willing to pay premiums varying from \$0 to \$10. Point A indicates that 34 percent of the subset of uninsured homeowners would be willing to pay more than the average rate for earthquake coverage. Point B indicates that 27 percent would be willing to pay more than the current subsidized flood insurance rate. Had they been aware of the actual premium, these nonpolicyholders <u>should</u> have been willing to buy coverage.

One of the arguments raised against a system of liberal disaster relief in the form of forgiveness grants and low-interest loans is that it discourages individuals from purchasing insurance in the

FIGURE 20.1

Subjective Estimates by Individuals of Cost of Flood
or Earthquake Insurance per $1,000 Coverage

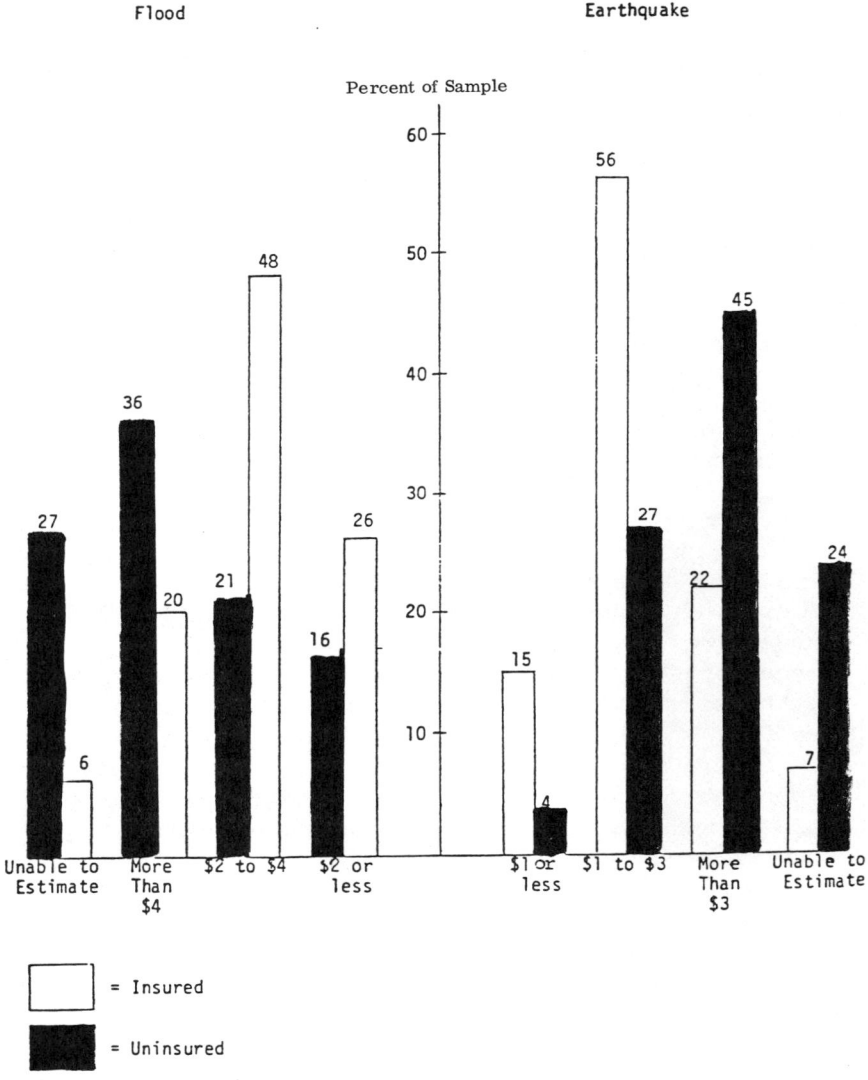

Source: Constructed by the authors.

FIGURE 20.2

Maximum Premium Uninsured Are Willing to Pay
for Insurance per $1,000 Coverage

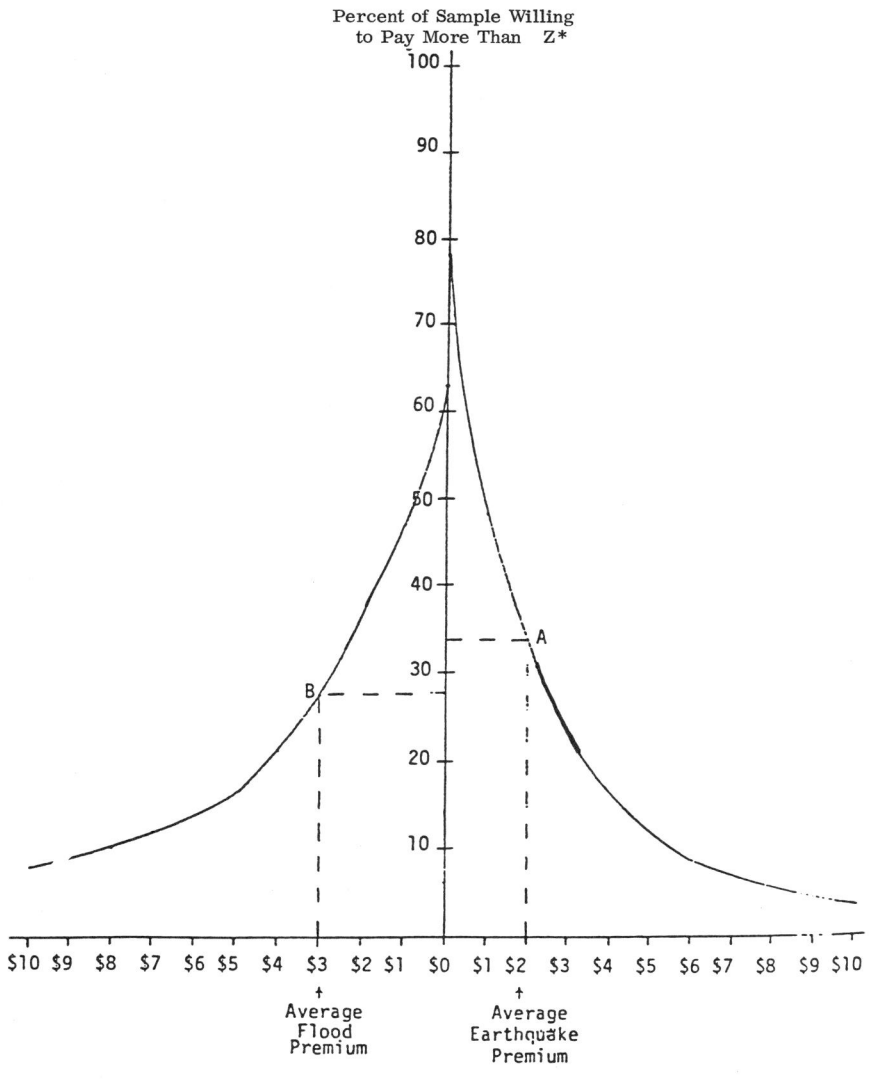

Source: Constructed by the authors.

predisaster period. We therefore questioned the homeowners in our sample as to their anticipated receipt of federal disaster relief should they suffer losses from a future disaster. Each respondent was asked to enumerate the expected dollar amounts that might be derived from different sources to restore their property and contents from damage resulting from a severe flood or earthquake. The majority of both insured and uninsured homeowners expected to receive <u>no aid</u> at all from the federal government, even though this source was specified in the question as one of several possible alternatives. This holds regardless of the estimated loss from a future disaster. It is clear that insured homeowners will have no need to rely on the federal government for relief except to cover the deductible portion of their policy or the loss in excess of their total coverage. Lack of knowledge among the uninsured, in spite of the need, is less predictable. When the losses are $10,000 or less, then over three-quarters of both the flood- and earthquake-uninsured respondents expect no aid. Even for homeowners who anticipate large losses, the majority expect no federal relief.

These findings suggest that prior to a disaster, most individuals feel that the federal government will not help them if they suffer severe losses. In fact, it may very well be the case that they have not considered how they would recover in the wake of a flood or earthquake. After a disaster, many of these victims will undoubtedly be anxious to obtain available federal relief to aid in their recovery.

Determining Attractiveness of Insurance

For those individuals able to provide estimates of the probability of a future disaster and the insurance premium, we were interested in whether their decision to purchase insurance was generally consistent with their maximizing expected utility as envisaged in the second behavioral assumption above. Using a straightforward contingent claims model described in Kunreuther (1976) a contingency price ratio (R), similar to one derived by Eisner and Strotz (1965), was utilized to determine the costs of insurance in relation to its potential benefits. If R is less than or equal to 1, insurance should be attractive to risk-averse individuals. As the value of R exceeds 1, insurance becomes progressively less attractive to the homeowner.

Figure 20.3 shows the percentage of insured and uninsured homeowners with subjective estimates of R below any given value R* in the range from 1 to 1,000. Point A marks the proportion of insured individuals whose estimates yield values of R above 10.

FIGURE 20.3

Contingency Price Ratio (R) for Insured and Uninsured

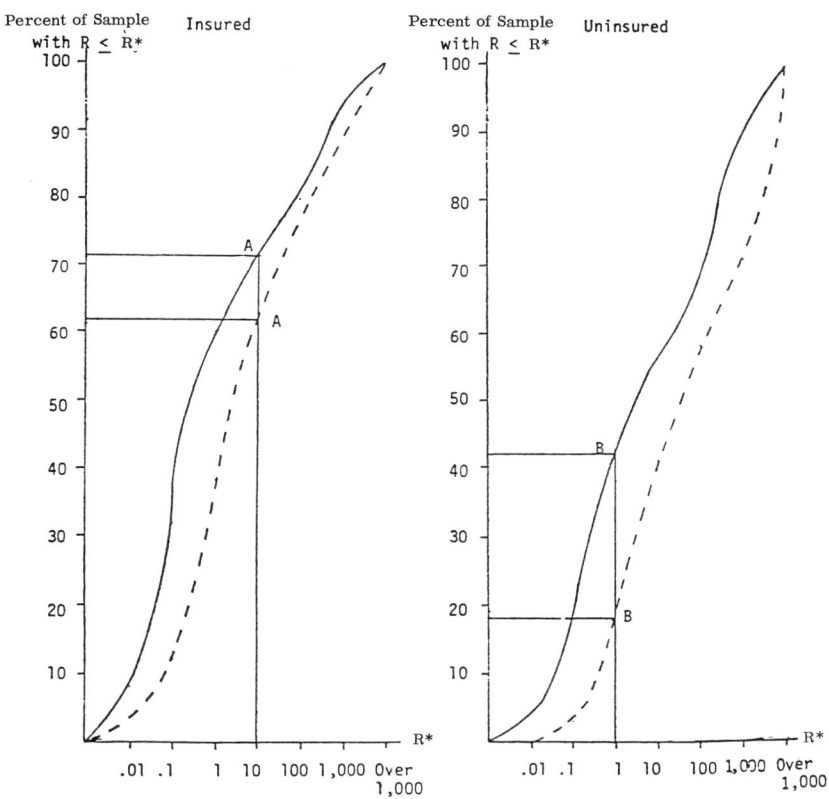

———— = Flood Survey

— — — — = Earthquake Survey

Source: Constructed by the authors.

If R exceeds this magnitude, then the cost of insurance in relation to its potential benefits is so high that it is unlikely that a person would have voluntarily protected himself/herself against flood and earthquake losses if he/she were maximizing expected utility. Almost 30 percent of insured homeowners in the flood sample and almost 40 percent of the insured homeowners in the earthquake sample fall into this category. In fact, there were a number of insured individuals who estimated such a low probability of a future severe disaster that their value of R exceeded 100.

Point B indicates that over 40 percent of the uninsured homeowners in the flood sample and almost 20 percent in the earthquake sample had estimates of R below 1 and, hence, should have purchased insurance if they were trying to maximize expected utility. A large number of uninsured homeowners in the flood sample had values of R less than .1, a ratio implying that their annual expected loss was approximately ten times the premium.

Factors Influencing Insurance Purchase

Given these findings about the level of information and likely calculations made by homeowners, we now turn to additional factors that might influence their actions. Our conclusions are based partly on the survey discussed above and partly on a series of experiments, carried out by Slovic and his associates at Decision Research (Slovic et al. 1977), designed to complement the survey and probe causal relationships more deeply than in a cross-sectional analysis.

To account for the behavior of the respondents in both the field survey and the experiments, three sets of factors are pertinent: (1) factors that led individuals to consider or ignore the risky event and its consequences in the first place, (2) factors related to the alternative protective mechanisms considered and the way these are characterized, and (3) factors related to the way alternatives are evaluated and compared.

They may be thought of as shaping three stages of a decision process, in which the concepts of information and attention play central roles. In our discussion, we focus on the heuristic rules that individuals seem to follow at each stage of the process.

Attending to the Hazard and Its Consequences

In the survey, one of the most important determinants of insurance purchase—by itself accounting for about a 25 percent difference in purchase probability—was whether the respondent considered floods or earthquakes a "serious problem." The low subscription rates for both types of coverage suggests that most people pay little attention to these hazards. The meaning of seriousness in our question was deliberately left unspecified, so that we could explore how respondents themselves interpreted it.* Based on their own evaluations, we then tried to determine what factors were related to their level of concern. Two possibilities and their combination were anticipated: focus on the consequences of the disaster and/or focus on the probability of its occurrence.

The ordinary least squares regression analysis presented in Table 20.1 indicates that although the effects of probability and estimated future damage per se are statistically significant, their impact on seriousness is relatively small.† Those homeowners who estimated the probability and damage from a future flood or earthquake as relatively high were somewhat more likely to treat the problem as being serious than those who felt the chances and losses from such a disaster were very small, but even with large differences in these factors, the likelihood of thinking the disaster a serious problem changes but little.

By contrast, other variables, such as location of home in relation to hazard, disaster experience, and knowledge of hazard prior to moving into the area, which might themselves be determinants of probability and damage estimates, were important. For example, homeowners who had suffered losses from past disasters were also more likely to view the hazard as a serious problem than uninitiated residents. Past experience may affect an individual's judgment of the consequences by making the losses vivid in the respondent's mind or by affecting the probability judgment of individuals who estimated likelihood by the availability or imaginability of examples (Tversky and Kahneman [1974]; Slovic, Kunreuther, and White [1974]; Kahneman and Tversky [1979]).

---

*Respondents were classified as perceiving the hazard to be serious, minor, or important, using a composite scale based on their responses to two survey questions. In the first question, they were asked whether they considered their immediate neighborhood to be an area where floods (earthquakes) could occur. The second question asked them to rank flood (earthquake) as a problem in their neighborhood in relation to four other ones (crime, education, housing, and public transportation).

†These ordinary least squares regressions yield essentially the same results in terms of t-test and the estimates of the dependent variable as logit regressions. For detailed comparisons, see Kunreuther et al. (1978, chap. 6, pp. 124-64).

TABLE 20.1

Determinants of Awareness of Problem

Name of Variable	Ordinary Least Squares	
	Coefficient	T-Ratio
Hazard is a serious problem	Dependent variable	
Constant term*	.240	
Knew area hazard prone when moved in:		
Yes	.280	10.4
Disaster experience:		
One disaster	.184	6.4
More than one disaster	.367	10.0
Log (probability)	.037/unit	7.0
Future damage:		
Cannot estimate	-.027	0.24
No damage	-.072	-2.5
Some damage	.0011/$1,000	2.8
Years lived in house and type of hazard:		
Coastal zone A	.263 - .0034/year	7.9
Coastal zone B	.038 + .0012/year	0.89
Riverine zone A	.292 + .0017/year	6.4
Riverine zone B	.093 + .0017/year	1.8
Earthquake	.000 - .0041/year	2.5
R^2 = .231		

*Estimated probability of homeowner thinking hazard is a serious problem who: (1) did not know area was hazard prone when moved in or has lived there whole life, (2) has never experienced a disaster, and (3) expects $1 future damage.

Source: Compiled by the authors.

Other analyses indicate that when probability is controlled, the effects of estimated future damage on seriousness may lose even statistical significance, although collinearity renders the survey results inconclusive on this point.

The results of the experiments are, however, much clearer. Subjects were presented with a series of gambles, each of which involved the possibility of losing a given amount with a specified probability. Losses and probabilities were varied, so that all gambles had the same expected loss. In one experiment, subjects were permitted to buy insurance against the loss at an actuarially fair rate. Parallel experiments varied the premiums so that insurance was offered at subsidized rates and commercial rates (that is, premiums lower and higher than expected loss).

Risk-averse subjects should find the subsidized or fair insurance attractive regardless of the particular probabilities and potential losses involved. Moreover, as Slovic et al. (1977) note, if transaction costs or computational limitations are introduced to account for nonpurchase of insurance, subjects should most likely insure against low-probability high-loss outcomes, since these involve the largest difference between the disutility of the premium and the expected disutility of the event. On the contrary, however, subjects showed a strong tendency to buy insurance only for high-probability low-loss events, regardless of the premium to expected loss ratio, and rejected insurance in situations where the probability of loss was low and the potential losses high.

Subject behavior can be explained (Slovic et al. 1977) in terms of a probability threshold, the level of which may vary from individual to individual and situation to situation. Events with probabilities below the threshold are simply dismissed from further consideration. This heuristic—ignore low probability events—was offered by subjects themselves as a reason for their actions. For example, in the experiments, where drawing a blue ball from an urn indicated disaster, subjects reported:

> "Only in urns number 7 and 8 were the probabilities high enough to warrant buying insurance."
>
> "I thought the odds of my coming up with a blue ball had grown sufficiently by urn number 4 to start taking insurance."
>
> "In the first two, the chances of picking the blue ball are too small to worry about. The remainder caused increasing concern for me."

The experimental protocols are, unfortunately, not detailed enough to determine how the threshold is set, nor do they enable one to specify the sources of individual invariability. Further, one cannot be sure to what extent the "low-probability-event" heuristic is used in other settings and, in particular, whether it was important for our respondents in the survey. Nevertheless, as a description of subject behavior, it seems better than expected utility models.

Attending to Insurance as an Option

Aside from perceived seriousness of the problem, the dominant factor differentiating survey purchasers of insurance from nonpurchasers is knowing someone who has insurance. These two factors interact in the sense that if both are positive, the individual is all the more likely to have insurance than one would expect on the basis of each of these factors taken separately.

The survey data do not reveal whether discussions with friends or neighbors took place before or after a homeowner had purchased coverage. There are two principal reasons for believing that in most cases, this type of interchange took place prior to the purchase of coverage. For one thing, substantial empirical research on the adoption of new products suggests that most individuals learn about a particular innovation through impersonal sources, such as the mass media, but that friends or neighbors are the most frequent channel leading to the actual adoption.* For example, in a classic study by Ryan and Gross (1943) on the adoption of a new type of hybrid corn by farmers in two small Iowa communities, most farmers learned about the innovation from salesmen or the mass media, but neighbors were the most frequent channel leading to the actual adoption of the product. Similar findings are reported by Coleman, Katz, and Menzel (1966) in a study on the adoption of a new drug by doctors in four midwestern communities.

The field survey results are consistent with this pattern. Most homeowners first learned about the availability of flood or earthquake coverage from the mass media or their insurance agent. In fact, only 15 percent first became aware of such insurance by talking with friends, neighbors, or relatives. With respect to the second stage in the adoption process, the survey revealed that over half of the policyholders had discussed insurance with personal acquaintances, while less than 20 percent of the uninsured respondents had ever had such conversations.

---

*The seminal work suggesting the importance of personal influence in the adoption process is by Katz and Lazarsfeld (1955). A summary of other studies can be found in Rogers with Shoemaker (1971) and Robertson (1971).

A second reason for believing that such interchanges are likely to occur prior to the purchase decision is the anecdotal evidence obtained from group depth interviews with insured and uninsured homeowners, as well as pretests of the questionnaire with residents in hazard-prone areas. One revealing incident illustrates this point. In a pretest in San Francisco, a homeowner, who was aware that earthquake coverage was available, responded to a question on his current status by saying that he was not insured. A friend, listening to the interview, could not resist commenting that he himself had purchased such insurance a couple of years before. The respondent was dumbfounded and asked the friend about where he could get coverage and its cost, adding, "I am going to have to look into earthquake insurance myself."

We hypothesize that friends and neighbors play a subtle role in the decision process, by inducing the individual to take insurance seriously, by reinforcing a decision to buy which has already been made, and by providing a source of additional information for a person who has been primed by other means to accept it. The interaction effect with seriousness of the problem revealed by the survey data analysis suggest that friends and neighbors supply information on the hazard, as well as on insurance.

These results indicate the crucial role of information channels in conjunction with individual decision processes as determinants of institutional performance. They also point up the need for detailed study of the efficiency properties of different information sources—personal contact, mass media, salesmen and agents, and prices—in alternative organizational settings.

The Decision to Purchase Insurance

Given that individuals take the hazard seriously and are aware of the availability of insurance, their decision to actually purchase coverage depends on how it is characterized and evaluated relative to other options. At the outset, we should note that for one reason or another, individuals are very reluctant to buy insurance. To quote Bernstein (1972) again:

> Most property owners simply do not buy insurance voluntarily, regardless of the amount of equity they have at stake. It was not until banks and other lending institutions united in requiring fire insurance from their mortgagors that most people got around to purchasing it. It was also many years after its introduction that the new popular homeowners insurance caught on. At one time, too, insurers could not give away crime

insurance, and we just need look at our automobile insurance laws to recognize that unless we force that insurance down the throats of the drivers, many thousands of people would be unprotected on highways. People do not buy insurance voluntarily unless there is pressure on them from one source or another (p. 23).

One reason for this resistance may be that individuals treat insurance purchase as an "investment" from which they expect a tangible and timely return. Such a view would contrast with the treatment of insurance as a contingent claim.* The investment interpretation is compatible with the findings of the controlled experiments and provides an alternative explanation as to the use of the low-probability heuristic. Subjects would now only find insurance attractive when probabilities are sufficiently high for them to feel that a return on their investment is likely. For example, one subject in the experiments commented: "I bought insurance only if the chances of selecting a blue ball was significant."

We cannot tell from the survey or experimental data just how prevalent such reasoning is. That insurance can be viewed as an investment rather than as a meaningful protective mechanism is, however, borne out by several other studies. Schoemaker and Kunreuther (1979) found, for example, that subjects preferred insurance with low rather than high deductibles—which would make a cash return more likely—even when it was clear to them that the extra premium would far exceed expected benefits. A preference for minimum deductibles on automobile insurance was reported by Pashigian, Schkade, and Menefee (1966), and an attempt by Governor Milton Shapp of Pennsylvania to institute a mandatory deductible of $100 for collision coverage was rescinded because of consumer opposition (Cummins et al. 1974). Finally, in a recent advertisement, Aetna Insurance Company stated:

Although Aetna has been stressing the value of deductibles and co-insurance since the mid-1950's . . . we are still writing insurance plans that have no deductibles for hospital charges. The pressure to "give

---

*For illustrations of the application of a contingent claims model to insurance decisions, see Kihlstrom and Pauly (1971), Ehrlich and Becker (1972), Arrow (1973), Zeckhauser (1973), and Marshall (1974).

the customer what he wants" is a constant in business. Aetna, like most insurers, has given in to it too many times when it may not have been in society's long-term interest.

IMPLICATIONS FOR POLICY

The results of the field survey and laboratory experiments strongly suggest that whatever the merits of the adverse selection argument as an explanation of supply side problems in disaster insurance markets, there are serious problems on the demand side as well. These have to do with the information people have about insurance and the risks facing them, the way they process that information, and the way they decide what action to take. Many individuals do not use insurance as a means of transferring risk from themselves to others because they have either not paid attention to the hazard itself or have not collected information on the terms of insurance coverage. Those who have such data frequently do not consider buying coverage because they view insurance as a poor investment rather than as a meaningful protective activity.

It is tempting to dismiss these phenomena by asserting that individuals are economizing on bounded rationality and search time. However, the data suggest that the way they "economize" when faced with low-probability catastropic events seems to be systematic rather than random and that these systematic biases do not wash out in the aggregate as far as institutional performance is concerned. Accordingly, the policy maker must not only cope with adverse selection problems as perceived by the supplier but, also, must focus on the information imperfections on the demand side of the transaction. Without this more complete treatment, it is unlikely that programs will work as well as anticipated.

The National Flood Insurance Program, for example, was designed to overcome the failure of privately marketed flood coverage, which had been attributed to problems associated with adverse selection. It was designed to shift the risks of the flood hazard gradually from the public to the private sector, by having communities voluntarily purchase coverage, and regulating new developments in flood-prone areas through building codes, land use restrictions, and rates reflecting risk.* As we noted, the program did not work

---

*See Kunreuther (1973), Anderson (1974), Brown and Lind (1976), and Platt (1976) for a detailed evaluation of the National Flood Insurance Program as it relates to flood plain management.

out as expected. Despite highly subsidized rates, the lack of interest in insurance was undoubtedly an important reason why few communities felt any pressure to join the program. By doing so, officials would have been forced to enact land use regulations without perceiving any compensating benefits for residents in their areas.

The failure of the voluntary flood program led to the passage of the Flood Disaster Protection Act of 1973, which through the use of more coercive requirements has in fact substantially increased the number of policies in force. Specifically, an identified flood-prone community has the choice of participating in the program or forfeiting most federally related financing for projects that would be located in flood-prone areas, as well as most mortgage money for property. If a community becomes eligible, homes and businesses in high-hazard areas are required to purchase flood insurance as a prerequisite for receiving types of federally related financial assistance for new acquisition or construction purposes. If a homeowner eligible for flood insurance does not purchase coverage and suffers flood damage, s/he can still receive a federal disaster loan from the Small Business Administration or Farmers Home Administration. As a condition for such assistance, however, s/he will be required to purchase flood insurance.*

Designing social programs by using the wrong behavioral model would be of little concern were it not for the fact that these programs frequently generate enormous private and social costs. As a result of the failure of the National Flood Insurance Program, new construction was not discouraged in most flood-prone regions throughout the United States. Individuals made their location decisions with little concern as to the potential risks facing them. By continuing to provide liberal relief to uninsured victims, the social costs have been enormous, as illustrated by the magnitude of the SBA loan and forgiveness grants triggered by tropical storm Agnes alone. Homeowners are also subject to severe private risks from

---

*The positive impact that this legislation has had on the sales of flood insurance is best illustrated by comparing the number of policies in force and insurance claims paid in areas affected by both tropical storm Agnes in 1972 and hurricane Eloise in 1975. Although Eloise caused approximately 60 percent less damage to homes and contents than Agnes, the amount of insurance claims resulting from the 1975 hurricane was more than ten times greater than it had been after the 1972 storm. The number of policies in force in all states affected by both disasters rose from 61,000 to 258,000 in this three-year period.

a voluntary flood program should they suffer serious damage from a disaster. Vinso (1977) has shown that many uninsured victims in Wilkes-Barre, Pennsylvania, were saddled with large debts following tropical storm Agnes. They were thus financially crippled despite the generous SBA loan policy.

We mentioned in the introduction that insurance has been taken as a paradigm by Arrow (1970), Williamson (1975), Akerlof (1970), Rothschild and Stiglitz (1976), and others in analyzing a wide variety of organizational problems involving risk and uncertainty. We strongly subscribe to this view. On the basis of the evidence presented in this chapter, however, we feel that the features of insurance that have been abstracted by economic theory to explain the inadequacy of the market and other social institutions under conditions of risk are not the only ones to which policy makers should be paying attention. Rather than assuming relatively precise knowledge by consumers of probabilities and consequences of uncertain events, and hence attending exclusively to adverse selection and transaction costs, we should also be paying attention to the information-gathering processes and to computational heuristics utilized by these same consumers if we are to change their behavior and improve social outcomes.

REFERENCES

Akerlof, G. 1970. "The Market for 'Lemons': Quality Uncertainty and the Market Mechanism." Quarterly Journal of Economics 84: 488-500.

Anderson, D. C. 1974. "The National Flood Insurance Program— Problems and Potential." Journal of Risk and Insurance 41: 579-99.

Arrow, K. J. 1963. "Uncertainty and the Welfare Economics of Medical Care." American Economic Review 53: 941-73.

_____. 1973. Optimal Insurance and Generalized Deductibles. RAND Report R-1108-(E). Santa Monica, Calif.: RAND.

Bernstein, G. K. 1973. Testimony before the U.S. 92nd Congress, Senate Subcommittee on Housing and Urban Affairs on the Flood Disaster Protection Act of 1973. June 11, 1973. Washington, D.C.: Government Printing Office.

Brown, J., and Lind, R. 1976. "An Economic Impact Analysis of the National Flood Insurance Program." Mimeographed. Washington, D.C.: Federal Insurance Administration.

Coleman, J. S.; Katz, E.; and Menzel, R. 1966. Medical Innovation: A Diffusion Study. Indianapolis, Ind.: Bobbs-Merrill.

Cummins, J. D., et al. 1974. Consumer Attitudes Toward Auto and Homeowners Insurance. Philadelphia: Department of Insurance, The Wharton School, University of Pennsylvania.

Ehrlich, I., and Becker, G. S. 1972. "Market Insurance, Self-Insurance and Self-Protection." Journal of Political Economy 80 (July-August): 623-48.

Eisner, R., and Strotz, R. 1965. "Flight Insurance and the Theory of Choice." Journal of Political Economy 69: 355-68.

Insurance Executives Association. 1952. Report on Floods and Flood Damage. Cited in U.S., Congress, Senate Report no. 1313, Federal Disaster Insurance. 89th Cong., 2d sess. Washington, D.C.: Government Printing Office.

Kahneman, D., and Tversky, A. 1979. "Prospect Theory: An Analysis of Decision Under Risk." Econometrica 47: 263-91.

Katz, E., and Lazarsfeld, P. F. 1955. Personal Influence. New York: Free Press.

Kihlstrom, R., and Pauly, M. 1971. "The Role of Insurance in the Allocation of Risk." American Economic Review Proceedings 61: 371-79.

Kunreuther, H. 1973. Recovery from Natural Disasters: Insurance or Federal Aid? Washington, D.C.: American Enterprise Institute.

_____. 1976. "Limited Knowledge and Insurance Protection." Public Policy 24: 227-61.

Kunreuther, H., et al. 1978. Disaster Insurance Protection: Public Policy Lessons. New York: Wiley-Interscience.

Manes, A. 1938. Insurance: Facts and Problems. New York: Harper.

Marshall, J. 1974. "Insurance as a Market in Contingent Claims: Structure and Performance." Bell Journal of Economics and Management Science 5: 670-82.

Pashigian, B.; Schkade, L.; and Menefee, G. 1966. "The Solution of an Optimal Deductible for a Given Insurance Policy." The Journal of Business 39: 35-44.

Pauly, M. 1974. "Overinsurance and Public Provision of Insurance: The Roles of Moral Hazard and Adverse Selection." Quarterly Journal of Economics 88: 44-62.

Platt, R. 1976. "The National Flood Insurance Program: Some Midstream Perspectives." American Institute of Planners Journal 42: 303-13.

Riley, J. G. 1976. "Informational Equilibrium." RAND Discussion Paper, R2059. Santa Monica, Calif.: RAND.

Robertson, R. S. 1971. Innovative Behavior and Communication. New York: Holt, Rinehart & Winston.

Rogers, E., with Shoemaker, F. 1971. Communication of Innovation. New York: Free Press.

Rothschild, M., and Stiglitz, J. 1976. "Equilibrium in Competitive Insurance Markets: An Essay in the Economics of Imperfect Information." Quarterly Journal of Economics 90: 629-49.

Ryan, B., and Gross, N. C. 1943. "The Diffusion of Hybrid Seed Corn in Two Iowa Communities." Rural Sociology 8: 15-24.

Schoemaker, P., and Kunreuther, H. 1979. "An Experimental Study of Insurance Decisions." The Journal of Risk and Insurance 46 (December): 603-18.

Simon, H. A. 1959. "Theories in Decision-Making in Economics and Behavioral Science." American Economic Review 49: 253-83.

Slovic, P., et al. 1977. "Preference for Insuring Against Probable Small Losses: Insurance Implications." Journal of Risk and Insurance 44: 237-58.

Slovic, P.; Kunreuther, H.; and White, G. 1974. "Decision Processes, Rationality and Adjustments to Natural Hazards." In

Natural Hazards: Local, National, and Global, edited by G. F. White, pp. 187-205. New York: Oxford University Press.

Spence, M. 1977. "Product Differentiation and Consumer Choice in Insurance Markets." Harvard Institute of Economic Research Discussion Paper No. 585 (mimeographed).

Syfert, R. 1972. "The Unwilling Market for Earthquake Insurance." *Best's Review* 73: 14-18.

Tversky, A., and Kahneman, D. 1974. "Judgement Under Uncertainty: Heuristics and Biases." *Science* 185: 1124-31.

Vinso, J. D. 1977. "Financial Implications of Natural Disasters: Some Preliminary Indications." *Mass Emergencies* 2.

Williamson, O. 1975. *Markets and Hierarchies: Implications for Anti-Trust Policy*. New York: Free Press.

Wilson, C. 1977. "A Model of Insurance Markets with Incomplete Information." *Journal of Economic Theory* 16 (December): 167-207.

Zeckhauser, R. 1973. "Coverage for Catastrophic Illness." *Public Policy* (Spring): 149-72.

21
HESITATION PHENOMENA AND CONVERSATIONAL STYLE: INDICATIONS OF UNCERTAINTY IN FAMILY SITUATIONS
Fern L. Johnson
Leslie K. Davis

INTRODUCTION

Even the most fluent and eloquent speakers inevitably find themselves in situations where they stammer, unnecessarily repeat themselves, are unable to finish the sentences they begin, fill their utterances with "ahs" and "ums," or are simply stymied into silence when they are expected to speak. Psycholinguists have for some time labeled such nonfluencies <u>hesitation phenomena</u> (Maclay and Osgood 1959) and attributed their occurrence to something other than random error (Mahl 1956; Maclay and Osgood 1959; Goldman-Eisler 1968). The presence of hesitation phenomena may result from a variety of personal states—anxiety, the quest for precision in wording, uncertainty of ideas, surprise—but no matter what the cause, they presumably occur at points of high uncertainty where the speaker must engage in verbal planning and organization.

This chapter is a report of a research project on the nature and frequency of hesitation phenomena present in a series of family conversations that were broadcast over the Westinghouse television stations and public television in 1977. The analysis of hesitation phenomena is interpreted within the context of the "conversational styles" in which they occur. We posited that conversations can be generally differentiated by the global functions they serve and that these functions vary in the degree to which corresponding utterances are "programmed" and fluent rather than uncertain and nonfluent. Less linguistic uncertainty should exist, for example, in exchanges about making dinner than in the working out of visitation privileges between a separated couple who have children.

To place the research in the context of work on both hesitation phenomena and conversational style, a brief review of each precedes our research report.

HESITATION PHENOMENA

Hesitation Types

Maclay and Osgood (1959) identified four types of hesitation, and these constitute the hesitation class for the study reported here.

1. Repetitions: iterations of linguistic elements that do not contribute semantically or serve as emphasis. We divided repetitions into three classes: phonemic—for example, g-got, th-thanks; one word—for example, what-what you're saying?; and multiword—for example, I'm simply not-simply not going to.
2. False starts: incomplete or self-interrupted utterances. There are two classes of false starts: retracted, which occur when the speaker interrupts her/his utterance and begins again—for example, If you want to-well you should do what you think's best; and unretracted, which are utterance fragments—for example, I read a really—.
3. Filled pauses: aural but nonlexical elements that can be phonetically represented and which serve to fill gaps between verbal elements, to interrupt silences within utterances, or to commence an utterance—for example, I ah don't like this; Would you (pause) ah (pause) help me?; Um let's talk to her.
4. Unfilled pauses: periods of silence within utterances—for example, If you want my opinion (two-second pause), I think we should go ahead.

Hesitation Placement

Prior research on hesitation placement is difficult to distill, primarily because varying methods have been used, and several controversies exist in the literature. There are, however, some major points to be made, particularly with reference to the functions of hesitation in speech. Two general comments are necessary at the outset. First, with the exception of a few studies (Maclay and Osgood 1959; Ragsdale 1976), data have not been derived from spontaneous, naturally occurring conversations. Utterance samples are usually taken from interviews about predetermined topics or in response to some stimulus material presented to the subjects (cartoons, TAT cards, and so forth). Second, many studies may have limited generalizability because the majority of research focuses on pausal properties rather than the full array of hesitation phenomena (Mahl and Schulze 1964). With these reservations in mind, several lines of investigation can be differentiated.

At the global level, the presence of hesitation phenomena is said to be related to subsequent information (or points of low redundancy and low predictability). Goldman-Eisler's work (1958a; 1958b; 1958c; 1961) is well-known on this topic. She has concluded (1958b) that pauses anticipate both sudden increases of information and uncertainty about message content. More specifically, her early work (1958a, 1958c) indicated that pauses are associated with low predictability of words, while fluency corresponds with high predictability of words. Silences within the stream of discourse occur, according to Goldman-Eisler (1961), when the speaker is engaged in cognitive activity; the length of pausing is directly related to difficulty of the cognitive task. Tannenbaum, Williams, and Hillier (1965) extended all of this work by demonstrating that words before and after filled and unfilled pauses, repetitions, and false starts are less predictable than in other contexts.

Goldman-Eisler and her associates (Goldman-Eisler 1958a; Henderson, Goldman-Eisler, and Skarbek 1966) have also shown that the placement of unfilled pauses in spontaneous speech is not simply governed by natural grammatical junctures. When they compared pausal placement in the reading of texts contrasted with spontaneous speech, the results were striking: most pauses in reading fall at grammatical junctures, while only about half in spontaneous speech fall at grammatical junctures. Pausing at grammatical junctures reflects the natural rhythm of language, but ungrammatical pausing is under the control of the process of cognition and its formative energy.

The relationship between cognitive demands and hesitation is considered more specifically by several other researchers. Lay and Paivio (1969) manipulated the level of abstraction required in speech by having their subjects give self-descriptions, descriptions of a cartoon, and evaluation of pairs of proverbs. They found filled and unfilled pauses increased in frequency with increases in the presumed level of abstractness in content. In Siegman and Pope's (1966) work, TAT cards, ranging from low to high ambiguity, were presented to subjects, who were asked to discuss their content. The ratio of filled pauses to number of words spoken was found to increase as the TAT cards became more ambiguous. Finally, Levin, Silverman, and Ford (1967) found that the length and frequency of unfilled pauses are greater in children's explanations of a physical demonstration than in their descriptions of the same demonstration.

What has come to be a somewhat common approach to the issue of hesitation and information was ushered in by Maclay and Osgood (1959), who distinguished between hesitations occurring before lexical words (nouns, verbs, adjectives, adverbs) and those occurring before <u>function</u> words (articles, prepositions, connectives, auxiliaries, and so forth). Their analysis of presentations at a professional conference revealed a tendency for filled and unfilled pauses to occur before lexical words, false starts to occur with lexical words, and repetitions to be of function words but to precede lexical words. Neither Cook's (1971) analysis of undergraduates' discussions of college life nor Kowal, O'Connell, and Sabin's (1975) work with youngsters supports these findings. Yet, the role of hesitation in preparing for lexical, that is, content, words is simply not clear because both methods and sample characteristics varied considerably in the three studies.

Another line of research on the function of pauses makes use of temporal analysis. In the 1960s, Goldman-Eisler and her associates conducted several studies which advance that spontaneous speech contains alternating periods of hesitancy and fluency (Goldman-Eisler 1967; Henderson, Goldman-Eisler, and Skarbek 1966). Hesitancy periods allow the speaker time to plan for the productive, fluency periods. Jaffe, Breskin, and Gerstman (1972) challenged the findings, but Butterworth (1975) has since supported the original work.

The last body of research on hesitation phenomena relevant to our study focuses on the ways in which speaker-anxiety and stress relate to hesitations. Mahl's (1956) work with the speech of subjects engaged in clinical interviews and stressful role-playing situations established that the degree of client-anxiety positively correlates with such dysfluencies as repetitions and false starts, but negatively correlates with filled pauses. Ragsdale (1976) found the same pattern of hesitation for students in a group discussion, who scored as highly anxious on a standardized measure.

In other research, anxiety has been correlated with both the frequency and duration of unfilled pauses (Siegman and Pope 1965; Cassotta, Feldstein, and Jaffe 1967). Filled pauses are much less likely to differentiate the speech of high-anxious and low-anxious speakers (Kasl and Mahl 1965; Siegman and Pope 1965), but Rochester (1973) concludes that the relationship between filled pauses and anxiety is not conclusive because of methodological issues in the research.

In sum, there is a well-developed body of research to support a strong positive relationship of certain measures of hesitation with high informational content, abstractness, and difficulty of the speaker's task, as well as the anxiety and stress level experienced by the speaker. Hesitation phenomena seem, then, to be quite normal features in the speech of individuals placed in situations with certain cognitive and emotion-laden attributes.

CONVERSATIONAL STYLE

There is no well-developed literature on the nature and features of conversational style. Style, per se, has long been an interest of rhetoricians and literary scholars, but the former tend to view style as a revelation of the individual speaker's persona (Weaver 1953), while the latter concern themselves with style as a formal feature of literary discourse (Herrnstein Smith 1978). Interest in conversational style concerns the formal properties of oral discourse produced within the context of interpersonal interactions, and the features of interest are those that normatively, rather than idiographically, define that discourse. We posit that everyday discourse is stylistically differentiated in terms of global purposes and their corresponding organizations of verbal and extraverbal means. Foundations for this approach lie in several areas of linguistic and sociolinguistic research, and our prior work with television conversations (Johnson and Davis 1979) presents our first attempt to relate conversational style to hesitation phenomena.

Joos (1961) discusses styles of English usage as a way of describing the impact of context on the nature of discourse; he sees the value of his work "in its helpful classification and accurate description of the situations in which we communicate, and in connecting each of these with certain linguistic features characteristic of the style of discourse" (p. xii). Hymes (1974) invokes the concept of style to aid our understanding of how language is actually used; linguistic features are organized in relation to "a community or other social context" (p. 59). Hymes's term, conversational genre (p. 61), further directs our attention to the formal characteristics differentiating one style from another. A third foundation for the notion of conversational style comes from work on functional stylistics conducted in the Prague and Russian schools of linguistics. Functional stylistics approaches language analysis with the assumption that verbal communication can be differentiated according to <u>functions</u> and <u>forms</u> of expression (Dolezel 1968). Kozina (1976) argues that a functional style implies both a sphere of communication and a form of social consciousness that work together to create specific norms for speech selection and organization.

In all treatments of conversational style, underlying and global purposes of conversation are assumed to be the contextualizing device accounting for variability in formal features. Topic, itself, is not a definiens of conversational style because the same topic may be developed differently, depending on underlying purpose.

Our conceptualization of conversational style was heavily influenced by the work of Tallman (1979). Over the past five years, she has analyzed a considerable amount of conversational data and has culled descriptions of four conversational styles, naming them after Hall's (1966) categories of interpersonal space—public, social, personal, and intimate. The organizing principle behind her typology (and Hall's) is the degree of interpersonal distance circumscribing the interaction.

Departing somewhat from Tallman's work, we conceptualized conversational style into four types that correspond to four different global purposes of oral interaction. <u>Casual style</u> occurs when the global purpose is to manage the exchange of routine and matter-of-fact reports and information. <u>Personal style</u> occurs when persons and their activities are defined through the offering of information and opinion; it functions by providing considerable background information and individualized opinion. <u>Intimate style</u> occurs when conversations develop private meanings for self and relationships, where self is central; it exists especially in situations of affection, self-disclosure, crisis, and interpersonal conflict. <u>Ritualistic style</u> occurs in those instances where the interaction is essentially "scripted" in advance and the script rigidly enforced (for example, meal ceremonies, chanting, song response). Any conversation may be unitary in style or may show change in focus and purpose, thus including multiple styles.

HYPOTHESES

Two hypotheses were tested regarding the nature of hesitation phenomena in stylistically differentiated conversations.

First, because prior work suggests that cognitive demand and level of emotional intensity precipitate hesitations, different global purposes of conversation should also reflect varying hesitation levels. As people move from mundane and routine purposes to the disclosure of private meanings and the confrontation of conflict, their speech should reflect more uncertainty: thus, hypothesis 1—the incidence of hesitation phenomena in familial conversations increases from casual to personal to intimate style.

Second, because pauses in spontaneous speech are less often markers of grammatical juncture than pauses in reading, we expect that the incidence of ungrammatical pausing should increase as the style of conversation becomes more demanding of personal statements: thus, hypothesis 2—the ungrammatical placement of all pausal hesitations increases from casual to personal to intimate style of conversation.

METHODS

Sample

The television documentary series, "Six American Families," constituted the sample for this study. The series was broadcast by Westinghouse and Public Broadcasting Service in the spring of 1977 as six separate one-hour programs. Each program featured a different family; the families had been chosen to represent a range of life-styles, geographic locales, socioeconomic classes, and ethnic heritages. The documentary series was done in verité style, which means that the intent was to record family situations as they occur—in this case, to present family members in naturalistic interaction with one another.

Our intent was to include each episode in the analysis, but one episode featuring an Appalachian family contained many portions that were difficult to understand (subtitles were even used in some instances). Thus, the final sample consisted of five of the six episodes and included approximately 280 minutes of narration and interactional footage.

Each episode was divided into segments of family conversation. To be included as a unit of analysis, the segment had to feature only family members related by birth or through marriage. A conversational segment was defined as all discourse from the first verbal or phonetically transcribable element to the last in a situation with a fixed and stable grouping of family members. A new segment occurred when (1) a family member(s) entered or left the conversational environment, (2) a non-family member(s) entered the conversational environment, (3) narration occurred, or (4) a new grouping of family members appeared. This procedure yielded a total of 120 segments for the five episodes.

Four trained transcribers compiled verbatim transcripts of the conversational segments. Transcription conventions developed by Sachs, Schegloff, and Jefferson (1974) were used. Transcriptions were organized by conversational turn and included verbal elements, filled pauses, unfilled pauses, and symbols for false starts and repetitions. Three types of temporal information were also included: total time for segment, time taken for each turn, and duration of all unfilled pauses exceeding .5 seconds.

Procedures

Hesitation Coding

The first author coded each conversational segment for incidence of false starts (both retracted and unretracted), repetitions (phonemic, one word, and multiword), filled pauses, and unfilled pauses. Both the total number of each type of hesitation phenomenon and the mean number per conversational turn were noted. For unfilled pauses, mean length was calculated.

All filled and unfilled pauses were characterized by defining the point of their occurrence as <u>grammatical</u> or <u>ungrammatical</u>. Rules for classification follow the work of Goldman-Eisler and Henderson (Goldman-Eisler 1968, p. 13).

Grammatical junctures are as follows:

1. "Natural" punctuation points, for example, the end of a sentence, following a form of address, following low information, and initial verbal elements, such as "well" and "so"; for filled pauses, the first element of the utterance
2. Immediately preceding or following either a coordinating or subordinating conjunction
3. Before relative and interrogative pronouns
4. Following a question that is indirect or implied
5. Before all adverbial clauses of time, manner, or place
6. Before and after complete parenthetical expressions

Ungrammatical junctures are as follows:

1. In the middle or at the end of a phrase
2. Between repeated phonemes, words, or phrases
3. Following a false start that disrupts the utterance
4. In the middle of a verbal compound

The video record of each conversational segment was assessed for the incidence of conversational style (singular or multistyle): casual, personal, intimate, or ritual. Subsequent to determining an intercoder reliability of .97 (Scott's Pi: Scott 1955), both investigators worked together to code the segments for style features.

RESULTS

Assessing the relationship between hesitation phenomena and conversational style first demanded a determination of the stylistic composition of the sample. Of the 120 conversational segments, 100 were single style (64 casual, 16 personal, 14 intimate, and six ritual). Because the ritualistic segments did not truly constitute conversations (they consisted of such things as chants, meal prayers, and riddles), they were dropped from the analysis. The remaining single-style segments (n = 94) were isolated for analysis, and they totaled approximately 50 minutes of family interaction.

Two different sets of analyses were performed. First, hesitation measures for the three stylistic categories were compared through use of a one-way analysis of variance. Second, to allow more general comparisons of the hesitation characteristics of casual style with those of personal and intimate styles combined, t-tests were employed. Such analysis is useful in differentiating the routine in family conversation from more personalized purposes, in which a greater degree of uncertainty should occur.

Hesitation Phenomena and Single-style Conversations

Each measure of hesitation was compared for the three style categories. In cases where significant differences occurred, the Student-Newman-Keuls a posteriori procedure (alpha < .05) was used. Means for each measure according to style of conversation are shown in Table 21.1.

False Starts

Three of the four measures of false starts proved to differentiate styles of conversation. The number of retracted false starts per segment differed $F(2, 91) = 14.984$, $p < .0000$, and the posttest indicated that the differences between each style were significant in the direction predicted by hypothesis 1. Unretracted false starts differed both by segment and conversational turn, $F(2, 91) = 12.896$, $p < .0000$, and $F(2, 91) = 6.940$, $p < .002$. Here, the differences in conversational segments were as predicted, but the posttest revealed that the number of unretracted false starts per turn was different when both casual and personal and casual and intimate styles were compared, but that personal and intimate styles did not differ on this measure.

Typical of the use of false starts are the following examples taken from a conversation about the employment prospects of the theatrical-minded son of a Chicago sanitation worker and his wife.

    Mother: You gotta make a living Gary.
    Son: Yeah but you can't expect a person to suc-suc to totally succeed at something overnight. . .
    Father: You-you don't mind the risk I can tell that.
    Son: No I was gonna ah it's what I-I
    Father: I wanted him to be ah I thought he should be a garbage truck driver he'd be a good lookin driver truck driver.

TABLE 21.1

Means for Hesitation Frequency, by Style of Conversation

Hesitation Measure	Style		
	Casual	Personal	Intimate
Retracted false starts/segment[a]	.375	1.125	2.214
Retracted false starts/turn	.055	.074	.132
Unretracted false starts/segment[a]	.281	.938	1.643
Unretracted false starts/turn[b]	.025	.065	.091
Repetitions/segment[a]	.547	1.312	2.571
Repetitions/turn	.086	.092	.134
Percent phoneme repetitions	2.500	5.000	8.929
Percent one-word repetitions[c]	14.141	25.000	42.500
Percent multiword repetitions[d]	10.547	12.857	28.750
Filled pauses/segment[b]	.531	.625	2.429
Filled pauses/turn	.026	.074	.101
Unfilled pauses/segment[c]	2.750	4.875	6.500
Unfilled pauses/turn	.464	.464	.642

[a] $p < .0000$.
[b] $p < .002$.
[c] $p < .03$.
[d] $p < .08$.
Source: Compiled by the authors.

Repetitions

The number of repetitions per segment of conversation differed significantly according to style of conversation, $F(2, 91) = p < .0000$. The pattern actually discovered by the posttest established that although the frequency of repetitions increases with style as predicted, the significant differences are between intimate style and both casual and personal styles; the difference in repetitions between casual and intimate styles was not significant.

The most common repetitions were of single words: for all segments in the sample (regardless of whether they included repetitions or not), one-word repetitions constituted 14 percent of all repetitions in casual style, 25 percent in personal style, and 42 percent in intimate style. Use of these one-word repetitions varied significantly by style, $F(2, 91) = 4.0285$, $p < .03$. The difference was accounted for by a significantly greater portion of these repetitions in intimate as compared with casual style. There was also a trend for style to affect the proportion of multiword repetitions, F (2, 91) = 2.667, $p < .08$; the pattern here appeared to be one where casual and personal styles both differed from intimate style but not from each other.

An example from a conversation between husband and wife about the wife's pursuit of a college degree "now that the children are older" illustrates both the way the repetitions occur and how they function.

> Husband: Joan <u>do you-do you</u> ever do the same thing I was telling Nancy [their daughter] <u>do you-ah-do you</u> think you would've gone to college for example if you wouldn't had known me. . . .
> Wife: <u>I'm not-I'm not</u> in that position <u>I-I</u> don't know what I would have done then I mean <u>I was sure-I was sure</u> to marry you so I just went on to work to save money

In each case, the repetition seems to function as a transition vehicle to the point made subsequent to it.

Filled Pauses

The use of utterance fillers such as <u>ah</u>, <u>um</u>, and <u>eh</u> in conversational segments differed when the three styles were compared, F (2,91) = 7.181, $p < .002$. The contrasts of significance were between filled pauses in casual and intimate segments and between filled pauses in personal and intimate segments. Clearly, it was intimate style that evoked this type of hesitation phenomenon.

Two examples from intimate style conversations are provided here to show how filled pauses are used. The first is from a separated couple who were struggling over the husband's visitation of the children.

> Wife: Okay how come <u>ah</u> normally when you spend just Saturday with them you usually don't spend Sunday how come you're <u>um</u> involved with Sunday tomorrow
> Husband: I'm not involved I <u>ah</u> thought that maybe if all of us you know if you are going to go <u>ah</u> <u>ah</u> bike riding that <u>ah</u> we'd <u>ah</u> do it together cause I talked <u>ah</u> to them about doing bike riding before you. . .

The second illustration comes from a family discussion revolving around the topic of which attributes of the children each parent was responsible for; the conversation is in the context of considerable parental dissatisfaction with a son's professional choices.

> Father: Gerard as far as music if he likes it I tell ya I-I think I-I always enjoy music I think I <u>eh</u> I got music inside of me and <u>ah</u> he if he did get it he probably got that <u>ah</u> from me <u>ah</u> Gary like I say <u>um</u> far as being for artish <u>ah</u> acting it's not from my side anyhow

Unfilled Pauses

The frequency of unfilled pauses per conversational segment differed on the basis of style, $\underline{F}$ (2, 91) = 4.891, $\underline{p}$< .01. The post-test revealed significantly more unfilled pauses in intimate than in casual style. These pauses did not significantly differ between casual and personal or personal and intimate styles.

The following example of intimate style demonstrates typical points at which unfilled pauses occur. Here, a black couple is discussing their life together "before the kids were born."

> Husband: I-I'd like to see this again (<u>2.6 seconds</u>) I think th-that was some of the best times in our lives because of the fact that it was just us
> Wife: Was just the two of us (<u>1.2 seconds</u>) and then we had the two of us to worry about
> Husband: unhum (<u>1.6 seconds</u>) I'd like to see that again

For those segments exhibiting unfilled pauses, mean length of pausal duration was noted. There was no pattern of significant differences when these means were related to conversational style, but it was generally the case that short pauses (.5 to 1.9 seconds) were almost typical for all segments, while there was a greater proportion of longer pauses (2.0 to 2.9 seconds) in intimate as opposed to casual and personal styles. The only instances of pauses lasting five seconds or more were in intimate style, and even there, they were rare.

Placement of Pausal Hesitations

The second hypothesis, which predicted that ungrammatical placement of pausal hesitations—both filled and unfilled—would increase from casual to personal to intimate style was not supported.

Hesitation Phenomena in Casual versus Personal and Intimate Styles

Because the comparisons for this set of analyses involved two levels of style (casual versus personal and intimate), conversational segments containing both personal and intimate styles (multistylistic) could be included: there were eight such segments in the sample. Comparisons were thus based on 64 casual segments and 38 personal, intimate, and personal/intimate segments.

All t-tests reported indicate one-tail probabilities. Each t-value is specified as either pooled variance or separate variance estimate, depending on whether the group variances were unequal or equal ($p < .05$). Table 21.2 displays the means for each hesitation measure in the two style categories.

TABLE 21.2

Means for Hesitation Frequency: Casual versus Personal and Intimate Styles

Hesitation Measure	Style	
	Casual	Personal and Intimate
Retracted false starts/segment[a]	.3750	2.2105
Retracted false starts/turn[b]	.0547	.1232
Unretracted false starts/segment[a]	.2813	1.4474
Unretracted false starts/turn[a]	.0252	.0808
Repetitions/segment[a]	.5469	2.4737
Repetitions/turn	.0922	.1316
Percent phoneme repetitions	5.0000	8.7632
Percent one-word repetitions[c]	14.1406	37.2895
Percent multiword repetitions[b]	10.5469	22.3421
Filled pauses/segment[d]	.5313	2.1579
Filled pauses/turn	.0741	.0955
Unfilled pauses/segment[c]	2.7500	8.1053
Unfilled pauses/turn	.4639	.5805

[a] $p < .0000$.
[b] $p < .05$.
[c] $p < .01$.
[d] $p < .001$.
Source: Compiled by the authors.

False Starts

All four measures of false starts significantly differed when the two style groups were compared. Personal and intimate style conversations have more retracted false starts per segment and per turn than conversations in casual style, t (100) = 4.52, $p < .000$ (separate variance), and t (100) = 2.29, $p < .02$ (separate variance). Unretracted false starts were also more abundant in both segments and turns conducted in personal and intimate styles compared with casual style, t (100) = 5.42, $p < .000$ (pooled variance), and t (100) = 3.97, $p < .000$ (pooled variance). Both types of false start seem to provide planning or to indicate some reason for disrupting the stream of speech in those conversations that depart from the routine and banal matters of everyday life.

Repetitions

Segments of personal- and intimate-style conversation demonstrated significantly more repetitions than those of casual-style conversation, t (100) = 4.27, $p < .000$ (separate variance). The percentage of phoneme repetitions is roughly similar in the two style categories, but conversations in personal and intimate styles evidence both more one-word repetitions, t (100) = 3.10, $p < .002$ (separate variance), and more multiword repetitions, t (100) = 1.95, $p < .03$ (separate variance), than conversations in casual style.

Filled Pauses

Filled pauses significantly differentiated causal from personal and intimate styles, t (100) = 3.30, $p < .0005$ (pooled variance). Segments in casual style contained less than half the number of filled pauses than those in personal and intimate styles.

Unfilled Pauses

Gaps of silence within utterances differed in the two categories of style, t (100) = 3.16, $p < .002$ (separate variance). Segments in personal and intimate styles had about four times as many unfilled pauses as segments in casual style. For all segments (including those without unfilled pauses), there were differences in the proportion of pauses of various durations. Pauses of 1.0 to 1.9 seconds accounted for a greater proportion of all pauses in personal and intimate conversations (42 percent) as compared with casual conversations (26 percent), t (100) = 2.44, $p < .01$ (separate variance). A greater proportion of pauses of 3.0 to 4.9 seconds also characterized personal and intimate conversations (7 percent) when compared with casual conversations (2 percent), t (100) = 1.67, $p < .05$

(separate variance). Thus, not only are unfilled pauses more frequent in segments of personal and intimate conversations, but these pauses also tend to be longer.

Placement of Pausal Hesitations

Grouping conversations in personal and intimate styles was useful in that it revealed an important difference between these styles and casual style. While we would expect pauses to be placed in ungrammatical junctures in many spontaneous utterances, the placement of pauses—both filled and unfilled—was more often ungrammatical in personal and intimate styles as compared with casual style, t (100) = 2.36, $p < .01$ (separate variance). The pauses in personal and intimate styles occurred at ungrammatical junctures 39 percent of the time as compared with casual style, where 19 percent of the pauses were at ungrammatical points.

An interesting and related finding occurred when the durations of both grammatical and ungrammatical unfilled pauses were compared for the two different style categories. While duration of grammatical pauses did not significantly vary according to style, the duration of ungrammatical pauses did: t (100) = 1.66, $p < .05$ (pooled variance). The mean length of ungrammatical pauses in personal and intimate styles was 1.4 seconds, while the mean length of ungrammatical pauses in casual style was .8 seconds.

DISCUSSION

Summary

The predicted relationship between frequency of hesitation phenomena and style of conversation was supported in some instances and not supported in others. Frequency of false starts conformed most closely to hypothesis 1. For other hesitation phenomena, the results were variable: (1) intimate-style conversations surpassed personal-style conversations in the incidence of repetitions and filled pauses; (2) intimate-style conversations surpassed casual-style conversations in the incidence of repetitions, percentage of one-word repetitions, and filled and unfilled pauses; (3) apart from the findings on false starts, there were no significant differences in frequency of hesitations for casual and personal styles of conversation.

When personal and intimate styles were combined and contrasted with casual style, the results were more striking: conversations in personal and intimate styles emerged as more dysfluent than those in casual style for measures of false starts, repetitions, percentage of one-word and multiword repetitions, filled and unfilled pauses, and the percentage of longer unfilled pauses.

Although hypothesis 2 was not supported when the three styles were compared, it was supported in the contrast of casual style with personal and intimate styles. The latter included a greater proportion of pauses at ungrammatical junctures than the former.

The Relationship of Style of Conversation
to Hesitation Phenomena

Some comments on the particular nature of family conversations in each style category are helpful in understanding the results of this study. Even though conversational topics, in and of themselves, are not stylistic markers, they do suggest stylistic differences. Conversations in casual style typically revolve around such matters as daily plans, clothing, paying bills, the weather, scheduling use of the bathroom or family car, and coordinating household chores. Examples of conversations in personal style range from career plans to personal characteristics of family members and friends to health issues to reminiscences about the past. Conversations in intimate style reflect more vulnerability, personal risk, self-disclosure, and conflict. The sample featured family members engaging in very interior explorations about their feelings for one another (both positive and negative), personality flaws, self-esteem, generational conflicts, hopes and fears about the future, competition, and racism.

One way of interpreting the results on hesitation frequency in the three styles of conversation draws on prior documentation that hesitancy is associated with cognitive planning, subsequent information, anxiety, and stress. When casual and intimate styles are compared, each type of hesitation emerges as more frequent in intimate style. This result is not surprising because intimate matters do involve a great deal of uncertainty—either in expressing ideas appropriately, that is, choosing the right words, or in responding to situations for which there are no matter-of-fact comments to be made. For example, one conversation in the sample featured a father and teen-age daughter involved in a very serious discussion about the daughter's sense that she was always competing with, and being compared with, her father. Quite understandably, the segment had many unfilled pauses, filled pauses, and false starts: the topic was emotional, self-disclosing, and probably novel.

Conversations in personal style, however, represent an intermediary point in hesitation frequency: they are more like casual style in incidence of repetitions and filled pauses, more like intimate style in incidence of false starts, and not significantly different from either casual or intimate style in incidence of unfilled pauses. This variation may reflect a tendency for personal style to combine both routine elements (things that "have been said before") and unpredictable conversational sequences. One illustration of this tendency occurred while a family was viewing slides of "dad's younger days." The segment begins with dad recounting some stories about how his father played around with him; this period is relatively fluent. Then dad shifts to what seems to be the moral of the story, that is, that his father taught him survival skills; in 15 seconds of speaking, dad produces three false starts, two repetitions, and three unfilled pauses.

Exactly why the level of hesitancy in personal style varies by type of hesitation phenomenon is not clear. For example, to the degree that conversations in personal style involve abstraction and ambiguity, the relatively low frequency of filled pauses would seem to contradict the work of Lay and Paivio (1969) and Siegman and Pope (1966). To the degree that conversations in personal style involve anxiety or stress, the data on filled pauses would seem to support prior work (Mahl 1956; Ragsdale 1976). These speculations are complicated by the fact that conversations in intimate style do exhibit more filled pauses than other conversational segments in the sample; that fact supports the research on filled pauses and level of abstraction/ambiguity, but does not support the research on filled pauses and level of anxiety/stress. It is most likely that hesitation phenomena—of any type—accompany personal style (and intimate style as well) when and if speakers experience content demands requiring cognitive planning or anxiety or uncertainty about the topics being discussed.

When personal and intimate styles are compared with casual style, a different profile of hesitation phenomena appears. Results here reflect a very general distinction between conversations functioning at the personal level and those functioning to manage the exchange of matter-of-fact information. More personalized conversations not only contain more instances of hesitancy, but they also exhibit longer repetitions and longer unfilled pauses. Repeating more elements, especially multiword elements, and pausing for a longer time allow speakers a greater opportunity to conceptualize and edit their utterances.

The placement of pauses proved helpful in contrasting casual with personal and intimate styles, but did not significantly differentiate each of the three styles from one another. The proportion of pauses at ungrammatical junctures for the entire sample was lower than for the speakers assessed by Goldman-Eisler and associates

(Goldman-Eisler 1958a; Henderson, Goldman-Eisler, and Skarbek 1966), but unlike earlier research, filled as well as unfilled pauses were included in the analysis. The easiest explanation for this difference is that filled pauses are not highly associated with anxiety and stress (Mahl 1956; Ragsdale 1976), but that explanation is not acceptable given the overall results on filled pauses and styles of conversation and past work documenting the tendency for filled pauses to increase with level of abstraction and ambiguity of the speaking task (Lay and Paivio 1969; Siegman and Pope 1966). We did classify filled pauses at the beginning of an utterance as <u>grammatical</u>, and this procedure may have inflated the grammatical category, thus reducing the proportion of pauses at ungrammatical points. In future research, a better estimate of pausal placement can be gained by separating filled and unfilled pauses and by treating initial filled pauses both in conjunction with and separate from other grammatical pauses.

Despite the lower-than-expected proportion of ungrammatical pauses, conversations in personal and intimate styles (combined) showed a greater proportion of ungrammatical pauses than conversations in casual style. The tendency for grammatical organization to govern pausing appears to diminish as conversational purposes change from routine to personalized.

Characteristics of the Sample

The sample of family conversations analyzed in this study is naturalistic, but several factors bring into question the degree to which that sample is representative of naturalistic conversation. A conversation is a sequence of utterances with a beginning, middle, and end. "Six American Families" was obviously edited, so that the programs consisted of both whole conversations and segments of whole conversations. The hesitation patterns might have differed somewhat had the sample included only whole conversations. The circumstances surrounding the filming may also have influenced the conversations in some way. It is impossible to estimate the degree to which family members' knowledge that they were being filmed for a television documentary affected the conversations they produced. Our impression is that most of the conversations "appeared" quite natural and candid.

We also noted a tendency for hesitancy rates to vary considerably within a number of conversational segments, that is, for several fluent turns to be followed by hesitant and longer turns, and so forth. By basing all analyses on mean frequencies of hesitation phenomena per segment and per turn, that qualitative distinction disappeared. Another option would be to inspect the most dysfluent portions of each conversational segment and to make comparisons of these across styles.

Implications

Analysis of the naturalistic conversations and conversational segments depicted in "Six American Families" offers several new insights on the nature and function of hesitation phenomena. First, it expands the small amount of extant work on hesitancy in real conversations. Second, it expands on that work by conceptualizing conversations as differentiated in global purpose. In this respect, the hesitation profiles discovered are useful for developing a conceptualization of conversational style. Finally, the data are a starting point in understanding the way in which various forms of uncertainty—cognitive and emotional—manifest themselves in the normal stream of conversational discourse.

REFERENCES

Butterworth, B. 1975. "Hesitation and Semantic Planning in Speech." Journal of Psycholinguistic Research 4: 75-87.

Cassotta, L.; Feldstein, S.; and Jaffe, J. 1967. "The Stability and Modifiability of Individual Vocal Characteristics in Stress and Nonstress Interviews." Research Bulletin no. 2. New York: William Alanson White Institute.

Cook, M. 1971. "The Incidence of Filled Pauses in Relation to Part of Speech." Language and Speech 14: 135-39.

Doležel, L. 1968. "Russian and Prague School Functional Stylistics." Style 2: 143-58.

Goldman-Eisler, F. 1958a. "The Predictability of Words in Context and the Length of Pauses in Speech." Language and Speech 1: 226-31.

_____. 1958b. "Speech Analysis and Mental Processes." Language and Speech 1: 59-75.

_____. 1958c. "Speech Production and the Predictability of Words in Context." Quarterly Journal of Experimental Psychology 10: 96-106.

_____. 1961. "A Comparative Study of Two Hesitation Phenomena." Language and Speech 4: 18-26.

_____. 1967. "Sequential Temporal Patterns and Cognitive Processes in Speech." Language and Speech 10: 122-32.

_____. 1968. Psycholinguistics: Experiments in Spontaneous Speech. New York: Academic Press.

Hall, E. T. 1966. The Hidden Dimension. Garden City, N.Y.: Doubleday.

Henderson, A.; Goldman-Eisler, F.; and Skarbek, A. 1966. "Sequential Temporal Patterns in Spontaneous Speech." Language and Speech 9: 207-16.

Herrnstein Smith, B. 1978. On the Margins of Discourse: The Relation of Literature to Language. Chicago: University of Chicago Press.

Hymes, D. 1974. Foundations in Sociolinguistics: An Ethnographic Approach. Philadelphia: University of Pennsylvania Press.

Jaffe, J.; Breskin, S.; and Gerstman, L. J. 1972. "Random Generation of Apparent Speech Rhythms." Language and Speech 15: 68-71.

Johnson, F. L., and Davis, L. K. 1979. "Hesitation Phenomena in Televised Family Conversations in the U.S.A." International Journal of Psycholinguistics 6: 29-45.

Joos, M. 1961. The Five Clocks: A Linguistic Excursion into the Five Styles of English Usage. New York: Harcourt, Brace & World.

Kasl, S. V., and Mahl, G. F. 1965. "The Relationship of Disturbances and Hesitations in Spontaneous Speech to Anxiety." Journal of Personality and Social Psychology 1: 425-33.

Kowal, S.; O'Connell, D. C.; and Sabin, E. J. 1975. "Development of Temporal Patterning and Vocal Hesitations in Spontaneous Narratives." Journal of Psycholinguistic Research 4: 195-207.

Kožina, M. 1976. "Some Basic Problems in the Theory of Functional Styles." In Soviet Studies in Language and Language

Behavior, edited by J. Průcha, pp. 50-61. Amsterdam: North-Holland.

Lay, C. H., and Paivio, A. 1969. "The Effects of Task Difficulty and Anxiety on Hesitations in Speech." Canadian Journal of Behavioral Science 1: 25-37.

Levin, H.; Silverman, I.; and Ford, B. L. 1967. "Hesitations in Children's Speech during Explanation and Description." Journal of Verbal Learning and Verbal Behavior 6: 560-64.

Maclay, H., and Osgood, C. E. 1959. "Hesitation Phenomena in Spontaneous English Speech." Word 15: 19-44.

Mahl, G. 1956. "Disturbances and Silences in the Patient's Speech in Psychotherapy." Journal of Abnormal and Social Psychology 53: 1-15.

Mahl, G. F., and Schulze, G. 1964. "Psychological Research in the Extralinguistic Area." In Approaches to Semiotics, edited by T. A. Sebeok, A. S. Hayes, and M. C. Bateson, pp. 51-124. The Hague: Mouton.

Ragsdale, J. D. 1976. "Relationships between Hesitation Phenomena, Anxiety, and Self-Control in a Normal Conversation Situation." Language and Speech 19: 257-65.

Rochester, S. R. 1973. "The Significance of Pauses in Spontaneous Speech." Journal of Psycholinguistic Research 2: 51-81.

Sachs, H.; Schegloff, E. A.; and Jefferson, G. 1974. "A Simplest Systematics for the Organization of Turn-Taking for Conversation." Language 50: 696-735.

Scott, W. A. "Reliability of Content Analysis: The Case of Nominal Scale Coding." Public Opinion Quarterly 19: 321-25.

Siegman, A. W., and Pope, B. 1965. "Effects of Question Specificity and Anxiety Producing Messages on Verbal Fluency in the Initial Interview." Journal of Personality and Social Psychology 2: 522-30.

_____. 1966. "Ambiguity and Verbal Fluency in the TAT." Journal of Consulting and Clinical Psychology 30: 239-45.

Tallman, J. 1979. "Ways of Speaking: Styles in Conversation." Ph.D. dissertation, University of California-Berkeley.

Tannenbaum, P. H.; Williams, F.; and Hillier, C. S. 1965. "Word Predictability in the Environment of Hesitations." *Journal of Verbal Learning and Verbal Behavior* 4: 134-40.

Weaver, R. M. 1953. *The Ethics of Rhetoric*. Chicago: Regnery.

22
UNCERTAINTY IN VOLUNTARY ORGANIZATIONS: THE CASE OF CONSUMER FOOD COOPERATIVES
Michael Nagy

Uncertainty is a very useful concept for the sociological understanding of organizations. This chapter will examine the "unfolding of uncertainty" as a natural history in an organizational context well-suited to the task: consumer food cooperatives.*
Food coops are community-based voluntary organizations through which members combine their houshold buying power to purchase food collectively in bulk—thereby obtaining wholesale prices and reducing the per unit cost of the food. The food is then broken down into household-sized units by the members and distributed among them through common effort—thus, they realize their savings individually. No profit is made on the food the coop handles; a markup over wholesale cost is charged to just cover expenses. The owners of the coop, the workers, and the customers are one-in-the-same

---

*<u>Natural history</u> refers to the fact that we will consider the coop-organization developmental sequence described to be necessary for the occurrence of the resulting structure (at least at this point in the history of the "food cooperative movement")—that is, if we find a cooperative exhibiting size and structural features characteristic of cooperatives at the end of the developmental sequence, we will argue that the cooperative must necessarily have traversed the sequence as a whole. Cooperatives may, however, exit the sequence at any point, failing by choice, chance, or error to attain the necessary conditions to continue. This approach is adapted from Howard S. Becker's approach to becoming a marijuana smoker (Becker 1953).

group. Consequently, food cooperatives are an organizational alternative to private capital food retailers.

We will trace the way that uncertainty unfolds in food cooperatives across levels of analysis (from individual to organization) and across spheres of activity (from intraorganizational to extraorganizational) over time, changes in organizational size, and the types of food the coop handles. We will see how a coop's organizational structure (the "stable residue of the organizing process" [Weick 1969, p. 11]) at any given point in time is the product of continuing responses of members to uncertainty. That there is a similarity of structure among cooperatives similar in size and products indicates the uncertainty exists in patterned ways and that members of cooperatives, in organizing to cope with uncertainty, have a similar, limited set of resources at their disposal.

THEORETICAL APPROACH

The theoretical point of departure for our investigation will be the "contingency theory" branch of organizational analysis. Contingency theorists have made uncertainty and responses to it a major theme of their work. Their line of inquiry sees organizations as open systems, that is, as systems containing more variables than can be comprehended at one time and subject to influences beyond the control of members (Thompson 1967, p. 6). Contingency theory stands in opposition to earlier theoretical approaches, which saw organizational structure as an independent variable manipulable by managers and sought the "one best way" to organize for maximum effectiveness (Perrow 1970, pp. 88-89).

For contingency theorists, "the central problem for complex organizations is one of coping with uncertainty" (Thompson 1967, p. 13). Uncertainty may come from many different spheres of organizational activity, and different theorists emphasize different spheres: technology (Gouldner 1954; Woodward 1965; Harvey 1968); the competitive environment (Selznick 1948; Chandler 1962; Lawrence and Lorsch 1967); or the perceived nature of raw materials (Perrow 1970; Goffman 1961). Nonetheless, all see the organization as developing responses to uncertainty.

We will be interested in the way that organizational responses to uncertainty are enacted in organizations. Perhaps the theorist who has gone furthest in projecting the direction of the growth of complex organizations in response to uncertainty is James D. Thompson. Using the technology and task environment of the organization as independent variables, Thompson presents propositions to predict the course of development of complex organizations.* Most generally, he states (Thompson 1967, p. 54):

> Our basic assumption is that structure is a fundamental vehicle by which organizations achieve bounded rationality. By delimiting responsibilities, control over resources, and other matters, organizations provide their participating members with boundaries within which efficiency may be a reasonable expectation. But if structure affords numerous spheres of bounded rationality, it must also facilitate the <u>coordinated</u> action of these <u>interdependent</u> elements.

Through an understanding of the nature of uncertainty generated by particular technologies and task environments, we can (and Thompson does) predict the way structure is likely to develop in complex organizations. But notice that creating boundaries to achieve rationality in some parts of the organization creates, at the very least, the problematic situation of then having to coordinate activity between those now-bounded parts.

Thus, reducing uncertainty becomes a basis for concerting members' activity as they attempt to "cope." But, when members organize to reduce uncertainty in one area crucial to organizational operations, they inevitably increase uncertainty in other areas. These areas of newly increased uncertainty consequently gain in their relative importance. Members find themselves continuously having to adjust and readjust activity in response, not only to changes in the external environment of the organization but, also, to changes in intraorganizational relationships resulting from previous adjustments. The continuing effort of members to reduce uncertainty provides the "marching orders" for organizational development. It is these marching orders, how they are perceived and how they are followed by food cooperatives, which we will be investigating.

An additional facet of the investigation needs to be introduced before beginning to examine the empirical case before us. Contingency theorists, for the most part, consider people only in their

---

*Thompson's definition of technology can be paraphrased as those activities that are judged to produce desired outcomes as dictated by man's beliefs (1967, p. 14). <u>Task environment</u> is defined as "those parts of the environment which are 'relevant or potentially relevant to goal setting and goal attainment.'" (1967, p. 27)

organizational context. The person is not taken into account <u>qua</u> individual, with a home, family, hopes, and needs, rather, "the structural viewpoint considers the roles people play, rather than the nature of the personalities in these roles" (Perrow 1970, p. 2). Our investigation will not consider the personalities per se of the people involved in food cooperatives. However, since we are dealing with voluntary organizations, we will find it necessary to consider extraorganizational roles and needs of members.

Voluntary organizations neither coerce their members into joining nor, having joined, into remaining in the organization. Members will be no worse off if they quit the coop than if they had never joined. They will not have lost their job, gone AWOL, escaped, or violated religious tenets. Members must, therefore, see the time they invest in the coop as being spent in a "worthwhile" fashion. What is seen as worthwhile in the case of voluntary organizations is very much influenced by extraorganizational roles and needs.

We will find ourselves examining not only organizational uncertainty, but personal uncertainty among members as they question the worthwhileness of their participation. Uncertainty is not only a structural concept, but a social psychological one as well. In voluntary organizations of the size and strong community base of coops, the social psychological and structural are in particularly high relief as they condition one another.

Finally, the contingency theory approach has been developed through examining, and with reference to, "complex organizations."* Food cooperatives do not qualify for the appellation <u>complex</u> (which is the way most of their members like it). The size of the organizations need not be our concern in this chapter because the same processes are at work regarding uncertainty and members' responses to it in coops as in much larger organizations. Weick (1969, p. 1), in his concise and insightful book, makes the same point:

---

*For example, the second paragraph of Perrow's <u>Organizational Analysis: A Sociological View</u> (1970) begins: "The purpose of this book is to present a distinctive viewpoint regarding complex organizations" (p. 1). Thompson (1967, p. 3) starts his first chapter: "Complex organizations—manufacturing firms, hospitals, schools, armies, community agencies—are ubiquitous in modern societies." The defining features of <u>complexity</u>, however, remain undisclosed.

If you're going to learn about organizations, it is not
necessary that you assume immediately that they are
complex, or that they differ from groups of smaller
size. Instead, assume that there are processes which
create, maintain, and dissolve social collectivities,
that these processes constitute the work of organizing,
and that the ways in which these processes are continuously executed are the organization.

We will examine the way members are able to continuously
execute the activities that constitute the food cooperative, the uncertainties they face in accomplishing that execution, and the responses they make to allow the execution to smoothly continue.

Our focus will be on three areas of activity that are relevant
to the existence of coops: (1) the extraorganizational environment,
from which the coop obtains the food that is processed and distributed to members, presents the initial source of uncertainty for cooperatives ("How do we get the food we want?"); (2) the intraorganizational environment, the relations of members to each other and
to the organization as a whole, presents uncertainty, especially as
larger amounts of food must be handled due to growth ("Who's supposed to do what?"); (3) the "movement environment," the development of the food cooperative movement present the relations of
coop organizations to one another and uncertainty as cooperatives
try to increase their long-term organizational viability ("Where do
we go now that we're moving?").

Each of these areas will be examined in turn. They form a
rough developmental sequence. Responses to uncertainty in obtaining food lead to confusion over organizational roles. Attachment of
particular people to particular roles reduces organizational uncertainty, but increases personal uncertainty, as those who are most
involved begin to find voluntary involvement less and less worthwhile. Paying people for their work is a successful compromise
between organizational and personal needs, but it generates uncertainty as to the political "purity" of the cooperative. Overarching
all these considerations is the question of the possibility of coops
becoming viable over the long term, a question that emerges most
strongly among those cooperatives who have successfully dealt with
uncertainty to the point where short-term viability is less problematic.

THE SETTING: FOOD COOPERATIVES
IN WESTERN "YANKEE STATE"

The study area is particularly well-adapted to examining the
developmental questions we are investigating. At the time the

research on which this chapter is based was conducted, there were 41 food cooperatives in the study area: the western third of "Yankee State" and immediately adjacent areas in three neighboring states. The coops studied range in size from nine member-households and $200 worth of food handled per month to more than 500 member-households and $29,700 worth of food a month (the median values being 49 member-households and $2,000 per month in food). The range of ages for the coops was from three months to more than six years (with a median age of 24 months).

We will be able to doubly observe organizational development in response to uncertainty. First, we can observe particular organizations over the course of time. Nine months of research was conducted in the study area. Intensive participant-observation was done in three selected cooperatives and the local federation of cooperatives. In addition, interviewing and some observing was done in eight other cooperatives and two other coalition organizations. Consequently, in single organizations, we can observe members' perceptions of the nature of the uncertainty they face in "doing" the cooperative and the way in which they concert activities to meet that uncertainty.

Second, as field work was ending, an organizational survey was conducted among the area's coops. Thirty-seven coops (90.2 percent) responded to the survey. We can, therefore, compare the organizational structures of cooperatives that are similar in size and age. Similarity of structure among them can be taken as evidence that the same sorts of processes are at work and that members have made similar responses to uncertainty. The use of multiple methods enables us to take advantage of the "natural laboratory" provided by the research setting.

There is another empirical advantage in using food cooperatives in western Yankee State for our investigation of organizational development in response to uncertainty. Food cooperatives are a comparatively recent organizational innovation, and as has been mentioned, they are community-based and run by members. This means that they are neither subject to a priori organizational designs developed and imposed by distant sponsors nor is there much established conventional wisdom to use as a guide. The organizational responses to uncertainty that we observe are constructed by members in response to the contingencies of operation that they themselves take into account. We have a relatively pristine and "uncontaminated" setting for observing the marching orders of organizational uncertainty as directed to small, voluntary organizations.

"HOW DO WE GET THE FOOD WE WANT ?":
EXTRAORGANIZATIONAL UNCERTAINTY

The initial question with regard to operating a food cooperative is how to obtain the food members desire; that, after all, is the reason for a food coop—to procure good food at a reasonable price. Generally, sources of food can be found. Contacting an existing cooperative for sources is usually possible. In fact, fully 51.7 percent of the cooperatives responding to the survey reported either having been started as a result of a group of members of an existing coop forming their own organization or receiving aid and guidance from another coop. They had ready-made knowledge of sources.

However, locating possible sources of food by no means resolves the uncertainty associated with actually getting the food that members want. Two sources of uncertainty deriving from the extraorganizational environment will be discussed: (1) the uncertainty generated by the nature of the raw material, food; and (2) uncertainty concerning the actual selection and purchasing of foodstuffs by the coop. We will examine the way in which the coops' responses to these two extraorganizational sources of uncertainty serve to cope with uncertainty in the food procurement sphere of activity, but increase uncertainty in the intraorganizational sphere, by fundamentally altering the relationships among the members of the cooperative.

The Nature of the Raw Material

The nature of the raw material of the organization is a theoretically prominent source of uncertainty for contingency theorists (see especially the discussion by Perrow 1970, pp. 75-80). The raw material of coops—food—is very much a source of uncertainty for members. Food is perishable, and once it spoils, it's worthless. Members must not only get food that is of acceptable quality to begin with, they must be able to distribute it and consume it before it spoils. However, food is to be purchased in wholesale quantities. Therein lies the uncertainty. Once food is purchased, it must be sold and used before it spoils, or the coop and its members must take a financial loss.* There are three ways coop members

---

*Briefly, for a coop to operate, a pool of capital is created by deposits, fees, or prepayment. This money is used to purchase foodstuffs ordered by members. The food is then sold to members

can cope with the uncertainty generated by the nature of the raw material coming in from the extraorganizational environment: the coop can use a long distribution cycle, the coop can grow, or the coop can become part of a buying coalition.

Long Distribution Cycles

Operating with at least a month in between distributions is the primary way the smallest coops (from nine to 20 households) are able to handle wholesale quantities of food. It simply takes them that long to get together a wholesale-sized order. Small coops are, in consequence, limited to handling nonperishable foods: grain flours, beans and seeds, nuts and nut butters, and cheese. Produce is not handled by small coops (usually called <u>buying clubs</u>); lettuce and bananas will not keep for a month.

Since the length of time between distributions and the sorts of food that can be handled are so closely linked, monthly distribution is a relatively poor means of coping with uncertainty in getting desired types of food; variety is very limited. One cooperative responded to the survey question asking "What are the one or two things that your coop is currently working the hardest at?," as follows: "Trying to get a larger membership which, in turn, will allow us to expand items carried and, hopefully, carry some stock of items—overpurchase allowance, if you will."*

Growth

A larger membership base in the coop increases the flexibility of the cooperative in purchasing food by reducing the uncertainty

---

(unless, as in buying clubs, they have prepaid for their food). Included in the sale price is a "markup." The sale price is the cost of the food plus a percentage markup to pay for the expenses of operation. If the pool of capital is not recouped following distribution of the food, the coop has lost money and must increase the markup to regain a solvent financial position. In essence, the deposit money constitutes an interest-free loan from the member to the coop. This money must be on hand if the member should decide to withdraw from the coop and demand his/her money back.

*Quotations not otherwise cited are from my fieldnotes, mimeoed letters, newsletters, and so forth, or from survey questionnaire responses. All proper names are fictitious.

associated with having food on hand. Smaller coops face a financial risk that food that has been purchased will not be sold. The coordinator of a small coop (35 households) explained the risks involved when produce is handled by the coop:

> Lisa said that they often do overbuy produce. They are forced to do so, however. She mentioned spinach as a case in point. Spinach must be purchased in ten-pound lots, so, for example, if there are only seven pounds ordered, the case will be purchased and the rest of the spinach sold as "extras." She outlined the situation: "It's real perishable stuff. We have to buy extras to meet case requirements. But once it's bought, it can't be stored until the next week's distribution." She said that she does not want to think about it in the refrigerator going rotten, so at the end of the night, it's sold at half-price.

On the other hand, Foxfire Food Coop, the largest cooperative in the study area, routinely "buffers" the amount of food order. The large size of the membership (about 500 households), coupled with the practice of selling extras to nonmembers (at an increased markup), assures that food left over from case lots not completely ordered will be sold.

More people in the coop "absorbs" the uncertainty associated with the purchase of a highly perishable commodity. However, a growing membership alters the relationships among the individual member-households. Small cooperatives most often comprise personal friendship-relations among members. Growing means that the identicality of member and friend will be lost. The member-friends may prefer the surety of friendship in spite of the operational uncertainty of smallness. In fact, at the time of the study, three of the five "buying clubs" had closed themselves to new members for just this reason.

Growing does not eliminate uncertainty. It reduces the extra-organizational uncertainty associated with getting the food desired, but increases the uncertainty of members with regard to their mutual relations to each other and the coop organization. We see that members' response to uncertainty in one sphere of activity is a means of coping in that sphere, but increases uncertainty in another sphere.

Coalition Buying

Another way cooperatives can reduce the uncertainty inherent in case lot purchases is through coalition. Instead of (or, usually, in addition to) individual coops growing internally, a number of cooperatives may come together and form a buying coalition. This means of coping with uncertainty increases flexibility in purchasing by expanding volume to the level of all the cooperatives put together.

A number of buying coalitions exist in the study area. They can be differentiated in terms of geographic area and the products regularly handled. The largest in volume and most widespread areally is Western Yankee Cooperatives, Inc. Western Yankee Coops is a federation of cooperatives, a "cooperative of cooperatives." It is owned by its coop organization members. Each coop that is a member of the federation must pay a nominal membership fee ($5) and contribute to the capital of the federation via an "equity markup" equal to 1 percent of their month's purchases. This is in addition to an operating markup that just covers the cost of doing business.

The federation was initially formed out of a desire on the part of a number of coops near one another to regularize making joint purchases with each other and the willingness of some of the members of those coops to coordinate these "deals." It has grown rapidly in size since its inception and now serves the entire western Yankee area, handling about three-quarters of a million dollars in foodstuffs (all nonperishables) per year.

Coalition buying enables member-organizations to "place their boundaries around" core activities and reduce the uncertainty associated with having to deal directly with the raw materials supplying environment (see Thompson 1967, pp. 35-36, 39-41). Buying coalitions serve this purpose for all the cooperatives at once. The core activity (distributing wholesale lots of food broken down to household size) of each coop is "once removed" from its supply environment by the interposing of coalition buying organizations.

Formation of coalition buying organizations has created an "alternative food distribution system," rather than simply an aggregate of individual cooperatives. Member cooperatives, in concert through Western Yankee, have the buying power to purchase boxcar loads of goods directly from producers. Joint purchasing by the four New England federations serves to "insulate" cooperative core activity even further. Sources of supply become more and more certain the greater the volume of purchases. The cooperative movement is building an assured financial base.

But, as we might expect, uncertainty is not eliminated through coalition. What uncertainty remains is extraorganizational for individual coops, but internal to the cooperative food distribution system itself. It becomes a practical and technical problem, rather than a life and death (for the coop) matter. But since the technology of the operations of cooperatives is not complicated (involving only changes in "package size," not substance), making connections between handling organizations is the crucial link in the alternative food distribution system. The schedules that are established become practical contingencies around which cooperative activity is organized. Their necessity is explained as a matter of practicality, and not ideology. The fact that more than one organization operates on a given schedule gives the schedule a relative permanence, based on the work that would be involved were all the organizations in the coalition to have to change their operating schedules.

In summary, one final note of theoretical importance: Western Yankee Coops is an organization itself. Its operational activities are analogous to those of an individual coop, except that its members are themselves organizations. The history of the coalition organization provides a parallel case study to the examination of individual coops. In the period just following its establishment, Western Yankee Coops distributed food monthly, when member cooperatives were able to get together on a joint purchase. The ordering, handling, and bookkeeping were rotated among the member coops each month. As the federation grew, distribution became more frequent (trucks now run twice a week), and the variety of foods, and even nonfood items, expanded, necessitating occupancy of a warehouse and, subsequently, another, larger one. Through the process we will examine, rotation of work stopped, and the "bulk buying collective" emerged. The federation itself now acts as a party to joint purchases, thus insulating its own core activities. The similarity in development between the federation and individual coops indicates similar sources of uncertainty are responded to with mobilization of similar resources—time, people, and cooperative relationships—with similar results: the mitigation of extraorganizational uncertainty.

Selecting and Purchasing Food

Contingency theorists argue that since organizations seek to reduce uncertainty, those individuals in a position to reduce uncertainty for the organization through their actions increase their importance to the organization (Crozier 1964, pp. 108-10; Thompson 1967, pp. 110-12). Regarding interorganizational exchanges, Thompson (1967, p. 112) argues that "jobs at contingent boundaries enable individuals to reduce uncertainties for the organization. To the extent that he can contain contingencies and to the extent that the contingencies are important to the organization, the individual is powerful in the bargaining process."

Thompson's argument is made with reference to complex organizations. We are dealing with relatively small, relatively new organizations. Thompson's explication can be adapted for our use as follows: in an organization that is initially undifferentiated with respect to the division of labor, the first positions to be named and staffed will be those that deal directly with contingencies surrounding the core activities of the organization. That is, given that the organization is just starting, all the possible positions, all the jobs to be done, would seem to be equally likely to be staffed either by one person or by a number of persons (assuming the "cooperative ethos" of equality of participation). We would argue that those positions which mediate the boundaries of the organization will be the ones that will initially be named as positions to be held and will be staffed by a single person or a restricted group of persons in rotation. This will be the case even though other tasks in the cooperative may be unnamed specifically or staffed by anyone wanting the job.

We can examine the emergence of contingent boundary positions by noting the resources that the position holder (or, to begin with in our case, simply, "the person doing the job") develops that begin to separate her/him from the rest of the members in terms of being able to make a unique (or, at least, closely shared) contribution to reducing the uncertainty generated by the extraorganizational environment.

The person who mediates the boundary of the organization with respect to the procurement of food develops three resources that she/he can bring to the operation of the organization that others cannot: a knowledge of sources, personal friendships with vendors, and a knowledge of prices. All of these relate to features of the environment outside the boundaries of the organization. The nature of the environment itself restricts the possibility of their being widespread among members.

A knowledge of sources is the easiest of the three resources mentioned to share. Still, for example, at Greengrocer Food Coop, the coordinator has an index card tacked on the wall with the telephone numbers of the coop's suppliers. The suppliers are listed only secondarily by the name of the supplying organization. Most are listed by the first name of the person who actually delivers the goods, for example, "Tony (Pepperidge Farm)—phone number." Knowledge about sources is somewhat incompletely communicated. Additionally, the importance of personal relationships with vendors is suggested.

A personal relationship with the person dealt with in the supplying organization cannot easily be shared—and the nature of personal relationships means that not everyone in the coop can develop a personal relationship with suppliers. The importance of personal friendship and mutual respect between buyers and sellers was especially emphasized to me in connection with buying at the produce market.

> I asked Ron how he got to know the people and processes when he first started buying produce in the market. "You buy a lot of bad produce." He said that buying produce was like learning a game, "a good game." "When you get good at it, that's when it starts to get fun." He emphasized that everything depends on the relationship that you have to the sellers. "They have to respect your knowledge of produce and prices and they try to take every advantage they can."

The members of the cooperative cannot easily rotate the job of buying produce the way they can easily rotate the job of taking it out of crates and putting it into bags. The person buying produce must be "in the flow" of the market so that she/he knows what is a good price and what is not. Being in the flow is a product of continuously doing the job of buying. It cannot be transferred and is person-specific. It is to the benefit of all the members to get good prices, and one person can get good prices far more efficiently than can a group. That person mediates the boundary of the coop with the supply environment and (perhaps with one or two others) becomes the "buyer" for the coop.

Conclusion

We have seen how the members of food cooperatives cope with the uncertainties that occur when they try to obtain food from outside the organization. Coping is accomplished with the resources coops can muster: time, people, and cooperation. A long distribution cycle and coalition buying cope with uncertainty without changing the coop organization itself very much. What uncertainty remains is still extraorganizationally generated: making case-lot limits, connecting with other organizations to transfer goods, supplier shortages of foods, and maintaining relations with coalition partners. But changes involving people—the growth and the emergence of boundary-task doers—fundamentally alter relationships within the organization. Uncertainty about obtaining from outside the organization is mitigated, but uncertainty about intraorganizational roles is exacerbated.

"WHO IS SUPPOSED TO DO WHAT?": INTRAORGANIZATIONAL UNCERTAINTY

This section examines the uncertainty associated with processing food once it is within the boundaries of the food cooperative. The specific tasks performed to do "breakdown" are simple in themselves. Produce is weighed out of crates; nonperishables are rebagged in wholesale-sized sacks; wheels of cheese are cut to household-sized quantities; floors are swept; and money is taken in and change is made. Once members are there to execute the tasks so the food is smoothly transferred from wholesale lots to household quantities to the possession of the proper household, uncertainty is reduced to zero—the organization successfully accomplishes its purpose for that distribution. But therein lies the uncertainty: How are people to be brought together at the right time and place to accomplish the transfer, and who is supposed to do what?

We will examine three ways in which cooperatives cope with the uncertainty of coordinating intraorganizational activity: (1) coops may introduce work schedules of various degrees of "tightness"; (2) coops may establish work requirements for members; and (3) "condensation of involvement" occurs, increasing operational efficiency.

When we examined responses to extraorganizational uncertainty, the cooperative was viewed as comparatively homogeneous in terms of members' time-involvement in its operation. Only in the discussion of boundary-mediating task-doers did we see the emergence of a differentiation among members. In this section, we shall see that a "hierarchy of involvement" among members results as the "residue of the organizing process" through which uncertainty in internal operations is reduced.

Work Schedules

The simplest way for people to be brought together at the proper time and place to do the distributing of food among the coop members is for all the members to show up when the order arrives and divide it up among themselves. This is the way that the smallest cooperatives distribute food. When there are only a dozen or so households in the cooperative, phone calls can be made notifying people when the food will arrive, and all the members can gather. Scheduling is done informally. So, for example, when asked by the survey: "What are the times of distribution of your coop?," two of the friendship-based buying clubs replied: "Whenever the order arrives," and, "To the availability of members." Given a small membership and nonperishable foodstuffs, this mechanism works well.

However, when there are as few as 25 households and perhaps as many as 200 to be getting food, when there are a number of sources supplying different products according to their schedule, and when the food itself is highly perishable, to have everyone get their own food would be chaotic.* Schedules must be set up to insure that someone will be at the coop to do "breakdown" and "setup" prior to distribution and that others will be there to make certain that members will get the food they ordered. The more frequently the cooperative distributes food—and thus, the more time that must be accounted for during which workers must be present—the "tighter" the scheduling is.

The survey requested that cooperatives supply scheduling information for each job that a member might do. The information obtained included the names for specific roles that members might play in the work process of the food coop. For each job, it was requested that the day and time period when the job was performed be given, as well as the number of workers needed to do the job. Some coops, for some jobs, listed only the job, with no reference to the day or time period of its performance. Other jobs were listed with the day of performance, but no time period. Other coops were able to respond with a job name, day, and time period for each task. Table 22.1 compares the distribution frequency of coops with the precision with which coop tasks are referenced in time.

We can observe a difference in the mechanism for coordinating the activity of members with respect to performing essential tasks in distribution between coops that distribute food on a monthly basis and those distributing food more frequently. We are not positing a necessarily developmental sequence (in fact, buying clubs have chosen not to develop). However, none of the cooperatives in the study area began as large and frequently distributing organizations. If the cooperative grows (and we have seen how it might grow to reduce uncertainty), scheduling distribution through personal, informal contact becomes too uncertain a way of making sure that people are at the right place at the right time. There is more, and more

---

*The largest cooperative in the study, Foxfire, has been identified as having almost 500 members. The discrepancy between its size and the example of 200 households awaiting food is accounted for by the fact that not every household orders every week, and that the coop has two distributions each week, to accommodate all its members in the church basement that is used.

perishable, food distributed to more households, more frequently. The response of members in coping with this uncertainty is to formalize and impersonalize mechanisms for coordinating members' execution of tasks.

TABLE 22.1

"Tightness" of Scheduling, by Distribution Frequency

Work Sheet Listings	Coop Distribution		
	More Often Than Once a Week	Weekly or Biweekly	Monthly or Sporadically
Day and time for all jobs	100.0 (4)	40.9 (9)	0.0 (0)
Day and time and job and day	0.0 (0)	54.5 (12)	0.0 (0)
Job and day or job only	0.0 (0)	4.5 (1)	100.0 (5)

Note: $X^2 = 30.296$; $V = .69903$; $a < .005$; and $\lambda = .34615$.
Source: Compiled by the author.

It is important to note theoretically here that organizational structure—a schedule of working times for members—does not begin full-blown. Rather, structure is the result of members' attempts to cope with uncertainty, which threatens the smooth execution of core activities.

However, scheduling times for participation does not necessarily mean that people will conform to the schedule. How do coops get members to abide by impersonal mechanisms of coordination, given the voluntary nature of their operation?

Work Requirements for Members

A rule in the cooperative requiring members to work in the coop was reported by 91.9 percent of the cooperatives in the study area. Seventy-three percent reported sanctions imposed on members failing to meet the requirement. The most common sanction (reported by 70.4 percent of those reporting sanctions) was the loss of buying rights. Getting members to work is not accomplished through appeals to voluntary cooperation with other members, but through the threatened loss of the material benefits of membership.

Food cooperatives are organizations that offer members material rewards for participation: savings on food.* The fact that coops are voluntary organizations means, however, that the rewards for participation are not made stronger in relation to the costs of not participating, as would be the case if one were to quit a job, go AWOL, escape, or violate religious tenets; the savings in the coop are the same whether the member helps or not. Coops are dual-nature organizations. They operate in the cash nexus of society, which requires them to be financially solvent or collapse, while, at the same time, they have very limited sanctions available to ensure adequate participation.

The necessity of material sanctions suggests that most members of the coop have what Etzioni (1961, p. 12) terms calculative involvement in the organization. In general, average members of a food coop (those whose involvement extends only to fulfilling work requirements) are seen by more active members to be attached to the coop primarily through "cheap food." Active members (those who work more than is required and/or attend coop policy-making meetings) do not receive any extra savings for their extra time. The attachment of active members is "moral" as well as "calculative."

The differentiation between active and average members of the cooperative suggests differences in participation not present at the inception of the organization, when activity was informally scheduled and all participated. The next section will examine the way in which differential participation reduces uncertainty in the organization, as well as the "residue of structure" that it leaves.

---

*Foxfire Food Coop does periodic price comparisons between the coop, the local outlet of a large New England supermarket chain, and a locally owned grocery store. A typical monthly comparison, by item category, found that for 38 items of produce, both private stores were priced 31 percent over the coop; for 14 dairy items, the supermarket prices were 21 percent higher and the grocery prices were 18 percent above the coop; for 16 types of bread, both private stores were 17 percent higher than Foxfire; and for ten canned good items, the grocery price was 10 percent higher and the supermarket price was 4 percent lower. It should be noted that coops do not offer coupons, stamps, or cash giveaways that mitigate price. Also, the price comparison list represents about one-half of all Foxfire sells, but only a small fraction of what is available at the grocery or supermarket.

Condensation of Involvement

Condensation of involvement refers to the fact that as the coop organization increases its membership and the amount of food it distributes, a smaller number of people do more work individually for the coop.

Condensation of involvement occurs in response to sources of uncertainty, which increase with organizational growth and which would threaten core task execution if it did not occur. First, essential tasks—that is, buying food, keeping books, and coordinating larger distributions—become more complex as the volume of food handled and size of the membership grow. Second, with the greater complexity of tasks comes increasing importance in communicating "what's going on" to fellow workers, as well as increasing difficulty in making that communication effectively to dilettante average members. The coop has gotten to where "you can't still be a volunteer and know what's going on." But again, these circumstances do not suddenly appear full-blown. Changes take place over time, as members make adjustments to the uncertainty that threatens the smooth operation of the coop. We shall look briefly at the way condensation of involvement in the cooperative results in paid positions in the coop.

Payments to Members

There are three identifiable stages of payments made to members of the cooperative: direct reimbursement, payment for people, and, finally, payment to the incumbents of positions. These stages are distinguishable along three dimensions: (1) the temporal relationship between the performance of a payable act, and payment for it; (2) the degree to which the possibility of payment is restricted to specifiable people and whether those people are self-selected or selected by others; and (3) whether payment is made for discrete acts or for time spent on coop business.

Direct Reimbursement

This is the most basic of payment mechanisms. All coops, if the situation arises, make direct reimbursement payments. Payment is made for acts in which a member has incurred an out-of-pocket expense. Payment is made following the discrete, payable act (spending one's own money on behalf of the coop). Who gets paid is self-selected. The person who makes the expenditure gets reimbursed. This is only fair, after all; no individual members of the coop should have to foot the bill for acts, carried out for the coop, which will benefit all the members. In general, the amounts of money involved are small enough and the circumstances of the individual's expenditure clear-cut enough so that reimbursement is handled in a perfunctory manner.

Payment for People

As the cooperative organization grows in its volume of sales, its operations become more regularized and continuous in nature (as indicated by scheduling). The following quotation from an open letter to western Yankee State cooperative community illustrates the manner in which regularized operations, which have become incongruous with discrete-act-based payment, leads to personal uncertainty for the time-involved "condensed" group in Western Yankee Coops:

> The bulk buying is presently going through a minor crisis. We have grown rapidly in the past months—in April 16 coops put in orders. A tremendous amount of time and energy is required to keep the whole operation running smoothly. . . . When Western Yankee Coops first got together it was agreed that any individual who put together a deal could collect a $25 salary. For the past six weeks members of the bulk buying collective have been collecting $25 salaries either weekly or every other week. But to do this we have to try to frantically create as many separate deals as needed salaries. We think that this is a ridiculous and unfair way to get paid. . . . It would be helpful if coops could talk about this at their meetings. Do you agree that coop workers should not be exploited?

In an interview with one of the workers, she characterized the payment mechanism as "crazy . . . a stupid rule . . . outdated," as indeed it was. The rule for payment no longer matches the situation of the people being paid. They are working for the organization on a continuous (albeit part-time) basis, but being paid by discrete acts. This creates personal uncertainty for them. The time that they have to spend in coop work, increasing as it is, begins to eat into their ability to "make a living." The uncertainty leads them to question whether their involvement is "worth it" and to see their relationship to the coop organization as one of "exploitation." One worker expressed the dilemma very clearly:

> Ellen said that she will quit the bulk-buying collective if she cannot get an adequate wage. She says she is at present cleaning houses and baby-sitting to fill in for the $25 per deal she is getting. She said: "I'm not willing to do it as a part-time thing anymore. I'm not going to work five jobs. It's not fair. I'll be damned if I'm going to starve for Western Yankee Coops. It's a business—a cooperative business—I'd like to get a salary I can live on."

The membership of the federation approved money to be paid to four part-time staff people at the rate of $25 per week. There was no one hired to perform the work being paid for; rather, those persons who had been working as members of the bulk-buying collective, and regularly receiving $25 per deal as reimbursement, were instated as staff people.

Temporally, the payment mechanism has now caught up with the operational situation: people are paid on a continuous basis for work performed on a continuous basis. Those who have the possibility of receiving payment are now specifiable before the fact, although they are self-selected. Paying people is the result of a compromise between the need of the organization to reduce uncertainty, by having essential tasks accomplished smoothly, and the workers' need to make a living. Reduction of uncertainty through essential task execution is attached to a few specific individuals, who now have the "responsibility" for execution as part of a quid pro quo exchange that simultaneously reduces their own uncertainty about making a living.

Here, we have the basis for increasingly differentiated participation. Paying people solidifies the status of those who are now, in effect, employees of the cooperative. It closes off the group who will be receiving money. Paid people are those whose moral involvement in the cooperative was so strong that it began to cut into their ability to make a living. But notice that they are now those with the strongest calculative involvement as well. A volunteer member is no worse off for quitting the coop. A paid employee is losing his or her job.

Payment for Incumbents of Positions

We have argued that growth is a necessary condition of condensing involvement. The open letter quoted above suggests that this is the case. Table 22.2 indicates that there is a similarity of structure among cooperatives of similar size. The same processes that have been described are at work in all the cooperatives in the study area. The patterned features of uncertainty in food coop organizations, with their similar core activities, leads to similarity of structure developed in responding to that uncertainty.

TABLE 22.2

Types of Payment to People, by Coop Sales Volume

Types of Payments	Coop Sales Volume (monthly)	
	$2,000	$2,000
Coop makes no payments or reimbursements only	88.2 (15)	29.4 (5)
Coop pays people and/or positions	11.8 (2)	70.6 (12)

Note: $X^2 = 12.143$; $\phi = .59761$; $a < .005$; and $\lambda = .54839$.
Source: Compiled by the author.

A few (only five at present) of the very largest cooperative organizations in western Yankee State have completed the third step in the progression and have positions held by paid incumbents. The rationale behind this step continues the condensation process: "Chris said that hiring someone to join the bulk-buying collective is a way to improve efficiency. Having four part-time workers is sporadic. It's hard to collect four part-time workers into being full-time, because people have to continually catch each other up on what is going on."

Two of the four people paid by Western Yankee Coops resigned; one additional person was hired from among 24 applicants to work full-time, and the two remaining people increased their work to full-time. All three are now incumbents of paid positions.

Paying the incumbents of positions represents the culmination of the process of condensation of involvement. The work to be done for the organization is considered as an entity in itself, separate from who is to do it. It has become an abstract task-set, performed in trust by the incumbent.

Temporally, the person being paid as the incumbent of a position begins to receive payment with their first taking over the position. They are paid in prospect for the work that they will be doing for the organization, concurrently with the passage of time, rather than for discrete acts performed in the past. The closure of the paid group is now complete. Workers are no longer self-selected. Rather, there is a formal application and hiring process mediated by other people.

Paid positions have further reduced both the internal organizational uncertainty of the cooperative and the personal uncertainty of worker-members, but it also generates new uncertainty as a result of the fundamental change in the relationship between a member and the organization. Where before there had been relationships between persons and the organization, there is now a person-position-organization relationship, the ground rules of which need to be worked out.

After Paid Positions

Those individuals who carry on the business of the organization and get paid for their services are no longer directly tied to the organization if they are incumbents of paid positions, since people in paid positions are paid in prospect for what they will be doing for the cooperative. Over time, the uncertainty of what they will be doing may lead people in positions to seek clarification of their duties; or lack of congruence between what others see as what they will be doing and what, at a given time, they may have been doing might lead others to seek some sort of clarification of duties or, even, the ouster of the person from the position.

For example, the call for the firing of one of the managers (a paid position) at Earth's Bounty Food Cooperative resulted in a great deal of controversy, as detracters and supporters lined up on opposite sides, with the majority of coop members uncommitted in between. A five-hour general meeting of the coop, attended by over 100 people (only about 6 percent of the total membership), finally passed a resolution to "suspend proceedings and commence an evaluation procedure that would start with Ben A. [the embattled manager] and be completed by November 30."

For the large majority, who were not declared proponents of either firing or retention, the compromise of a formal evaluation procedure defused the existing controversy; through establishing new organizational rules, they tried to insure that it would not happen again. The outcome of the incident is that present uncertainty is accepted and ignored in favor of (hopefully) less uncertainty in the future. That reduction is to take place through formalization of relationships.

At the federation, it was the people holding the paid positions themselves who requested that they be "reviewed" as to the acceptability of their performance. As one worker expressed it: "I would like a review. It would make my relation to the organization clearer. We don't have a formal mechanism for feedback from coops." Again, the means for reducing uncertainty is the institution of procedures that result in the increased formalization of relationships.

Conclusion

This section has examined the course of organizational development in response to intraorganizational uncertainty. Uncertainty is generated by the need for the core activities of the cooperative to be executed smoothly. This is especially true given the perishable nature of the organizational product, food. We have seen that the principal way of coping with operational uncertainty is to increasingly formalize the relationships among members. This occurs through tightening work schedules, instituting work requirements for members, and through the condensing of time-involvement, which ends in the voluntary organization losing its voluntary character, at least for some members. In trying to cope with uncertainty, the initially undifferentiated labor of the coop moves by increments to a formalized structure left as the "residue" of organizing to cope with recurring, patterned uncertainty.

"WHERE DO WE GO, NOW THAT WE'RE MOVING?": MOVEMENT UNCERTAINTY

So far, our discussion has been concerned with members' responses to the uncertainty inherent in the operation of food cooperatives as food-distributing organizations. This final section will shift the discussion somewhat to examine the uncertainty generated by food cooperatives as a social movement. We shall examine alternative "visions of the movement."

As a whole, the food coop movement is nothing apart from the organizations that are its practical accomplishment as an innovation and alternative to private-capital retailers of food. Uncertainty with respect to the cooperative movement as a whole, therefore, revolves around the question of whether or not viable organizations can be built and the strategies that might make viable organizations more likely. Two different, although not necessarily opposing, strategies will be seen in the following outlines of the "western Yankee philosophy" and "coop chauvinism."

The "western Yankee philisophy" argues for a strong federation of cooperatives. Its logic runs as follows:

1. Large-volume quantity purchasing is required to obtain discounts from suppliers.
2. To achieve the largest volume it can, the federation must include in its purchases as much of the volume of its member coops as possible.
3. The heart of the argument is that large coops should subsidize the purchases of small coops for the benefit of all.
4. The principle is that it's worth paying a little more (Western Yankee Coop's markup) for something that you believe in.

The operational directive for coops, then, is to purchase everything they can through the federation rather than looking for lower prices at private capital wholesalers.

The "coop chauvinist" position is an individualist position. It argues for strong, autonomous local cooperatives. Its logic runs this way:

1. The coop was formed to save money on the retail price of food by circumventing centralized private capital.
2. The federation represents a potential centralization of supply reminiscent of centralized private capital.
3. It is in the best interests of the coop organization that there be as many sellers as possible to obtain competitive prices and services.
4. The principle is that the first responsibility of the food coop is to its members.

The operational directive for coops in this case is to look around for the best prices and services. The federation should be treated as first of a number of possible suppliers, but the focus should be on the local organization rather than on the area as a whole.

These two philosophical approaches to the coop movement are not incompatible with one another because, as we have said, the movement is based on building organizational viability. So far, the federation has become more viable because it can offer low prices and good services to member-coops. Likewise, through looking around for the best prices, individual coops have been able to increase their own viability. There are different interpretations of the level (local coop or federation) that should be the focus of the movement, but thus far, there has been little need to cope with "movement uncertainty."

However, the ultimate purpose of the movement remains ambiguous: is it "community service" or "community feeling"? Some of the differences that we have seen in cooperative organizations are expressions of differences in visions of the food cooperative movement. Closing memberships is an example. A member of a buying club stated her perspective that "a cooperative ceases to be a cooperative when it gets bigger than 15 to 20 families." In contrast, a member of another cooperative argued for the growth of the coop and its obtaining a storefront: "The exclusiveness of not growing rubs me the wrong way. A storefront would facilitate membership for more people. The coop could offer the opportunity of membership to segments of the population that should really be reached. For instance, old people need to be served."*

Increasing success of the movement, that is, more people being served by more viable coop organizations, may, in fact, increase movement uncertainty in the future. Thus far, food cooperatives have not made a noticeable dent in the retail food distribution market. Presently, the relative size of the losses that would have to be sustained by large retailers to undercut the prices of coops and drive them out of business, balanced against the increase in revenue to be obtained if they succeeded, is such that direct competition is very unlikely. Success for coop might change this.

The uncertainty that is present is of the sort that we have discussed: how to build viable organizations and how to continue the execution of core activities—and even make that execution smoother and less uncertain. Here members exhaust the uncertainty of organizing a new social and economic organizational type. There is a certain excitement in doing things for the first time. Members may discover new foods that they were not familiar with and new ways of cooking and eating. The food coop movement is closely aligned through its members with the surge of interest in health "naturalness" (in childbirth, physical activity, energy production, and, of course, food). The uncertainty associated with forming a community organization and trying to make it work smoothly is exciting.

---

*We can see a distinction between exclusive and inclusive social movement organizations. In the case of coops in western Yankee state, inclusive organizations are in the overwhelming majority. We have seen the practical reasons for this. There are also, as indicated by the growth advocate, reasons of ideology. After all, it would hardly be "cooperative" to refuse membership to those who want it. Open membership is a long-standing tenet of consumer cooperatives.

SUMMARY AND CONCLUSION

The course of development we have traced in these voluntary organizations—food cooperatives—is neither a result of following a set of organizational blueprints nor, in most cases, of deliberate planning by members. The course of development of food cooperatives is a result of members of the coops making constant adjustments to cope with the uncertainty that threatens the continuous execution of tasks which constitute the core activities of the cooperative.

When Thompson (1967, p. 1) introduces his book by saying, "We will argue that organizations do some of the basic things they do because they must—or else!" he indicates the way that uncertainty sets directions (gives marching orders) which organizations must follow if they are to continue operation.* Although Thompson explicitly excludes "organizations of a 'voluntary' nature, such as religious or ideological associations" (1967, p. viii), from his consideration, his propositions fit our purposes well. This is a reflection of the limited, purely ideological content of the food cooperative movement. The food coop movement is at root an organizational social movement. It rests on the establishment of innovative organizations that utilize cooperative rather than private capital, participatory democratic decision-making rather than hierarchy, members' rather than hired labor, and discounted prices rather than profit.

One reason that food cooperatives have been a good setting in which to examine uncertainty as a patterned feature of organizing is that because coops are innovative organizations, members' responses to uncertainty are not habituated by experience. As food cooperatives expand in size and number, as they appear to be doing, the developmental sequence that we have outlined may tend to be more direct. Members may institute structure in response to their knowledge of what a coop is "supposed" to look like, rather than as

---

*Thompson's perspective is from the point of view of profit-making, survival-seeking organizations. Rothschild-Whitt, on the other hand (1976a, pp. 78-79), cites a "transitory orientation" as a condition facilitating participatory democracy in organizations. Food cooperatives are, by design and intent, participatory democracies. It is an open question whether, given the sorts of practical considerations discussed, they will remain so or whether we are presenting a specific example of the operation of the "iron law of oligarchy."

a response to uncertainty in its operations. Over time, we may expect to see a reduction in the variety of organizational forms, as experience suggests what "works." There is even now a growing literature of a "how to do it" kind about coops (Stern 1974; Co-op Handbook Collective 1975; Vellela 1975). There is also increasing scholarly interest in alternative organizations (Curhan and Wertheim 1972, 1975; Ronco 1974; Freeman 1975; Wertheim 1976; Bernstein 1976; Rothschild-Whitt 1976a, 1976b).

If the perspective on which our analysis has been based is correct, organizational variety of coops will be reduced because uncertainty of operation will be reduced. Western Yankee Coops and other large cooperative organizations are now in a position to offer both "technical assistance" and a limited amount of financial aid. The increasing viability of these organizations itself is a result of successfully coping with uncertainty. The formation of new channels of interorganizational communication and new channels for the distribution of food changes the pattern of uncertainty newly begun cooperatives face. To the degree that uncertainty is reduced, so also will the variability needed to "do" a food coop successfully be reduced. If the patterning of uncertainty has conditioned the development of food cooperatives, food cooperatives, through sucessfully coping with uncertainty, may find themselves able to mold that pattern, and consequently themselves.

REFERENCES

Becker, Howard S. 1953. "Becoming a Marihuana User." American Journal of Sociology 59, no. 6 (November): 235-42.

Bernstein, Paul. 1976. Workplace Democratization: Its Internal Dynamics. Kent, Ohio: Kent State University Press.

Chandler, Alfred D., Jr. 1962. Strategy and Structure: Chapters in the History of the Industrial Enterprise. Cambridge, Mass.: Massachusetts Institute of Technology Press.

Co-op Handbook Collective. 1975. The Food Co-op Handbook: How to Bypass Supermarkets to Control the Quality and Price of Your Food. Boston: Houghton Mifflin.

Crozier, Michael. 1964. The Bureaucratic Phenomenon. Chicago: University of Chicago Press.

Curhan, Ronald C., and Wertheim, Edward G. 1972-73. "Consumer Food Buying Cooperatives—A Market Examined." Journal of Retailing 48, no. 4 (December): 29-39.

———. 1975. "Consumer Food Buying Cooperatives Revisited: A Comparison from 1971 to 1974." Journal of Retailing 51, no. 4 (December): 22-32, 87.

Etzioni, Amitai. 1961. A Comparative Analysis of Complex Organizations: On Power, Involvement, and Their Correlates. New York: Free Press of Glencoe.

Freeman, Jo. 1975. "Political Organization and the Feminist Movement." Acta Sociologica 18, no. 2-3 (Summer-Fall): 222-44.

Goffman, Erving. 1961. Asylums: Essays on the Social Situation of Mental Patients and Other Inmates. Garden City, N.Y.: Anchor Books.

Gouldner, Alvin W. 1954. Patterns of Industrial Bureaucracy. New York: Free Press.

Harvey, Edward. 1968. "Technology and the Structure of Organizations." American Sociological Review 33, no. 2 (April): 247-59.

Lawrence, Paul R., and Lorsch, Jay W. 1967. Organization and Environment: Managing Differentiation and Integration. Cambridge, Mass.: Harvard University Press.

Perrow, Charles. 1970. Organizational Analysis: A Sociological Perspective. Monterey, Calif.: Brooks/Cole.

Ronco, William. 1974. Food Co-ops: An Alternative to Shopping in Supermarkets. Boston: Beacon Press.

Rothschild-Whitt, Joyce. 1976a. "Conditions Facilitating Participatory-Democratic Organizations." Sociological Inquiry 46, no. 2 (June): 75-86.

———. 1976b. "Problems of Democracy." Working Papers for a New Society 4, no. 5 (September): 41-45.

Selznick, Philip. 1948. "Foundations of the Theory of Organizations." <u>American Sociological Review</u> 13, no. 1 (February): 25-35.

Stern, Gloria. 1974. <u>How to Start Your Own Food Co-op</u>. New York: Walker.

Thompson, James D. 1967. <u>Organizations in Action: Social Science Bases of Administrative Theory</u>. New York: McGraw-Hill.

Vellela, Tony. 1975. <u>Food Co-ops for Small Groups</u>. New York: Workman.

Weick, Karl E. 1969. <u>The Social Psychology of Organizing</u>. Reading, Mass.: Addison-Wesley.

Wertheim, Edward G. 1976. "Evolution of Structure and Process in Voluntary Organizations: A Study of Thirty-Five Consumer Food Cooperatives." <u>Journal of Voluntary Action Research</u> 5, no. 1 (January): 4-15.

Woodward, Joan. 1965. <u>Industrial Organization: Theory and Practice</u>. London: Oxford University Press.

ABOUT THE EDITOR AND CONTRIBUTORS

The late SEYMOUR FIDDLE was Associate Professor of Sociology, Hunter College, New York.

PAUL MONTAGNA is Associate Professor of Sociology, Brooklyn College, New York.

ALLEN LERNER is Associate Professor of Political Science, University of Illinois, Chicago.

MARIE JAHODA is Professor of Psychology, University of Sussex, England.

TERRY CONNOLLY is Associate Professor, Georgia Institute of Technology, Atlanta.

RICHARD E. SYKES is Associate Professor of Sociology, University of Minnesota.

JAMES G. HOUGHLAND, JR., is Assistant Professor of Sociology, University of Kentucky.

JON M. SHEPARD is Professor of Business Administration and Sociology, University of Kentucky.

BARUCH FISCHHOFF is Research Associate of Decision Research, Branch of Perceptronics, Rutgers, Oregon.

EMMANUEL DEMBY directs his own marketing research agency, MPT, in New York City.

The late TALCOTT PARSONS was Emeritus Professor of Sociology, Harvard University.

GEORGE KATONA is Professor of Psychology and attached to The Michigan Survey Research Center.

VINCENT B. ROBINSON is Visiting Assistant Professor, Department Urban Studies, University of Akron.

ROBERT MASON is Professor of Sociology and attached to Survey Research Center, Oregon State University, Gorvallis, Oregon.

G. DAVID FAULKENBERRY is Associate Professor of Statistics and attached to Survey Research Center, Oregon State University, Gorvallis, Oregon.

EUGENE J. ALPERT is Assistant Professor of Political Science, Texas Christian University.

ANDREW CHERLIN is Assistant Professor of Sociology, Johns Hopkins University.

C. E. BRIAN FROST is with the Division of Economic Studies, University of Sheffield, England.

DANIEL J. KLENOW is Assistant Professor of Sociology and Anthropology, North Dakota University.

FABIO B. Dasilva is Assistant Professor of Sociology and Anthropology, University of Notre Dame.

PETER LORENZI is Assistant Professor of Business Administration, University of Kansas, Fargo, North Dakota.

ROBERT E. CLARK is Associate Professor of Sociology, Midwestern State University.

LARRY HALFORD is Associate Professor of Sociology, Washburn University, Topeka.

RALPH B. GINSBERG is Professor of Regional Science, Sociology, and Public Policy Analysis at the University of Pennsylvania. He is editor of the Journal of Mathematical Sociology.

HOWARD KUNREUTHER is Chairman, Department of Decision Sciences, The Wharton School, University of Pennsylvania.

FERN L. JOHNSON is a linguist at the University of Massachusetts Department of Communication where she is Assistant Professor.

LESLIE K. DAVIS is an Assistant Professor in the University of Massachusetts Department of Communication.

MICHAEL NAGY is Assistant Professor of Sociology, Concord College, Athens, West Virginia.